To my beautiful wife Michelle:

Thank you for believing in me;
thank you for your ongoing love and dedication;
and, most of all, thank you, thank you
for never being naked in a movie.

THE BABES ARE BACK IN TOWN!

WINNER
UNPRECEDENTED
7 RAZZIE AWARDS!
INCLUDING WORST PICTURE

"A RICH SLEAZY
KITSCH-FEST!"
—JAY CARR, BOSTON GLOBE

PAUL VERHOEVEN's

"THIS IS LIKE THE
RESURRECTION AFTER
THE CRUCIFIXION."
—PAUL VERHOEVEN, DIRECTOR

"...IT IS
'ALL ABOUT EVE'
IN A G-STRING!"
SISKEL & EBERT

SHOW GIRLS

"...AN INSTANT
CAMP CLASSIC!"
—JANET MASLIN, NY TIMES

"'SHOWGIRLS' IS A
MORALITY TALE."
JOE ESZTERHAS, SCREENWRITER

"...A MASTERPIECE OF
FLASHY TACKINESS!"
—MICK LASALLE, SAN FRANCISCO CHRONICLE

"...GLITTERY, GLEEFULLY
VULGAR!"
—TERRY LAWSON, DAYTON DAILY NEWS

Contents

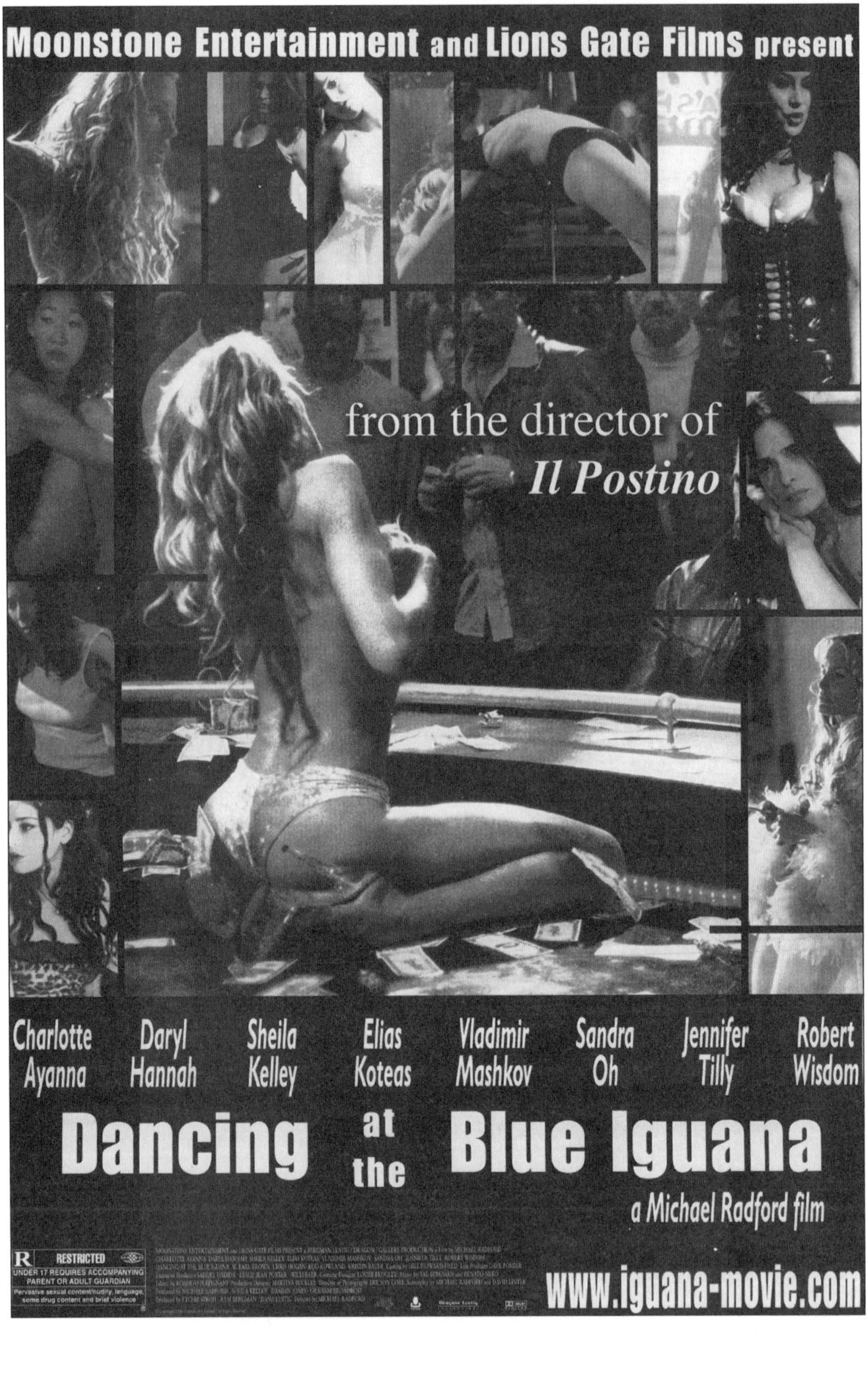

Moonstone Entertainment and Lions Gate Films present
from the director of
Il Postino
Charlotte Ayanna
Daryl Hannah
Sheila Kelley
Elias Koteas
Vladimir Mashkov
Sandra Oh
Jennifer Tilly
Robert Wisdom
Dancing at the Blue Iguana
a Michael Radford film
R RESTRICTED
UNDER 17 REQUIRES ACCOMPANYING PARENT OR ADULT GUARDIAN
Pervasive sexual content/nudity, language, some drug content and brief violence
www.iguana-movie.com

Skintroduction

Hi. I'm Mr. Skin.

Maybe you know me from my website, MrSkin.com—the world's number-one resource for celebrating nudity in film.

Or maybe you know me from *The Howard Stern Show*, where I regularly sit in live with Howard and the gang and where, every Thursday, Howard 100 News airs the weekly "Mr. Skin Minute."

Of course, you may also know me from one of the more than five hundred other radio shows I've appeared on, or from my being "skinterviewed" on CNN, VH1, and E!, or from when I was written up in *USA Today*, *Maxim*, and *Playboy*.

Or maybe you just saw the words "Sex & Nudity on DVD" emblazoned across the cover of this book and . . . well, here we are.

Upon the arrival of cable TV and a VCR in my suburban home when I was an adolescent, my life's passion has been collecting, reviewing, and revealing the skinny on nude scenes in PG- and R-rated movies (as long as the nudity is female!). That's how I got the name "Mr. Skin." Since 1999, that's also been the mission of my website, MrSkin.com.

Part of the challenge has been keeping up with developing technology when it comes to capturing skin on-screen. Perhaps no leap forward has been more beneficial to bare-starlet buffs than the DVD revolution of the past decade or so.

This brings me to the reason for *Mr. Skin's Skintastic Video Guide*. There seem to be more *skin*-stantly accessible movies on DVD than were ever available to the general public before. So how does a fan of famous funbags sift through all those millions of discs to pick out the peak of the peeks?

He doesn't.

I do.

And, assisted by a tireless platoon of Skin Skouts, that's exactly the task I undertook in order to complete this *Skintastic* volume. It was a dirty job. And don't think for a second that I'd let anybody else do it.

So after countless hours of watching DVDs, tallying up bare body parts, and reviewing both the plot of each movie and the quality of its flesh content, the results are in the palm of your (one free) hand—*Mr. Skin's Skintastic Video Guide: The 501 Greatest Movies for Sex & Nudity on DVD.*

Of course, there were some guidelines. **To qualify for inclusion, a movie had to have an official North American DVD release. In addition, the disc had to be playable in Region 1 DVD players.**

Each movie also has to be easy to purchase online. I didn't want to send readers out in search of bootlegs or videos that wouldn't work when inserted into their machines (inserting them anywhere else is none of my business).

Other than that, I had five decades of DVDs in a vast array of genres from which to choose. The final results arose from *my* personal opinions regarding the *quality* of the sex and nudity content. This incorporates factors such as star power ("Look! Nicole Kidman's pubes!"), the element of surprise ("Look! Julie Andrews's boobs!"), and historical importance ("Look! Jayne Mansfield's everything! In 1963!").

Consider *Mr. Skin's Skintastic Video Guide,* then, the ultimate tool when it comes to fast-forwarding to the good parts.

Skincerely,

Mr. Skin

T&Acknowledgments

Mr. Skin would like to thank Howard Stern, Jimmy Kimmel, Richard Roeper, and Judd Apatow.

Now for the nonmillionaires. *Skin*-ormous thanks go to:

David Wilk, our heroic publishing consultant.

Christine Marra and her staff at Marrathon Production Services.

Mark Suchomel, Jen Wisnowski, and the entire ace staff at IPG.

Elise Canon and Kevin Votel.

Adam Parfrey of Feral House Publishing and Process Books.

Kristina McBride, who serves as all things to all people at MrSkin.com. You are gracious, meticulous, tireless, good-humored, and utterly essential to our every effort.

Our crack skin-house design team of Steve Svoboda, Erik Westra, and Chris Dilts. Mr. Westra also created the cover.

Sam Rakowski, who spearheaded a great effort to gather materials. Sam was assisted by Melinda Fries, Ryan McClughen, Dan Reed, Matt Shadis, and Jim "The Marinator" Mariner.

Praise to our "boob-counting" skinterns, Jesse Bernstein, William "Doc" Heath, Rob Koleszar, Alexandra Snell, and Tanner Servoss. Special thanks to Jenny Speciale.

All MrSkin.com editorial contributors, including James Hollis Smith, Rin Kelly, Sam Henderson, Rob Hauschild, L.A. Simington, Nathan Hogan, Kim Martin, and Brian Collins.

Nudity gurus Celebrity Skin and Scoopy; as well as Michael Liuzza, whose knowledge of non-American nakedness is a national treasure.

My father, Pa Skin, for being a skinspiration.

Ma Skin, for her tireless hard work, which definitely did not end in the delivery room.

Mrs. Skin, Baby Skin, and Skin Jr.

Extra special thanks go to the many members, visitors, and supporters of MrSkin.com. Without you, I'd just be some mook in his mom's basement with a stack of movies and an extremely suspicious hobby.

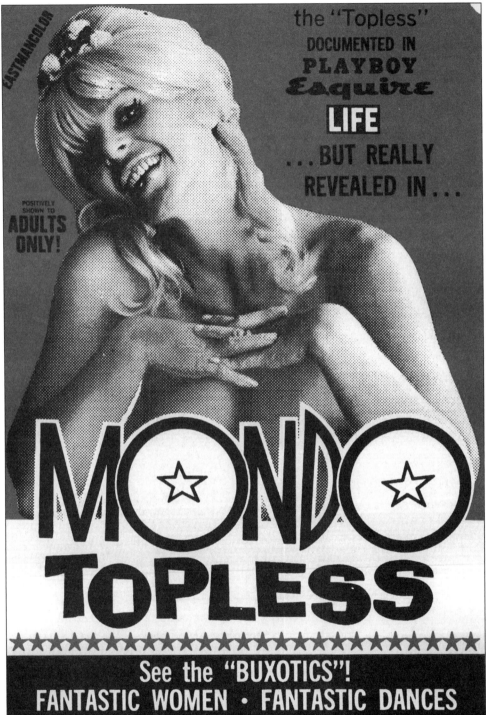

Who Wrote This Book

Mr. Skin set the T&A template from which all the following words emanate. If he had never coined the term *furburgerage,* none of this would be possible (and only a few of the following individuals would be employed).

Mike McPadden is the editorial director of MrSkin.com, and also of this book, and also of Chicago shock-rock ensemble Gays in the Military, which is good, because he's not much of a guitar player. Or a singer. Or a dresser. Or anything else that doesn't involve staring at nudie pics all day and concocting madcap synonyms for nipples.

Kara Edington copyedited, proofread, managed the unmanageable Mr. McPadden, and contributed choice chunks to this volume. Kara's limitless commitment and intense application of highbrow linguistic sciences to sentences containing words such as *funbaggables* is nearly as ironic as the fact that she looks like she's not old enough to see any of the movies in this book.

Funniest funnylady alive **Keara Shipe** never fails to astound with her wondrous wit and endlessly inventive way with a (dirty) word. She is the titanically talented pride of all Riot Grrls, Class of '92 (maybe '93).

Peter Landau is a nice Jewish boy with a Catholic wife, two uncircumcised sons, and a *goyishe kopf* when it comes to career choices. And best friends.

Allan MacDonell is one flowery son-of-a-Scotsman. Buy his book—*Prisoner of X: Twenty Years in the Hole at Hustler Magazine* (Feral House).

J. R. Taylor riles the Left-leaning benighted regularly at RightWingTrash.com.

Meghan McCarville, a.k.a. **Lil Princess**, remains a constant editorial skinspiration.

White skin on the black market

The dirty dolls of devil's island.

You can meet them for a price!

IN METROCOLOR

R

WOMEN IN CAGES

starring
JENNIFER GAN · JUDY BROWN · ROBERTA COLLINS · PAMELA GRIER
produced by
CIRIO SANTIAGO · written by DAVID OSTERHOUT & JIM WATKINS · directed by JERRY deLEON · A NEW WORLD PICTURES RELEASE

And now,
in glorious alphabetical order,
Mr. Skin
presents...

The 501
Greatest Movies for
Sex & Nudity
on DVD

10 (1979)

Director: Blake Edwards

Breasts: 18; **Butts**: 4;
  Bushes: 2

Nude Stars: **Bo Derek** (Breasts, Butt);
  Annette Haven (Breasts); **Dorothy
  Le May** (Breasts, Butt); **Constance
  Money** (Breasts); **Dee Wallace-Stone** (Butt)

Anonymous Nudes: 7

Dudley Moore is the pint-size embodiment of middle-aged
lust in *10*. He's got everything but Bo Derek, who makes
one of filmdom's most arousing entrances jogging—all jiggly
jugs—through the surf. For a little Bo peek, you'll have to
wait until the third reel when Bo finally lets Dudley get dirty
on her perfect-10 body.

Perfect *10*'s

Director Blake Edwards pilfered the cream of
Hollywood's then-burgeoning hardcore movie
industry to cast the swing-party scenes in *10*.
Among the X-rated royalty turning up (and on) are
Serena, Constance Money, Dorothy Le May, Annette
Haven, Harry Reems, and Ron Jeremy.

skinfo

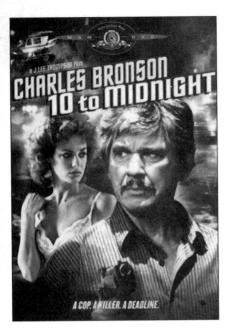

10 to Midnight (1983)

Director: J. Lee Thompson

Breasts: 8; **Butts**: 2; **Bushes**: 1

Nude Stars: **June Gilbert** (Full Frontal, Butt);
Jeane Manson (Breasts); **Ola Ray** (Breasts, Butt);
Patti Tippo (Breasts)

Ultimate tough guy Charles Bronson chases a serial killer in *10 to Midnight* and gets kicked off the force after planting evidence on the creep. Chuck catches the murderer anyway, handcuffs him naked, and, when the nut pleads insanity, blows him away. What a kook! It doesn't get much better than this, but it does thanks to many topless and fully naked turns from June Gilbert, Jeane Manson, Ola Ray, and Patti Tippo.

Midnight massive

Throughout the 1970s, Clint Eastwood and Charles Bronson competed for international A-list superstar status. By the Reagan era, Eastwood was both a huge mainstream draw and a high-class filmmaker, while Bronson hitched his wagon to Israeli exploitation powerhouse Canon Films. Naturally, Mr. Skin prefers Chuck's '80s efforts, beginning with the savage *Death Wish II* (1982) and culminating in the Yakuza kiddie-prostitution epic *Kinjite: Forbidden Subjects* (1989). Bronson's finest dialogue moment, however, occurs in *10 to Midnight*. Upon discovering a complex and not-terribly-comfortable-looking sexual aid hidden in the bad guy's lair, Chuck erupts: "You know what this is for? It's for JERKIN' OFF!"

skinfo

1984 (1984)

Director: Michael Radford

Breasts: 2; **Butts**: 1; **Bushes**: 2

Nude Stars: **Suzanna Hamilton** (Full Frontal, Butt);
Shirley Stelfox (Bush)

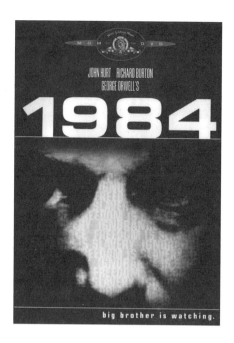

A bleak vision of a populace of human drones held in
the repressive vise of a totalitarian government, *1984* is
rendered with reverence, chilling ambiance, and a few
fleeting moments of glorious freedom as experienced
through authority-defying, flesh-flaunting sexuality. Suzanna
Hamilton starts a blaze down below by warming her totally
naked form over a campfire in the great outdoors. Her
bouncy boobage and booming bush are enough of a rush
to make Big Brother blush.

2 Days in the Valley (1996)

Director: John Herzfeld

Breasts: 2

Nude Star: **Charlize Theron** (Breasts)

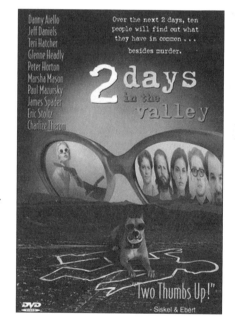

2 Days in the Valley revolves around intersecting California
characters, most notably Charlize Theron and Teri Hatcher.
The lovelies engage in a brutal catfight that makes audiences
purr with delight. James Spader's got game when he bites off
Charlize's teddy and gets a handful of her pint-size fun balls
to play catch. We could use a few more days in this valley.

The 40-Year-Old Virgin (2005)
Unrated Edition
Director: Judd Apatow

Breasts: 8; **Bushes**: 1

Nude Stars: **Laura Bottrell** (Breasts); **Stormy Daniels** (Full Frontal); **Catherine Keener** (Right Nip Slip); **Jamie Elle Mann** (Breasts); **Kimberly Page** (Right Breast)

With *The 40-Year-Old Virgin*, the conflict is will he or won't he? It becomes the sole goal of his coworkers to get Steve Carell laid. That means picking up drunk chicks, hooking up with a tranny hooker, and sharing porno. He practices his newfound technique on blonde cutie Elizabeth Banks, but it's Catherine Keener who captures Steve's heart-on.

Virgin Viewing
The R-rated theatrical cut of *The 40-Year-Old Virgin* contained scant female nudity. Fortunately the unrated DVD made up for it with enough mounds to pop any horndog's eye cherries.

skinfo

8½ Women (1999)

Director: Peter Greenaway

Breasts: 11; **Butts**: 3; **Bushes**: 3

Nude Stars: **Natacha Amal** (Breasts); **Toni Collette** (Full Frontal); **Annie Shizuka Inoh** (Right Breast, Butt); **Kirina Mano** (Breasts); **Amanda Plummer** (Full Frontal, Butt); **Polly Walker** (Full Frontal, Butt)

After a horny man's wife dies in *8½ Women,* he turns his country estate into a cunty-estate brothel. There's oodles of nudeness from Toni Collette (in a fully shaved frontal!), Annie Shizuka Inoh, Kirina Mano, Amanda Plummer (getting off bareback on a horse), and Polly Walker. As with any movie about whores, well, you get what you pay for. This one's more than worth the price of admission. *8½ Women* will give you 8½ inches.

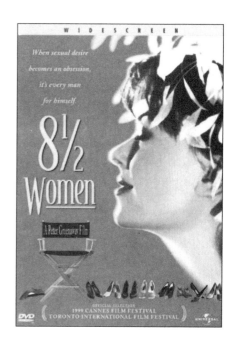

Women trouble

8½ Women director Peter Greenaway rose to art-film prominence after his kinky culinary hit *The Cook, the Thief, His Wife & Her Lover* (1989). Shocking imagery always figured prominently on Greenaway's palette, but his seventeenth-century-set opus *The Baby of Mâcon* (1993) proved too potent to find a distributor outside of Europe. In the movie, Julia Ormond plays a virgin mother who gets sentenced to be raped 113 times. And Greenaway's camera depicts each one.

skinfo

9¹/₂ Weeks (1986)

Director: Adrian Lyne

Uncut, Uncensored Version

Breasts: 5; **Butts**: 1

Nude Stars: **Kim Basinger** (Breasts, Butt); **Petina Cole** (Breasts); **Cintia Cruz** (Left Breast)

Before Mickey Rourke used his face for a speed bag, he was known for erotic think pieces like *9¹/₂ Weeks*. Kim Basinger never again reached this level of nonstop erotic overload. Here, Mickey exposes Kim to sensual boundary breaking, from cross-dressing to sadomasochism to voyeurism to an attempted threesome. And, ah, that moment when Mickey and Kim use each other as dinner plates. Hello lips, hello tongue, look out nipples, here it comes.

9½ peaks

Controversial and critically debated upon its 1986 release, *9½ Weeks* was no box-office blockbuster. But it did play in some theaters for unusually extended runs, developing a cult following the old-fashioned way—on the big screen. Of course, *9½ Weeks* truly flourished on home video and ultimately spawned two sequels: *Another 9½ Weeks* (1997) and *The First 9½ Weeks* (1998). Mickey Rourke returned for the first. Kim Basinger had moved on, somehow, to lamer things.

skinfo

The Abductors (1972)

Director: Don Schain

Ginger's the sexiest super-sleuth ever to subdue mankind!

GINGER

Starring Cheri Caffaro

THE ABDUCTORS

They took what they wanted, but they wanted more!

Breasts: 12; **Butts**: 4; **Bushes**: 6

Nude Stars: **Gerie Bronson** (Breasts, Butt, Bush);
Jennifer Brooks (Breasts, Bush); **Cheri Caffaro** (Full
Frontal, Butt); **Jeramie Rain** (Full Frontal, Butt);
Ined Som (Full Frontal); **Honey Well** (Full Frontal,
Butt)

Cheri Caffaro embodies platinum-blonde private dick
Ginger in *The Abductors.* The flick follows the plight and
eventual liberation of one beauty queen and three
cheerleaders snatched off the streets by a white-slavery ring.
Delight to a triple-header of hairy 1970s muff as fair
abductees Jeramie Rain, Honey Well, and Ined Som stand
and strip for the pleasure of their captors. The malefactors
didn't count on the grit and gonadal dexterity of Ms.
Caffaro. But you can.

H.O.T.S. for *Ginger*

Ginger star Cheri Caffaro exposed even more of her
talents when she penned the screenplay for the
naked sorority-house classic *H.O.T.S.* (1979).

skinfo

About Last Night . . . (1986)

Director: Edward Zwick

Breasts: 2; **Butts**: 4; **Bushes**: 1

Nude Star: **Demi Moore** (Breasts, Butt)

Anonymous Nudes: 3

About Last Night . . . is adapted from a David Mamet play originally titled *Sexual Perversity in Chicago* and delves into the titillated but somehow tortured psyches of two Windy City couples who struggle with the boundaries between love and lust. But, really, it's all about the naked body of young Demi Moore. There's a lingering bedroom scene with her pre-op boobs, with a full moon to bring out the wolf in viewers.

Action Jackson (1988)

Director: Craig R. Baxley

Breasts: 4; **Butts**: 1

Nude Stars: **Sharon Stone** (Breasts, Butt);
   Vanity (Breasts)

Ex-jock Carl Weathers storms through Detroit like a black Dirty Harry in *Action Jackson*. Your jackson will be stiff with pleasure watching both Vanity and Sharon Stone heat up this high-octane flick with their ample toplessness. *Action Jackson* is a rush!

Alfie (2004)

Director: Charles Shyer

Breasts: 3; **Butts**: 1

Nude Stars: **Jane Krakowski** (Left Breast, Butt); **Sienna Miller** (Breasts, Thong)

Jude Law revises the role of the British cad that made Michael Caine a star in *Alfie*. Law gets a piece of ass (and we get a peek) from Jane Krakowski. Later, Law hooks up with Sienna Miller, who struts her topless stuff. Susan Sarandon shows up as a rich bitch, and Nia Long adds some dark delights. And that's what it's all about, Alfie!

Anatomy Awards - *n. pl.*

Mr. Skin's annual one-armed salute to the very breast in the previous year's nudity in film and television.

Alice in Wonderland (1976)

Director: Bud Townsend

Breasts: 21; Butts: 8; Bushes: 8

Nude Stars: **Kristine DeBell** (Full Frontal, Butt); **Juliet Graham** (Full Frontal, Butt); **Sue Tsengoles** (Full Frontal, Butt)

Anonymous Nudes: 10

Explore Kristine DeBell's rabbit hole in *Alice in Wonderland!* Director Bud Townsend's nude musical adaptation of the revered Lewis Carroll children's classic is a piece of time-capsule magic, a special moment in the history of hardcore. Only in the '70s, kiddies!

Wonder Gland

Not only did the X-rated *Alice in Wonderland* play in nonporn neighborhood theaters, but its *Playboy* centerfold star, Kristine DeBell, also crossed over to unequaled mainstream success. After baring (and filling) her rabbit hole in *Alice*, Kristine co-starred in *Meatballs* (1979) and *The Big Brawl* (1980), and played a lead role on the soap *The Young and the Restless.*

skinfo

Alley Cat (1984)

Director: Edward Victor

Breasts: 14; **Butts**: 4; **Bushes**: 4

Nude Stars: **Britt Helfer** (Breasts); **Karin Mani** (Full Frontal, Butt); **Moriah Shannon** (Full Frontal)

Anonymous Nudes: 4

A pretty, fragile-looking sweet face is attacked by a crude and style-challenged gang of street toughs in *Alley Cat,* and the cops don't do diddly-squat to apprehend the louts. Does *Alley Cat's* heroine pout and join a victims' support group? Or does she undertake a crash course in killer martial arts and exact her bloody payback? You'll be yelling, "You go, girl!" as slim and fit vaginal vigilante Karin Mani kicks ass and flashes grass.

All the Right Moves (1983)

Director: Michael Chapman

Breasts: 2; **Butts**: 1; **Bushes**: 1

Nude Star: **Lea Thompson** (Full Frontal, Butt)

High-school football hotshot Tom Cruise butts heads with coach Craig T. Nelson in *All the Right Moves.* Tom's got to choose—a scholarship or doing the right thing and sticking to his guns. He can't have both. Or can he? And does it matter when we get to see Lea Thompson's lickables?

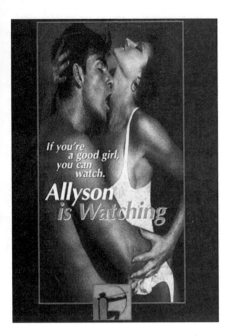

If you're a good girl, you can watch.

Allyson is Watching

Allyson Is Watching (1997)
Director: Robert Kubilos

Breasts: 4; Butts: 2; Bushes: 2
Nude Stars: **Caroline Ambrose** (Breasts, Butt, Bush, Thong); **Jennifer Hammon** (Full Frontal, Butt)

Beautiful women are at their most attractive when solving murder mysteries, as exemplified by *Allyson Is Watching*, especially when the murder victim is a high-breasted, sweet-thighed, sugar-assed hooker. It also helps when the deceased has recently displayed every prurient facet of her fleshly charms in a lesbianic lick-down with the stacked eye pleaser who is now attempting to solve the murder.

Arthouse - *adj.*
Sophisticated films made for a highbrow audience, but often kind enough to include down-and-dirty nudity and sex.

SKIN·finition

Almost Pregnant (1992)

Director: Michael DeLuise

Breasts: 4; **Butts**: 3; **Bushes**: 1

Nude Stars: **Lisa Comshaw** (Butt); **Tanya Roberts** (Full Frontal, Butt); **Joan Severance** (Breasts, Butt, Thong)

Almost Pregnant is a sex farce that follows the tribulations of Tanya Roberts as a woman whose biological clock is sounding the alarm. Tanya seeks the help of her neighbor and an in-law. Naturally, Tanya is naked throughout, and Joan Severance adds to the skinful affair as a naughty neighbor. Watching this sexy flick is sure to get someone pregnant.

Amazon Women on the Moon (1987)

Directors: Joe Dante, Carl Gottlieb, Peter Horton, John Landis, Robert K. Weiss

Breasts: 5; **Butts**: 1; **Bushes**: 1

Nude Stars: **Monique Gabrielle** (Full Frontal, Butt); **Tracy Hutchinson** (Right Breast); **Corinne Wahl** (Breasts)

Amazon Women on the Moon is a sketch-comedy revue that doesn't skimp on the big laughs and bare ladies. Most nudeworthy is Monique Gabrielle as a *Penthouse* Pet of the Month who poses all of her fine skin for the camera and then goes for a walk around L.A. without a stitch on, commenting on her likes and dislikes in typical centerfold fashion. Corinne Wahl also offers some topless action as a video-dating girl.

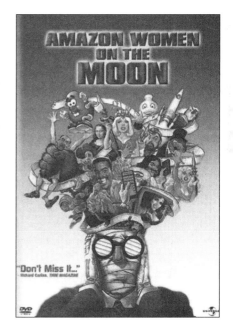

There's something about your first piece.

American Pie (1999)

Director: Paul Weitz

Breasts: 3

Nude Star: **Shannon Elizabeth** (Breasts)

Anonymous Nudes: 1

American Pie is classic teen-sex-comedy fodder: High-school buddies pledge to lose their virginity by graduation. Sex ensues, and never more hilariously than when geeky hero Jason Biggs samples the warm apple concoction of the title—only *not* with his mouth. We also get to peek in on a web-cast strip show by sexy and uninhibited foreign-exchange student Shannon Elizabeth. *American Pie* is hot *and* sweet.

Pie Light

Although the acronym M.I.L.F. (Mom I'd Like to Fuck) may well have existed in schoolyards and locker rooms prior to the release of *American Pie*, it was Jennifer Coolidge as Stifler's mom who truly entered the term into the common lexicon.

skinfo

American Pie Presents Band Camp
(2005) Unrated Edition
Director: Steve Rash

Breasts: 10; **Butts**: 3; **Bushes**: 1

Nude Stars: **Ginger Lynn Allen** (Breasts, Butt, Bush);
Tara Killian (Breasts); **Angela Little** (Breasts, Butt);
Rachel Veltri (Breasts); **Jennifer Walcott** (Breasts,
Butt)

In *American Pie Presents Band Camp,* the fourth installment
of the *American Pie* franchise, an unruly adolescent is forced
by his parents to attend band camp as atonement for his
teenage derelictions. Naturally, as soon as the young
reprobate arrives, he sets about installing secret cameras in
the girls' shower stalls. The weird thing is that this normal
high-school guy falls in love and embarks on a program of
self-betterment. Can good intentions survive on this island
of nubile temptations? Does a flute make an excellent
improvised marital aid?

American Pie
Have another piece!

American Pie (1999) popped hot out of the oven and was slapped onto crotches across the
country, uniting sex and laughs in a way that didn't leave the audience limp. *American Pie 2*
(2001) upped the ante. Shannon Elizabeth returns but keeps her breast bits covered. Not so
with Lisa Arturo and Denise Faye as bisexuals who double the fun. *American Wedding* (2003)
features Amanda Swisten in a French maid costume and Nikki Schieler Ziering as a topless cop.
Talk about getting busted! Audiences remained hungry for more, and an onslaught of direct-
to-DVD sequels resulted in the skinstant classics *American Pie Presents Band Camp* (2005) and
American Pie Presents The Naked Mile (2006).

Top 501 DVDs: *American Pie* (1999), *American Pie Presents Band Camp* (2005), *American Pie
Presents The Naked Mile* (2006)

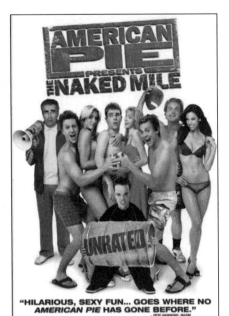

"HILARIOUS, SEXY FUN... GOES WHERE NO
AMERICAN PIE HAS GONE BEFORE."
— PETE HAMMOND, MAXIM

American Pie Presents The Naked Mile (2006)

Unrated Edition

Director: Joe Nussbaum

Breasts: 110; **Butts**: 53;
  Bushes: 7

Nude Stars: **Michelle Cormier** (Breasts); **Candace Kroslak** (Breasts, Butt); **Angel Lewis** (Breasts, Butt, Thong); **Alyssa Nicole Pallett** (Breasts); **Stephany Sexton** (Breasts); **Jaclyn A. Smith** (Breasts, Butt)

Anonymous Nudes: 98

Yet another Stifler ignites chaos in *American Pie Presents The Naked Mile*. This time it's virginal cousin Erik Stifler (John White), who visits a nearby college for an annual nude run. All the expected pranks and hijinks ensue. What you won't expect is the ass-tonishing amount of bare coed bodies on hand. You'll be a mile long.

Mr. Skin's TOP 69

16

TOP 5

Movies for Butts

5. *Bacchanales Sexuelles* (1974) – 20 butts

4. *Salon Kitty* (1976) – 28 butts

3. *Immoral Tales* (1974) – 31 butts

2. *Caligula* (1979) – 41 butts

1. American Pie Presents The Naked Mile (2006) 53 Butts!

American Psycho (2000)
Uncut Collector's Edition
Director: Mary Harron

Breasts: 8; **Butts**: 2

Nude Stars: **Samantha Mathis** (Right Breast); **Cara Seymour** (Breasts, Butt); **Krista Sutton** (Breasts, Butt, Thong); **Guinevere Turner** (Breasts)

Anonymous Nudes: 1

In *American Psycho,* Christian Bale plays a cool financial whiz in the go-go '80s. He's also a whack job who rapes, mutilates, and murders strangers. Nobody's perfect. *American Psycho* also features some crazy-hot females in the form of Samantha Mathis, Chloë Sevigny, and Reese Witherspoon. Don't miss serial driller Bale posing in the mirror during an over-the-top threesome with hookers Krista Sutton and Cara Seymour.

The Amorous Mis-Adventures of Casanova (1977)
Director: Franz Antel

Breasts: 33; **Butts**: 7; **Bushes**: 5

Nude Stars: **Jenny Arasse** (Full Frontal, Butt); **Jeannie Bell** (Breasts); **Marisa Berenson** (Right Breast); **Britt Ekland** (Left Breast); **Sylva Koscina** (Breasts); **Marisa Mell** (Left Breast); **Lillian Müller** (Full Frontal, Butt); **Olivia Pascal** (Full Frontal); **Carla Romanelli** (Breasts, Butt)

Anonymous Nudes: 9

The Amorous Mis-Adventures of Casanova casts Tony Curtis as the dandy-dressed fop of the title. Mostly, though, costumes don't play much of a part in this comedic sexploitation flick about the lothario and a look-alike making their way to Venice to bed an Arabian caliph's wife. Along the way they both get to have sex on the run with such classic hotties as Britt Ekland, Jeannie Bell, Sylva Koscina, Olivia Pascal, Marisa Berenson, Marisa Mell, and Carla Romanelli.

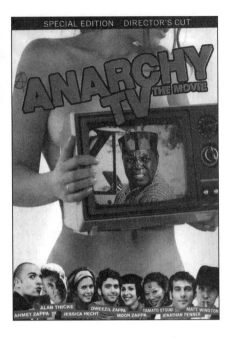

Anarchy TV (1997)
Director: Jonathan Blank

Breasts: 7; **Butts**: 2; **Bushes**: 2

Nude Stars: **Jessica Hecht** (Full Frontal, Butt);
   Tamayo Otsuki (Full Frontal, Butt)

Anonymous Nudes: 2

Shows broadcast on Channel 69 should be dirty, as evidenced in *Anarchy TV.* The protests of televangelist Alan Thicke bring out the real rebels in the station managers, and they decide to fulfill the promise of the station's call numbers with full-frontal nudity! It's a ratings booster, as well as a pants lifter. Talk about "Muff-See TV"!

Angel (1984)
Director: Robert Vincent O'Neill

Breasts: 18; **Butts**: 4; **Bushes**: 5

Nude Stars: **Donna McDaniel** (Breasts);
   Graem McGavin (Breasts)

Anonymous Nudes: 7

Honor student Donna Wilkes, in *Angel,* has been supporting herself as a hooker since she was twelve years old. Now someone is killing the streetwalkers, and our girl becomes an avenging angel with a gun. Donna McDaniel is ogled topless, and Graem McGavin gets to show off her treasured chest. There's also a shower scene in which there's more muff than you can get your hands on, though Mr. Skin suggests you try.

Angel III: The Final Chapter (1988)

Director: Tom DeSimone

Breasts: 29

Nude Stars: **Laura Albert** (Breasts, Thong); **Bella Donna** (Breasts, Thong); **Barbara Hammond** (Breasts); **Roxanna Hernandez** (Right Breast); **Julie K. Smith** (Breasts, Thong)

Anonymous Nudes: 10

Angel III: The Final Chapter finds avenging hooker Angel played by Mitzi Kapture. Finding out that her long-lost mother and sister are involved in a porno, drug, white-slavery ring, Angel goes typically ballistic. Laura Albert, Bella Donna, Roxanna Hernandez, and Barbara Hammond add some titty, but it's Julie K. Smith who steals the show by showing off her video-vixen T&A on the porno set. *Angel III* will make you a horny devil.

Angel: Heaven's Harlot
Honor student by day . . . in your VCR every night!

Heaven would be full if not for all the fallen angels who have tumbled from the heights and landed on the curbs of Hollywood Boulevard to ply their pearly gates. Where can these outcast cherubs look for succor, protection, and vengeance? The cops just want to lock 'em up, shake 'em down, and bang 'em for free. Their boyfriends are too busy acting like pimps to be of any use. A girl, if she is to survive with any tattered shred of dignity, is forced to take her destiny into her own hands and strike out like a cunning she devil. See bruised, innocent hell break loose in *Angel* (1984), *Avenging Angel* (1985), *Angel III: The Final Chapter* (1988), and *Angel 4: Undercover* (1993).

Top 501 DVDs: *Angel* (1984), *Angel III: The Final Chapter* (1988)

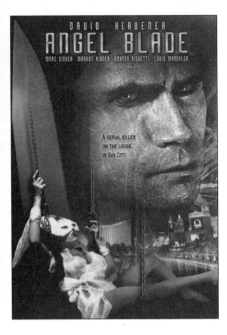

Angel Blade (2002)

Director: David Heavener

Breasts: 40; **Butts**: 7; **Bushes**: 3

Nude Stars: **Kathleen Pederson** (Breasts);
   Amanda Righetti (Breasts, Butt, Thong)

Anonymous Nudes: 23

Angel Blade is the story of a cop obsessed with a string of gruesome murders of pregnant prostitutes. His investigation leads him into the underbelly of the Las Vegas sex underground and to lingerie model Amanda Righetti. Amanda not only models skimpy thongs but also wears decidedly less in very hot and disturbing sex scenes with director and star David Heavener. It's a heated noir that mixes bondage and other extreme sexual expressions into a pants boiler of a hit.

Angelfist (1991)

Director: Cirio H. Santiago

Breasts: 16; **Butts**: 6; **Bushes**: 6

Nude Stars: **Denise Buick** (Full Frontal, Butt);
   Melissa Anne Moore (Breasts, Butt, Bush);
   Catya Sassoon (Full Frontal)

Anonymous Nudes: 5

Angelfist is the perfect union of hot chicks (the angel) and kick-ass action (the fist). It stars Catya Sassoon as an LAPD officer who travels to the Philippines to track down her sister's killer. She goes undercover as a kickboxer, which means a lot of hard-bodied females beating the living daylights out of one another—and, even better, showering together. *Angelfist* packs quite the punch . . . and it hits below the belt!

Angel Heart (1987)

Director: Alan Parker

Breasts: 9

Nude Stars: **Lisa Bonet** (Breasts); **Charlotte Rampling** (Right Breast); **Elizabeth Whitcraft** (Breasts)

Anonymous Nudes: 3

Mickey Rourke is a private dick in *Angel Heart* hired by Louis Cyphre (Robert De Niro) to find Johnny Favorite. That leads to voodoo and hoodoo and not a wee bit of whoopee with occult knockout Lisa Bonet. Lisa's brown breast bonnets pop hard in a water-splashed sex romp with Mickey. Mickey loses his mind, but along the way his dick is no longer as private. Lisa will give you a Bonet.

Fallen *Angel*
The MPAA initially branded *Angel Heart* with an X rating, due mostly to the plasma-dripping voodoo canoodling between Lisa Bonet and Mickey Rourke. A few snips later, and they had an R-rated change of *Heart.*

skinfo

Angel of H.E.A.T. (1982)
Director: Myrl A. Schreibman

Breasts: 18; **Bushes**: 2

Nude Stars: **Marilyn Chambers** (Full Frontal);
   Remy O'Neill (Breasts); **Mary Woronov** (Full Frontal)

Anonymous Nudes: 6

Angel of H.E.A.T. stars Marilyn Chambers as a secret agent
out to bust up a devious plan by a mad scientist to conquer
the world—and she ends up busting out of her clothes to
do it! Mary Woronov also shows off her bush *and* nakedly
mud wrestles Remy O'Neill. Now that's some kind of
H.E.A.T.

Angels Hard as They Come (1971)
Director: Joe Viola

Breasts: 9

Nude Stars: **Becki Cross** (Breasts); **Neva
   Davis** (Breasts); **Gilda Texter** (Left Breast);
   Janet Wood (Breasts)

Anonymous Nudes: 1

Angels Hard as They Come chronicles what goes on (and
comes off) when three Hells Angels are invited by the
Dragons into a hippie commune. A drunken, drug- and
sex-crazed orgy ignites, and there are a lot of heavy hooters
from Janet Wood, Neva Davis, and Becki Cross. Thanks to
them, not only the angels are coming . . . hard.

Animal House (1978)

Director: John Landis

Breasts: 11; **Butts**: 1

Nude Stars: **Karen Allen** (Butt);
Lisa Baur (Left Breast);
Sarah Holcomb (Breasts);
Mary Louise Weller (Breasts)

Anonymous Nudes: 3

It's the three R's of collegiate life: raunch, retching, and 'rections. They're all present and accounted for in this uproarious T&A masterpiece that made all the world a wild toga party. The drunken perverts of *Animal House* put high, hard fun in higher education as they wage war on so-called decency, repressed homoerotic frat houses, and a disciplinarian dean. *Animal House* is all about Belushi, boobs, beer, and bombastic blowouts. And you can't beat that (but you can beat *off* to it).

Prefab *House*-ing

National Lampoon editor Chris Miller, who co-scripted *Animal House,* revealed in a 2006 Skinterview on MrSkin.com that Mary Louise Weller's swellers were man-made. "She had had some sort of '70s boob job," Miller said. "Have you noticed in the movie? They don't move when she moves! Don't mean to spoil things for anyone, but these were titties o' plastic!"

skinfo

Animal Instincts (1992)

Director: Gregory Dark

Breasts: 28; **Butts**: 4; **Bushes**: 1

Nude Stars: **Delia Sheppard** (Breasts);
   Shannon Whirry (Full Frontal, Butt, Thong)

Anonymous Nudes: 12

Animal Instincts revolves around a cop who's married to firebrand Shannon Whirry yet somehow can't make his love gun work. Seems the piece officer can raise his nightstick only when he's peeping on Shannon having shenanigans with other men. Shannon gladly appeases hubby's kink by having cable guy Jan-Michael Vincent lay some cable between her legs. As a bonus, Lynette O'Connell and Delia Sheppard also suck Sapphic.

Animal Instincts II (1994)

Director: Gregory Dark

Breasts: 18; **Butts**: 3; **Bushes**: 3

Nude Stars: **Debra K. Beatty** (Full Frontal); **Shannon McLeod** (Breasts); **Elizabeth Sandifer** (Breasts, Butt); **Shannon Whirry** (Full Frontal, Butt, Thong)

Anonymous Nudes: 5

Shannon Whirry is back in *Animal Instincts II,* and this time she's got friends. Debra K. Beatty, Shannon McLeod, and Elizabeth Sandifer offer up a plethora of flesh. There's a plot, too, of course: something about beautiful twins, one being an evil murderer. Never mind that—just know that the twins are both played by Shannon, which means about sixty pounds of booby meat.

Animal Instincts III (1995)

Director: Gregory Dark

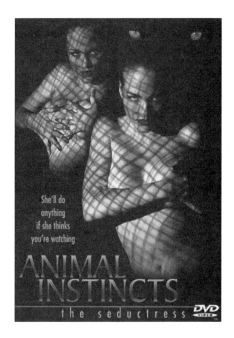

Breasts: 18; **Butts**: 5; **Bushes**: 3

Nude Stars: **Taylor Hayes** (Breasts, Bush); **Jenteal** (Full Frontal, Butt, Thong); **Jacqueline Lovell** (Breasts, Butt, Thong); **Wendy Schumacher** (Full Frontal, Butt, Thong)

Anonymous Nudes: 6

Wendy Schumacher will make you roar in the sex zoo *Animal Instincts III.* Wendy is a best-selling author and exhibitionist who gets involved with a blind record producer and has sex with everyone in front of him. Now here's the spoiler: he isn't blind but gets off on watching. Don't be upset by the plot twist; there's enough twisted sex exposed throughout the torrid tale to keep you howling.

Animal III–It Don't Stink!

The third installment in the *Animal Instincts* series was scripted by a young genius named Selwyn Harris, publisher of the underground zine *Happyland*, *Hustler* entertainment editor from 1993 to 1995, and screenwriter of the hardcore Gregory Dark-directed classics *The Devil in Miss Jones 5* (1994) and *Sex Freaks* (1996). Selwyn Harris is a prince.

skinfo

The Anniversary Party (2001)

Directors: Alan Cumming, Jennifer Jason Leigh

Breasts: 4

Nude Stars: **Jane Adams** (Breasts);
    Parker Posey (Breasts)

Jennifer Jason Leigh and Alan Cumming play a couple
who has recently reconciled after a yearlong separation in
The Anniversary Party. They throw a sixth-anniversary party
for themselves and invite their closest friends, including
Gwyneth Paltrow, Phoebe Cates, Parker Posey, and Jennifer
Beals. The celebration's highlights include Parker's posies
blooming during an underwater swim with adorably mini-
jugged Jane Adams.

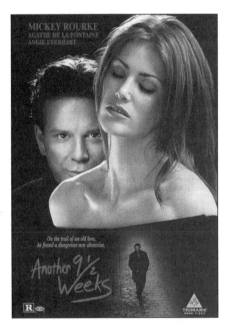

Another 9½ Weeks (1997)

Director: Anne Goursaud

Breasts: 7; **Butts**: 1; **Bushes**: 1

Nude Stars: **Agathe de La Fontaine** (Left Breast);
    Angie Everhart (Full Frontal, Thong);
    Phillipa Mathews (Breasts)

Anonymous Nudes: 1

Part-time boxer, full-time mess Mickey Rourke stars in the
sequel *Another 9½ Weeks*. The original's Kim Basinger is
replaced by Angie Everhart. Mickey and Angie throw back
a few shots of absinthe, attend fashion shows, and throw
around anger and passion in equal amounts, but it's up to
Angie to provide enough nudity for another 9½ erections.

Aria (1987)

Directors: Robert Altman, Bruce Beresford, Bill Bryden, Jean-Luc Godard, Derek Jarman, Franc Roddam, Nicolas Roeg, Ken Russell, Charles Sturridge, Julien Temple

Breasts: 17; **Butts**: 5; **Bushes**: 2

Nude Stars: **Valerie Allain** (Full Frontal, Butt); **Linzi Drew** (Breasts); **Bridget Fonda** (Breasts, Butt); **Elizabeth Hurley** (Breasts, Butt); **Marion Peterson** (Full Frontal, Butt)

Anonymous Nudes: 5

What happens when you put ten big-time directors together, each responsible for bringing to life a different opera aria? You get *Aria*. Scratching your head, huh? Well, move that hand a little lower, for what this movie lacks in cohesiveness, it more than makes up for with a boobful of young and naked Elizabeth Hurley, Bridget Fonda, Linzi Drew, Marion Peterson, and Valerie Allain.

Ask the Dust (2006)

Director: Robert Towne

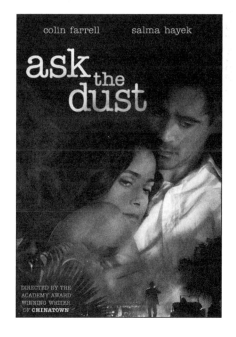

Breasts: 2; **Butts**: 2; **Bushes**: 1

Nude Stars: **Salma Hayek** (Full Frontal, Butt); **Idina Menzel** (Butt)

Ask the Dust features Salma Hayek full-frontally nude. Need to know more? She plays a Mexican immigrant looking to marry into America when sidetracked by Colin Farrell as a boozy author. The romance may not always be beautiful or lead the characters to their ambitions, but who can blame Colin for wanting Salma no matter what the cost? You've got to crack a few eggs to make it with this Spanish omelet.

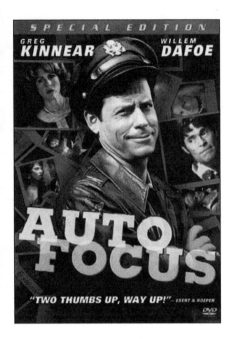

Auto Focus (2002)

Director: Paul Schrader

Breasts: 39; **Butts**: 1; **Bushes**: 3

Nude Stars: **Kitana Baker** (Breasts); **Maria Bello** (Breasts); **Teri Geary** (Full Frontal, Butt, Thong); **Amber Griebel** (Breasts); **Katie Lohmann** (Full Frontal); **Alex Meneses** (Breasts); **Zen** (Breasts); **Zero** (Breasts)

Anonymous Nudes: 13

Auto Focus focuses on *Hogan's Heroes* star Bob Crane, played by Greg Kinnear. Crane was an amateur photographer and a professional pervert who filmed his sexploits. Women such as Maria Bello, Alex Meneses, and Amber Griebel supply Crane with searing skin for his leering lens.

Auto Erotica

Scotty Crane, the real-life son of *Auto Focus* subject Bob Crane, was so upset by what he claimed were inaccuracies in the biopic that he launched BobCrane.com. The website offered actual pics and clips of the senior Crane engaged in kinky shenanigans. Alas, Scotty has since declared, "The movie is long forgotten . . . and so the film and photo proof we offered here—showing you how *Auto Focus* got it dead wrong—is no longer necessary."

skinfo

Baberellas (2003)

Director: Chuck Cirino

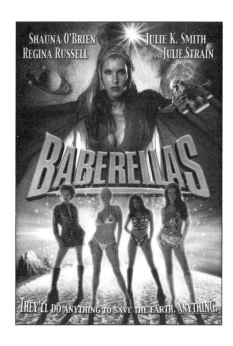

Breasts: 26; **Butts**: 5; **Bushes**: 5

Nude Stars: **Athena Demos** (Full Frontal, Butt); **Bettie Dewar** (Breasts); **Deborah Dutch** (Breasts, Thong); **Shauna O'Brien** (Breasts, Thong); **Jana Oujeska** (Breasts); **Sasha Peralto** (Breasts, Thong); **Regina Russell** (Full Frontal, Butt, Thong); **Julie K. Smith** (Breasts, Thong); **Julie Strain** (Full Frontal); **Linda Vox** (Breasts, Thong); **Zen** (Full Frontal, Butt); **Zero** (Full Frontal, Butt)

Anonymous Nudes: 1

Who's going to save the world from evil alien Julie Strain and her plan to destroy Earth in a bid for higher ratings for her extraterrestrial TV show? The all-female rock band the Baberellas is a pretty good candidate—or maybe not, since Strain's plot relies on stealing our planet's sexual essence. These gals certainly seem set with a never-ending supply of the stuff. So does *Baberellas,* thanks to an amazingly unclad cast.

Bacchanales Sexuelles (1974)

Director: Jean Rollin

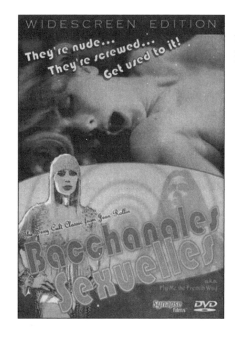

Breasts: 71; **Butts**: 20; **Bushes**: 9

Nude Stars: **Joëlle Coeur** (Full Frontal, Butt); **Brigitte De Borghese** (Full Frontal, Butt); **Minia Malove** (Full Frontal); **Marie-France Morel** (Full Frontal, Butt); **Jenny Trochu** (Full Frontal, Butt)

Anonymous Nudes: 49

The title *Bacchanales Sexuelles* says it all, even if you don't know what it's saying at all. The plot revolves around Joëlle Coeur house-sitting for her cousin. She's frightened to be alone in the large, empty house so uses gal pal Marie-France Morel's fully nude body as a security blanket. We later learn that Joëlle's cousin is a member of a secret sex society. And, yes, the ladies join in.

Bachelor Party (1984)

Director: Neal Israel

Breasts: 10; **Bushes**: 1

Nude Star: **Monique Gabrielle** (Full Frontal)

Anonymous Nudes: 4

Tom Hanks is a bus driver engaged to rich socialite Tawny Kitaen in *Bachelor Party*. A ball of a bachelor party is thrown for him at a posh hotel, and it's a cavalcade of hookers, drugs, debauchery, and even a barnyard animal. There's a lot of in-the-background nudity, plus Monique Gabrielle peels down to her girl fur as Hanks's wank-come-flesh bachelor present.

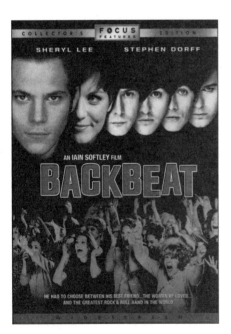

Backbeat (1994)

Director: Iain Softley

Breasts: 10; **Butts**: 3; **Bushes**: 4

Nude Stars: **Finola Geraghty** (Full Frontal, Butt);
    Sheryl Lee (Full Frontal, Butt)

Anonymous Nudes: 3

Backbeat is the story of the Beatles before they were the Fab Four. The band works the bottom rung of the sex, drugs, and rock-and-roll circuit and gets sidetracked by naked and stacked Sheryl Lee. *Backbeat* will leave you beating off to the oldies.

Bad Bizness (2003)

Director: Jim Wynorski

Breasts: 12; **Butts**: 2; **Bushes**: 1

Nude Stars: **Kira Eggers** (Breasts, Thong); **Belinda Gavin** (Full Frontal, Butt); **Kim Maddox** (Breasts, Butt); **Regina Russell** (Breasts); **Julie K. Smith** (Breasts); **Mia Zottoli** (Breasts)

Traci Bingham is head of security at an Indonesian resort in *Bad Bizness*. Business is good—if you happen to be a murdering psycho who loves to kill promiscuous young models. Mia Zottoli and Kira Eggers bare boobage. Kim Maddox scorches a hot tub with some man meat, while Regina Russell and Julie K. Smith prove you don't need a man to keep things heated.

TOP 5
Jim Wynorski Movies

5. *The Bare Wench Project* (1999)

4. *Big Bad Mama II* (1987)

3. *Not of This Earth* (1988)

2. *Sorority House Massacre II* (1990)

1. Bad Bizness (2003)

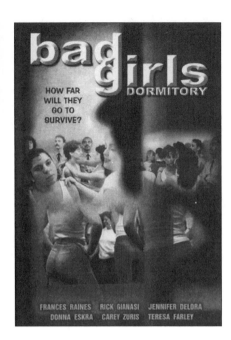

HOW FAR
WILL THEY
GO TO
SURVIVE?

FRANCES RAINES   RICK GIANASI   JENNIFER DELORA
DONNA ESKRA   CAREY ZURIS   TERESA FARLEY

Bad Girls' Dormitory (1984)

Director: Tim Kincaid

Breasts: 20; **Butts**: 6; **Bushes**: 6

Nude Stars: **Renata Cobbs** (Full Frontal, Butt);
Jennifer Delora (Breasts); **Jane Donadio**
(Breasts); **Charmagne Eckert** (Full Frontal, Butt);
Donna Eskra (Breasts); **Natalie O'Connell** (Full
Frontal, Butt); **Frances Raines** (Breasts, Butt);
Carey Zuris (Full Frontal)

Anonymous Nudes: 2

The action in *Bad Girls' Dormitory* takes place behind bars,
where first-and-only-time skinsters Renata Cobbs,
Charmagne Eckert, Donna Eskra, Carey Zuris, and Jane
Donadio are brutalized by a sadistic warden and plan their
escape—from their clothes!

Body Double - *n.*

A professional naked stand-in whose stunt privates
substitute for a star who's too skingy to perform a nude
scene herself.

Ss

SKIN·
finition

Bad Girls from Mars (1990)

Director: Fred Olen Ray

Breasts: 10

Nude Stars: **Dana Bentley** (Breasts); **Greta Carlson** (Breasts, Thong); **Jasae** (Breasts); **Brinke Stevens** (Breasts); **Edy Williams** (Breasts, Thong)

The story of homicidal difficulties faced during filming of a low-budget, high-skinterest flick, *Bad Girls from Mars* starts as a sci-fi peek-a-boob thriller and morphs into a peek-a-boob serial-killer thriller, never taking its eyes off the prizes, especially those residing on the chests of Edy Williams and Dana Bentley. The two go head-to-head and tit-to-tit in a topless wrestling match. The only problem: who to root for!

Fred Olen Ray
B-movies with all three Bs.

In 2007 Fred Olen Ray celebrated thirty years as a movie director, with nearly one hundred(!) titles to his credit. A lifelong fan of B-movies, professional wrestling, and bare bosoms, Fred Olen Ray's name on a movie is a guarantee of quality. Not "quality" the way your mom might define the word, but in a way that suits Mr. Skin just fine.

Top 501 DVDs: *Bad Girls from Mars* (1990), *Bikini Airways* (2003), *Bikini Drive-In* (1995), *Evil Toons* (1992), *Masseuse* (1996), *Scream Queen Hot Tub Party* (1991)

SKIN VISIONARIES

Bad Lieutenant (1992)

Director: Abel Ferrara

Breasts: 4; **Butts**: 1; **Bushes**: 1

Nude Stars: **Victoria Bastel** (Breasts);
Frankie Thorn (Full Frontal, Butt)

The Bad Lieutenant (Harvey Keitel) is a crooked, crack-smoking New York cop. And he's put on one of history's most foul cases: that of a nun raped on the altar. The fact that Frankie Thorn, playing the nun, shows off her holy, habitless body adds to Keitel's conflicting emotions and proves that nuns are best when the clothing they're wearing is none—and their burning bush is a fiery red!

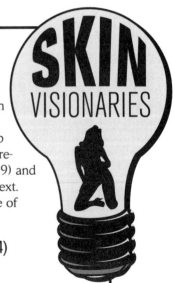

Abel Ferrara
Dirty doings in New York City.

Manhattan madman Abel Ferrara broke big in the independent film business by directing the splatter-horror favorite *The Driller Killer* (1979), which he also starred in—very convincingly. He followed up with the rape-and-revenge opus *Ms. 45* (1981) and the Times-square-gone-wild thriller *Fear City* (1984). The kinked out *Cat Chaser* (1989) and the Christopher Walken ass-kicker *King of New York* (1990) came next. Then, with *Bad Lieutenant* (1992), Ferrara reinvented himself as one of cinema's true wild cards. And he's no joker.

Top 501 DVDs: *Bad Lieutenant* (1992), *Cat Chaser* (1989), *Fear City* (1984)

Barbarella (1968)

Director: Roger Vadim

Breasts: 12; **Butts**: 1; **Bushes**: 1

Nude Star: **Jane Fonda** (Breasts, Butt)

Anonymous Nudes: 5

Barbarella is a sci-fi skinedelic classic that follows Jane Fonda in the title role as she saves the universe from an evil mastermind who wants to end the reign of peace and free love. No plain Jane, *Barbarella* boasts Fonda's fantastic form, groovy see-through clothing, death by orgasm, and, amazingly, a PG rating!

Breast Sizes

Small - *adj.*
Taut and tiny; more nip than knocker. Sunken treasures and carpenter's dreams who flat-out beautify the Itty-Bitty Titty Committee. (Misty Mundae, Parker Posey)

Medium - *adj.*
The A-list of B- and C-cups. Happy handfuls of sufficiently sumptuous boobage adorning B-cup beauties and C-cup cuties. (Gina Gershon, Maggie Gyllenhaal)

Large - *adj.*
Bodaciously bountiful bra-busting bazoombas. Meaty sweeties; big and bouncy. Much more than a mouthful, no less than twin volcanoes of titanic voluptitude. (Rosanna Arquette, Jennifer Connelly)

JAMAMBO! - *adj.*
Superhumanly over-endowed dairy queens. Beyond the valley of the ultimate mega-boobage! The hugest, heaviest, most back-breakingly bombastic and ravishingly rotund monster mashers in all of Mamdom! (Uschi Digard, Mimi Rogers)

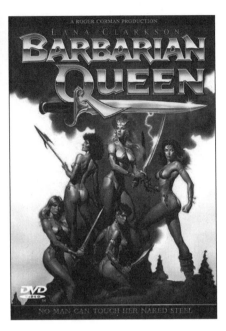

Barbarian Queen (1985)

Director: Héctor Olivera

Breasts: 38; **Butts**: 3; **Bushes**: 4

Nude Stars: **Lana Clarkson** (Breasts);
  Dawn Dunlap (Breasts);
  Katt Shea (Breasts);
  Susana Traverso (Breasts)

Anonymous Nudes: 15

Lana Clarkson is joined by a slew of savage beauties in *Barbarian Queen,* including Katt Shea, Dawn Dunlap, and Susana Traverso. The ladies' saga tells of freeing oppressed people from cruel Roman rule. A lot of clothing gets freed from bodies too, including one megamammary and blast-of-bush scene featuring fifteen naked extras.

The *Queen* Is Dead

Buxom blonde Lana Clarkson, who so nobly filled out the titular breastplate in both *Barbarian Queen* and *Barbarian Queen II: The Empress Strikes Back* (1989), was shot to death at the home of hot-shot record producer Phil Spector in 2003.

skinfo

The Bare Wench Project (1999)

Director: Jim Wynorski

Breasts: 10; **Butts**: 4; **Bushes**: 4

Nude Stars: **Antonia Dorian** (Breasts); **Nikki Fritz**
(Breasts, Butt, Bush); **Lorissa McComas** (Full Frontal,
Butt); **Julie K. Smith** (Full Frontal, Butt); **Julie Strain**
(Full Frontal, Butt)

The setup of *The Bare Wench Project* is "four sorority sisters
disappeared into the woods near Bareassville, Delaware,
while shooting a documentary. A week later their footage
was found." It's a titillating premise made more so by the
tit-flashing cast that includes Julie Strain as the Bare Wench
and such softcore starlets as Julie K. Smith, Lorissa
McComas, and Nikki Fritz.

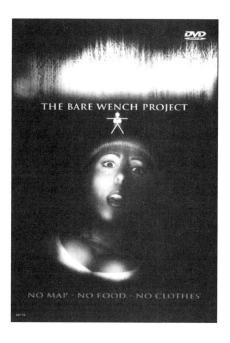

All's Bare

The Bare Wench Project was just one of a slew of *Blair
Witch Project* parodies to storm the cultural landscape
at the turn of the millennium. Among the others: The
Erotic Witch Project (1999), *The Blair Bitch Project Starring
Linda Blair* (1999), *The Blair Clown Project* (1999), *The
Blair Warner Project* (1999), and *The Blair Thumb* (2002).
There was also *The Bare Wench Project 2:
Scared Topless* (2001).

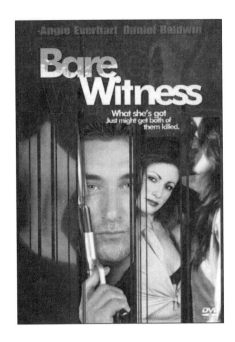

Bare Witness (2001)

Director: Kelley Cauthen

Breasts: 10; **Butts**: 5; **Bushes**: 5

Nude Stars: **Angie Everhart** (Full Frontal, Butt); **Catalina Larranaga** (Full Frontal, Butt); **Linda Molnar** (Full Frontal, Butt, Thong); **Lauren Reina** (Full Frontal, Butt); **Keri Windsor** (Full Frontal, Butt)

Bare Witness is the kind of thriller that makes guys wish they grew up to be cynical cops like Daniel Baldwin. Angie Everhart is rooming with hooker Catalina Larranaga. Trouble is, one john is an assassin who blabs about offing a political hotshot. Now Catalina is in his crosshairs, though not before we get to see her pubic hairs—and a cupful of tits and ass for good measure.

SKINEMA SENSATIONS!

Erotic Thrillers
Not just whodunits—nude-done-its!

In its infancy, late-night-cable-television programming was often studded with penetration-edited hardcore porn and/or European soft-sex imports. Taking a cue from flesh-intensive Hollywood potboilers like *Body Heat* (1981), *Fatal Attraction* (1987), and *Sea of Love* (1989), B-movie studios sowed fertile seeds into the after-hours TV landscape with low-budget smashes that mixed murder and mammaries such as *Night Eyes* (1990) and *Mirror Images* (1991). These films rapidly blossomed into one of the most prolific sexploitation subgenres in all of skinema. The Erotic Thriller has generated its own superstars (Shannon Tweed, Shannon Whirry, Angie Everhart), signature directors (Gregory Hippolyte, a.k.a. Gregory Dark), and enduring film series (*Animal Instincts, Secret Games, Body Chemistry*).

Top 501 DVDs: *Animal Instincts* (1992), *Animal Instincts 2* (1994), *Animal Instincts III* (1995), *Bare Witness* (2001), *Diary of a Sex Addict* (2001), *Naked Souls* (1995), *Sexual Predator* (2001), *Stripped to Kill* (1987)

Basic Instinct (1992)
Unrated Ultimate Edition
Director: Paul Verhoeven

Breasts: 4; **Butts**: 2; **Bushes**: 1

Nude Stars: **Sharon Stone** (Full Frontal, Butt); **Jeanne Tripplehorn** (Breasts, Butt, Thong)

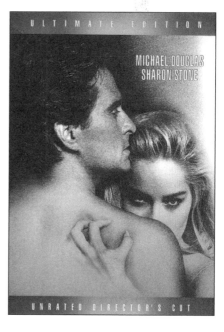

If you're not familiar with *Basic Instinct,* you may have to relearn the basics of big-screen nudity. Michael Douglas plays a cop seeking an ice-pick-wielding murderer. Sharon Stone is the key suspect, and Douglas becomes dangerously enamored of her lethal charms. There's sick sex, lesbianism, crazy car chases, and, of course, Sharon's thigh-parting breakthrough moment.

TOP 5

Movies from 1992

5. *The Lover*

4. *La Belle Noiseuse*

3. *Innocent Blood*

2. *Blown Away*

1. Basic Instinct

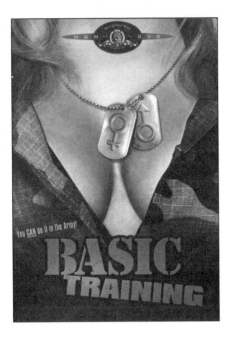

Basic Training (1985)

Director: Andrew Sugerman

Breasts: 38; **Butts**: 1; **Bushes**: 2

Nude Stars: **Angela Aames** (Breasts); **Erika Dockery** (Breasts); **Ann Dusenberry** (Breasts); **Barbara Peckinpaugh** (Full Frontal); **Rhonda Shear** (Breasts)

Anonymous Nudes: 14

Basic Training is the recipe for world peace—that is, by giving guys a piece of ass. Ann Dusenberry plays a Pentagon worker who lets down her arms so the brass can lie down with her. Angela Aames proves her aim is true, and Rhonda Shear flashes jug while riding a whale of a guy to the big O.

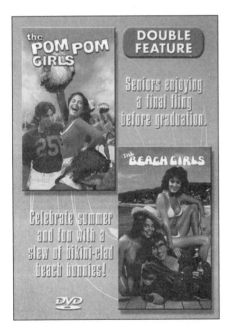

The Beach Girls (1982)

Director: Bud Townsend

Breasts: 32; **Butts**: 11

Nude Stars: **Debra Blee** (Breasts); **Val Kline** (Breasts, Butt); **Jeanette Linne** (Breasts); **Jeana Tomasina** (Breasts, Butt)

Anonymous Nudes: 12

In *The Beach Girls,* one virginal high-school grad moves into a beach house with two wild and crazy gals who teach her the joy of anonymous sex with pizza delivery boys and TV repairmen. The orgy is fueled by six oversized trash bags of marijuana that mysteriously wash ashore; soon everyone is partying naked! Life sure is a beach for these girls.

Beer League (2006)

Director: Bud Townsend

Breasts: 14

Nude Stars: **Charlene Biton** (Breasts, Thong);
   Keisha (Breasts)

Anonymous Nudes: 5

Enormously affable stand-up-comedy superstar and Howard
Stern sidekick Artie Lange spills onto the big screen with all
his hilarity intact via the extremely tactless brews-boobs-and-
baseball epic *Beer League*. Best described as "The Bad News
Bears grow up to become insane alcoholics," *Beer League*
chronicles Artie leading his hard-luck softball squad in and
out of all manner of foul-mouthed, bodily-function-intensive
misadventures. *Beer League* scores a home run on laughs,
and in terms of naked Jersey bar babes, it's flat-out
in-*fox*-icating!

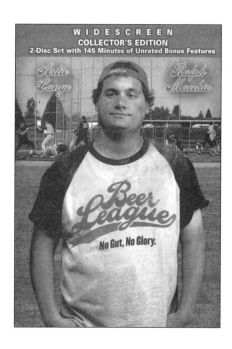

Behind Locked Doors (1968)

Director: Charles Romine

Breasts: 21; **Butts**: 2; **Bushes**: 2

Nude Stars: **Joyce Danner** (Breasts, Butt); **Madeleine
   Le Roux** (Breasts); **Eve Reeves** (Full Frontal, Butt)

Anonymous Nudes: 8

A brother and sister abduct go-go dancers in *Behind Locked
Doors*. The brother is experimenting on live nude girls to
create the perfect sexual plaything. He's got good fodder
with Joyce Danner and Eve Reeves. They show off their
hippie hooters and even lez out, while redheaded beauty
Madeleine Le Roux lets it all hang out.

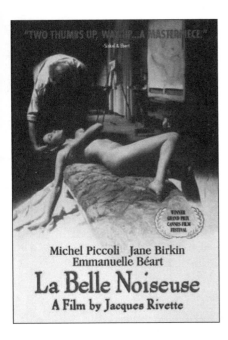

La Belle Noiseuse (1992)

Director: Jacques Rivette

Breasts: 2; **Butts**: 1; **Bushes**: 1

Nude Star: **Emmanuelle Béart** (Full Frontal, Butt)

La Belle Noiseuse is a four-hour nudie loop of star Emmanuelle Béart. It's officially a French tale of a frustrated older painter who has Emmanuelle as his muse and naked model. Almost the entire film takes place in the artist's studio, with Emmanuelle posing in the buff. It's all fodder for great art and better masturbation.

Below the Belt (1971)

Director: Bethel Buckalew

Breasts: 16; **Butts**: 8; **Bushes**: 7

Nude Stars: **Rene Bond** (Full Frontal, Butt); **Uschi Digard** (Full Frontal, Butt); **Terri Johnson** (Breasts, Butt); **Mirka Madnadraszky** (Full Frontal, Butt); **Jane Tsentas** (Full Frontal, Butt)

Anonymous Nudes: 3

Below the Belt is a pants boiler about boxing with a double combination sure to KO viewers. The first hit comes from top-heavy Uschi Digard, followed by a body shot from Rene Bond. Mirka Madnadraszky makes her nude debut, while Terri Johnson ensures this movie leaves you *up* for the count.

Beneath the Valley of the Ultra-Vixens (1979)

Director: Russ Meyer

Breasts: 12; **Butts**: 4; **Bushes**: 4

Nude Stars: **Ann Marie** (Full Frontal, Butt); **Uschi Digard** (Breasts, Butt); **Sharon Hill** (Full Frontal, Butt); **June Mack** (Breasts, Bush); **Francesca Natividad** (Full Frontal, Butt)

Anonymous Nudes: 1

Russ Meyer returns with another big-boob satire on middle-class values in the softcore sextravaganza *Beneath the Valley of the Ultra-Vixens*. Meyer regular Francesca "Kitten" Natividad is as sex crazed as always, but she's not turned on by her boyfriend's backdoor fetish. This leads to infidelity with bosomy Sharon Hill, chesty Ann Marie, and super jugs Candy Samples—and who wouldn't want to sample her candy? None of this makes narrative sense, but your tight pants will prove that sometimes a good story doesn't need a good story.

Beneath, Beneath, good for your heart, the more you eat ...

With hardcore X-rated movies exploding in adults-only theaters the world over, Russ Meyer—the Supreme Viscount of Soft-sex Voluptuousness—went out with a gas in the mountainously full-bodied form of *Beneath the Valley of the Ultra-Vixens*. Not only did Meyer co-write the movie with Roger Ebert, he also directed, photographed, edited, and distributed it, and, he claimed, the love scenes are scored with recordings of Russ's own flatulence!

skinfo

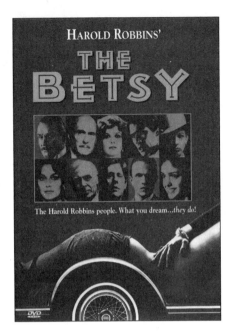

The Harold Robbins people. What you dream...*they do!*

The Betsy (1978)

Director: Daniel Petrie

Breasts: 4; **Butts**: 1; **Bushes**: 1

Nude Stars: **Kathleen Beller** (Full Frontal);
   Lesley-Anne Down (Left Breast, Butt);
   Katharine Ross (Left Breast)

Mr. Skin misses the '70s, when big-name stars like Laurence Olivier and Robert Duvall would star in big-budget vulgarathons like *The Betsy*. Olivier and Duvall play auto mavens eager to show off their latest model, the Betsy. But what gives this vehicle gas is the gash: Kathleen Beller in one of the all-time great skinny-dips, Lesley-Anne Down baring ass crack, and Katharine Ross breast-feeding for all us big babies.

Wet? See *Betsy*

Kathleen Beller kicks *The Betsy* into overdrive early on with the most fur-tastically fabulous full-frontal skinny dip of all time. In real life, the former Kirby of TV's *Dynasty* has been married to "She Blinded Me with Science" geek Thomas Dolby since 1988.

skinfo

Betty Blue (1986)
Director: Jean-Jacques Beineix

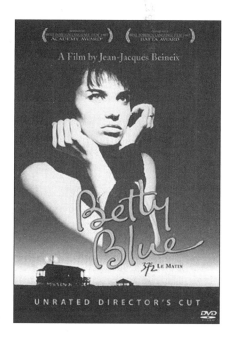

Breasts: 3; **Butts**: 1; **Bushes**: 1

Nude Stars: **Clémentine Célarié** (Right Breast);
Béatrice Dalle (Full Frontal, Butt)

A French repairman gets a monkey wrench thrown into his mild-mannered existence when he falls for wild child Betty (Béatrice Dalle) in *Betty Blue*. First charming and disarming, Betty's energy and insane exploits send both of their lives spinning out of control. What will happen when this handyman realizes that no amount of tinkering can fix poor Betty's blue moods? Betty may be batty, but boy is she insanely hot.

Midnight Movies
Cult happenings for hip insomniacs.

What's the roving cinefile/skinefile to do when the weekend night is old but the eyes are wide awake? Stake out the local arthouse movie theater, where the enterprising owners have taken to maximizing Friday and Saturday-night profits by putting on a special event that follows the last show of the evening. What's on the bill? *Beyond the Valley of the Dolls* (1970), *El Topo* (1970), *The Rocky Horror Picture Show* (1975), *Summer School Teachers* (1975), *Forbidden Zone* (1980), *Pink Floyd the Wall* (1982), as well as anything directed by maniacal movie mavericks David Lynch and John Waters, are standard fare for this decidedly unstandard audience.

Top 501 DVDs: *Angel Heart* (1987), *Barbarella* (1968), *Beyond the Valley of the Dolls* (1970), *Bloodducking Freaks* (1976), *Blue Velvet* (1986), *Café Flesh* (1982), *A Clockwork Orange* (1971), *Eating Raoul* (1982), *Forbidden Zone* (1980), *The Hunger* (1983), *Ilsa, She Wolf of the S.S.* (1974), *The Kentucky Fried Movie* (1977), *Lost Highway* (1997), *The Man Who Fell to Earth* (1976), *Massacre at Central High* (1976), *Mulholland Dr.* (2001), *Pink Flamingos* (1972), *Wild at Heart* (1990)

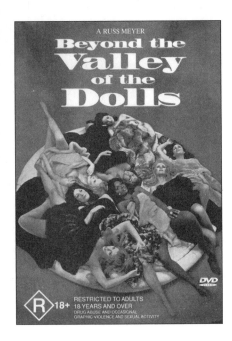

Beyond the Valley of the Dolls (1970)

Director: Russ Meyer

Breasts: 18; **Butts**: 2; **Bushes**: 1

Nude Stars: **Erica Gavin** (Breasts); **Marcia McBroom** (Breasts); **Cynthia Myers** (Breasts, Butt); **Angel Ray** (Full Frontal, Butt); **Dolly Read** (Breasts); **Susan Reed** (Breasts); **Samantha Scott** (Breasts)

Anonymous Nudes: 2

Beyond the Valley of the Dolls is sex, jugs, and rock and roll, Russ Meyer style. Delicious Dolly Read heads the Carrie Nations—the swingingest girl group to wow the L.A. scene. Along the way the girls contend with a Nazi, a hermaphrodite, topless dancer Angel Ray, and Edy Williams in her prime. After glimpsing Marcia McBroom's superduper, all-natural cocoa cupcakes you'll need a McBroom to clean up! This is Mr. Skin's happening, and it freaks me out!

Valley Whirls

Time named *Beyond the Valley of the Dolls* one of the ten best films of the 1970s. As a bridge between hippies, acid rock, and punk, *BVD* so captivated the members of the Sex Pistols that they hired Russ Meyer and Roger Ebert to create their own feature film, to be titled *Who Killed Bambi?* Due to personality clashes, the project ultimately went the way of Sid Vicious's love life.

skinfo

Big Bad Mama (1974)

Director: Steve Carver

Breasts: 10; **Butts**: 6;
  Bushes: 1

Nude Stars: **Shannon Christie** (Butt);
  Angie Dickinson (Full Frontal, Butt);
  Sally Kirkland (Breasts, Butt);
  Robbie Lee (Breasts, Butt); **Joan Prather** (Breasts,
  Butt); **Susan Sennett** (Breasts, Butt)

Angie Dickinson keeps it in the family by working with her delicious daughters to rob banks in *Big Bad Mama*. The family that steals together ends up getting naked together. Angie displays all three big bad B's and has sex with both Tom Skerritt and William Shatner (watch out for Captain Kirk's man ass, though!). Shannon Christie, Sally Kirkland, Robbie Lee, Joan Prather, and Susan Sennett all show off their young, svelte bodies. Bang 'em while you've got 'em!

Big Good *Mamas*

Don't confuse *Big Bad Mama* with producer Roger Corman's *Bloody Mama* (1970) starring Shelley Winters or Cloris Leachman's turn as *Crazy Mama* (1975). Only Angie's Mama got naked—and it's no wonder then that she's the only one who also earned a sequel.

skinfo

Big Bad Mama II (1987)

Director: Jim Wynorski

Breasts: 6; **Butts**: 1; **Bushes**: 1

Nude Stars: **Danielle Brisebois** (Breasts);
   Angie Dickinson (Full Frontal, Butt);
   Julie McCullough (Breasts)

In *Big Bad Mama II,* it's back to a life of crime for Angie Dickinson. She teams up with daughters Danielle Brisebois and Julie McCullough to start knocking over banks. This gangster saga includes a nostalgic look back at Dickinson's full-frontal nudity from the first film—which is vital, since Angie relies on a body double for her nude scenes here.

TOP 5

Movies from 1974

5. *The Night Porter*

4. *Double Agent 73*

3. *Caged Heat*

2. *Emmanuelle*

1. Big Bad Mama

The Big Bird Cage (1972)

Director: Jack Hill

Breasts: 25; **Butts**: 7; **Bushes**: 2

Nude Stars: **Teda Bracci** (Breasts); **Rizza Fabia** (Breasts); **Anitra Ford** (Left Breast, Butt, Bush); **Wendy Green** (Right Breast); **Pam Grier** (Breasts); **Karen McKevic** (Full Frontal, Butt); **Candice Roman** (Butt); **Carol Speed** (Left Breast)

Anonymous Nudes: 9

The Big Bird Cage, the follow-up to the 1971 hit *The Big Doll House,* follows its predecessor's successful formula: hot broads behind bars, catfights, shower scenes, and an all-hell-breaks-loose climactic riot. The prison is guarded by homosexuals to keep the chicks from tempting dicks, but don't worry—the ladies find other reasons to lose their hot pants and halter tops when out in the fields picking sugar cane.

Women in Prison
W.I.P. it! W.I.P. it good!

Some things we hold to be self-evident, such as the appeal of films that follow the triumphs and travails of attractive females who happen to be detained in houses of correction. An inmate's entry to such an institution involves the inevitable strip search, followed by the mandatory group shower, leading to the requisite catfight, which predictably but enticingly segues into budding respect born of amorous affections shared by the two former combatants, until finally—after intermittent violence and brutality—everybody is happy, both on the screen and in the audience. You know the drill, now line up!

Top 501 DVDs: *Alley Cat* (1984), *Bad Girls' Dormitory* (1984), *Behind Locked Doors* (1968), *The Big Bird Cage* (1972), *Caged Heat* (1974), *Cellblock Sisters: Banished Behind Bars* (1995), *Ilsa, the Wicked Warden* (1980), *Love Camp 7* (1969), *Reform School Girls* (1986), *Women in Cages* (1971)

Bikini Airways (2003)

Director: Fred Olen Ray

Breasts: 10; **Butts**: 4; **Bushes**: 5

Nude Stars: **Maya Divine** (Full Frontal); **Belinda Gavin** (Full Frontal, Butt, Thong); **Amy Lindsay** (Full Frontal, Butt, Thong); **Kimber Lynn** (Full Frontal, Butt, Thong); **Regina Russell** (Full Frontal, Butt, Thong)

The heroine of *Bikini Airways* boasts beauty, charm, a stupendous rack, and an airline she's inherited. Alas, running a network of passenger planes is not a no-brainer. Even the highest of highfliers might go under. Luckily, the new CEO is an idea ma'am—she cleverly charters her jets to sporting swains who want to throw their bachelor parties at 69,000 feet.

TOP 5

Fred Olen Ray Movies

5. *Hollywood Chainsaw Hookers* (1988)

4. *Scream Queen Hot Tub Party* (1991)

3. *Bikini Airways* (2003)

2. *Masseuse* (1996)

1. Bikini Drive-In (1995)

Bikini Bistro (1995)

Director: Ernest G. Sauer

Breasts: 10; **Butts**: 3; **Bushes**: 4

Nude Stars: **Amy Lynn Baxter** (Full Frontal, Butt, Thong);
   Marilyn Chambers (Full Frontal, Butt); **Isabelle
   Fortea** (Full Frontal, Butt); **Joan Gerardi** (Full Frontal)

Anonymous Nudes: 1

When Amy Lynn Baxter fears for her vegetarian restaurant
in *Bikini Bistro*, she calls on Marilyn Chambers to help save it.
Marilyn's plan is simple and already given away by the
movie's title—she has the sexy wait staff wear as little as
humanly possible, and the sales go through the roof while
customers' veggie dogs go through their pants!

The Bikini Carwash Company (1992)

Director: Ed Hansen

Breasts: 18; **Butts**: 5; **Bushes**: 4

Nude Stars: **Kimberly Bee** (Breasts); **Rikki
   Brando** (Breasts); **Sara Suzanne Brown** (Breasts);
   Neriah Davis (Breasts, Butt); **Kristi Ducati** (Breasts,
   Butt, Bush); **Brook Lynn Page** (Breasts); **Missy
   Warner** (Breasts)

Anonymous Nudes: 3

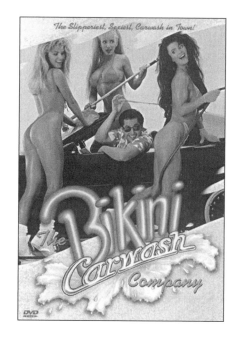

When a car wash improves its business by hiring scantily
clad honeys to sweeten its return, the authorities try to
shut it down. *The Bikini Carwash Company* is the stirring tale
of those stirring tails, including Missy Warner, Sara Suzanne
Brown, Rikki Brando, Kristi Ducati, Neriah Davis, and
Kimberly Bee, among many topless others.

Bikini Drive-In (1995)

Director: Fred Olen Ray

Breasts: 24; **Butts**: 5; **Bushes**: 2

Nude Stars: **Michelle Bauer** (Breasts, Thong); **Roxanne Blaze** (Breasts); **Deborah Dutch** (Breasts, Thong); **Nikki Fritz** (Full Frontal, Butt, Thong); **Becky LeBeau** (Breasts); **Toni Lynn** (Breasts); **Tane McClure** (Breasts); **Melissa Anne Moore** (Breasts); **Ashlie Rhey** (Breasts, Butt)

Anonymous Nudes: 3

When a movie has a name like *Bikini Drive-In,* you may be disappointed to learn that many of the cuties here are seen *without* their bikinis—that is, if you're crazy! Among the many bared boobs, most notable are Michelle Bauer, Nikki Fritz, Roxanne Blaze, Deborah Dutch, Becky LeBeau, Tane McClure, Melissa Anne Moore, and Ashlie Rhey, who are seen bathing topless, in wet T-shirt contests, and dancing naked.

Bikini Summer 2 (1992)

Director: Jeff Conaway

Breasts: 17; **Butts**: 3

Nude Stars: **Avalon Anders** (Breasts, Thong); **Melinda Armstrong** (Breasts, Butt, Thong); **Carrie Bittner** (Breasts, Thong); **Tracy Dali** (Breasts, Thong); **Maureen Flaherty** (Breasts, Thong); **Tammy Marcel** (Breasts, Thong)

Anonymous Nudes: 4

Bikini Summer 2 focuses on rich girls who take a beach bum home and start a rock band. Sounds plausible. Meanwhile, the father of one of the girls submits to blonde dominatrix Avalon Anders. Yet he has the stunning Jessica Hahn at home as his horny wife. Go figure—and what a figure! Add lots of bikinied and French-maid-outfitted cuties and, oh, if only this bikini were an endless summer.

Bilitis (1977)

Director: David Hamilton

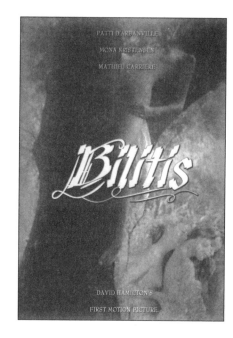

Breasts: 28; **Butts**: 12; **Bushes**: 12

Nude Stars: **Patti D'Arbanville** (Full Frontal, Butt); **Mona Kristensen** (Breasts); **Catherine Leprince** (Breasts)

Anonymous Nudes: 11

Lush and erotic, *Bilitis* tells the tale of a young French schoolgirl away at boarding school. Along the way the viewer is treated to complex themes of power, lesbian romance, and the confusion of adolescence. Patti D'Arbanville is fantastic as Bilitis, especially when she peels off her bathing suit, exposing as nubile a pair of nubbins as you will ever see.

David Hamilton
From high-art stills to big-screen thrills.

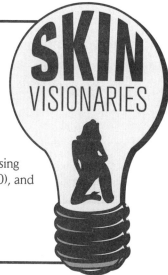

There's no mistaking the passion of British art photographer David Hamilton. Published books of his nude figure studies include the titles *Dreams of a Young Girl* (1971), *Sisters* (1972), *The Young Girl* (1973), and *The Age of Innocence* (1995). Training his keen eye on moving images, Hamilton helmed some of skinema's most arousing coming-of-age stories, including *Bilitis* (1977), *Tendres Cousines* (1980), and *First Desires* (1983).

Top 501 DVDs: *Bilitis* (1977)

Billy Bathgate (1991)

Director: Robert Benton

Breasts: 2; **Butts**: 1; **Bushes**: 1

Nude Star: **Nicole Kidman** (Full Frontal, Butt)

It's the dusk of mobster Dutch Schultz's criminal career. In those twilight years, though, Dutch is kept happy by the perfectly perverse Nicole Kidman, who's so naked throughout *Billy Bathgate* that the rest of the plot becomes as fuzzy as her oft-seen muff.

Billy Jack (1971)

Director: Tom Laughlin

Breasts: 4; **Butts**: 2; **Bushes**: 2

Nude Stars: **Delores Taylor** (Full Frontal, Butt)

Anonymous Nudes: 1

Tom Laughlin is a half-Indian, ex–Green Beret, fully kick-ass pacifist in *Billy Jack*. Laughlin's real-life wife, Delores Taylor, plays Billy Jack's earth-mother squeeze, who's an alternative-school teacher in a small New Mexico town. Billy Jack keeps the local rednecks from running rampant over the school's proto-alterna-kids, many of whom are hot, barely covered hippie chicks in the lush bloom of free-lovin' youth.

The Bitch (1979)

Director: Gerry O'Hara

Breasts: 26; **Butts**: 5; **Bushes**: 6

Nude Stars: **Joan Collins** (Breasts, Butt); **Sue Lloyd** (Breasts, Butt); **Pamela Salem** (Breasts, Butt, Bush)

Anonymous Nudes: 10

Joan Collins embodies sister Jackie Collins in *The Bitch*, playing a disco diva in this adaptation of Jackie's novel. She's a club owner who's got plenty of problems with all the adoring men in her life. There's plenty of tawdry action, with Joan frequently dropping her top to tally some tickets. Still, she gets some competition from the young bods of youngbloods Sue Lloyd and Pamela Salem.

Black Mama, White Mama (1972)

Director: Eddie Romero

Breasts: 26; **Butts**: 5; **Bushes**: 1

Nude Stars: **Alona Alegre** (Breasts); **Wendy Green** (Breasts, Butt); **Pam Grier** (Breasts); **Margaret Markov** (Breasts)

Anonymous Nudes: 12

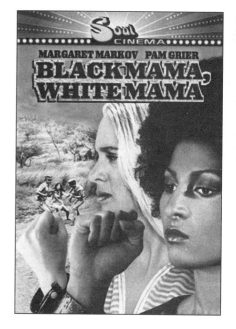

Black Mama, White Mama kicks off when Pam Grier and Margaret Markov escape a jungle prison while shackled to one another, and cultural barriers—like the ladies' tops— eventually come down. The girls pool their efforts to save their own skins and further the cause of banana-republic revolutionaries in this raucous, shoot-'em-up mix of bounding racks and archvillainy.

Black Shampoo (1976)

Director: Greydon Clark

Breasts: 13; **Butts**: 1; **Bushes**: 5

Nude Stars: **Tanya Boyd** (Full Frontal, Butt);
    Diana St. Clair (Right Breast, Bush)

Anonymous Nudes: 5

The supercool hero of *Black Shampoo* just wants to run his Sunset Strip hair salon and bone his steady stream of female admirers. Don't interfere with the happiness of his trusted receptionist, the beautiful Tanya Boyd, not even if you are top dog in the Mob. You should know to leave the stud to his own devices, unless you are prepared to take the shaft yourself.

Black Venus (1983)

Director: Claude Mulot

Breasts: 15; **Butts**: 5; **Bushes**: 4

Nude Stars: **Monique Gabrielle** (Full Frontal, Butt);
    Florence Guérin (Full Frontal, Butt); **Josephine
    Jacqueline Jones** (Full Frontal, Butt); **Karin
    Schubert** (Full Frontal, Butt)

Anonymous Nudes: 4

Poor sculptor José Antonio Ceinos has completely lost his inspiration in *Black Venus*. Fortunately, he finds a muse in the form of gorgeous Josephine Jacqueline Jones. She's a bisexual prostitute in a very artistic brothel run by Mandy Rice-Davies. Soon Josephine provides inspiration to both José and horny home viewers—with assistance from such patrons of the arts as Monique Gabrielle, Florence Guérin, and Karin Schubert.

Blame It on Rio (1984)

Director: Stanley Donen

Breasts: 86; **Butts**: 1;
  Bushes: 1

Nude Stars: **Michelle Johnson** (Full Frontal, Butt); **Demi Moore** (Right Breast)

Anonymous Nudes: 43

Blame It on Rio is the ultimate midlife-crisis caper about a pair of jiggly, nude nubiles who can't get enough of a low-swinging, shriveled scrotum. One old ball is Michael Caine, who's got a crush on the best friend (Michelle Johnson) of his daughter (Demi Moore) as they vacation on Brazil's bawdy beaches. Demi exposes one of her sweetly teeny pre-op chest plums, but it's the naturally bazoombastic Michelle who gets naked early and often.

TOP 5

Movies from 1984

5. *Fear City*

4. *Body Double*

3. *Sheena*

2. *Gwendoline*

1. Blame it on Rio

Blame Tit on Rio

Blame It on Rio is based on the 1977 French comedy *Un moment d'égarement,* a.k.a. *One Wild Moment,* which features much less nudity than its raunchy American cousin. That's a refreshing switch from *le norm!*

skinfo

Blaze Starr Goes Nudist (1960)

Director: Doris Wishman

Breasts: 20; **Butts**: 10; **Bushes**: 2

Nude Star: **Blaze Starr** (Full Frontal, Butt)

Anonymous Nudes: 9

The classic exploitation flick *Blaze Starr Goes Nudist,* directed by Doris Wishman, follows Blaze as she runs away from autograph hounds, escaping into a theater playing a nudist film. The living looks sleazy, so she joins up, and viewers are teated to her swimming naked, engaging in chess with all her pieces exposed, and playing archery in the buff, which will sharpen audiences' arrowheads.

Something Weird Video
Seattle's retro-sexploitation powerhouse.

In a way, Something Weird Video invented the DVD bonus feature. The company, founded by former Dead Kennedys manager Mike Vraney, pioneered the field in collecting trailers, deleted scenes, posters, and photos and issuing them along with the ultrarare and extremely groovy vintage sexploitation titles that they (oftentimes literally) unearthed. As times and technology changed, Something Weird adapted and remains the go-to source for go-go-girl flicks, nudie loops, and other crazy ephemera of the days when sex-on-screen was America's favorite secret sin.

Top 501 DVDs: *Below the Belt* (1971), *Blaze Starr Goes Nudist* (1960), *Deadly Weapons* (1973), *Double Agent 73* (1974), *The Godson* (1971), *Mantis in Lace* (1968), *The Pigkeeper's Daughter* (1972), *Sassy Sue* (1972), *Tobacco Roody* (1970), *Wham Bam Thank You Spaceman* (1975)

SKIN VISIONARIES

Blind Date (1984)

Director: Nico Mastorakis

Breasts: 10; **Bushes**: 1

Nude Stars: **Kirstie Alley** (Breasts); **Antigone Amanitis** (Breasts); **Lana Clarkson** (Breasts, Bush); **Kathy Hill** (Breasts); **Marina Sirtis** (Breasts)

Blind Date casts Joseph Bottoms as a blind ad exec pursuing a serial killer. Fortunately, he's got an electronic device that allows him to see the world like a bad '80s video game. Home viewers, of course, get a perfect look at the amazing beauties who are stalked by the psycho—including young Kirstie Alley.

Blind Luck

Kirstie Alley fans had to wait for *Blind Date* to hit DVD to witness the full impact of her sex scene. The initial theatrical cut was heavily censored. Most of the DVD comes from "ungraded dailies," but it ups the Alley sensationally. Cheers!

skinfo

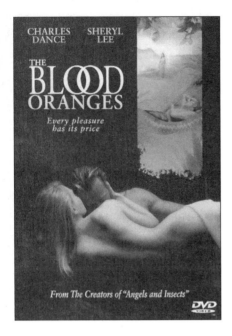

The Blood Oranges (1997)

Director: Philip Haas

Breasts: 6; **Butts**: 1; **Bushes**: 1

Nude Stars: **Sheryl Lee** (Breasts); **Aida Lopez** (Full Frontal, Butt); **Laila Robins** (Breasts)

Longtime married couple Sheryl Lee and Charles Dance go off to a lovely beach town to indulge some wild oats—and we don't just mean using the hot tub at the resort. Instead, they're soon swapping mates with Laila Robins and her photographer husband, Colin Lane. Sadly, we're not talking about Laila and Sheryl hooking up. Still, the interconnecting canoodling in *The Blood Oranges* makes for a pretty hot tale. Nice vitamin C-cups!

Bloodsucking Freaks (1976)

Director: Joel M. Reed

Breasts: 56; **Butts**: 14; **Bushes**: 21

Nude Star: **Viju Krem** (Breasts, Butt)

Anonymous Nudes: 27

Bloodsucking Freaks centers around a theater of the macabre in the SoHo district of New York City. Master Sardu (Seamus O'Brien) and his dwarf assistant run a show featuring naked, tortured, and dismembered women. O'Brien captures Viju Krem, playing a ballerina, whom he breaks for his greatest showstopper. Along the way, completely nude victims are tortured to death in a variety of creative ways that both repel and attract the sicko viewer.

Blown Away (1992)

Director: Brenton Spencer

Breasts: 2; **Butts**: 1

Nude Star: **Nicole Eggert** (Breasts, Butt)

In some circles, *Blown Away* is known as *The Tale of Two Coreys,* or, alternatively, *Former Child-Star Orgy.* Corey Haim and Corey Feldman play brothers working at a ski resort. Their lives turn to slush with the arrival of Nicole Eggert. She wants nothing more than to have sex with Corey Haim in hopes that he'll off her daddy. Does morality stand a chance in the face of so much nudity?

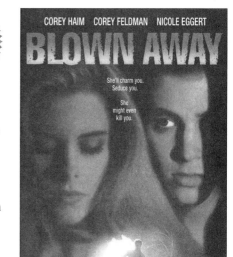

COREY HAIM   COREY FELDMAN   NICOLE EGGERT

BLOWN AWAY

She'll charm you.
Seduce you.

She
might even
kill you.

ARTISAN

Freaks You!

Bloodsucking Freaks may or may not have been rated X by the MPAA. It was definitely protested on New York's skinfamous 42nd Street by the organization Women Against Pornography, but they were tipped off to the movie's outrages by the movie's producers, looking for free publicity. Luis De Jesus, who plays the vile (yet charming) dwarf Ralphus, was a stage dancer with Parliament Funkadelic and once costarred in a hardcore porn loop with Vanessa Del Rio.

skinfo

Bluebeard (1972)

Directors: Edward Dmytryk, Luciano Sacripanti

Breasts: 12; **Butts**: 2

Nude Stars: **Agostina Belli** (Breasts); **Sybil Danning** (Breasts); **Nathalie Delon** (Breasts); **Joey Heatherton** (Breasts); **Karin Schubert** (Breasts, Butt); **Marilù Tolo** (Breasts, Butt)

Richard Burton is a serial groom in the kinky thriller *Bluebeard*. His trophies include the likes of Raquel Welch, Joey Heatherton, and Nathalie Delon. Of course, Burton's character is kind of cheating, since he racks up the honeymoons by killing off his unlucky spouses. This amazing oddity features an incredible cast of naked beauties, even though a good number of them end up dead.

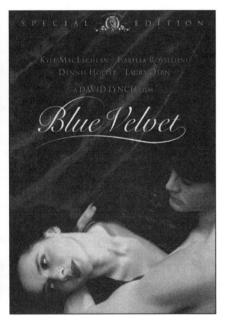

Blue Velvet (1986)

Director: David Lynch

Breasts: 2; **Butts**: 1; **Bushes**: 1

Nude Star: **Isabella Rossellini** (Full Frontal, Butt)

The suburbia conjured up in *Blue Velvet* teems with perversity. While trying to solve the mystery of a severed ear, Kyle MacLachlan stumbles into the hidden world of Isabella Rossellini's sordid sex life and finds it hard to turn away from her full-frontal form. And, of course, Dennis Hopper shows up as a snorting psychopath who really loves the F word—or, in other words, Dennis Hopper.

Boarding School (1978)

Director: André Farwagi

Breasts: 10; **Bushes**: 1

Nude Stars: **Véronique Delbourg** (Breasts); **Nastassja Kinski** (Full Frontal); **Marion Kracht** (Breasts); **Carolin Ohrner** (Breasts)

Anonymous Nudes: 1

Just as we suspected, boarding schools for girls are full of young nymphos who are ready to pose as prostitutes in order to lose their virginity. Fortunately, the girls in *Boarding School* have plenty of eager clients at a boys' boarding school right down the road. But in the grand tradition of the teenage sex comedy, everybody still has a hard time getting laid.

Boarding drool

Nineteen-year-old Nastassja Kinski turned the whole world on in *Boarding School*. So much so that one might wonder what effect gamine fräulein Nastassja must have had on her own father—renowned cinematic madman Klaus Kinski. In his 1997 autobiography, *Kinski Uncut*, Klaus claims to have had incestuous relations with his own mother and sister—and, what's more, he loved it!

skinfo

Boat Trip (2002)
Unrated Edition
Director: Mort Nathan

Breasts: 14

Nude Stars: **Deanna Brooks** (Breasts); **Jami Ferrell** (Breasts); **Michelle Ruben** (Breasts); **Natalia Sokolova** (Breasts)

Anonymous Nudes: 3

Straight dudes Cuba Gooding Jr. and Horatio Sanz are mistakenly booked on a cruise for gay men in *Boat Trip*. The two leads soon discover that the ladies are quick to expose themselves around homosexual males. The real (s)exposure comes before the film even starts, however, as the filmmakers added a DVD menu that includes bonus toplessness from Deanna Brooks, Jami Ferrell, and Natalia Sokolova. Talk about special features!

TOP 5
DVD Special Features
5. *Blind Date* (1984)

4. *Sunset Grill* (1993)

3. *The 40-Year-Old Virgin* (2005)

2. *Final Destination 3* (2006)

1. Boat Trip (2002)

Double Trouble
Early on, *Body Double* director Brian De Palma considered casting adult-film star Annette Haven as the film's female lead. The studio balked, and Melanie Griffith got the job, although Annette stayed on as a technical consultant.

skinfo

Body and Soul (1981)

Director: George Bowers

Breasts: 11; **Butts**: 1

Nude Stars: **Ingrid Greer** (Breasts); **Azizi Johari** (Breasts); **Rosanne Katon** (Breasts); **Jayne Kennedy** (Right Breast); **Ola Ray** (Breasts, Butt); **Laurie Senit** (Breasts)

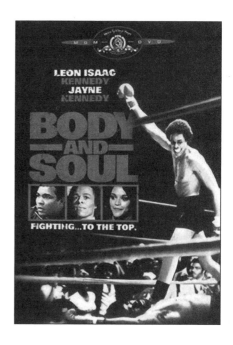

Body and Soul charts bruiser Leon Isaac Kennedy as he punches his way to the top of the boxing heap. Actually, most of his battles occur far from the ring. His greatest matchup is in a frisky foursome with Ingrid Greer, Ola Ray, and Laurie Senit, three of the top-heaviest hookers, who love their jobs and devour the champ for a T&A KO.

Body Double (1984)

Director: Brian De Palma

Breasts: 15; **Butts**: 2; **Bushes**: 1

Nude Stars: **Barbara Crampton** (Full Frontal); **Melanie Griffith** (Breasts, Butt, Thong); **Mindi Miller** (Breasts); **Barbara Peckinpaugh** (Breasts); **Linda Shaw** (Left Breast); **Brinke Stevens** (Breasts)

Anonymous Nudes: 3

MR. SKIN'S **TOP 69**

55

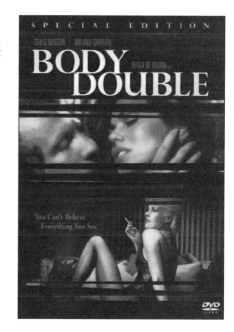

Director Brian De Palma gets his Hitchcock on in *Body Double*. Struggling actor Craig Wasson uses a telescope to spy on beautiful neighbor Deborah Shelton while she undresses. He also sees her get murdered. Then he meets porn star Melanie Griffith, who has just taken a job posing as the late Deborah. Now just add a crazy, drill-wielding Native American, and you've got a kink classic!

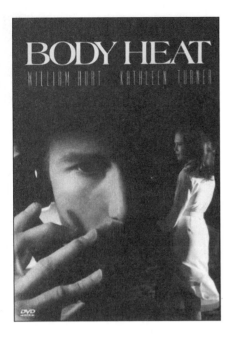

Body Heat (1981)

Director: Lawrence Kasdan

Breasts: 2; **Butts**: 1; **Bushes**: 1

Nude Star: **Kathleen Turner** (Full Frontal, Butt)

If you can't quite remember why Kathleen Turner still
inhabits the realm of A-list celebrity, return to Lawrence
Kasdan's master work *Body Heat* and witness her stunning
debut. Take one look at her delectable full-frontal nudity
and turn one ear to her distinctive, breathy whisper, and
you'll be clawing your way to the front of the line past
William Hurt yelling, "Me! Me! Let me kill your husband!"

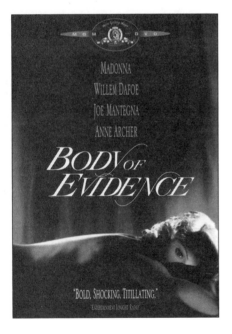

Body of Evidence (1993)

Director: Uli Edel

Breasts: 6; **Butts**: 3; **Bushes**: 2

Nude Stars: **Anne Archer** (Breasts, Butt, Bush);
Madonna (Full Frontal, Butt); **Julianne Moore**
(Breasts, Butt)

After *Basic Instinct* it seemed perfectly logical to make a
courtroom thriller about a woman who's accused of fucking
her lover to death. And who better to play the murder
weapon than Madonna? The result is *Body of Evidence,* a
box-office bomb panned by mainstream critics yet hailed
here as a skinema landmark, as Madonna's crotch shots
forever confirm that Papa Don't Bleach.

Body Shots (1999)

Director: Michael Cristofer

Breasts: 4; **Butts**: 1

Nude Stars: **Emily Procter** (Breasts, Thong);
   Tara Reid (Breasts, Butt)

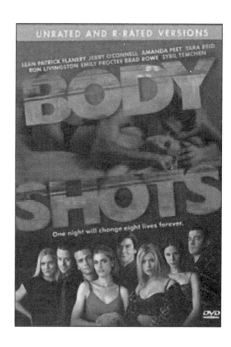

Body Shots chronicles the alleged rape of Tara Reid by Jerry O'Connell. Listen in as Tara tells her side of the story to friends Amanda Peet and Emily Procter, and watch as the film recounts both sides of the sordid tale. Tara's character may be in a compromised position, but you always know that it's just acting, so you can take pleasure in the hot shots of Tara's body.

Bolero (1984)

Director: John Derek

Breasts: 10; **Butts**: 2; **Bushes**: 3

Nude Stars: **Olivia d'Abo** (Full Frontal, Butt);
   Bo Derek (Full Frontal, Butt); **Mirta Miller** (Breasts);
   Ana Obregón (Breasts, Bush)

Anonymous Nudes: 1

Bo Derek plays an English boarding-school student whose graduation present is to get laid in *Bolero*. She sheiks her booty in Arabia, then gets horny with a bullfighter in Spain. When Bo thinks she's found the man of her dreams, she lures him like a bee to deflower her by spreading honey all over her heaving bosom. He licks, and Mr. Skin moans.

Boogie Nights (1997)

Director: Paul Thomas Anderson

Breasts: 11; **Butts**: 2; **Bushes**: 1

Nude Stars: **Skye Blue** (Breasts, Butt);
   Summer Cummings (Breasts);
   Heather Graham (Full Frontal, Butt,
   Thong); **Nina Hartley** (Right Breast);
   Julianne Moore (Breasts); **Nicole Ari
   Parker** (Breasts)

A sprawling spelunk into the '70s porn industry, *Boogie Nights* revolves around Mark Wahlberg as donkey-donged porn stud Dirk Diggler and his dysfunctional, adult-filmmaking surrogate family. Diggler gets to take digs at red-hot redhead Julianne Moore and Heather Graham—who, as Rollergirl, never even takes off her skates. And real-life porn stars Nina Hartley, Skye Blue, and Summer Cummings bring authenticity to the adults-only shenanigans—by getting naked!

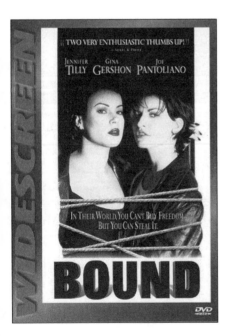

Bound (1996)

Directors: Andy Wachowski, Larry Wachowski

Breasts: 2; **Butts**: 1

Nude Stars: **Gina Gershon** (Left Breast); **Jennifer
   Tilly** (Right Breast, Butt)

Mafia moll Jennifer Tilly finds love in the guise of ex-con handy "man" Gina Gershon in *Bound.* The two clam-digging divas connive their way to two million in mob money and plan to ride off into the Sapphic sunset until they're caught and, yes, bound together, but not before our hair pie–happy heroines enjoy a scorching bedroom chow-down.

Boys Don't Cry (1999)

Director: Kimberly Peirce

Breasts: 3; **Butts**: 1; **Bushes**: 1

Nude Stars: **Chloë Sevigny** (Breasts); **Hilary Swank** (Right Breast, Butt, Bush)

Based on the true story of Brandon Teena, a female who passed herself off as male, *Boys Don't Cry* recounts a tragic murder. Slender but busty Hilary Swank plays Brandon, who hooks up with Chloë Sevigny. It's not long, though, before Brandon's secret comes out, and his tough-guy friends feel betrayed. Bad stuff goes down, but it's sweetened by the sight of Hilary's biological (and furry) femaleness.

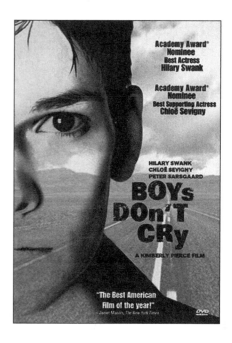

Glory *Bound*

Bound creators Andy and Larry Wachowski followed up their lesbian noir cult fave by making *The Matrix* (1999) and essentially changing popular culture forevermore.

skinfo

DAVID SCHWIMMER CHRIS COOPER

BREAST MEN

TWO YOUNG DOCTORS WITH A DREAM OF MAKING IT BIG...

REALLY BIG.

NEVER BEFORE HAS ONE INVENTION GIVEN AMERICA SUCH A LIFT.

DVD

Breast Men (1997)

Director: Lawrence O'Neil

Breasts: 101

Nude Stars: **Mary Deno** (Breasts); **Lisa Falcone** (Breasts, Thong); **Amanda Foreman** (Breasts); **Tiffany Granath** (Breasts); **Emily Procter** (Breasts); **Rena Riffel** (Breasts)

Anonymous Nudes: 45

Mr. Skin's TOP 69

52

HBO knew that plenty of guys would tune in to see a film based on the history of fake boobies, and you'll be fascinated by the bouncing abundance of before-and-after suckables in *Breast Men*. The film boasts an amazing array of avocados, including the lung pillows of lovely starlets such as Tiffany Granath, Rena Riffel, Mary Deno, Amanda Foreman, and Lisa Falcone, as well as a pom-pom-filled parade of anonymous knockers.

TOP 5

Movies for Breasts

5. *Summer Lovers* (1982) – 93 breasts

4. *Rapa Nui* (1994) – 97 breasts

3. *Breast Men* (1997) – 101 breasts

2. *The Naked Mile* (2006) – 110 breasts

1. Caligula (1979) 112 Breasts!

Breathless (1983)

Director: Jim McBride

Breasts: 2; **Butts**: 1; **Bushes**: 1

Nude Star: **Valérie Kaprisky** (Full Frontal, Butt)

Breathless is the Hollywood remake of Jean-Luc Godard's 1959 classic about a young cop killer and his scorching sexpot girlfriend. Richard Gere lets himself go buck wild— and buck naked, unfortunately—but the real find is the equally peeled Valérie Kaprisky in the role originally played by sexy '60s pixie Jean Seberg. Unlike with the original, audiences don't go breastless with this film, and our favorite scene has Gere toweling down lovely Valérie for some full-frontal French furburgerage.

Breeders (1986)

Director: Tim Kincaid

Breasts: 11; **Butts**: 3; **Bushes**: 1

Nude Stars: **LeeAnne Baker** (Breasts, Butt); **Amy Brentano** (Breasts); **Teresa Farley** (Right Nip Slip); **Adriane Lee** (Breasts); **Natalie O'Connell** (Breasts, Butt); **Frances Raines** (Full Frontal, Butt)

The monstrous aliens of *Breeders* are in danger of dwindling out of existence. Their only hope is to foist their other-worldly affections on the virginal damsels of Earth. In the process of impregnating our fair lasses, the intergalactic horndogs cause these comely specimens to wander about the streets completely nude, seriously undercutting anyone's motivations to put a halt to the activities.

Broadcast Bombshells (1995)

Director: Ernest G. Sauer

Breasts: 12; **Butts**: 3; **Bushes**: 3

Nude Stars: **Amy Lynn Baxter** (Full Frontal, Butt);
Elizabeth Heyman (Breasts); **Debbie Rochon** (Full
Frontal, Thong)

Anonymous Nudes: 3

In *Broadcast Bombshells,* the on-screen talent and behind-the-scenes movers and shakers (how they do shake) of television station WSEX are predominantly female and uniformly ballooning of bust. Witness a triple treat of top-shelf teat as stacked temptresses Amy Lynn Baxter, Elizabeth Heyman, and Debbie Rochon sit around with their tops off, unable to make up their minds about what to wear. Career guidance has never been so clear or exciting.

Broken Flowers (2005)

Director: Jim Jarmusch

Breasts: 2; **Butts**: 1; **Bushes**: 1

Nude Star: **Alexis Dziena** (Full Frontal, Butt)

Bill Murray plays an aging womanizer paying visits to his ex-flames, including Julie Delpy, Frances Conroy, Tilda Swinton, and Jessica Lange, in *Broken Flowers.* But it's Sharon Stone's daughter Lolita, played by Alexis Dziena, who makes this flower bloom. She entertains Murray in a short robe, offering him a popsicle and then popping viewers' sticks with a full-frontal view.

Bully (2001)

Director: Larry Clark

Breasts: 5; **Butts**: 3; **Bushes**: 2

Nude Stars: **Kelli Garner** (Right Breast, Butt); **Rachel Miner** (Full Frontal, Butt); **Bijou Phillips** (Full Frontal, Butt)

Inspired by a true story of high-school stoners turned killers, director Larry Clark's *Bully* has its share of explicit violence and, more important, shockingly explicit full-frontal nudity from the nubile likes of Bijou Phillips and Rachel Miner. Rachel has enough fur and enough steamy sex to last her through any cold winter. There's even a close-up of Bijou's camel-toe white panties with a quick glimpse of a loose lip that raises Mr. Skin's ship.

FROM THE DIRECTOR OF "KIDS"

Brad Renfro   Bijou Phillips   Rachel Miner   Michael Pitt   Leo Fitzpatrick   Nick Stahl

a film by LARRY CLARK

"POWERFUL"
- Jamie Malanowski, New York Times

"...A MASTERPIECE"
- Roger Ebert, Chicago Sun-Times

"TWO THUMBS WAY UP!"
- Ebert & Roeper and the Movies

TOP 5

Movies from 2001

5. *Y tu mamá también*

4. *Sex and Lucia*

3. *Bully*

2. *Mulholland Dr.*

1. Monster's Ball

Busted (1996)

Director: Corey Feldman

Breasts: 12; Butts: 5; Bushes: 4

Nude Stars: **Devin DeVasquez** (Full Frontal, Butt, Thong);
Griffin Drew (Breasts, Butt, Thong); **Ava Fabian** (Full
Frontal, Butt, Thong); **Mariana Morgan** (Breasts);
Monique Parent (Full Frontal, Butt, Thong); **Julie
Strain** (Full Frontal, Butt)

Busted is the story of a police precinct under the control of
a stuck-up female officer, so Corey Feldman and his fellow
flatfoots do their breast to loosen her up. That means loads
of unholstered hooters! The movie opens with Devin
DeVasquez and Ava Fabian making a Feldman sandwich
and ends with Mariana Morgan riding Feldman on top of
a desk. Well, since he directed this comedy, he may as well
get in on the joke!

Adjust yourself for *Busted*

Go back up and look at who directed *Busted*. Corey
Feldman. Yes. *Corey Feldman*. To date, *Busted* remains
Mr. Feldman's only directorial effort, but for his
sort-of-beloved 1989 head-scratcher *Dream a Little
Dream*, the Feld Man also served as choreographer.
Wait! Make that a . . . *Corey*-ographer.

skinfo

Caddyshack (1980)

Director: Harold Ramis

Breasts: 2

Nude Star: **Cindy Morgan** (Breasts)

It's the snobs versus the slobs in the golf-club comedy *Caddyshack*. And who wins? Anyone who likes laughs straight up, with some jiggling topless action as a chaser. Sarah Holcomb and Cindy Morgan add spice to the punch lines. Plus, it's got the most lovable rodent on film that's not a beaver.

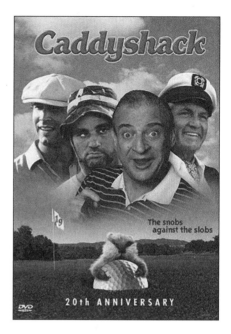

Cheek Peek - *n.*

Accidental exposure of the bottom of the buttocks.

THE TIME... Five Years After the Nuclear War.
THE SURVIVORS... Post-Nuke Thrill Freaks Lookin' for a Kick.

VCR INTERACTIVE
SETTING THE STANDARD OF EXCELLENCE

The Creators of NIGHTDREAMS present a motion picture too hot for a world with a future.

Café Flesh (1982)

Director: Stephen Sayadian

Breasts: 15; **Butts**: 8; **Bushes**: 5

Nude Stars: **Michelle Bauer** (Breasts, Butt, Bush); **Terri Copeland** (Full Frontal); **Becky Savage** (Breasts, Bush); **Marie Sharp** (Breasts, Butt, Bush)

Anonymous Nudes: 6

An immorality tale of postapocalyptic sex, *Café Flesh* is that rare successful blend of a functioning art film and full carnal insertion. Director Stephen Sayadian's vision of the bombed-out future includes enervated radiation victims gathering in survivalist nightclubs to watch those humans who are still able to achieve sexual relations engage in that activity onstage. *Café Flesh* burns.

TOP 5

Sci-Fi Movies

5. *The Man Who Fell to Earth* (1976)

4. *Breeders* (1986)

3. *Café Flesh* (1982)

2. *Species* (1995)

1. Lifeforce (1985)

Caged Heat (1974)

Director: Jonathan Demme

Breasts: 42; **Butts**: 7; **Bushes**: 8

Nude Stars: **Juanita Brown** (Breasts);
Roberta Collins (Breasts); **Erica
Gavin** (Breasts, Butt); **Lynda Gold**
(Breasts); **Ella Reid** (Breasts, Butt);
Cheryl "Rainbeaux" Smith (Full Frontal, Butt)

Anonymous Nudes: 19

Caged Heat is another Roger Corman–produced bush-
behind-bars flick, with ample boobies but only implied
lesbianism. That said, Roberta Collins, Erica Gavin, and
Cheryl "Rainbeaux" Smith undress at the drop of a
nightstick, and there are some genuinely disturbing dream
sequences that show off skin and take unexpected twists,
keeping this prison picture positively perverted.

TOP 5
Women-in-Prison Movies

5. *Under Lock and Key* (1995)

4. *Women in Cages* (1971)

3. *Cellblock Sisters* (1995)

2. *Ilsa, She Wolf of the S.S.* (1974)

1. Caged Heat (1974)

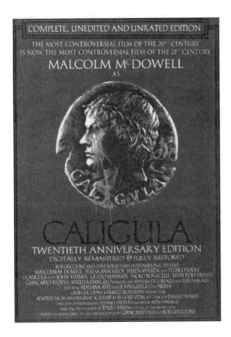

Caligula (1979)

Directors: Bob Guccione, Tinto Brass

Breasts: 112; **Butts**: 41;
Bushes: 46

Nude Stars: **Adriana Asti** (Breasts);
Mirella D'Angelo (Full Frontal, Butt);
Anneka Di Lorenzo (Full Frontal,
Butt); **Helen Mirren** (Full Frontal); **Teresa Ann Savoy**
(Full Frontal, Butt); **Lori Wagner** (Full Frontal, Butt)

Anonymous Nudes: 80

Sir John Gielgud, Helen Mirren, Malcolm McDowell, and
Peter O'Toole star in this porn epic about the decadence
that was Rome. Written by Gore Vidal and financed by
Penthouse, Caligula tells of the famously insane Roman
emperor, complete with come shots, full penetration, spread
beavers, slurped schlongs, and lap-liquefying lesbianism.
Teresa Ann Savoy goes full frontal, and Lori Wagner and
Anneka Di Lorenzo engage in Sapphic escapades. Mirella
D'Angelo gets it on with McDowell, who then shoves his fist
up some greased man butt. That's art.

Caligula's Roman Hands

Penthouse publisher Bob Guccione is credited as
Caligula's director, but most of the film was shot by
master European eroticist Tinto Brass. After four
years and $22 million spent, *Caligula* debuted at
New York's Penthouse East theater, where tickets
cost $7.50 (the NYC average was $5). The movie
then opened wide to big box office, and it ran for
years in certain locations.

skinfo

Tinto Brass
Tits and Brass.

Born in the country of the Pope, filmmaker Tinto Brass first courted controversy with the Nazi whorehouse epic *Salon Kitty* (1976), which prompted *Penthouse* magazine publisher Bob Guccione to tap the director to helm the mighty *Caligula* (1979). From then on, Brass dedicated himself to mastering cinematic erotica via tantalizing triumphs such as *The Key* (1983), *Paprika* (1991), *All Ladies Do It* (1992), and *Fallo!* (2003). Quite rightly, Brass himself once declared: "I put two balls and a big cock between the legs of the Italian cinema!"

Top 501 DVDs: *Caligula* (1979), *Salon Kitty* (1976)

The Candy Snatchers (1973)
Director: Guerdon Trueblood

Breasts: 4; **Butts**: 1

Nude Stars: **Tiffany Bolling** (Breasts, Butt); **Susan Sennett** (Breasts)

Criminals are rarely more brutal than the ones who kidnap teenage heiress Candy (Susan Sennett) in *The Candy Snatchers*. Where some movies revel in the struggle between good and evil, this one slithers along its plot points of dismemberment, rape, murder, and blood betrayal with an "only-in-the-'70s" abandon. And that's sweet!

They'll give you fast-fast-fast relief!

Playing doctor was never like this!

Keep abreast of the medical world with the
candy stripe nurses

CANDICE RIALSON • ROBIN MATTSON • MARIA ROJO • KIMBERLY HYDE WRITTEN and DIRECTED by ALLAN HOLLEB
METROCOLOR   A NEW WORLD PICTURE

Candy Stripe Nurses (1974)

Director: Alan Holleb

Breasts: 12; **Butts**: 1; **Bushes**: 2

Nude Stars: **Elana Casey** (Breasts); **Kimberly Hyde** (Breasts); **Robin Mattson** (Breasts, Butt, Bush); **Candice Rialson** (Breasts); **María Rojo** (Breasts)

Anonymous Nudes: 1

The nurse trainees of *Candy Stripe Nurses* are all eager to shuck their candy-striper tunics and engage in holistic hanky-panky with doctors and patients alike. The many skin scenes are active, well lit, and lingering. The featured girls hail from near the top of the B pantheon, with one—Robin Mattson—of soap-opera quality. Robin traipses across a sex-rumpled bed, flexing her fully feminine funbags and twisting her tight tush.

SKINEMA SENSATIONS!

Naughty Nurses
Bawdy bedside manner.

Going to the doctor is a drag, and being in the hospital is even worse. It's a wonder we don't all stay away from our medical manhandlers. More of us would lick our own wounds far away from professional attention if not for the existence of nurses. These soft-eyed, soft-thighed administrators of pain pills and sponge baths are not called Sisters of Mercy for nothing. Next time a health emergency descends, put yourself in their capable and caressing hands. For a preview of how you should behave, study the patient-nurse interactions in *The Student Nurses* (1970), *Night Call Nurses* (1972), *Candy Stripe Nurses* (1974), and *The Sensuous Nurse* (1975).

Top 501 DVDs: *Candy Stripe Nurses* (1974), *Night Call Nurses* (1972), *The Sensuous Nurse* (1975)

Cannibal Holocaust (1980)

Director: Ruggero Deodato

Breasts: 40; **Butts**: 9; **Bushes**: 9

Nude Star: **Francesca Ciardi** (Full Frontal, Butt)

Anonymous Nudes: 20

25th Anniversary Collector's Edition

CANNIBAL HOLOCAUST

WARNING
Due to its
SHOCKING and VIOLENT
subject matter
No one under 17
should view this film.

THE MOST CONTROVERSIAL MOVIE EVER MADE.

Cannibal Holocaust is Italian gore-meister Ruggero Deodato's ultimate excursion into cinematic savagery sopped with blood, brains, gullets, and guts. Robert Kerman plays an anthropology professor dispatched to the jungles of Colombia to find out what happened to a documentary crew who had ventured there sometime earlier. And it's ugly. Francesca Ciardi makes for an appetizing (in every sense) naked blonde interloper, and nudity among the local females is up-front and all-out from beginning to end.

TOP 5

Banned Movies

5. *The Last House on the Left* (1972)

4. *Flesh for Frankenstein* (1974)

3. *Cannibal Holocaust* (1980)

2. *I Spit on Your Grave* (1978)

1. Bloodsucking Freaks (1976)

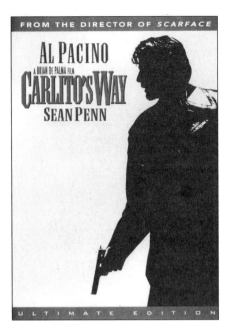

Carlito's Way (1993)

Director: Brian De Palma

Breasts: 12

Nude Star: **Penelope Ann Miller** (Breasts)

Anonymous Nudes: 5

Puerto Rican ex-con Carlito Brigante (Al Pacino) longs to lounge in the sun with his girl (Penelope Ann Miller) in *Carlito's Way*. And when you see her strip-club routine, you'll understand why. But first Carlito must help his lawyer knock off the Mafia don who is after him and run from several thugs looking to whack him. Soon there's a whole lot of banging going on.

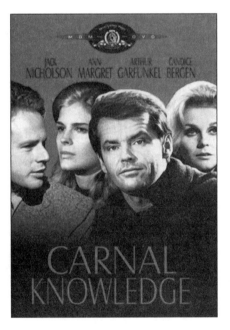

Carnal Knowledge (1971)

Director: Mike Nichols

Breasts: 2; **Butts**: 1

Nude Star: **Ann-Margret** (Breasts, Butt)

Mr. Skin's
TOP
69

53

Carnal Knowledge chronicles Jack Nicholson and Art Garfunkel as two men who spend their entire lives in pursuit of the perfect woman. Art takes his turn with classy Candice Bergen, and Jack sets off flesh bomb Ann-Margret and takes prostitute Rita Moreno for a ride. The knowledge of Ann-Margret's Swedish meat-butt will make you want to get carnal again and again.

Carrie (1976)

Director: Brian De Palma

Breasts: 18; **Butts**: 3; **Bushes**: 8

Nude Stars: **Nancy Allen** (Full Frontal); **Sissy Spacek** (Full Frontal, Butt)

Anonymous Nudes: 9

Much has been said in praise of Brian De Palma's gripping and jolting adaptation of writer Stephen King's novel *Carrie*. But not enough has been said, or could ever be said, of the gripping views of buoyant booties and boobies suspended from the fresh forms of actresses Sissy Spacek and Nancy Allen. *Carrie* will leave you covered in something hot and sticky, but it won't be pig's blood.

Carried Away (1996)

Director: Bruno Barreto

Breasts: 4; **Butts**: 2; **Bushes**: 2

Nude Stars: **Amy Irving** (Full Frontal, Butt); **Amy Locane** (Full Frontal, Butt)

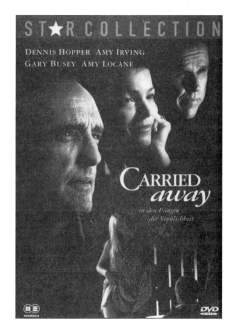

Dennis Hopper plays a moping high-school teacher in *Carried Away*. His rote relationship with girlfriend Amy Irving doesn't stand a chance once vivacious blonde Amy Locane comes on-screen. *Carried Away* explores the complex textures and weaves within the fabric of human relations, as well as examines practically every inch of skin on the two Amys, Irving and Locane.

Castle Erotica (2001)

Director: Madison Monroe

Breasts: 12; **Butts**: 4; **Bushes**: 5

Nude Stars: **Loredana Bontempi** (Breasts, Bush); **Silvia Gogovacinschi** (Breasts, Butt); **Amber Karney** (Full Frontal, Butt); **Catalina Larranaga** (Full Frontal); **Evita Pascual** (Full Frontal, Butt); **Holly Sampson** (Full Frontal, Butt)

Guess what happens when two foxy female cousins visit Italy for a summer vacation at a place called *Castle Erotica*. Here's a hint: One of the stunners, played by Holly Sampson, is quiet and bookish. The other, Amber Karney, is a babe with a video camera who yearns to bring home a record of hot action with Latin-lover playboys. Naturally, the video vixen prevails! This castle boasts many damsels in undress.

Pussy *Cat*

The British theatrical-cut version of *Cat Chaser* runs one hour and thirty-eight minutes. Fifty-nine minutes in, Kelly McGillis graphically spreads her legs, providing lucky viewers with something to really witness.

skinfo

Cat Chaser (1989)

Director: Abel Ferrara

Breasts: 2; **Butts**: 1; **Bushes**: 1

Nude Star: **Kelly McGillis** (Full Frontal, Butt)

In *Cat Chaser*, Peter Weller stars as a potentially violent
wayfarer lured to an exotic, dangerous locale, where he
succumbs to the potent sexual allure of an adventurous
enchantress, played by Kelly McGillis, and risks the wrath
of her murderous husband. Sexy Kelly may be worth
both dying and killing for. Though couched in shadow
and flickering light, Kelly McGillis's triple-B trifecta of
boobs, butt, and beaver is an eye-popping highlight.

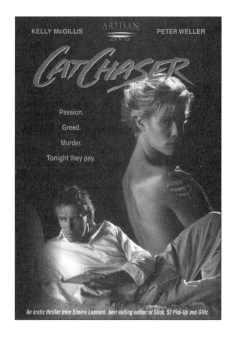

Cat People (1982)

Director: Paul Schrader

Breasts: 8; **Butts**: 2; **Bushes**: 1

Nude Stars: **Nastassja Kinski** (Full Frontal, Butt); **Lynn
Lowry** (Breasts); **Annette O'Toole** (Breasts); **Tessa
Richarde** (Breasts, Butt)

In *Cat People*, Nastassja Kinski is the sexiest virgin in
New Orleans, where she's visiting her brother, Malcolm
McDowell. Turns out bro and sis are descended from a race
of "cat people" who, unless they mate with their own, turn
into ferocious pussies that must kill to revert back to human
form. McDowell wants Kinski for his own—and who can
blame him?—but she's hot for a zookeeper, with fur-raising
consequences. Mee-*yow!*

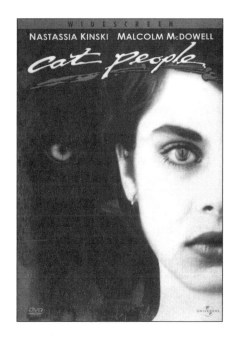

Cellblock Sisters: Banished Behind Bars (1995)

Director: Henri Charr

Breasts: 27; Butts: 7; Bushes: 4

Nude Stars: **Jenna Bodnar** (Full Frontal, Butt); **Gail Harris** (Breasts, Butt, Bush); **Annie Wood** (Breasts)

Anonymous Nudes: 12

Cellblock Sisters: Banished Behind Bars is the kind of female-empowerment flick that even guys can get into. Separated siblings May (Gail Harris) and April (Annie Wood) rediscover their familial bonds in a women's prison, where they get to shower naked and fight equally skinful honeys such as Jenna Bodnar. Sisterhood was never so sexy.

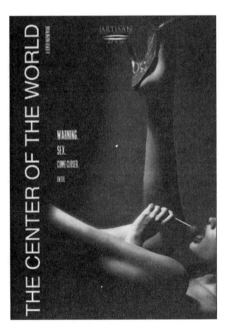

The Center of the World (2000)

Director: Wayne Wang

Breasts: 6; Butts: 1; Bushes: 1

Nude Stars: **Alisha Klass** (Breasts, Bush); **Molly Parker** (Breasts, Butt)

Anonymous Nudes: 1

Molly Parker stars in *The Center of the World* as a savvy stripper who agrees to spend a weekend in Las Vegas with a megarich computer nerd for ten thousand dollars. The stripper environment is presented with enough nudity to earn an NC-17 rating, and the guy does not get the girl in the end. Sex pro Alisha Klass dampens a lollipop between her lower lips during a stage dance. That'll rock your world.

The Cheerleaders (1973)

Director: Paul Glickler

Breasts: 14; **Butts**: 7; **Bushes**: 6

Nude Stars: **Jovita Bush** (Full Frontal, Butt); **Denise Dillaway** (Full Frontal, Butt, Thong); **Sandy Evans** (Breasts, Butt, Bush); **Stephanie Fondue** (Full Frontal, Butt); **Kimberly Hyde** (Breasts, Butt); **Terri Teague** (Full Frontal, Butt); **Brandy Woods** (Breasts, Butt, Bush)

Remember your high-school fantasies of perky-breasted nubiles thumbing their budding sexuality beneath sputtering nozzles? That suspicion that a few really adventurous girls were practicing bedroom moves on one another? The certainty that the cheerleading teams routinely gathered for massive orgies with the jocks? It was all true, and it's all right here in *The Cheerleaders*. Rah-rah-sis-boob-bah!

TOP 5
Cheerleader Movies

5. *The Swinging Cheerleaders* (1974)

4. *Just One of the Girls* (1992)

3. *The Pom Pom Girls* (1976)

2. *Revenge of the Cheerleaders* (1976)

1. The Cheerleaders (1973)

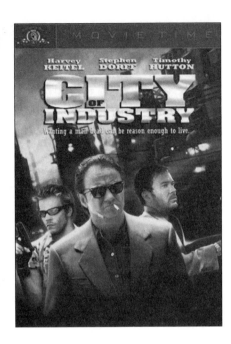

City of Industry (1997)

Director: John Irvin

Breasts: 9; **Butts**: 1; **Bushes**: 1

Nude Stars: **Dana Barron** (Butt); **Lucy Liu** (Breasts)

Anonymous Nudes: 4

City of Industry is propelled by angry jewel thief Harvey Keitel, who is out to do in the rat who done him wrong. *City of Industry* achieves an atmosphere of menace largely through its musical score and low-life locations, both of which come into play during the film's plentiful strip-club footage. Also coming into play at the stripatorium is Lucy Liu, who turns this into a city of skindustry.

Caged Monkey - *n.*

Pubic hair that sticks out of the sides of bikini bottoms or underpants.

Ss

SKIN·finition

A Clockwork Orange (1971)

Director: Stanley Kubrick

Breasts: 21; **Butts**: 4; **Bushes**: 5

Nude Stars: **Adrienne Corri** (Full Frontal); **Carol Drinkwater** (Breasts); **Cheryl Grunwald** (Breasts); **Gillian Hills** (Full Frontal, Butt); **Shirley Jaffe** (Full Frontal, Butt); **Barbara Scott** (Full Frontal, Butt); **Virginia Wetherell** (Breasts); **Katya Wyeth** (Full Frontal)

Anonymous Nudes: 3

Sex and violence have never been more intricately intertwined than in *A Clockwork Orange.* Director Stanley Kubrick's vision of moral decay extends from street thugs to government policy makers. The sex is plentiful, and no affection is ever attached to any of it. As Alex, Malcolm McDowell has a three-way with a pair of drugged-up teenyboppers that is one of the most hyperkinetic and humorous sex scenes ever committed to film.

Rock around the *Clockwork*

One early concept for the movie version of Anthony Burgess's sci-fi novel *A Clockwork Orange* would have cast Mick Jagger as Alex and the other Rolling Stones as the Droogs. Albums by the Beatles and Pink Floyd appear in a record-store scene (as does the soundtrack for director Kubrick's *2001: A Space Odyssey*), while two fictitious band names were later appropriated by real-life groups who scored New Wave hits in the early 1980s: Haircut 100 and Heaven 17.

skinfo

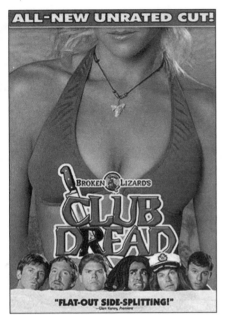

ALL-NEW UNRATED CUT!

BROKEN LIZARD'S
CLUB DREAD

"FLAT-OUT SIDE-SPLITTING!"
—Glen Kenny, Premiere

Club Dread (2004)
Director: Jay Chandrasekhar

Breasts: 6

Nude Stars: **Jordan Ladd** (Breasts); **Elena Lyons**
(Breasts); **Tanja Reichert** (Breasts)

The Broken Lizard comedy troupe turns its wit on topical
holidays and slasher flicks alike in *Club Dread*. Elena Lyons
and Tanja Reichert open things up by opening up one
another during a threesome. Hooterific Hollywood legacy
Jordan Ladd makes a dazzling nude debut while riding a
lucky laddie. Every other hottie is barely dressed beyond a
skimpy bikini, and Brittany Daniel wears something so slight
it might as well not even be there.

Broken Lizard
Tits and laughs.

The gaggle of funny dudes calling themselves Broken Lizard boasts
a perfect (t)rack record: they've made three movies to date—*Super
Troopers* (2001), *Club Dread* (2004), and *Beerfest* (2006)—and each one
peppers its knee-slapping guffaws with bone-popping nude starlets.

Top 501 DVDs: *Club Dread (2004)*

SKIN
VISIONARIES

Coach (1978)

Director: Bud Townsend

Breasts: 10

Nude Stars: **Cathy Lee Crosby** (Breasts); **Kristine Greco** (Breasts); **Rosanne Katon** (Breasts); **Lenka Novak** (Breasts); **Robyn Pohle** (Breasts)

Cathy Lee Crosby plays a foxy female athlete who is hired sight unseen to coach a boys' basketball team in *Coach*. Aside from looking terrific in 1970s-style basketball shorts, Cathy Lee has the panache to carry off the portrayal of a grown woman who has an affair with her starting point guard, and she manages to flop out her basketballs a few times.

Coach Class

There is no excuse for confusing *Coach* star Cathy Lee Crosby with Kathie Lee Gifford. Cathy Lee Crosby has been a pinup poster model, a leggy dancer as one of Dean Martin's Golddiggers, and a top-ranked tennis player who competed at Wimbledon twice. Kathie Lee Gifford will be discussed at some other time.

Coffy (1973)
Director: Jack Hill

Breasts: 15; **Butts**: 2

Nude Stars: **Lisa Farringer** (Breasts, Butt); **Pam Grier** (Breasts, Butt); **Marilyn Joi** (Breasts)

Anonymous Nudes: 6

Pam Grier is mad as hell, and she's not going to take it anymore! In *Coffy,* she plays a nurse by day and vigilante by night who uses her big guns to lure in drug dealers and pimps before cleaning the streets of their scummy ilk. She also engages in a catfight with dozens of buxom hookers. Black is more than beautiful; it's heart-stopping when Pam sheds her groovy threads. *Coffy* will cream you!

Blaxploitation
Afros, Macks, and sweet, brown racks.

In the early 1970s, B-movie producers expanded their gaze beyond drive-ins to the grindhouse theaters of America's inner cities. The blockbuster success of *Shaft* (1971), featuring Richard Roundtree as a suave, two-fisted African-American private eye, provided a template, and Blaxploitation was born. Marked by funky fashions, free-flowing 'fros, revolutionary stands against "The Man," bombastic violence, and black beauties the likes of which had never been freed upon the screen, Blaxploitation made an instant and indelible imprint on cinema history. And in the form of its knockout Nubian queen, Pam Grier, an eternal icon of celluloid sensuality.

Top 501 DVDs: *Black Mama, White Mama* (1972), *Black Shampoo* (1976), *Coffy* (1973), *Foxy Brown* (1974)

Color of Night (1994)

Director: Richard Rush

Breasts: 4; **Butts**: 1; **Bushes**: 2

Nude Star: **Jane March** (Full Frontal, Butt)

Anonymous Nudes: 1

Bruce Willis's fellow psychiatrist friend is murdered in
Color of Night, so he takes over the dead doc's therapy
sessions to find the killer. He also hopes for a different kind
of session with Jane March. Before long, the two are playing
die hard in a pool, in the shower, and in the bathtub. There
are sumptuous views of Jane's grapefruit-size tits, juicy butt,
and head-case hair pie, but watch out for Willis's willy.

BRUCE WILLIS

DIRECTOR'S CUT
15 Extra Steamy Minutes!

COLOR OF
NIGHT

Flesh *Color*

In *Color of Night,* Jane March gives one of skinema
history's all-time-great over-the-top-and-out-of-her-
clothes performances. SPOILER WARNING: She
even wears a mustache. END SPOILER. *Color* was
a fitting follow-up to Jane's bare debut in *The Lover*
(1992), and it's even funnier than Howard Stern's
appraisal of Jane in *Tarzan and the Lost City* (1998).
According to the King of All Media, Jane
"looks like a monkey–but hot."

skinfo

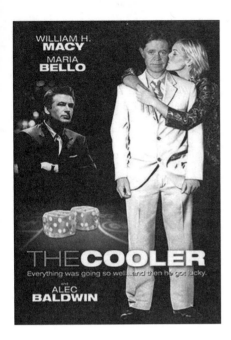

The Cooler (2003)

Director: Wayne Kramer

Breasts: 6; **Butts**: 1; **Bushes**: 1

Nude Star: **Maria Bello** (Full Frontal, Butt, Thong)

Anonymous Nudes: 3

In *The Cooler,* unlucky loser William H. Macy's misfortune is so contagious that mobsters hire him to "cool down" gamblers on a hot streak. When he falls for cocktail waitress Maria Bello, Lady Luck suddenly turns everything in his favor . . . except the opinion of his maligned Mafia bosses. Enjoy Maria's bouncing Bellos as she bops atop William's wango in bed. Her bonus bush baring makes this movie all the more aces.

Hotter *Cooler*

Be sure to watch the full-screen DVD of the Vegas comedy *The Cooler* to see what Maria Bello's got below. The wide-screen version cuts off Maria B's bush at the thirty-nine-minute mark, while the full-screen shows a close-up, and better butt shots.

skinfo

The Cool Surface (1994)

Director: Erik Anjou

Breasts: 2

Nude Star: **Teri Hatcher** (Breasts)

The Cool Surface showcases Teri Hatcher as an aspiring actress whose playwright neighbor (Robert Patrick) spies on her. He watches her fight with an abusive boyfriend, then ride the baloney pony all night long, then fight again, then ride the . . . You get the idea. Pretty soon, Mr. Playwright begins to use that imagination to program his own dreams about Teri into his work and out of her clothes.

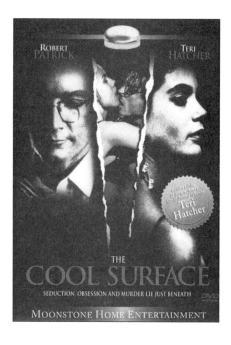

Crash (1996)

Director: David Cronenberg

Breasts: 7; **Butts**: 1; **Bushes**: 2

Nude Stars: **Rosanna Arquette** (Left Breast); **Holly Hunter** (Left Breast, Bush); **Yolande Julian** (Breasts, Thong); **Alice Poon** (Breasts); **Deborah Kara Unger** (Right Breast, Butt, Bush)

In the David Cronenberg–directed mindblower *Crash,* James Spader and Deborah Kara Unger try to spice up their love life by having affairs and then telling the other the lurid details. Then Spader gets involved with a cult of freaky collision fetishists who get erections for automotive destruction. Don't think twisted steel and broken glass are hot? How about a collision course of casabas from Holly Hunter, Rosanna Arquette, and the enticingly named Alice Poon?

Crazed (1978)

Director: István Ventilla

Breasts: 4

Nude Stars: **Catherine Bach** (Breasts);
  Leslie Caron (Breasts)

Is there anything better than when a childhood sex symbol is found to have done some early sexy skinema? *The Dukes of Hazzard* star Catherine Bach started a stock-car race in our pants when we discovered the early bizarre lesbian drama *Nicole,* later retitled *Crazed.* Even better, fans of cinema's golden age can enjoy legendary dancer Leslie Caron as Catherine's psychotic older lover—who, incidentally, was still in great shape at the age of forty-seven.

Troma Films
NYC's anti-Hollywood on the Hudson.

Yale students Lloyd Kaufman and Michael Herz founded Troma Films in 1974. Among the company's early releases were the breathtakingly sadistic *Bloodsucking Freaks* (1976) and *Mother's Day* (1980). Their big breakthrough came, however, with the sexy softball farce *Squeeze Play* (1980), which they followed with more nudity-enriched comedies before perfecting their trademark hard-gore, lunatic-slapstick, and bare-boobies formula with *The Toxic Avenger* (1985). Fiercely independent, Troma continues to make one-of-a-kind shock romps on the order of *Tromeo and Juliet* (1996), while also reissuing B-movie nuggets like *Crazed* (1978). Their annual road trips to the Cannes Film Festival are the stuff of legend.

Top 501 DVDs: *Bloodsucking Freaks* (1976), *Crazed* (1978), *Cry Uncle!* (1971), *The G.I. Executioner* (1973), *Sizzle Beach, U.S.A.* (1986), *Sugar Cookies* (1973), *Tromeo and Juliet* (1996)

SKIN VISIONARIES

Cruel Intentions 2 (2000)

Director: Roger Kumble

Breasts: 4

Nude Stars: **Alicia Lorén** (Breasts);
   Annie Sorell (Breasts)

Though chronologically a follow-up to the box-office smash of almost identical name, *Cruel Intentions 2* covers a span of years directly prior to the events in the original flick. As might be eagerly anticipated, the brother-and-sister tandem celebrated for their evil intent are just as prone to carnal mischief in their formative prep-school years as they will be during their scholastic primes. And their classmates make adorable topless playthings.

Drool, *Intentions*

Cruel Intentions 2 was actually culled from episodes of *Manchester Prep*, a Fox TV series spun off from *Cruel Intentions* (1999). A controversial scene of Amy Adams giving orgasmic horseback-riding lessons to Keri Lynn Pratt aired once on *Entertainment Tonight,* and the show was scrapped. Be grateful, then, for the direct-to-DVD sequel market, where nude scenes were added and this proper follow-up was born.

Cry Uncle! (1971)

Director: John G. Avildsen

Breasts: 11; Butts: 5; Bushes: 5

Nude Stars: **Maureen Byrnes** (Full Frontal, Butt); **Liz Ferroll** (Left Breast); **Pamela Gruen** (Full Frontal, Butt); **Madeleine Le Roux** (Full Frontal, Butt); **Debbi Morgan** (Full Frontal, Butt); **Nancy Salmon** (Full Frontal, Butt)

It was a brave new world after the late '60s—and *Cry Uncle!* was determined to turn mainstream moviemaking into a brave *nude* world. Allen Garfield strips down as a private dick who dicks his clients—even one who's dead. And, of course, a lot of tickets were sold thanks to the real, live nudity of Maureen Byrnes, Pamela Gruen, Debbi Morgan, and others.

Cry Boobies

Cry Uncle!'s hardcore orgy scene at the seventeen-minute mark is shown in negative black-and-white. Top-notch technicians at MrSkin. com inverted the tones for the website and turned viewing the full-penetration party into quite the positive (s)experience!

skinfo

The Dallas Connection (1994)

Director: Christian Drew Sidaris

Breasts: 12; **Butts**: 2; **Bushes**: 1

Nude Stars: **Wendy Hamilton** (Breasts, Butt, Thong);
T.J. Myers (Breasts); **Samantha Phillips** (Breasts,
Thong); **Julie K. Smith** (Full Frontal, Butt, Thong);
Julie Strain (Breasts, Thong)

Anonymous Nudes: 1

T isn't only for Texas; it's also for tits, as some of
womanhood's biggest boobies get involved in action that
fills a ten-gallon hat in *The Dallas Connection.* That's because
vixens such as Julie Strain segue the ass-kicking with kick-ass
nudity. Look no further than former *Playboy* Playmate
Wendy Hamilton, who is joined for a pole-pleasing topless
dance by equally endowed hotties T.J. Myers and Julie K.
Smith, proving that girls just want to have funbags!

Dance with Death (1991)

Director: Charles Philip Moore

Breasts: 12

Nude Stars: **Alretha Baker** (Breasts, Thong); **Tracey
Burch** (Breasts, Thong); **Sean'a Mahoney** (Breasts,
Thong); **Jill Pierce** (Breasts, Thong); **Catya Sassoon**
(Breasts, Thong); **Barbara Alyn Woods** (Breasts,
Thong)

Anonymous Nudes: 1

In *Dance with Death,* a reporter is sent undercover to a strip
club, where a psycho killer is feasting more than his eyes on
the topless talent. But this movie is far more successful as a
who-done-who than as a whodunit. Alretha Baker, Tracey
Burch, Sean'a Mahoney, Jill Pierce, Catya Sassoon, and
Barbara Alyn Woods costar as peelers who grease the pole
with such aplomb that viewers will be greasing their own
poles a-plenty.

Dancing at the Blue Iguana (2000)

Director: Michael Radford

Breasts: 18; **Bushes**: 1

Nude Stars: **Charlotte Ayanna** (Breasts, Thong); **Kristin Bauer** (Full Frontal, Thong); **Daryl Hannah** (Breasts, Thong); **Sheila Kelley** (Breasts, Thong); **Sandra Oh** (Breasts, Thong); **Jennifer Tilly** (Breasts, Thong)

Anonymous Nudes: 3

A quick impression of the director: "Okay, I've got six hot women stripping, Jennifer Tilly's jiggling, Daryl Hannah's dancing . . . What have I forgotten? Oh, right, the script! Aw, screw it!" Okay, maybe that's not exactly the way director Michael Radford built *Dancing at the Blue Iguana,* but it must be close. The ladies were given free rein to improvise their parts, which were then scripted. The prevalence of skin here makes for nudity nirvana.

Mr. Skin's TOP 69

18

TOP 5

Movies from 2000

5. *Mercy*

4. *The Monkey's Mask*

3. *The Gift*

2. *Road Trip*

1. Dancing at the Blue Iguana

Down-Blouse - *n.*
An inadvertent overhead peek into the confines of a starlet's shirt, oftentimes resulting in a Nip-Slip.

SKIN·finition

Dark Harvest (2003)

Director: Paul Moore

Breasts: 5; **Butts**: 3; **Bushes**: 1

Nude Stars: **Jeanie Cheek** (Breasts, Butt); **Amiee Cox** (Full Frontal, Butt); **Jessica Dunphy** (Left Breast, Butt)

A young dolt inherits a farm in *Dark Harvest,* which he immediately populates with his girlfriend and other couples, including a pair of teenage lesbian lovers! A ghost appears, but it doesn't matter, as mound-munching gal pals Jeanie Cheek and Jessica Dunphy warm their fantastic forms on a dock. And everything is better when Jeanie, Jessica, and Amiee Cox get wetter skinny-dipping for some daytime fun in the sun.

DarkWolf (2003)

Director: Richard Friedman

Breasts: 15; **Butts**: 3

Nude Stars: **Jaime Bergman** (Breasts); **Andrea Bogart** (Breasts, Butt); **Katie Lohmann** (Breasts); **Sasha Williams** (Breasts, Butt)

Anonymous Nudes: 4

DarkWolf is the tale of a rubbery-looking lycanthrope who lusts for the last of his kind (the too clothed Samaire Armstrong) and kills anyone who dares to slow his pursuit. Fortunately for us, it's mostly strippers (Katie Lohmann), nude models, and Jaime Bergman who fall prey to Mr. Foamy-and-Hairy, providing ample anatomy samplings amid the oftentimes gory goings-on.

Deadly Weapons (1973)

Director: Doris Wishman

Breasts: 4; **Butts**: 2; **Bushes**: 1

Nude Star: **Chesty Morgan** (Breasts, Butt)

Anonymous Nudes: 1

Hell hath no fury like the gargantuan breasts of a gutsy and busty woman who has been wronged. The comely and courageous possessor of the titular Deadly Weapons is Chesty Morgan, playing the superstacked moll of a small-change crook who falls afoul of his gangster betters. Revenge is a dish best served in the smothering embrace of the grieving gal's grand glands. And, really, they don't call her "Chesty" Morgan for nothin'! Those are no Polish jokes, but they will give you a Polish sausage.

Heady *Weapons*

Liliana Wilczkowska—better known as *Deadly Weapons* star Chesty Morgan—was a Polish immigrant whose accent was so thick that her dialogue was redubbed by another actress. Nobody else could ever hope to stand in for Chesty's physical fortitude, however, which measured an astonishing 73FF-32-36.

skinfo

Death Game (1977)

Director: Peter S. Traynor

Breasts: 4; **Butts**: 2

Nude Stars: **Colleen Camp** (Breasts, Butt); **Sondra Locke** (Breasts, Butt)

In horror movies, the sexually immoral tend to go first, while the virgin avoids the reaper's scythe. So it goes in *Death Game*. Married hero Seymour Cassel finds himself in a heap o' trouble after he lets two skin-o-rific stray sociopaths (Sondra Locke and Colleen Camp) into his hot tub. Much whack-a-whack-a accompanies the waka-waka '70s musical score as the three have a steamy ménage à trois with a gruesome payoff. *Death Game* is killer.

"A male sex fantasy carried to the point of no return. VIOLENT AND UNNERVING!"
- Bruce Williamson
Playboy

Death Race 2000 (1975)

Director: Paul Bartel

Breasts: 8; **Butts**: 2; **Bushes**: 1

Nude Stars: **Roberta Collins** (Breasts); **Simone Griffeth** (Breasts, Butt); **Louisa Moritz** (Breasts, Butt); **Mary Woronov** (Breasts, Bush)

At the turn of the twenty-first century, people will run down pedestrians for points in cross-country car races. At least that's how the future of America was envisioned in *Death Race 2000*. Lucky for skinophiles, there are several "pit stops" along the way, featuring gratuitous "lube jobs" wherein nearly every female in the film gets nude! Yes, this movie has it all—death, guns, explosions, car racing, and, most important, boobies!

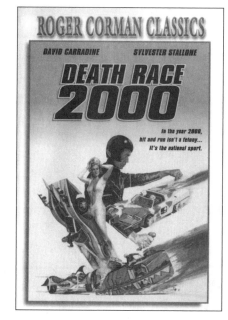

ROGER CORMAN CLASSICS

DAVID CARRADINE   SYLVESTER STALLONE

DEATH RACE 2000

In the year 2000,
hit and run isn't a felony...
it's the national sport.

Deathstalker (1983)

Director: John Watson

Breasts: 21; **Butts**: 4

Nude Stars: **Barbi Benton** (Breasts);
   Lana Clarkson (Breasts)

Anonymous Nudes: 10

Brawny and big-hearted *Deathstalker* is enlisted for the forces of good and sent on a mission to retrieve three mystical artifacts that will channel all the powers of creation. An evil demon lord has set about obtaining these all-powerful trinkets for ill-humored purposes of his own. Will nobility triumph over venality? Here's a hint: Barbi Benton's earthly bosom heaves on the side of fair play and sweetness. Also up for a little swordplay is Lana Clarkson.

Delta of Venus (1995)

Director: Zalman King

Breasts: 24; **Butts**: 5; **Bushes**: 7

Nude Stars: **Eva Duchkova** (Full Frontal, Butt);
   Audie England (Full Frontal, Butt); **Markéta Hrubesová** (Breasts)

Anonymous Nudes: 11

Full-frontal adventures abound in *Delta of Venus* as our heroine, Elena (Audie England), moves to 1940s Paris to write erotic fiction. She also feels she must actually commit the acts before committing them to paper and promptly assigns herself her first job as a nude artist's model. Before you can say *sacre bleu,* Audie is getting the old in-and-outie from plenty of Parisian *papas sucres* and even some *mamans.*

Demon Knight (1995)

Directors: Gilbert Adler, Ernest R. Dickerson

Breasts: 20

Nude Stars: **Brenda Bakke** (Left Breast); **Traci Bingham** (Breasts); **Tina Hollimon** (Left Breast); **Chasey Lain** (Breasts); **Peggy Trentini** (Breasts, Thong)

Anonymous Nudes: 6

If there is any basis in reality to *Demon Knight,* then one small vial of Jesus' blood still stands between mankind and total domination by the lords of hell. One more drop of the heavenly hemoglobin is required, and there will be hell to pay for the mere mortal who tries to keep the prize from the Collector's grasp.

Demon Rage (1981)

Director: James Polakof

Breasts: 3; **Bushes**: 2

Nude Star: **Lana Wood** (Breasts, Bush)

Anonymous Nudes: 1

Demon Rage depicts Lana Wood as a sexually unfulfilled wife who soon finds solace in the arms of Satan (hence the alternate title of this flick, *Satan's Mistress*). The devil, or the tall dark stranger, or whoever this ghostly S.O.B. is, pulls the bedcovers off our heroine in one scene, giving us a nice, prolonged view of her massive mammaries and even a slight peek at her bush. The devil will make you do something to that image. Like a demon.

VINTAGE COLLECTION

Desert Hearts (1985)
2-Disc Collector's Edition
Director: Donna Deitch

Breasts: 5

Nude Stars: **Andra Akers** (Left Breast); **Patricia Charbonneau** (Breasts); **Helen Shaver** (Breasts)

In *Desert Hearts,* unhappy 1950s housewife Helen Shaver moves to Nevada for a quickie divorce. There she falls for Patricia Charbonneau, an open and self-assured girl-lover. The two are soon naked and writhing in a scene sure to lasso your bucking bronco. All that girl-girl flesh against the rocky landscape is sure to give audiences a desert heart-on. And don't miss the dyke-alicious special 2-Disc Collector's Edition of *Desert Hearts.* It features bonus footage of Helen and Pat's famous femme-on-femme frottage.

Lesbian Independent Films
Butch nonchastity and the Sundance flicks.

Two girls are always better than one, especially if those two girls are doing each other. Lesbians are a very productive sort, and when they didn't see movies that turned them on, they turned them out by the reel. Some were just the girl-girl version of a peepshow loop, such as *Girls Who Like Girls*, where filmmaker Pauline Edwards spliced together her favorite lesbian sex scenes from the '60s and the '70s. Whatever floats your boat, and that boat is starting to break out into mainstream waters with movies such as *Better Than Chocolate* (1999), *Go Fish* (1994), and *Butterfly Kiss* (1996), which has Saskia Reeves checking out the plumbing on Amanda Plummer. With Hilary Swank and Charlize Theron winning Oscars for such Lesbian Independent Films as *Boys Don't Cry* (1999) and *Monster* (2003), respectively, the pie's the limit.

Top 501 DVDs: *Boys Don't Cry* (1999), *Desert Hearts* (1985), *Live Nude Girls* (1995), *Slaves to the Underground* (1997)

The Devil's Advocate (1997)

Director: Taylor Hackford

Breasts: 12; **Butts**: 1;
  Bushes: 2

Nude Stars: **Connie Nielsen** (Full
  Frontal, Butt); **Charlize Theron** (Full
  Frontal); **Tamara Tunie** (Breasts)

Anonymous Nudes: 3

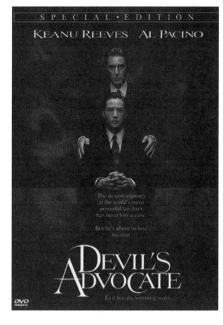

Keanu Reeves is a lawyer who discovers that his boss, Al
Pacino, is really Satan in *The Devil's Advocate*. This wild clash
of acting styles is further electrified by the naked Connie
Nielsen, as well as delectable South African sweetheart
Charlize Theron. Charlize desecrates—er, *decorates*—a church
with her Sun City nips and neatly trimmed diamond mine,
as she treats hubby Keanu to a most excellent adventure
that makes *Matrix* boy go mnemonic.

TOP 5

Horror Movies

5. *Cat People* (1982)

4. *Don't Look Now* (1973)

3. *Hostel* (2005)

2. *Embrace of the Vampire* (1994)

1. The Devil's Advocate (1997)

Drive-in Skinema - *n.*
Hard-drive, high-camp B-movie fun that got vans a-
rockin' in outdoor theaters from the 1960s to the mid-
1980s.

SKIN·finition

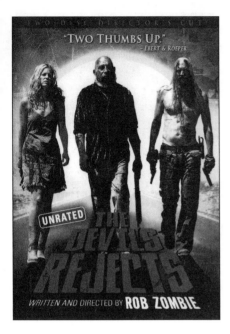

The Devil's Rejects (2005)
Director: Rob Zombie

Breasts: 12; **Butts**: 3; **Bushes**: 3

Nude Stars: **Ginger Lynn Allen** (Full Frontal, Butt);
Priscilla Barnes (Right Breast); **Jessica Helmer**
(Breasts); **Sheri Moon** (Right Breast, Butt); **Kate
Norby** (Full Frontal, Butt)

Anonymous Nudes: 2

The Devil's Rejects tracks a family of cannibalistic killers
on the lam from a Bible-thumping sheriff out to avenge
the death of his brother. Kate Norby, Priscilla Barnes,
Jessica Helmer, and Ginger Lynn Allen all provide skin,
but director Rob Zombie saves his most loving close-ups
for wife Sheri Moon, who shows more butt cleavage than
a drunken trucker.

Diary of a Sex Addict (2001)
Director: Joseph Brutsman

Breasts: 10

Nude Stars: **Tangie Ambrose** (Right Breast); **Rosanna
Arquette** (Left Breast); **Joey House** (Breasts); **Eva
Jenícková** (Breasts, Thong); **Shannan Leigh** (Breasts)

Anonymous Nudes: 1

Michael Des Barres is a sexual compulsive and Nastassja
Kinski is his shrink in *Diary of a Sex Addict*. This may be
the closest you'll ever get to seeing Rosanna Arquette,
Alexandra Paul, and Kinski in a porn video—that is, in the
sense of a nookie-riddled film shot directly on videotape. Of
those three, Arquette's the only one who doffs her top, but
you'll enjoy a bevy of breasties from lesser-known lovelies.

Different Strokes (1997)

Director: Michael Paul Girard

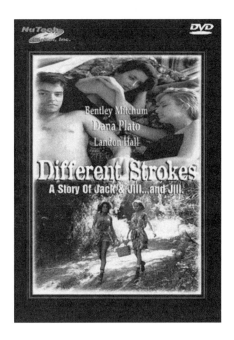

Breasts: 10; **Butts**: 4; **Bushes**: 4

Nude Stars: **Gabriella Hall** (Breasts, Butt, Bush);
Landon Hall (Full Frontal, Butt); **Dana Plato** (Full
Frontal, Butt); **Michelle Trongone** (Full Frontal)

Anonymous Nudes: 1

Different Strokes is the answer to every Dana Plato lover's wet
dream. The ex-star of *Diff'rent Strokes* is all grown up, and
her breasts are filled to surgical capacity. She plays a lesbian
photographer who seduces Landon Hall in a shower scene,
while Gabriella Hall and Michelle Trongone snog in the sack.
Dana remains the star attraction and doesn't fail to please
with her softcore shenanigans. "Whatchoo talkin' 'bout,
Mr. Skin?!"

Different Pokes

Dana Plato's final public appearance occurred
on the morning of May 8, 1999, when she sat in
live on *The Howard Stern Show. Different Strokes* was
in heavy late-night-cable-TV rotation at the time.
Later that evening, Dana overdosed on prescription
drugs and died.

skinfo

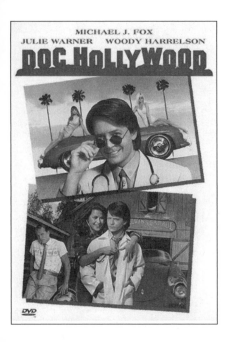

Doc Hollywood (1991)

Director: Michael Caton-Jones

Breasts: 2; **Bushes**: 1

Nude Star: **Julie Warner** (Full Frontal)

Michael J. Fox plays an arrogant doctor on his way from Washington, D.C., to a lucrative gig as a Hollywood plastic surgeon. But on the way his sports car breaks down in a small town. In the pleasant comedy *Doc Hollywood,* Fox learns the true value of life through arousing Julie Warner, who offers him the breast reason to stay: a view of her wet boobs while taking a naked swim.

Don't Look Now (1973)

Director: Nicolas Roeg

Breasts: 2; **Butts**: 1; **Bushes**: 1

Nude Star: **Julie Christie** (Full Frontal, Butt)

Donald Sutherland and Julie Christie play a married couple mourning their recently drowned daughter in the classic thriller *Don't Look Now.* As their child's spirit seems to be leading them on a chase through the canals of Venice, her loss bonds the couple further, resulting in one of the all-time-great graphic sex scenes. Look now—and hard!

Do or Die (1991)

Director: Andy Sidaris

Breasts: 12; **Butts**: 3

Nude Stars: **Cynthia Brimhall** (Breasts, Butt, Thong);
   Ava Cadell (Breasts, Butt, Thong); **Carolyn Liu**
   (Breasts); **Pandora Peaks** (Breasts); **Dona Speir**
   (Breasts, Butt); **Roberta Vasquez** (Breasts)

Do or Die, that is the question. Erik Estrada and Pat Morita
star and provide the acting chops, but the chest chops are
better represented by such heavy titters as Pandora Peaks,
Dona Speir, and the boob from Budapest, Ava Cadell.
And for lovers of Latin—the ladies, not the language—there
are the unnatural wonders of Roberta Vasquez. The *Playboy*
Playmate from October 1985 keeps things bouncy.
So do, do, do!

Andy Sidaris
Bombs, bullets, blood . . . and boobs!

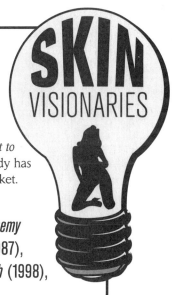

In terms of classic sexploitation, Andy Sidaris is the last man
shooting. His *Malibu Express* (1985) chronicles the adventures of
female super-agents who get naked and shoot guns in between
getting naked and blowing stuff up. They also do that in *Hard Ticket to
Hawaii* (1987), *Picasso Trigger* (1988), and *Savage Beach* (1989). Andy has
continued his "L.E.T.H.A.L. Ladies" saga for the direct-to-video market.
P.S. In Mamoriam: Mr. Sidaris passed away on March 7, 2007.

Top 501 DVDs: *The Dallas Connection* (1994), *Do or Die* (1991), *Enemy
Gold* (1993), *Fit to Kill* (1993), *Guns* (1990), *Hard Ticket to Hawaii* (1987),
Malibu Express (1985), *Picasso Trigger* (1988), *Return to Savage Beach* (1998),
Savage Beach (1989)

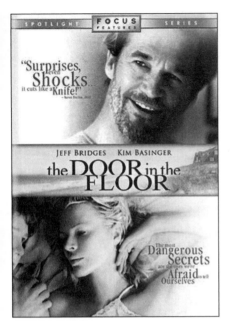

The Door in the Floor (2004)

Director: Tod Williams

Breasts: 3; **Butts**: 1; **Bushes**: 1

Nude Stars: **Kim Basinger** (Left Breast); **Mimi Rogers**
   (Full Frontal, Butt)

If there's one movie about a drunken children's book author
that you must see, *The Door in the Floor* is it. Kim Basinger
plays the writer's wife who falls for her husband's assistant
after catching him masturbating with her panties. But Kim is
dwarfed by the titanic talents of Mimi Rogers, who busts it
all out for the bookworm, from her hairy pie to her
overstuffed dumplings.

The Doors (1991)

Director: Oliver Stone

Breasts: 37; **Butts**: 6; **Bushes**: 6

Nude Stars: **Kristina Fulton** (Breasts); **Kathleen
   Quinlan** (Breasts, Butt, Bush); **Meg Ryan**
   (Right Breast)

Anonymous Nudes: 16

Rock star Jim Morrison will forever be a sexy shaman in
leather pants, thanks in part to *The Doors*. Oliver Stone's
worshipful ode to hedonistic 1960s excess comes complete
with drugs, destructive sex, and enough wigs to cover the
heads of every drag queen in New York. Speaking of excess,
watch Meg Ryan put on some fake hair and shed her
cheerleader image, shoving a side of tit into camera range
as she attends to Val Kilmer's lizard king.

Double Agent 73 (1974)

Director: Doris Wishman

Breasts: 12; **Butts**: 6; **Bushes**: 1

Nude Stars: **Chesty Morgan** (Breasts); **Tempest Storm** (Left Breast)

Anonymous Nudes: 9

Double Agent 73 is the follow-up to *Deadly Weapons* (1973) and again features the aptly named Chesty Morgan in an eye-popping mamnificent performance. Whereas before Chesty killed with her bazooka-size boobs, she now plays a secret agent/assassin with a camera implanted in her jugs, which naturally gives the film ample opportunity to show off her bountiful treasure chest. Tempest Storm provides some backup boobage in one scene. That's double trouble.

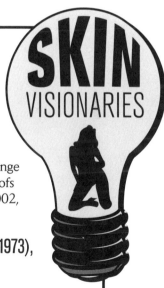

Doris Wishman
The high priestess of lowbrow cinema.

One of the most prolific female filmmakers of all time, Doris Wishman brought a unique sensibility to each of her low-budget, high-impact exploitation productions. Beginning with a series of "nudie cuties" in the early 1960s, Wishman evolved with the times, by turns cranking out rough-sex grindhouse fare, the bizarre sex-change documentary *Let Me Die a Woman* (1978), and überboobed spy spoofs starring the impossibly buxom Chesty Morgan. Wishman died in 2002, shortly following the completion of her final feature, *Dildo Heaven*.

Top 501 DVDs: *Blaze Starr Goes Nudist* (1960), *Deadly Weapons* (1973), *Double Agent 73* (1974)

Dr. Alien (1988)

Director: David DeCoteau

Breasts: 16

Nude Stars: **Laura Albert** (Breasts); **Ginger Lynn Allen** (Breasts); **Michelle Bauer** (Breasts); **Julie Gray** (Breasts); **Linnea Quigley** (Breasts); **Karen Russell** (Breasts); **Edy Williams** (Breasts)

Anonymous Nudes: 1

Dr. Alien serves up Judy Landers as Xenobia, an alien masquerading as a college professor who experiments on one of her students, turning him into a lady lover, though an antenna pops out of his head when he gets excited. He gets excited a lot thanks to a parade of nude screen sirens, including Ginger Lynn Allen, Michelle Bauer, Linnea Quigley, and Edy Williams.

T&Alien

Dr. Alien star Judy and her sister Audrey Landers put the boob in late-'70s and early-'80s boob tube, from *Vega$* to *B.J. and the Bear.* Sadly, the siblings never shared their hidden talents on-screen, though supposedly they liked to soak topless together in their Jacuzzi.

skinfo

Dr. T and the Women (2000)

Director: Robert Altman

Breasts: 5; **Butts**: 3; **Bushes**: 2

Nude Stars: **Farrah Fawcett** (Full Frontal); **Helen Hunt** (Breasts, Butt); **Holly Pelham** (Left Breast); **Janine Turner** (Butt)

Anonymous Nudes: 1

Richard Gere plays a gynecologist in *Dr. T and the Women,* and he really has it made. Not only does he have patients like Janine Turner, but he also has Helen Hunt for a topless mistress, and his wife (Farrah Fawcett) gets her kicks by dancing naked in a shopping-mall fountain. His daughter (Kate Hudson) even goes in for a bit of Sapphic salaciousness with Liv Tyler. Forget Dr. T—where's Dr. Feel-the-Goods when we need him most?

The Dreamers (2003)
Original Uncut Version
Director: Bernardo Bertolucci

Breasts: 2; **Butts**: 1; **Bushes**: 1

Nude Star: **Eva Green** (Full Frontal, Butt)

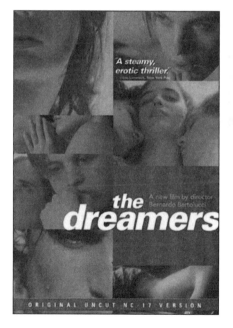

Set in swinging '60s Paris, *The Dreamers* revolves around Isabelle (Eva Green) and her twin brother, Theo (Louis Garrel), who invite Matthew (Michael Pitt), a kid from California, to play with them at their apartment. The three become tight when their shared love of skinema spills over into elaborate sexual games. Both brother and sis make happy carnal bliss, with outsider Matthew soon turning their taboo twosome into a dreamy threesome.

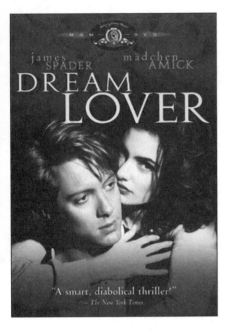

Dream Lover (1994)

Director: Nicholas Kazan

Breasts: 2; **Butts**: 1; **Bushes**: 1

Nude Star: **Mädchen Amick** (Full Frontal, Butt)

James Spader is a yuppie who marries Mädchen Amick. His dream lover, though, is hiding a dark secret—but not her gorgeous body. *Dream Lover* starts off nicely enough, with Mädchen's jugs peeking from beneath the sheets in bed with Spader. Then it takes off, as she gets out of bed and flashes tush before going into the bathroom and giving up the bush. Talk about a dream come true!

Dressed to Kill (1980)

Director: Brian De Palma

Breasts: 5; **Butts**: 2; **Bushes**: 1

Nude Stars: **Nancy Allen** (Breasts, Butt); **Angie Dickinson** (Left Breast, Butt); **Victoria Lynn Johnson** (Breasts, Bush)

Director Brian De Palma's *Dressed to Kill* is a stylish, female-obsessed murder thriller of the top tier—which means there's no lack of toplessness. Stunt-body supreme Victoria Lynn Johnson fills in for the fuzz and flappers of soapy siren Angie Dickinson. Waifish blonde Nancy Allen caught the eye of director De Palma by standing out in the crowded shower scene of *Carrie* (1976) and married him soon after. De Palma threw another shower for his bride in *Dressed to Kill.*

Drum (1976)

Director: Steve Carver

Breasts: 23; **Bushes**: 1

Nude Stars: **Pam Grier** (Breasts); **Fiona Lewis** (Breasts); **Cheryl "Rainbeaux" Smith** (Breasts); **Brenda Sykes** (Breasts); **Isela Vega** (Breasts)

Anonymous Nudes: 7

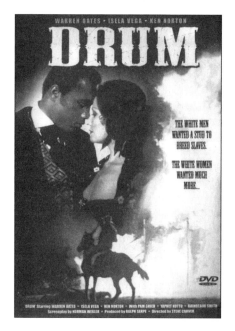

Ken Norton—a.k.a. *Drum*—dons slave rags in this sequel to *Mandingo* (1975) and proceeds to make all women steam under their petticoats. Plantation owner Warren Oates takes Drum's girl (Pam Grier) into his bed—that is, when he and his redneck friends aren't using the white sheets. Yaphet Kotto is along for the ride, and hot 'n' spicy Isela Vega is *en fuego* with raw sensuality. Cheryl "Rainbeaux" Smith plays the master's daughter with a taste for blacksnake.

Brian De Palma
Hitched cock.

Suspense-meister Brian De Palma built a brand name on his highly stylized thrillers that typically feature acrobatic camera work, overpowering musical scores, and, wherever possible, dazzling damsels in naked distress.

Top 501 DVDs: *Body Double* (1984), *Carlito's Way* (1993), *Carrie* (1976), *Dressed to Kill* (1980)

The Dukes of Hazzard (2005)
Unrated Edition
Director: Jay Chandrasekhar

Breasts: 18; **Butts**: 6

Nude Stars: **Nikki Griffin** (Breasts); **Jacqui Maxwell** (Breasts)

Anonymous Nudes: 7

The Dukes of Hazzard reunites cornpone TV fans with Boss Hogg (Burt Reynolds), Uncle Jesse (Willie Nelson), Bo (Seann William Scott) and Luke (Johnny Knoxville) Duke, and, of course, Daisy Duke (Jessica Simpson). Jessica lives up to the double-D perv-fection of original Daisy, Catherine Bach, appearing in little more than ass-hugging cutaways and halter tops, plus a too small red bikini. More than just the South is going to rise again!

Delicious *Dukes*

Although Daisy still keeps her Dukes covered, the unrated DVD of *The Dukes of Hazzard* movie–which featured no nakedness at all in its PG-13 theatrical form–contains some hugely intoxicating bonus nudity. Talk about moonshine jugs!

skinfo

Eating Raoul (1982)

Director: Paul Bartel

Breasts: 12; **Butts**: 4

Nude Star: **Mary Woronov** (Breasts, Butt)

Anonymous Nudes: 6

Mary Woronov and Paul Bartel play Mr. and Mrs. Bland who play murderous "pimp 'n' ho" in *Eating Raoul*. Mary works hard to give her johns stiffies with her knockers, and then Paul knocks them off. Once the johns are truly stiff, they're rolled for their money and turned into dog food. Eventually, the Blands infiltrate the world of swingers, where it's no holes barred—and all clothes off!

A tasty comedy of bad manners.

EATING RAOUL

"OUTRAGEOUS... WICKEDLY FUNNY."
- Jack Kroll, NEWSWEEK

Eating Paul Bartel's dust

Paul Bartel, creator and star of *Eating Raoul*, arose from a remarkable school of 1970s filmmakers who flowered under exploitation producer Roger Corman. Among Bartel's peers were Martin Scorsese (*Boxcar Bertha*), Jonathan Demme (*Caged Heat*), and Ron Howard (*Eat My Dust*). Each may have surpassed Bartel in terms of Academy Awards, but, to date, none has made a movie as cool as *Death Race 2000* (1975). Bartel, who passed away, fittingly, in 2000, can perpetually claim that as his legacy.

skinfo

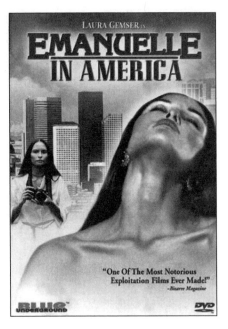

"One Of The Most Notorious
Exploitation Films Ever Made!"
–*Bizarre Magazine*

Emanuelle in America (1976)

Director: Joe D'Amato

Breasts: 49; **Butts**: 15; **Bushes**: 15

Nude Stars: **Lorraine De Selle** (Full Frontal, Butt); **Laura Gemser** (Full Frontal, Butt); **Paola Senatore** (Full Frontal, Butt)

Anonymous Nudes: 22

Laura Gemser stars in *Emanuelle in America,* the adventures of a fearless fashion photographer and investigative photojournalist. This film is not related to the Sylvia Kristel *Emmanuelle* films, and it doesn't have much to do with America either. But what's in a name when there's hot animal sex going on (and we do mean *animal*)? When she's not sating her bottomless appetite for sexual situations, Emanuelle is uncovering the fabled international snuff-film underground.

Emanu-Hell!

Visionary sci-fi director David Cronenberg was so stunned upon witnessing the atrocities of *Emanuelle in America* that it inspired him to create his own over-the-top masterpiece, *Videodrome* (1983), about perverse TV broadcasts that are rigged to cause tumors in the brains of anyone sick enough to watch them.

skinfo

Embrace of the Vampire
(1994)

Director: Anne Goursaud

Breasts: 10; **Butts**: 1;
Bushes: 1

Nude Stars: **Sabrina Allen** (Breasts);
Glori Gold (Breasts); **Alyssa Milano**
(Breasts, Butt, Bush); **Seana Ryan** (Breasts)

Anonymous Nudes: 2

Embrace of the Vampire reinvents Alyssa Milano as a student
trying to decide who'd be more exciting to have sex with:
her safe, handsome boyfriend or a dangerous, handsome
vampire. The vampire's influence turns Alyssa from a
demure virgin into a raging bisexual horndog, culminating
in one of the hottest lesbian kisses ever caught on camera
between Alyssa and Charlotte Lewis. Charlotte doesn't
show off her Sapphic skin, but Alyssa provides enough to
make this one hot embrace.

TOP 5

Movies from 1994

5. *My Breast*

4. *Ready to Wear*

3. *Embrace of the Vampire*

2. *Exit to Eden*

1. Sirens

Emmanuelle (1974)

Director: Just Jaeckin

Breasts: 17; **Butts**: 6; **Bushes**: 7

Nude Stars: **Christine Boisson** (Full Frontal, Butt); **Jeanne Colletin** (Full Frontal); **Marika Green** (Breasts, Butt); **Sylvia Kristel** (Full Frontal, Butt)

Anonymous Nudes: 5

Mr. Skin's
TOP
69

66

The bored, unfulfilled wife of a French diplomat gets a sexual awakening in Bangkok, which is aptly named for such things. This simple premise, accented with tons of sex, created a cottage industry of carnal delights. It was the money shot heard 'round the world. And you'll spew, too, when leading lust object Sylvia Kristel shows off her goblets. *Emmanuelle* may have become synonymous with sexy filmmaking, but first it was just a zipper-busting good time. Genitalmen, start your masturbating.

SKINEMA SENSATIONS!

Emmanuelle
Sex queen of the galaxy.

Nobody racks up frequent-flyer miles like this icon of Skinema. Making her bow in 1974 with *Emmanuelle*, the character has gone on to be . . . *in Africa*, . . . *on Taboo Island*, . . . *in Prison*, and more. Few of these titles are authentic *Emmanuelle* movies. Still, over twenty films have been adapted from the pioneering dirty books by "Emmanuelle Arsan"—a.k.a. Marayat Andriane. Other productions are often retitled with the *Emmanuelle* moniker (often spelled *Emanuelle*) because their starlet played the character in an earlier film. Sylvia Kristel is the original sex bomb, but others include Krista Allen, Laura Gemser, and Mia Nygren (actually billed as Emmanuelle IV in *Emmanuelle IV*).

Top 501 DVDs: *Emanuelle in America* (1976), *Emmanuelle* (1974)

Enemy Gold (1993)

Director: Christian Drew Sidaris

Breasts: 10; **Butts**: 4; **Bushes**: 2

Nude Stars: **Stacy Lynn Brown** (Breasts, Butt, Thong); **Tai Collins** (Full Frontal, Butt); **Suzi Simpson** (Full Frontal, Butt, Thong); **Julie Strain** (Breasts, Thong); **Angela Wright** (Breasts, Butt, Thong)

The narcs of *Enemy Gold* would seem to be making the best of a dirty job, but nothing is what it seems in the cracked-looking-glass world of drug enforcement. Mayhem and murder would reign supreme if not for the heroic efforts of a team of law-abiding beauties like Tai Collins, Suzi Simpson, and legendary skinstress Julie Strain. Bullets will fly, but prepare for special effects filled with bounce and body.

Erotique (1994)

Directors: Lizzie Borden, Clara Law, Ana Maria Magalhães, Monika Treut

Breasts: 14; **Butts**: 3; **Bushes**: 3

Nude Stars: **Priscilla Barnes** (Breasts, Butt); **Michelle Clunie** (Breasts, Thong); **Kamala Lopez-Dawson** (Bush); **Hayley Man** (Breasts, Butt); **Cláudia Ohana** (Breasts, Butt, Bush); **Camilla Søeberg** (Breasts)

Anonymous Nudes: 2

Really four films in one, *Erotique* gives us all the woman's point of view on different types of sexual relationships. All four segments include nudity, but Mr. Skin is most impressed with "Taboo Parlor," about two lesbians (Priscilla Barnes and Camilla Søeberg) who decide to take a man home, and the two clam-lapping lovelies decide to have some *fun* with him. Easy, guys, it's not the kind of fun you're thinking of. Trust me!

A FILM BY JESS FRANCO

Eugenie

...the story of her journey into perversion

Marie Liljedahl
Maria Rohm
Jack Taylor
Christopher Lee

BLUE UNDERGROUND

DVD

Eugenie . . . the Story of Her Journey into Perversion (1970)

Director: Jesus Franco

Breasts: 6; **Butts**: 2; **Bushes**: 3

Nude Stars: **Marie Liljedahl** (Full Frontal, Butt);
Maria Rohm (Full Frontal, Butt)

Anonymous Nudes: 1

Eugenie . . . the Story of Her Journey into Perversion tells the simple story of a young girl corrupted in a weekend of debauchery. Marie Liljedahl is the innocent. Maria Rohm is the other principal in the perverted film, and she shares ample boob and butt time on-screen with Marie. As journeys into perversion go, this one is not all wet, but you will be after watching.

Eugenie-us

With its reputation bolstered for decades by an unforgettably arousing still photo in *The Psychotronic Encyclopedia of Film* by Michael J. Weldon, *Eugenie...the Story of Her Journey into Perversion* made a fine and fitting DVD debut as the inaugural release from Blue Underground. The top-notch DVD label is headed by exploitation filmmaker William Lustig *(Maniac, Maniac Cop)*.

skinfo

EuroTrip (2004) Unrated Edition
Director: Jeff Schaffer

Breasts: 60; Butts: 1

Nude Stars: **Jessica Boehrs** (Breasts, Butt, Thong);
Tereza Brettschweiderova (Breasts); **Edita
Deveroux** (Breasts); **Lucie Kachtikova** (Breasts);
Barbora Navratilova (Breasts); **Molly Schade**
(Breasts); **Kristyna Simova** (Breasts); **Petra
Tomankova** (Breasts); **Tereza Zimova** (Breasts)

Anonymous Nudes: 24

The near-nonstop parade of international female flesh in
EuroTrip spurs on the cast of flagrantly inebriated, proudly
underachieving American youths as they rollick across
Europe, landing in one ludicrous and lascivious misunder-
standing after another. *EuroTrip* is a party-hearty love letter
to far-flung cultures. Never before have dipsomania and
diplomacy been so tightly intertwined.

Evil Toons (1992)
Director: Fred Olen Ray

Breasts: 16

Nude Stars: **Suzanne Ager** (Breasts, Thong); **Michelle
Bauer** (Breasts, Thong); **Barbara Dare** (Breasts);
Monique Gabrielle (Breasts); **Katie Jordan** (Breasts,
Thong); **Allanah Rhodes** (Breasts); **Madison Stone**
(Breasts, Thong)

Anonymous Nudes: 1

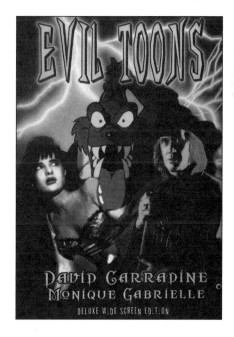

David Carradine has a book that contains a cartoon demon
in *Evil Toons,* a creative mix of live action and animation with
boobs and blood. A bunch of sexy cleaning girls played by
sexy ball cleaners Suzanne Ager, Michelle Bauer, and
Monique Gabrielle discover the book and unwittingly
release the evil toon. It possesses one of the girls, which
allows for some lesbian scenes and, of course, a lot of tits.
That's all, folks, but isn't (t)it enough?

Exit to Eden (1994)

Director: Garry Marshall

Breasts: 20; **Butts**: 1; **Bushes**: 2

Nude Stars: **Dana Delany** (Full Frontal, Butt); **Julie Hughes** (Breasts, Thong); **Alison Moir** (Breasts); **Stephanie Niznik** (Full Frontal); **Tanya Reid** (Breasts, Thong); **Sandra Taylor** (Breasts)

Anonymous Nudes: 4

Exit to Eden stars comedians Rosie O'Donnell and Dan Aykroyd as detectives after a diamond smuggler. *Exit to Eden* is also one of the hottest mainstream skintaculars ever released, taking place on an island paradise dedicated to fetish indulgence. The headmistress is Dana Delany, and when she's not sexily decked out in skintight dom gear, she's completely naked, revealing a lushly grown-out full-frontal Garden of Eden!

Every Which Way and Loose - *adj.*

All-encompassing, utterly overwhelming erotic appeal.

Eyes Wide Shut (1999)

Director: Stanley Kubrick

Breasts: 60; **Butts**: 20; **Bushes**: 5

Nude Stars: **Julienne Davis** (Full Frontal); **Abigail Good** (Full Frontal, Butt, Thong); **Nicole Kidman** (Breasts, Butt)

Anonymous Nudes: 41

Eyes Wide Shut is director Stanley Kubrick's swan song about a troubled Manhattan couple, played by Tom Cruise and Nicole Kidman. The movie opens with a full frontal by Julienne Davis; then Nicole exposes her flawless body. To achieve an R rating, *Eyes Wide Shut* used some of the most advanced computer-generated-imagery techniques to obscure or erase the genitalia from the orgy scene, truly making it a masked orgy. Still, this is one to watch with thighs wide open.

Eyeful Towers - *n. pl.*
French tits.

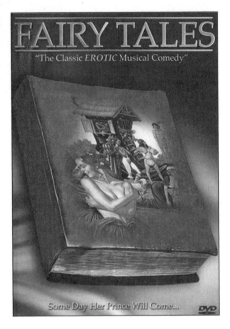

Fairy Tales (1979)

Director: Harry Hurwitz

Breasts: 23; **Butts**: 9; **Bushes**: 9

Nude Stars: **Angela Aames** (Full Frontal, Butt); **Nai Bonet** (Butt); **Sherry Bragg** (Full Frontal, Butt); **Marita Ditmar** (Full Frontal); **Brenda Fogarty** (Left Breast); **Lindsay Freeman** (Full Frontal, Butt); **Anne Gaybis** (Full Frontal, Butt); **Evelyn Guerrero** (Full Frontal, Butt); **Linnea Quigley** (Breasts, Butt); **Mariwin Roberts** (Full Frontal); **Idy Tripoldi** (Full Frontal, Butt); **Melinda Utal** (Full Frontal, Butt)

Anonymous Nudes: 1

Fairy Tales spins the wooly yarn of a prince who needs to create an heir to the throne but just can't consummate the deal. Not much of a plot, but who needs more to propel a good softcore movie? Along the way, classic fairy-tale characters are introduced, such as Angela Aames as Little Bo Peep, Linnea Quigley as Sleeping Beauty, Melinda Utal as Little Red Riding Hood, and Marita Ditmar and Evelyn Guerrero as S&M dancers who make their hairies *and* tails magically appear.

Fairy Tales for Adults
Bedtime stories. For real.

It is true that very few Americans born after 1950 have any desire to grow up. The only thing that's different now from when these guys and dolls were marble-shooting tykes on the playground is that sex is taking place. Which brings us to a suitable explanation for the popularity of such adult-entertainment (read: heavily nude and dripping with erotic juice) fairy-tale flicks as *The Erotic Adventures of Pinocchio* (1971), *Alice in Wonderland* (1976), *Cinderella* (1977), and *Fairy Tales* (1979). These irresistible flights of flesh-fueled fantasy combine infantilism and eroticism, a magic potion conjured specifically for the eternal adolescent as he or she dodders toward the last orgasm of senescence.

Top 501 DVDs: *Alice in Wonderland* (1976), *Fairy Tales* (1979)

Fanny Hill (1983)

Director: Gerry O'Hara

Breasts: 21; **Butts**: 4; **Bushes**: 4

Nude Stars: **Lisa Foster** (Full Frontal, Butt); **Maria Harper** (Full Frontal, Butt)

Anonymous Nudes: 9

Fanny Hill is a masturbation piece based on the skinfamous banned novel. Oliver Reed and Shelley Winters add class to this production of an innocent's fall into prostitution to survive. For the ass, there's Lisa Foster as Fanny and Maria Harper as the whore Phoebe. Both women are free with their bodies, showing everything in a lesbian love scene that's sure to give viewers a hill in their pants.

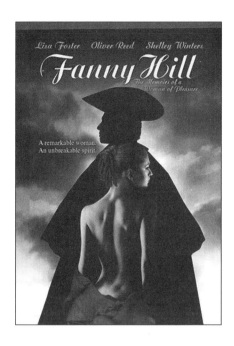

Fantasm (1976)

Director: Richard Franklin

Breasts: 27; **Butts**: 8; **Bushes**: 11

Nude Stars: **Maria Aronoff** (Full Frontal, Butt); **Rene Bond** (Full Frontal, Butt); **Roxanne Brewer** (Breasts, Butt); **Wendy Cavanaugh** (Breasts); **Uschi Digard** (Full Frontal); **Gretchen Gayle** (Left Breast, Bush); **Dee Dee Levitt** (Breasts, Bush); **Maria Lutra** (Full Frontal, Butt); **Helen O'Connell** (Breasts); **Candy Samples** (Full Frontal, Butt); **Serena** (Full Frontal); **Shayne** (Breasts, Butt, Bush, Thong); **Maria Welton** (Full Frontal, Butt)

Anonymous Nudes: 1

Fantasm features a professor lecturing on female fantasies, whether they are Rene Bond banging in a boxing ring or a card game in which the winner gets to bonk the loser's wife (Maria Aronoff). There's even a devil-sacrifice fantasy with porn star Serena. Roxanne Brewer brews up a bouncy turn-on for the breast fetishist by exposing her huge hooters, as do lung-heavy legends Uschi Digard and Candy Samples.

Fantasm Comes Again (1977)

Director: Colin Eggleston

Breasts: 43; Butts: 14; Bushes: 19

Nude Stars: **Michael Barton** (Full Frontal, Butt); **Rene Bond** (Breasts, Bush); **Elaine Collins** (Breasts, Bush); **Christine De Shaffer** (Breasts, Bush); **Uschi Digard** (Full Frontal, Butt); **Brenda Fogarty** (Full Frontal, Butt); **Dee Dee Levitt** (Breasts, Butt, Bush); **Nancy Mann** (Full Frontal); **Angela Menzies-Wills** (Right Breast); **Helen O'Connell** (Full Frontal, Butt); **Lois Owens** (Breasts); **Candy Samples** (Full Frontal); **Serena** (Full Frontal, Butt); **Cheryl "Rainbeaux" Smith** (Full Frontal); **Liz Wolfe** (Breasts, Butt)

Anonymous Nudes: 7

Two self-help columnists dispense love-life etiquette in *Fantasm Comes Again.* They review carnal conundrums ranging from how to fuel a three-way frolic to mastering the intricacies of library venery. Difficulties and solutions are played out in the instructional big-screen format, with highlights including the God-given glands of breast-blessed Uschi Digard and Dee Dee Levitt being mashed together from neckline to mons.

Fire on the Hole! - *n.*

Naturally red pubic hair.

SKIN·finition

Fast Times at Ridgemont High (1982)

Director: Amy Heckerling

Breasts: 4

Nude Stars: **Phoebe Cates** (Breasts);
   Jennifer Jason Leigh (Breasts)

Great gags, soon-to-be stars, deep-throated carrots, nubile nudity, and Spicoli versus Mr. Hand all blend into one gut-busting student-body bouillabaisse in *Fast Times at Ridgemont High*. Jennifer Jason Leigh serves up sweet stuff twice. And then there is Phoebe Cates stepping out of the pool and popping open her bikini top to the delight of gavel-stroking Judge Reinhold. It doesn't get any higher than that.

Faster *Times*

The ultimate teen sex comedy, *Fast Times at Ridgemont High* was initially slapped with an X rating due to Jennifer Jason Leigh's awkward pool-house poke with Robert Romanus. Despite a TV cut that includes numerous new scenes, the uncensored sex footage has never turned up. And that is *not* awesome, totally awesome!

skinfo

Fear City (1984)

Director: Abel Ferrara

Breasts: 29

Nude Stars: **Rae Dawn Chong** (Breasts, Thong); **Emilia Crow** (Breasts, Thong); **Melanie Griffith** (Breasts, Thong)

Anonymous Nudes: 12

There's a nut stalking and murdering the innocent naked women of topless bars in *Fear City*. The investigation allows the film to focus on a lot of striptease acts, such as funnyman Tommy Chong's daughter Rae Dawn Chong, Melanie Griffith, and Emilia Crow all shaking their things for our things. Maria Conchita Alonso also plays a stripper, though not a very good one, as she shows neither rear nor titty in *Fear City*.

Felicity (1979)

Unrated Director's Cut

Director: John D. Lamond

Breasts: 27; **Butts**: 12; **Bushes**: 12

Nude Stars: **Glory Annen** (Full Frontal, Butt); **Joni Flynn** (Full Frontal, Butt); **Jody Hanson** (Full Frontal, Butt); **Sarah Lee** (Full Frontal, Butt); **Angela Menzies-Wills** (Full Frontal); **Marilyn Rodgers** (Full Frontal, Butt)

Anonymous Nudes: 10

Glory Annen grows up—and out!—in the Australian softcore classic *Felicity*, and the unrated director's cut is every bit as first-rate as the movie itself. Glory is perfect as a curious teenager who tests exhibitionism, a lesbian tryst, skinny-dipping, heavy petting, and all the other pubescent sexual practices we've come to know and lust after in movies like this. Only few movies do it all as well as this one, and only *Felicity* features Glory Annen's booberangs, Australian outback, and gland down under.

Female Perversions (1997)

Director: Susan Streitfeld

Breasts: 14; **Butts**: 2; **Bushes**: 3

Nude Stars: **Marcia Cross** (Breasts);
Azalea Davila (Breasts); **Frances
Fisher** (Breasts, Bush, Thong); **Amy
Madigan** (Full Frontal, Butt); **Karen
Sillas** (Breasts); **Tilda Swinton** (Full Frontal, Butt)

Anonymous Nudes: 1

A pair of twisted sisters lay at the heart of *Female Perversions.*
One (Tilda Swinton) is a calculating corporate climber
whose sensual obsessions take her one rung closer to a
debauched bottom with each step she takes up the
achievement ladder. Her sibling (Amy Madigan) is a slinky
thief who busts a vaginal O with every successful steal.
Their perversions are your pleasure.

Femalien (1996)

Director: Cybil Richards

Breasts: 22; **Butts**: 6; **Bushes**: 11

Nude Stars: **Jacqueline Lovell** (Breasts, Bush);
Taylor St. Clair (Full Frontal, Butt); **Venesa Talor**
(Full Frontal, Butt)

Anonymous Nudes: 9

Venesa Talor plays *Femalien,* a space babe on a mission
to discover the emotional properties of human beings,
mostly when they're naked and on top of one another.
Her investigations involve all manner of coupling, with
copious nudity, including some lesbian encounters from
Jacqueline Lovell and Taylor St. Clair. Mission accomplished!

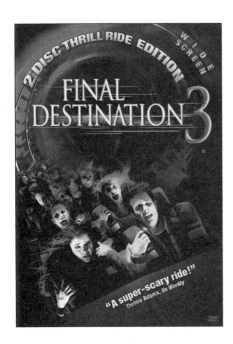

Final Destination 3 (2006)

2-Disc Special Edition

Director: James Wong

Breasts: 4; **Butts**: 1

Nude Stars: **Crystal Lowe** (Breasts, Butt); **Chelan Simmons** (Breasts)

Made in 3-D, which makes one really want to reach out and grab the ample skin on display, *Final Destination 3* is the third and arguably the best in the scare series. The story is basically the same, with a premonition of death on a roller coaster saving a group of students. But Death never takes a holiday and comes looking to redeem the lives owed him. The deaths are great—creative and satisfying for the horror fans in the audience. And for skin fans? It's the Final Breastination!

Final Sexamination

Viewers of *Final Destination 3* on DVD are enabled by a special feature to redirect the outcome of key scenes. And no scene is more key—or evocative of the word *outcome*—than the tanning-bed nudie-fry thirty-three minutes in. By choosing an alternate take, we get to see even more nakedness from Crystal Lowe and Chelan Simmons before their hot stuff *really* becomes hot stuff.

skinfo

Fiona (1998)

Director: Amos Kollek

Breasts: 7; **Butts**: 3; **Bushes**: 3

Nude Stars: **Anna Levine** (Full Frontal, Butt); **Alyssa Mulhern** (Left Breast, Butt); **Sue Ponczkowski** (Breasts, Butt)

Anonymous Nudes: 3

The low-life epic *Fiona* follows Anna Levine as a junkie whore who spends her day . . . well, doing what junkie whores do best. Nobody's being glamorized in this seedy masterpiece, though. In fact, Anna indulges in some very hot and sleazy sex scenes. Sue Ponczkowski is disturbingly real as a naked gal shooting up, while Alyssa Mulhern is totally fearless as Anna's lesbian lover. Alyssa even goes hardcore for some serious oral action in the name of art—or maybe money.

Firehouse (1987)

Director: J. Christian Ingvordsen

Breasts: 28

Nude Stars: **Martha Peterson** (Breasts); **Renee Raiford** (Breasts); **Gianna Rains** (Breasts); **Jennifer Stahl** (Breasts)

Anonymous Nudes: 10

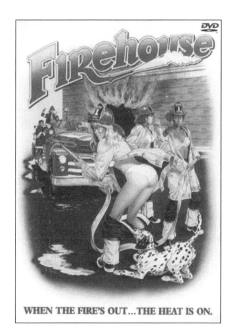

Firehouse is a sexy take on female firefighters and the ordeals they must endure from their male counterparts. Along their fight for equality there is much bosom exposed by Martha Peterson, Renee Raiford, Gianna Rains, and Jennifer Stahl, but the big question is whether this B movie is the debut of A-lister Julia Roberts. She's not naked, so who cares? Otherwise, *Firehouse* is smoking hot.

The First Nudie Musical (1976)

Directors: Mark Haggard, Bruce Kimmel

Breasts: 32; Butts: 17; Bushes: 17

Nude Stars: **Alexandra Morgan** (Full Frontal, Butt);
  Jane Ralston (Full Frontal, Butt); **Susan Stewart** (Full
  Frontal, Butt)

Anonymous Nudes: 16

An ailing studio attempts to regain its past glory by making *The First Nudie Musical.* That setup leads to punch lines such as the musical numbers "Lesbian Butch Dyke," "Orgasm," "Perversion," and "Dancing Dildos." Even better, there's no end to the naked parade of actresses, including Alexandra Morgan in her nude debut, Susan Stewart in her last skin on-screen, and Jane Ralston in her sole flesh scene. That's a lot of milestone mams!

TOP 5 Musicals

5. *Beyond the Valley of the Dolls* (1970)

4. *Fairy Tales* (1979)

3. *Oh! Calcutta!* (1972)

2. *Alice in Wonderland* (1976)

1. The First Nudie Musical (1976)

Nudie Musicals
Put out and sing.

Who among us has not sung in the shower or wished that he might be present to be serenaded by a favorite female entertainment figure while she is dripping wet and sudsy, belting out a love ballad in the steamy confines of a luxurious bathroom suite? Unfortunately, you can't have everything, but get off the can and search out some method with which to view *Oh! Calcutta!* (1972) and *The First Nudie Musical* (1976).

Top 501 DVDs: *Alice in Wonderland* (1976), *Beyond the Valley of the Dolls* (1970), *Fairy Tales* (1979), *The First Nudie Musical* (1976), *Forbidden Zone* (1980), *Oh! Calcutta!* (1972)

Fit to Kill (1993)
Director: Andy Sidaris

Breasts: 14; **Butts**: 1

Nude Stars: **Cynthia Brimhall** (Breasts); **Ava Cadell** (Breasts); **Carolyn Liu** (Breasts, Butt); **Dona Speir** (Breasts, Thong); **Julie Strain** (Breasts, Thong); **Roberta Vasquez** (Breasts, Thong); **Sandra Wild** (Breasts, Thong)

In *Fit to Kill,* Dona Speir and Roberta Vasquez search for a stolen diamond, and in the process they show off their treasured chests a lot. Julie Strain also returns as sexy villainess Blu Steele, and your steel will be blue watching her in various states of undress. She's joined by other plastic-fantastic lovers, such as Cynthia Brimhall, Sandra Wild, Ava Cadell, and Carolyn Liu. *Fit to Kill*'s tits are killer.

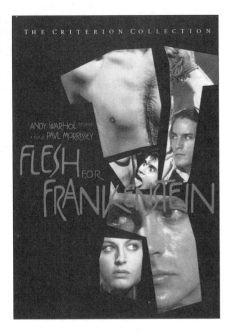

Flesh for Frankenstein (1974)

Director: Paul Morrissey

Breasts: 10; Bushes: 3

Nude Stars: **Dalila Di Lazzaro** (Breasts, Bush);
    Imelde Marani (Breasts); **Fiorella Masselli** (Breasts);
    Rosita Torosh (Full Frontal); **Monique van Vooren**
    (Breasts, Bush)

Flesh for Frankenstein casts Udo Kier as the diabolical doctor
who animates a delectable corpus delecti played by Dalila
Di Lazzaro. While he tries to piece together a man worthy
of this homemade hottie, the baron's neglected bride,
Monique van Vooren, is staying animated with studly stable
boy Joe Dallesandro. You'll go va-voom over Monique van
Vooren, and Fiorella Masselli, Rosita Torosh, and Imelde
Marani make for a lovely trio of trollops.

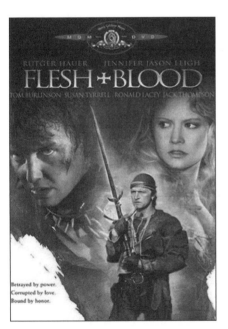

Flesh + Blood (1985)

Director: Paul Verhoeven

Breasts: 11; Butts: 1; Bushes: 2

Nude Stars: **Nancy Cartwright** (Breasts); **Jennifer Jason
    Leigh** (Full Frontal, Butt); **Blanca Marsillach** (Full
    Frontal); **Marina Saura** (Breasts); **Susan Tyrrell**
    (Right Breast)

Anonymous Nudes: 1

Set in plague-ridden medieval times, *Flesh + Blood* brings
to vivid life an era when rape and murder are casual acts,
and the sweet innocent, as portrayed by Jennifer Jason Leigh
at the film's beginning, is soon strutting fully nude. Blanca
Marsillach gives thumping flashes of fur and fury. And
Nancy Cartwright, the off-camera voice of TV's Bart
Simpson, busts out her Lenny and Carls. Ay caramboobs!

Flypaper (1997)

Director: Klaus Hoch

Breasts: 4; **Butts**: 1

Nude Stars: **Sadie Frost** (Breasts);
   Lucy Liu (Breasts, Butt)

It's just another day in the quirky world of '90s hipster cinema, as violent drug dealer Craig Sheffer mingles with lovable eccentrics in an orgy of sex and violence. Fortunately, *Flypaper* is awfully creative on the sexual side of things. Talisa Soto and Sadie Frost heat things up as complicated gals who are worth the trouble. Lucy Liu, however, steals the film as a kinky, naked snake lover whose favorite sexual act requires plenty of venom antidote.

CRAIG SHEFFER ROBERT LOGGIA
SADIE FROST LUCY LIU

With friends
like these...
you're bound to
get stuck!

flypaper

Paul Verhoeven
Pretty little Dutch girls gone wild.

Paul Verhoeven grew up among Nazis. Literally. The Dutch village in which he was raised was occupied by the Third Reich until Verhoeven was five years old. He credits the experience with making his worldview . . . unique. Savage violence and sex that resembles savage violence are the touchstones of Verhoeven's films, from his European productions such as *Turkish Delight* (1973) and *Soldier of Orange* (1977) to his sci-fi blockbusters *RoboCop* (1987), *Total Recall* (1990), and *Starship Troopers* (1997). Verhoeven's collaborations with screenwriter Joe Eszterhas yielded two of the most exhilaratingly over-the-top sex epics ever made: *Basic Instinct* (1992) and *Showgirls* (1995).

Top 501 DVDs: *Basic Instinct* (1992), *Flesh + Blood* (1985), *Hollow Man* (2000), *Showgirls* (1995), *Starship Troopers* (1997), *Turkish Delight* (1973)

SKIN VISIONARIES

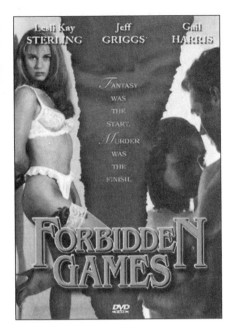

Forbidden Games (1995)

Director: Edward Holzman

Breasts: 35; **Butts**: 3; **Bushes**: 2

Nude Stars: **Griffin Drew** (Breasts); **Gail Harris** (Full Frontal, Butt); **Aleksandra Kaniak** (Breasts); **Becky Mullen** (Breasts, Thong); **Ashlie Rhey** (Breasts, Butt); **Amy Weber** (Breasts, Butt)

Anonymous Nudes: 12

The hook on which the clothing of such heavy-topped hitters as Griffin Drew, Gail Harris, and Ashlie Rhey is hung in *Forbidden Games* is that there's a murderer preying on the talent at a modeling agency. The psychic detective on the case then has visions of crazy sex, which may be a clue or just a personal perversion. Either way, it cleanses the sexual palette among strippers, lesbian sex, and the shower scenes that heat up these forbidden games.

Forbidden Zone (1980)

Director: Richard Elfman

Breasts: 22; **Butts**: 1; **Bushes**: 1

Nude Stars: **Marie-Pascale Elfman** (Left Breast); **Gisele Lindley** (Breasts); **Susan Tyrrell** (Breasts)

Anonymous Nudes: 9

Forbidden Zone is a journey into the sixth dimension where Hervé Villechaize rules a society of topless cuties and director Richard Elfman manages to combine the devil as a big-band leader, Max Fletcher animation, jazzy musical numbers, and characters in their underwear into the greatest (s)expressionistic film ever made. Gisele Lindley, as the princess of this netherworld, never wears a top, and her young, firm breasts stand out in a flick littered with tits.

The Forsaken (2001)

Director: J. S. Cardone

Breasts: 8

Nude Stars: **Izabella Miko** (Breasts); **Phina Oruche** (Breasts); **Julia Schultz** (Breasts); **Beth Ann Styne** (Breasts)

Dawson's Creek's Kerr Smith heads out to his sister's wedding in Miami and ends up tangling with a fashionable vampire coven out in the desert. Fortunately, *The Forsaken* reveals that vampirism is just a disease that can be cured with proper medication. Even better, a shotgun works just as well as a wooden stake. Vampires also have really great taste in their female victims, as seen by potential bloodsucker Izabella Miko, whose naked flesh is not in vein.

Forbidden Bone

Director Richard Elfman's midnight-movie masterpiece *Forbidden Zone*, which was out of print on video for years, erupted onto DVD in 2005 with a special edition from Fantoma.com that, for fans, is as mind-blowing as the frantic film itself. The disc's bonus scenes include additional nudity from puffy-nerped proto-Paris-Hilton Gisele Lindley, as well as a never-before-seen nip flash from Marie-Pascale Elfman (the director's wife) when Susan Tyrrell hungers for some breast meat.

skinfo

Foxfire (1996)

Director: Annette Haywood-Carter

Breasts: 6

Nude Stars: **Hedy Burress** (Breasts); **Angelina Jolie** (Breasts); **Jenny Shimizu** (Breasts)

Foxfire depicts wild schoolgirls who form a gang after they beat up a sexist schoolteacher. Angelina Jolie makes her first big splash as the ringleader. You'll also wonder why Hedy Burress isn't a star once she unveils her titanics during a tattoo scene. Real-life lesbian (and one-time Angelina bedmate) Jenny Shimizu is equally hot as the most Sapphic of the sweethearts.

Furburgerage - *n.*

Hair, beautiful hair, of the pubic persuasion. Oh, what a tangled web we weave when first we delve into the fluffy underworld of a woman's decorative genital shrouding!

Foxy Brown (1974)

Director: Jack Hill

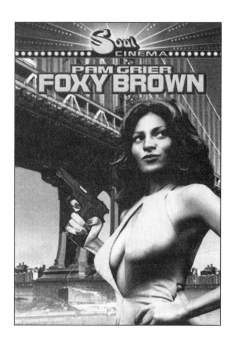

Breasts: 9

Nude Stars: **Pam Grier** (Breasts); **Sharon Kelly** (Breasts); **Sally Ann Stroud** (Breasts)

Anonymous Nudes: 2

Pam Grier plays the titular heroine of *Foxy Brown*. She avenges the killings of her dope-dealing brother and her cop boyfriend. If a craven male worm must suffer a merciless death as meted out by Foxy Brown, better that craven male worm not be you, and best yet that Foxy snuffs him up on the big screen so the rest of us worms can stand up and roar in appreciation. *Foxy Brown* won't let you down . . . even for a second.

TOP 5

Blaxploitation Films

5. *Foxy Brown* (1974)

4. *J.D.'s Revenge* (1976)

3. *Slaughter* (1972)

2. *Black Shampoo* (1976)

1. Coffy (1973)

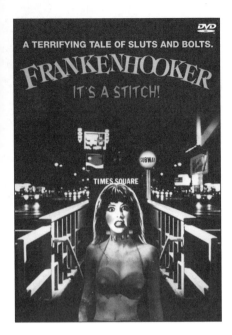

A TERRIFYING TALE OF SLUTS AND BOLTS.

FRANKENHOOKER

IT'S A STITCH!

Frankenhooker (1990)

Director: Frank Henenlotter

Breasts: 20; **Butts**: 1; **Bushes**: 1

Nude Stars: **Vicki Darnell** (Breasts); **Jennifer Delora** (Breasts); **Gittan Goding** (Full Frontal, Thong); **Charlotte J. Helmkamp** (Breasts); **Heather Hunter** (Breasts, Thong); **Patty Mullen** (Breasts, Butt); **Susan Napoli** (Breasts); **Kimberly Taylor** (Breasts)

Anonymous Nudes: 2

Frankenhooker recounts the story of mad electrician and scientist Jeffrey Franken (James Lorinz). Using "supercrack" as bait, Franken cruises for prostitutes to provide limbs for a new body he's building for his girlfriend, played by Patty Mullen. Patty was dismembered in a tragic lawn-mower accident, but don't worry—losing her head doesn't stop her from losing her threads! Look for a whole bevy of topless hookers, including Vicki Darnell and Jennifer Delora, to show their own supercracks.

Hooker Movies
The world's boldest profession.

Since biblical times, as evidenced by some of the oldest stories known to man, the righteous male has harbored an enduring fascination with whores. What's so interesting? First off, there is the actual physical activity of what a pro pussy does for a living. Add in the typical hooker's outlaw lifestyle, mix in the colorful cast of day-to-day characters that populate and pass through her sordid and insular world, throw in incidental and frequent violence, and you've accumulated enough cinematic high points to define an entire genre of modern-day filmic entertainment, for example: *Belle de Jour* (1967), *Klute* (1971), *The Happy Hooker* (1975), and *Crimes of Passion* (1984).

Top 501 DVDs: *Angel* (1984), *Angel III: The Final Chapter* (1988), *Beer League* (2006), *Frankenhooker* (1990), *Hardcore* (1979), *Porky's* (1982), *Salon Kitty* (1976), *Wild Orchid 2: Blue Movie Blue* (1992)

Fraternity Vacation (1985)

Director: James Frawley

Breasts: 8; **Butts**: 5; **Bushes**: 2

Nude Stars: **Barbara Crampton** (Breasts, Butt, Bush);
 Kathleen Kinmont (Breasts, Butt, Bush); **Sheree J.
 Wilson** (Breasts, Butt)

Anonymous Nudes: 3

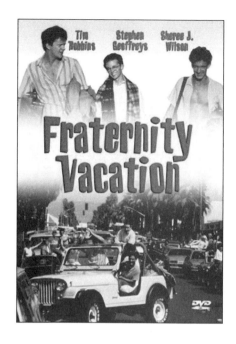

Fraternity Vacation boasts Tim Robbins as scheming frat
brother Larry "Mother" Tucker and übernerd Stephen
Geoffreys being accepted by his frat brothers once they
find out he has access to a condo in Palm Springs. Barbara
Crampton and Kathleen Kinmont provide plenty of raw
skinspiration.

Frida (2002)

Director: Julie Taymor

Breasts: 8; **Butts**: 3; **Bushes**: 1

Nude Stars: **Lucia Bravo** (Breasts); **Salma Hayek**
 (Breasts, Butt); **Mia Maestro** (Butt); **Karine
 Plantadit-Bageot** (Breasts, Butt); **Ivana Sejenovich**
 (Full Frontal)

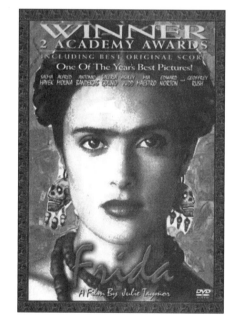

Bisexual artist Frida Kahlo liked to paint herself naked.
Starring as the sexy sketcher in *Frida* is south-of-the-border
bombshell Salma Hayek. The story follows Frida's life from a
crippling bus crash to her volatile marriage. Along the way
there are a lot of girl-on-girl good times. Ashley Judd nearly
flops out of her flapper dress during a scene where she and
Salma suck face. Overall, *Frida* is Salma's exhibition, and her
palette is fully exposed.

MIMI ROGERS   BRYAN BROWN

FULL BODY MASSAGE

A FILM BY NICOLAS ROEG

(M) Frequent nudity
Moderate sex
scenes

Full Body Massage (1995)

Director: Nicolas Roeg

Mr. Skin's TOP 69

4

Breasts: 6; **Butts**: 3; **Bushes**: 2

Nude Stars: **Elizabeth Barondes** (Full
Frontal, Butt); **Gabriella Hall** (Full
Frontal, Butt); **Mimi Rogers** (Breasts,
Butt, Thong)

The plot of *Full Body Massage* is deceptively simple: Mimi
Rogers savors a leisurely review of highlights from her
erotically charged lifetime while reclining naked on a
massage table being worked over by Bryan Brown, who
possesses the luckiest hands in human history. The greatest
aspect of this modern classic is that it doesn't matter what
point of the movie you play. It's all naked Mimi, all the time!
And those are some jolly Rogers!

Full Body barrage

The younger version of Mimi Rogers's character in *Full
Body Massage* is played, in flashbacks, by Gabriella Hall.
There are two crucial differences between the stacked
starlets. First, Mimi's jolly Rogers are all natural, while
Gabriella's are store bought. Second, despite baring her
titanic T&A nearly nonstop, Mimi keeps her muff covered,
while Gabriella flashes gash. It all adds up to endless
opportunities for you to *Massage* yourself.

skinfo

The Further Adventures of Tennessee Buck (1988)

Director: David Keith

Breasts: 12

Nude Star: **Kathy Shower** (Breasts)

Anonymous Nudes: 5

The titular character in *The Further Adventures of Tennessee Buck* is a boozer and jungle guide who takes a married couple on safari. Perhaps if Buck had laid off the juice and not been diverted by the sweet juices of native clam, he might have prevented his charges from falling prey to horny cannibals, who behead the husband and subject wife Kathy Shower (who really is a show-er) to a naked ordeal by boola-boola.

Full-Frontal Nudity (FFN) - *n.*

Simultaneous naked exposure of both breasts and pubic mound in a single shot.

The G.I. Executioner (1973)

Director: Joel M. Reed

Breasts: 10; **Butts**: 4; **Bushes**: 3

Nude Stars: **Angelique Pettyjohn** (Full Frontal, Butt, Thong); **Victoria Racimo** (Breasts, Butt, Bush); **Janet Wood** (Breasts, Thong)

Anonymous Nudes: 2

In *The G.I. Executioner,* former Vietnam vet turned nightclub king Tom Keena is hired by mercenaries as a one-man death squad in Southeast Asia. Mammy mayhem ensues when he gets mixed up with sultry stripper Angelique Pettyjohn, defecting Chinese citizen Victoria Racimo, and sexed-up red agent Janet Wood.

The Getaway (1994)

Director: Roger Donaldson

Breasts: 4; **Butts**: 2; **Bushes**: 1

Nude Stars: **Kim Basinger** (Breasts, Butt, Bush); **Jennifer Tilly** (Breasts, Butt)

When Alec Baldwin and Kim Basinger undertook the updating of a Sam Peckinpah gem with their version of *The Getaway,* they saw that more nudity would be their key to success, and they had the courage to implement that starkly skintastic vision. Basinger is far more forthcoming with fleshly delights in this shoot-'em-up saga than was any actress of the original flick. Way to getaway from your clothes, Kim!

Gia (1998)

Director: Michael Cristofer

Breasts: 6; **Butts**: 3

Nude Stars: **Angelina Jolie** (Breasts, Butt); **Elizabeth Mitchell** (Breasts, Butt)

Anonymous Nudes: 2

TOO BEAUTIFUL TO DIE.
TOO WILD TO LIVE.

GIA

based on the tragic life and times of america's first supermodel

What could compel a creature such as the late supermodel Gia Carangi (portrayed here by Angelina Jolie) to do anything other than loll stoned all day in bed with tweaking fingers trading off duty on nipples and love nub? The answer, according to the sexy biopic *Gia,* is that only another chick of equal appeal can capture the attention and motivate the affections of such a splendid narcissist. Take a long, hard look.

The Gift (2000)

Director: Sam Raimi

Breasts: 2

Nude Star: **Katie Holmes** (Breasts, Thong)

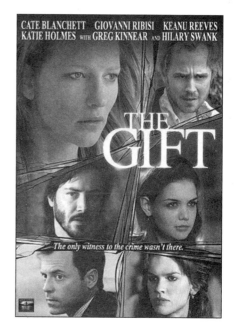

CATE BLANCHETT   GIOVANNI RIBISI   KEANU REEVES
KATIE HOLMES with GREG KINNEAR and HILARY SWANK

THE GIFT

The only witness to the crime wasn't there.

In *The Gift,* Cate Blanchett plays a psychic who is tormented by the death of her husband years earlier. She saw it coming in a vision and was powerless to stop him from dying. When police ask for her help to find missing girl Katie Holmes, all manner of suspense ensues, but none of the thrills equal what you'll feel waiting for Katie's famous unveiling of her Dawson's Peaks!

She's sinful... she's provocative... she's super spy "Ginger".

TOP SECRET

GINGER

Every man wants her,
No man can tame her!

Ginger (1971)

Director: Don Schain

Mr. Skin's TOP 69

58

Breasts: 9; **Butts**: 4; **Bushes**: 3

Nude Stars: **Cindy Barnett** (Left Breast, Butt); **Cheri Caffaro** (Full Frontal, Butt); **Michele Norris** (Full Frontal, Butt); **Linda Susoeff** (Breasts)

Anonymous Nudes: 1

Cheri Caffaro's *Ginger* is a high-society debutante who goes undercover to expose a kidnapping, drug, and prostitution ring! Ginger uses her powers of persuasion to seduce the bad guys—and girls! Cherry-busting Cheri gives us a nice close-up of her shag carpet while on top of Calvin Culver. Apparently, nothing gets between Cheri and her Calvins.

Group Shower - *n.*

Three or more naked actresses sharing a single shower area. It could be a bathroom shower, a shower room (as in a gym), or any other kind of overhead water-distribution system that requires female nudity and gets all steamy!

Ss

SKIN·finition

Girls Are for Loving (1973)

Director: Don Schain

Breasts: 6; **Butts**: 3; **Bushes**: 3

Nude Stars: **Cheri Caffaro** (Full Frontal, Butt);
    Jocelyne Peters (Full Frontal, Butt)

Anonymous Nudes: 1

The United States is about to sign a trade treaty with an
Asian country in *Girls Are for Loving,* so delicious but
deadly Ronnie St. Clair (Jocelyne Peters) tries to find out
some top-secret info so she can insider-trade her way to
riches. Ruthless Ronnie must be stopped! The CIA enlists
the help of Cheri Caffaro, reprising the role of hot
undercover agent Ginger MacAllister. Watch our girl
dance, strip, and sex her way to the info she needs in
this bullets 'n' boobs masterpiece!

Girls in Prison (1994)

Director: John McNaughton

Breasts: 10; **Butts**: 5; **Bushes**: 3

Nude Stars: **Anne Heche** (Breasts); **Ione Skye** (Right
    Breast); **Bahni Turpin** (Left Breast)

Anonymous Nudes: 8

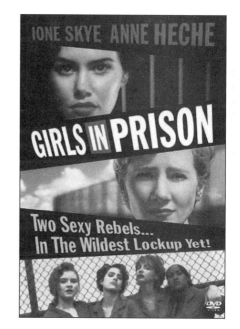

Girls in Prison is one part genre send-up, one part homage,
and one part straight-ahead chicks-in-prison flick. Its B-plus-
list talent gleefully submits to sadistic screws and suggestive
scrub downs. Leading lady inmates Anne Heche, Ione Skye,
and Bahni Turpin are all slick-skinned and soapy-sweet in
this institutional shower-stall treat.

Gladiator Eroticus (2001)

Director: John Bacchus

Breasts: 20; **Butts**: 7; **Bushes**: 9

Nude Stars: **Darian Caine** (Full Frontal); **Heidi Christine** (Full Frontal, Butt); **Jade Duboir** (Full Frontal); **Ashley Heart** (Full Frontal, Butt); **Katie Jordan** (Breasts, Butt, Bush); **A. J. Khan** (Breasts, Butt, Bush); **Ruby Larocca** (Breasts, Butt, Bush); **Misty Mundae** (Full Frontal, Butt); **Lilly Tiger** (Full Frontal, Butt); **Victoria Vega** (Breasts, Thong)

A softcore Sapphic *Gladiator* spoof that would make Russell crowe, *Gladiator Eroticus* is a hilarious tale of Roman Empire raunch with a bevy of boob-baring B-movie sirens. Darian Caine is Eroticus, Misty Mundae is Clitoris, and Jade Duboir is Orgasmus. What's in a name? Everything you need to know. Now you see 'em in the coliseum!

The Godson (1971)

Director: William Rotsler

Breasts: 20; **Butts**: 10; **Bushes**: 8

Nude Stars: **Jane Allyson** (Full Frontal, Butt); **Maria Aronoff** (Breasts, Butt); **Orita De Chadwick** (Breasts, Butt, Bush); **Uschi Digard** (Full Frontal, Butt); **Deborah McGuire** (Full Frontal, Butt); **Lois Mitchell** (Full Frontal)

Anonymous Nudes: 6

The Godson makes your pants an offer they can't refuse. Produced by exploitation king Harry Novak, it features a half dozen of softcore's hottest hitters, including the double hitters of Uschi Digard in a nearly explicit sex scene. Future Supervixen and super-chocolate-milk jugger Deborah McGuire adds color to the production. Audiences go gangbusters.

Golf Balls! (1999)

Director: Steve Procko

Breasts: 28; **Butts**: 2

Nude Stars: **Amy Lynn Baxter** (Breasts);
   Jennifer Steele (Breasts)

Anonymous Nudes: 12

Like *Caddyshack* (1980), *Golf Balls!* chronicles a country-club struggle between snobs and slobs. The conflict resolution comes down to a winner-take-all round of golf, the victor of which is never really in doubt. Where *Golf Balls!* does *Caddyshack* one better, or rather a pair of pairs better, is in deploying the racks and rears of an ample stable of amply blessed eye candy. *Golf Balls!* won't give you blue ones. It's in the hole!

Graveyard Tramps (1973)

Director: Denis Sanders

Breasts: 16; **Butts**: 5

Nude Stars: **Anna Aries** (Breasts, Butt); **Rene Bond** (Breasts); **Anitra Ford** (Breasts, Butt); **Sharon Kelly** (Breasts, Butt); **Susan Player** (Breasts); **Beverly Powers** (Breasts, Butt); **Victoria Vetri** (Breasts, Butt)

Anonymous Nudes: 1

Graveyard Tramps concerns a town of sexy women who experiment with a radiation-mutated bee serum that turns them into bee creatures that kill men with sex. Well, if you have to go . . . And if you don't want to go, at least you can watch as Anna Aries, Rene Bond, Anitra Ford, Sharon Kelly, Susan Player, Beverly Powers, and Victoria Vetri prove who's the most dangerous sex.

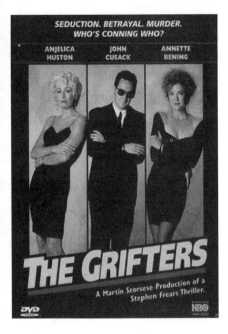

The Grifters (1990)

Director: Stephen Frears

Breasts: 2; **Butts**: 1; **Bushes**: 1

Nude Star: **Annette Bening** (Full Frontal, Butt)

A smart and suspenseful tale of competing Mom and son con artists Anjelica Huston and John Cusack, *The Grifters* is a film with style, violence, heat, and sex. Throw into this continual tug and pull of love and loathing the amorous advances of superambitious budding moll Annette Bening, add a triple-cross betrayal and a presumed murder, and the mother-son relationship becomes uncommonly strained. Where it will snap, nobody knows.

A Gun, a Car, a Blonde (1997)

Director: Stefani Ames

Breasts: 2; **Butts**: 1; **Bushes**: 1

Nude Star: **Andrea Thompson** (Full Frontal, Butt)

On the surface of it, a man in a wheelchair dying of spinal cancer might seem to be an unlikely protagonist for an action film, but as *A Gun, a Car, a Blonde* proves, though the body be confined, the imagination may be feverishly overactive. The movie delves into the rich fantasy life of a terminally ill patient who seems to have seen every film-noir detective flick ever, and his imaginary femme fatale is embodied by hardbody Andrea Thompson.

Guns (1990)

Director: Andy Sidaris

Breasts: 11; **Butts**: 1; **Bushes**: 2

Nude Stars: **Cynthia Brimhall** (Breasts, Thong); **Devin DeVasquez** (Full Frontal, Butt, Thong); **Kym Malin** (Full Frontal, Thong); **Donna Spangler** (Breasts, Thong); **Dona Speir** (Breasts, Thong); **Roberta Vasquez** (Right Breast)

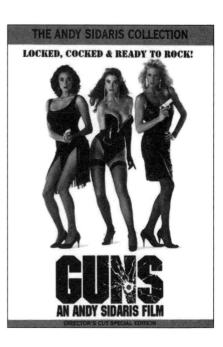

Be advised to stock up on ammo before pulling this pistol of a skin production out of its holster! *Guns* is true to form with model-quality babes flexing their breasts while tripping along intricate story lines that always find time for a revealing shower reverie or a down-and-dirty bout of tits-out mud wrestling. Quality entertainment to engage the senses and the brain! *Guns* is a double-barreled blast of milk bazookas.

Grindhouse - *n.*

The city equivalent of the rural and suburban drive-in, from the 1960s through the mid-1980s, a Grindhouse theater would typically showcase discount double and triple features composed of gory horror, kung-fu, softcore sex, blaxploitation, and other high-energy examples of skinema at its most (s)exciting.

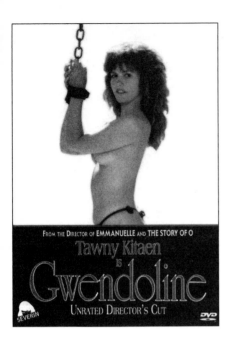

Gwendoline (1984)
Unrated Director's Cut
Director: Just Jaeckin

Breasts: 60; **Butts**: 1; **Bushes**: 1

Nude Stars: **Tawny Kitaen** (Breasts, Butt, Bush, Thong); **Zabou** (Breasts, Thong)

Anonymous Nudes: 29

Legendary lust director Just Jaeckin ended his erotic career with *The Perils of Gwendoline in the Land of the Yik Yak,* a.k.a. *Gwendoline,* an adaptation of a kinky comic book. Tawny Kitaen stars as the titular adventuress who frequently ends up being bound or topless or both. The lovely Zabou plays Tawny's vaguely butch sidekick, although any sense of andro-gyny disappears whenever the French *fille* doffs her top.

The Pearls of *Gwendoline*

Long out of print and better known by the exhausting moniker *The Perils of Gwendoline in the Land of the Yik Yak,* French eroticist Just Jaeckin's *Gwendoline* provided a perfect jumping-off point for the premium DVD label Severin Films. *Gwendoline: Unrated Director's Cut* was the company's first release, and it's followed with more top-notch T&A classics. Get the complete skinny at Severin-Films.com.

skinfo

H.O.T.S. (1979)

Director: Gerald Seth Sindell

Breasts: 32; **Butts**: 1

Nude Stars: **Angela Aames** (Breasts);
Lindsay Bloom (Breasts); **Pamela
Jean Bryant** (Breasts); **Kimberly
Carson** (Breasts); **Sandy Johnson**
(Breasts); **Susan Lynn Kiger** (Breasts);
Lisa London (Breasts); **K.C. Winkler** (Breasts)

Anonymous Nudes: 8

With a name like *H.O.T.S.*, it's got to be good. Well, it's better. First, start off with a slew of *Playboy* Playmates and put them in a picture with just enough plot to hang the countless bras. Two rival sororities compete like any big-breasted houses would, through wet T-shirt contests, skydiving contests, and the climactic strip-football game that's sure to raise your gridiron over the goalpost. *H.O.T.S.* is the S.H.I.T.!

H.O.T.S. or Not?

The enormous popularity of *H.O.T.S.* on early-1980s cable TV and during the fledgling days of home video would naturally have ignited thoughts of a sequel. Alas, caveat emptor when it comes to questionable-looking flicks titled *H.O.T.S. II* and/or *H.O.T.S. III.* Those are just cheap, repackaged versions of *The Swinging Cheerleaders* (1974) and *Revenge of the Cheerleaders* (1976), respectively. Each is a classic in its own right, and therefore each is worth owning in its proper, official DVD release.

skinfo

Halloween (1978)

Director: John Carpenter

Breasts: 4

Nude Stars: **Sandy Johnson** (Breasts);
    P.J. Soles (Breasts)

It's the granddaddy of slasher movies, giving audiences what they want: beautiful naked women screaming their nipples off. Many imitators followed *Halloween,* but few surpassed its mix of gore and goodies. Case in point (two cases, really) is P.J. Soles, who gets offed, but not before Mr. Skin gets off watching her Sole sisters set free from her shirt. Jamie Lee Curtis may not strip, but this flick offers enough treats to do the trick.

Hardcore (1979)

Director: Paul Schrader

Breasts: 26; **Butts**: 3; **Bushes**: 5

Nude Stars: **Leslie Ackerman** (Breasts); **Ilah Davis**
    (Breasts, Butt); **Season Hubley** (Full Frontal);
    Linda Morell (Breasts); **Serena** (Full Frontal);
    Gigi Vorgan (Breasts)

Anonymous Nudes: 7

George C. Scott plays an ultrareligious papa whose teenage offspring runs away to the land of fruits and nuts and immediately lands in the tits-and-ass industry in *Hardcore.* Scott ventures to Sin Angeles with the passion of Patton and, with the help of happy hooker Season Hubley, tries to find his lost little girl. But before Season can give old George a helping hand, she offers him a peeping clam as she spreads her legs in a peep booth.

Hard Hunted (1992)

Director: Christian Drew Sidaris

Breasts: 14

Nude Stars: **Cynthia Brimhall** (Breasts); **Ava Cadell** (Breasts); **Carolyn Liu** (Breasts); **Becky Mullen** (Breasts, Thong); **Mika Quintard** (Breasts); **Dona Speir** (Breasts); **Roberta Vasquez** (Breasts)

The agents of LETHAL, that intrepid antiterrorist organization that uses KSXY—the radio station with bikini-clad DJs who also strip in the adjacent bar—as a front for its co-pervert operations, are at it again in *Hard Hunted*. Agents Cynthia Brimhall, Mika Quintard, and Carolyn Liu spend almost as much time kicking the bad guys' butts as they do baring their tops. It's a sight for sore eyes and sorer crotches.

Hardcore Hubley

Spectacularly flat-chested Season Hubley portrays a tough, seen-it-all peepshow dancer in the antiporn freak-out *Hardcore*. In her second-best-known film, the grindhouse classic *Vice Squad* (1982), Season plays a hard-as-nails street hooker. Coincidence? Well . . . yeah.

skinfo

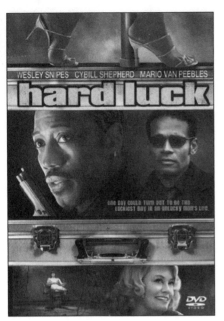

Hard Luck (2006)

Director: Mario Van Peebles

Breasts: 7; **Butts**: 1

Nude Star: **Jackie Quinones** (Breasts, Butt, Thong)

Anonymous Nudes: 3

Wesley Snipes heads up a twisty tale in *Hard Luck,* portraying an ex-pusher who comes across a heap of stolen dope. Further menacing Snipes is Mario Van Peebles as a cop with a vengeance and Cybill Shepherd(!) as a torture-happy serial murderer. Jackie Quinones repeatedly peels off on camera. She'll make more than just your luck hard.

Hard Ticket to Hawaii (1987)

Director: Andy Sidaris

Breasts: 10; **Butts**: 1

Nude Stars: **Cynthia Brimhall** (Breasts); **Hope Marie Carlton** (Breasts, Thong); **Patty Duffek** (Breasts); **Dona Speir** (Breasts, Butt); **Julie Strain** (Breasts)

Drug smugglers would be less inclined to avoid capture if all the agents assigned to catching them were as pretty as the scantily clad law-enforcement posse exposed in *Hard Ticket to Hawaii,* directed by bombs, bullets, and boobs visionary Andy Sidaris. The bad guys should know that the deck is stacked against them—way stacked.

Havoc (2005)
Unrated Edition
Director: Barbara Kopple

Breasts: 6; **Butts**: 1

Nude Stars: **Anne Hathaway** (Breasts, Butt); **Bijou Phillips** (Breasts)

Anonymous Nudes: 1

Under the influence of countless rap videos in *Havoc,* a pair of teenage Los Angeles princesses (Anne Hathaway and Bijou Phillips) indulge the delusion that they are two gangsta-hard hip-hoppers. The fantasy is fun until the whiter-than-white girls cross the line that separates the squeaky-clean streets of affluence from the gritty alleyways of low-rider culture. And *Princess Diaries* star Anne bares her dairy queens!

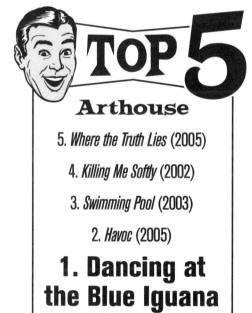

TOP 5
Arthouse

5. *Where the Truth Lies* (2005)

4. *Killing Me Softly* (2002)

3. *Swimming Pool* (2003)

2. *Havoc* (2005)

1. Dancing at the Blue Iguana (2000)

FRED WARD   UMA THURMAN   MARIA DE MEDEIROS
RICHARD E. GRANT   KEVIN SPACEY

Henry & June

UNE HISTOIRE VRAIE
PLUS ÉROTIQUE
QUE N'IMPORTE
QUEL FANTASME

DVD
VIDEO

UNIVERSAL

Henry & June (1990)

Director: Philip Kaufman

Breasts: 42; **Butts**: 17;
Bushes: 4

Nude Stars: **Maria de Medeiros**
(Breasts, Butt); **Brigitte Lahaie**
(Breasts, Butt); **Maïté Maillé**
(Breasts)

Anonymous Nudes: 33

Author Henry Miller spent much of his adult life among the easy-virtue ladies of Paris. *Henry & June,* a biographical bacchanal based on Miller and his wife, June, documents Miller's antics in France, and they make for prime movie entertainment. Maria de Medeiros watches a steamy lesbian tryst between frail and frilly blonde Brigitte Lahaie and bright-eyed, bitty-boobied brunette Maïté Maillé, then uses what she's learned on frustratingly clothed June Miller stand-in Uma Thurman.

Henry & June & Gene & Roger

After an ongoing campaign spearheaded by critics Gene Siskel and Roger Ebert for an "A rating" to be affixed to adult-themed, nonpornographic films, the MPAA devised the NC-17 rating to keep out the kiddies. The first release to hit theaters brandishing an NC-17 rating? *Henry & June.*

skinfo

Hitcher in the Dark (1989)

Director: Umberto Lenzi

Breasts: 12; **Butts**: 2

Nude Stars: **Josie Bissett** (Breasts, Butt);
  Oralee Sanders (Breasts)

Anonymous Nudes: 5

A sicko travels around in Dad's camper looking for women
to torture and kill in *Hitcher in the Dark*. He offs Oralee
Sanders, though not before letting her remove her top.
Then along comes Josie Bissett. He has a weird way of
showing his affection, namely, taking naked Polaroids of
her small wonders and cute ass. Hitch her in the dark . . .
poke her in the rear!

Hollow Man (2000)

Director: Paul Verhoeven

Breasts: 7

Nude Stars: **Kim Dickens** (Right Breast);
  Rhona Mitra (Breasts)

Anonymous Nudes: 2

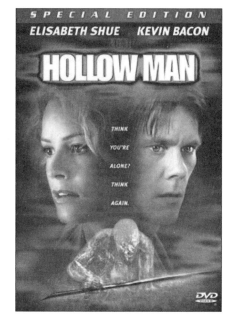

Hollow Man perversely updates the classic invisible-man yarn.
This time Kevin Bacon takes the potion and does what
every red-blooded American male would do in his place . . .
proceeds to peep on the pretty ladies. Kim Dickens and
Rhona Mitra in the buff? They won't leave you hollow, man.

THE STREET WHERE STARLETS ARE MADE!

HOLLYWOOD BOULEVARD

SHAMELESSLY LOADED WITH SEX AND VIOLENCE
CANDICE RIALSON · MARY WORONOV · RITA GEORGE · JEFFREY KRAMER
DICK MILLER · PAUL BARTEL · JONATHAN KAPLAN and GODZILLA
featuring: COMMANDER CODY and his LOST PLANET AIRMEN
Written by: PATRICK HOBBY · Produced by JON DAVISON · Directed by JOE DANTE and ALLAN ARKUSH
A NEW WORLD PICTURES RELEASE   R   METROCOLOR

Hollywood Boulevard (1976)

Directors: Allan Arkush, Joe Dante

Breasts: 7

Nude Stars: **Rita George** (Breasts); **Candice Rialson** (Breasts); **Tara Strohmeier** (Breasts)

Anonymous Nudes: 1

Is an exploitation movie still an exploitation movie when it's a parody of an exploitation movie? That's the philosophical nut to crack in *Hollywood Boulevard,* about a grade-Z movie studio and the girls who take it all off for its pictures. Those girls include Rita George, Candice Rialson, and Tara Strohmeier, who are all naked, and Mary Woronov, who isn't. This boulevard will give you holly wood.

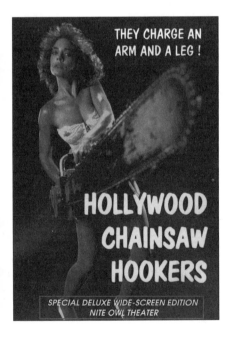

THEY CHARGE AN ARM AND A LEG !

HOLLYWOOD CHAINSAW HOOKERS

SPECIAL DELUXE WIDE-SCREEN EDITION
NITE OWL THEATER

Hollywood Chainsaw Hookers (1988)

Director: Fred Olen Ray

Breasts: 10; **Butts**: 1; **Bushes**: 2

Nude Stars: **Michelle Bauer** (Full Frontal, Butt, Thong); **Tricia Burns** (Breasts); **Esther Elise** (Breasts, Bush); **Linnea Quigley** (Breasts); **Susie Wilson** (Breasts)

In *Hollywood Chainsaw Hookers,* a private detective hired to track down and retrieve runaway Linnea Quigley discovers that she's fallen under the sway of a hooker cult that worships the ancient Egyptian god of chainsaws. This god is, befittingly, a bloodthirsty deity and demands human sacrifice along with copious amounts of rip-roaring, gratuitous hooker nudity. Special effects, aside from generous quantities of fleshly delights, include a pair of provoked prostitutes engaged in a heated chainsaw duel!

The Hollywood Knights (1980)

Director: Floyd Mutrux

Breasts: 8; **Butts**: 3; **Bushes**: 2

Nude Stars: **Dawn Clark** (Breasts); **Michele Drake** (Butt, Bush); **Kim Hopkins** (Breasts, Bush); **Carol Ann Williams** (Breasts)

Anonymous Nudes: 3

Tubby's Drive-in is closing on Halloween night, 1965, as a bunch of pledges try to get into a club called the Hollywood Knights. The knights drop their hopefuls off stark naked outside of town, and the newbies must wheel some auto tires back to Tubby's before closing. Dawn Clark and Kim Hopkins get topless, and Michele Drake is bottomless, bringing the *National Lampoon 1964 Yearbook* cover to life as she twirls in her cheerleader's skirt before a school assembly and reveals that she forgot her panties!

Holy Smoke! (1999)

Director: Jane Campion

Breasts: 2; **Bushes**: 1

Nude Star: **Kate Winslet** (Full Frontal)

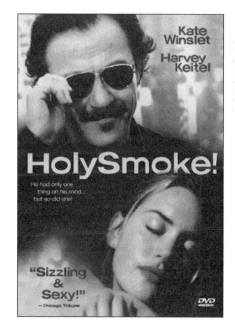

Kate Winslet searches for the meaning of life and finds it in a cult in *Holy Smoke!* Kate's parents lure her home and hire deprogrammer Harvey Keitel. Soon enough, Kate is the one leading Harvey on a search for the meaning of lust. The bad news: Harvey continues his full-frontal streak here. The great news: Kate keeps right up when it comes to taking it all off. Hole-y smoke!

EVERY YOUNG MAN NEEDS A TEACHER

with JOAN COLLINS As Sheila's Mother in

HOMEWORK

YOU CAN'T DO IT ENOUGH.

MAX J. ROSENBERG Presents "HOMEWORK"
Starring SHELL KEPLER • WINGS HAUSER • BETTY THOMAS
Written by MAURICE PETERSON and DON SAFRAN Executive Producer ROBERT L. FENTON
Produced and Directed by JAMES BESHEARS

Homework (1982)

Director: James Beshears

Breasts: 20; **Butts**: 2; **Bushes**: 2

Nude Stars: **Michelle Bauer** (Breasts); **Joy Michael** (Breasts); **Barbara Peckinpaugh** (Breasts)

Anonymous Nudes: 7

A punk rocker tries to get his rocks off with high-school girls in *Homework*. But this hardcore virgin is about to get the lesson of his life from lustful teacher Joan Collins. Joan's one nude scene is actually by body double Joy Michael. Michelle Bauer plays one of a trio of nudie groupies, and Barbara Peckinpaugh opens the show with an erotic photo session. This is the kind of homework you'll want to take home and work hard on!

Hairy Pieball - *n.*

Voyeurism, esp. when involved with spying on pubic hair; e.g., In *Porky's*, Pee-Wee gives the shower girls a *hairy pieball*.

SKIN·finition

Hostel (2005)
Unrated Edition
Director: Eli Roth

Breasts: 40; **Butts**: 5;
    Bushes: 5

Nude Stars: **Jana Kaderabkova**
    (Breasts, Thong); **Barbara**
    Nedeljakova (Breasts); **Sandy Style** (Full Frontal);
    Natali Tothova (Breasts, Butt); **Paula Wild**
    (Breasts, Thong)

Anonymous Nudes: 16

The horror hit *Hostel* features young ugly Americans
yahooing their way across Europe until sadists abduct them.
Thankfully, before all the bloody chainsaw action, they get
in some nice sightseeing. Jana Kaderabkova and Barbara
Nedeljakova undress, and there's tons of anonymous nudity,
including full frontals that are lip-smacking good. Sadly, the
high times end with a hangover no hair of the dog can cure.

Eli Roth
Modern horror's nude showman.

Cabin Fever (2002) positioned writer-director Eli Roth as a talent to
watch in the realm of twenty-first-century horror. It also showcased
Cerina Vincent naked. Roth's follow-up, the brutally cruel *Hostel*
(2005), made good on the filmmaker's early promise not only as a
master of fright, but also when it comes to splattering the screen with
gorgeous young ladies who have taken leave of their clothing.

Top 501 DVDs: *Hostel* (2005)

Hot Dog . . . The Movie (1984)

Director: Peter Markle

Breasts: 15; **Butts**: 3; **Bushes**: 2

Nude Stars: **Crystal Smith** (Full Frontal, Butt); **Tracy Smith** (Left Breast, Butt); **Shannon Tweed** (Full Frontal, Butt)

Anonymous Nudes: 5

Hot Dog . . . The Movie will please your wiener. Patrick Houser picks up hot hitchhiker Tracy Smith, and they check into the ski lodge where Crystal Smith is the nude bellhop. Shannon Tweed rounds out the flesh with a peek at her meaty top. There's a lot of freestyle skiing in between the freestyle screwing, making this hot dog perfect for a poke in the buns.

Hardwood Floor - *n.*

Bald-shaven female crotch.

SKIN·finition

The Hot Spot (1990)

Director: Dennis Hopper

Breasts: 23; **Butts**: 4;
   Bushes: 3

Nude Stars: **Debra Cole** (Breasts,
   Bush); **Jennifer Connelly** (Breasts,
   Butt); **Virginia Madsen** (Breasts,
   Butt)

Anonymous Nudes: 9

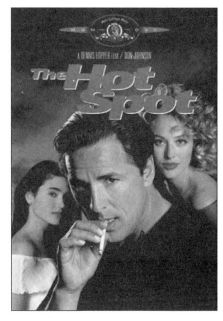

Drifter Don Johnson gets involved with the boss's wife, mountain-mammed Virginia Madsen, in this Southern-set modern noir. Before long, Don robs a bank, and the lid gets blown off a blackmail plot. But *The Hot Spot* is *really* all about the jugadocious perfection of Jennifer Connelly. Jen tans the hottest hootage in Hollywood history by a lake, and there's even a distant butt shot at such an angle that you almost get a glimpse of her tonsils. One of the greatest nude scenes of all time. Period.

Humanoids from the Deep (1980)

Director: Barbara Peters

Breasts: 8; **Butts**: 1; **Bushes**: 1

Nude Stars: **Lisa Glaser** (Full Frontal, Butt);
   Linda Shayne (Breasts); **Lynn Theel** (Breasts);
   Cindy Weintraub (Breasts)

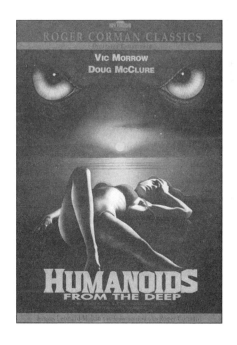

Humanoids from the Deep exists as a showcase for seaweed-encrusted, slime-oozing, bulky hulks who stumble up from the ocean bottom to chase down our pure, innocent women, assault them in a sexual manner, and discard their bodies on the shore for the stalwart men to find like so much weekend picnic trash. It's awesome.

The Hunger (1983)

Director: Tony Scott

Breasts: 6; **Butts**: 3

Nude Stars: **Catherine Deneuve** (Breasts, Butt); **Ann Magnuson** (Breasts); **Susan Sarandon** (Breasts)

Anonymous Nudes: 2

Three very different but equally sexy hotties heat up the arty vampire movie *The Hunger*. There's Ann Magnuson as a disco-dancing victim of bloodsuckers David Bowie and our second siren, Catherine Deneuve. Completing our torrid triangle is Susan Sarandon. She plays a doctor working on age reversal, which Catherine hopes will help her aging lover, Bowie. But soon the two are getting les-be-friendly, and Catherine easily forgets the crusty musician.

Lesbian Vampires
Fangs for the mammaries.

They vant to suck your girlfriend! Even back in 1936, guys knew what was going on when Gloria Holden stalked Marguerite Churchill in *Dracula's Daughter*. There was no mistaking what desires drove Ingrid Pitt in *The Vampire Lovers* (1970), and Soledad Miranda's seduction of Ewa Strömberg in *Vampyros Lesbos* (1970) needs no further explanation. By the time that Catherine Deneuve imbibed more than the blood of Susan Sarandon in *The Hunger* (1983), followed by Alyssa Milano's sanguinary sex with Charlotte Lewis in *Embrace of the Vampire* (1994), the groundwork was laid for Misty Mundae to star in softcore epics such as *An Erotic Vampire in Paris* (2002), *My Vampire Lover* (2002), and *Vampire Vixens* (2003).

Top 501 DVDs: *Embrace of the Vampire (1994), The Hunger (1983)*

If These Walls Could Talk 2 (2000)

Directors: Jane Anderson, Martha Coolidge, Anne Heche

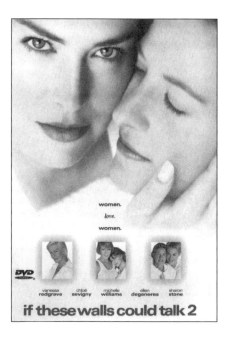

Breasts: 7; **Butts**: 1

Nude Stars: **Ellen DeGeneres** (Right Breast); **Chloë Sevigny** (Breasts); **Sharon Stone** (Breasts, Butt); **Michelle Williams** (Breasts)

Three short films connected by location (an old house inhabited by a succession of Sapphists) and sexual orientation, *If These Walls Could Talk 2* presents the difficult issues and profound rewards of the sister-suckling lifestyle with sensitivity, intelligence, and a triple dose of dramatic resolution. Your imagination will run wild when you witness real-life high-profile labe licker Ellen DeGeneres grappling in the naked grasp of Sharon Stone.

Chick Flicks
Movies for pussies. Literally.

The thing to remember about sappy romantic comedies and/or heartfelt indie-flick dramas is that you will forever have to endure them. But there's a payoff. So you witness the half-a-rebel male lead who can't see the love offered by the sweet, kind, and wholesomely hot gal in front of him because his gaze has been blinded by the glaring lust appeal of a nasty chick who only wants to toy with his emotions. His world crashes down around him, and, tail between his legs, he suddenly sees the appeal of the sweet, kind sexpot and pledges her his undying devotion. At this point in the film, every chick in the theater melts, down there below the waist, and is good to go. And so are you.

Top 501 DVDs: *Boys Don't Cry* (1999), *Holy Smoke!* (1999), *If These Walls Could Talk 2* (2000), *In the Cut* (2003), *Kama Sutra: A Tale of Love* (1996), *Live Nude Girls* (1995), *Love Letters* (1984), *Sirens* (1994)

Ilsa, Harem Keeper of the Oil Sheiks
(1976)

Director: Don Edmonds

Breasts: 34; **Butts**: 6; **Bushes**: 6

Nude Stars: **Tanya Boyd** (Breasts, Butt, Thong); **Uschi Digard** (Full Frontal, Butt); **Haji** (Breasts); **Marilyn Joi** (Full Frontal, Thong); **Sharon Kelly** (Full Frontal, Butt); **Su Ling** (Breasts, Butt, Bush); **Dyanne Thorne** (Breasts, Butt)

Anonymous Nudes: 10

In *Ilsa, Harem Keeper of the Oil Sheiks,* the titular sadist (Dyanne Thorne) oversees white slave girls (along with a couple of exotic-dancing black kung-fu lesbians) who are imported for rape, torture, and other amusements. When a Hollywood starlet and a tycoon's daughter turn up in Ilsa's clutches, the United States dispatches a Henry Kissinger stand-in to bring down the whole unholy operation. Dyanne is as dastardly as ever, and Uschi Digard, Sharon Kelly, and Haji up the rack ante.

Feeling *Ilsa*

Both *Ilsa, She Wolf of the S.S.* and its first sequel, *Ilsa, Harem Keeper of the Oil Sheiks* (1976), were directed by square-jawed actor Don Edmonds, who had previously appeared in fare such as *Gidget Goes Hawaiian* (1961) and on the *Disneyland* TV series.

skinfo

Ilsa, She Wolf of the S.S.
(1974)
Director: Don Edmonds

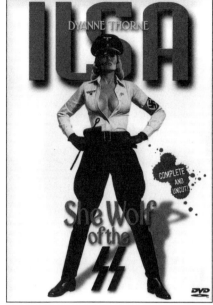

Breasts: 31; **Butts**: 4; **Bushes**: 5

Nude Stars: **Uschi Digard** (Breasts);
   Jackie Giroux (Full Frontal, Butt);
   Sharon Kelly (Full Frontal, Butt);
   Maria Marx (Full Frontal, Butt); **Sandy Richman** (Full
   Frontal); **Dyanne Thorne** (Breasts, Butt); **Donna
   Young** (Full Frontal)

Anonymous Nudes: 9

Dyanne Thorne is *Ilsa, She Wolf of the S.S.,* a sexually
insatiable commandant of a concentration camp. By day, she
conducts experiments to prove women can withstand more
pain than men. At night, she's humping every stiff joint she
can find . . . and then castrating it afterward. Sharon Kelly,
Uschi Digard, and Donna Young are just a few of the
comely prisoners at Dyanne's disposal.
Ilsa will make you spill, sir.

Ilsa
Queen of the sadistic bitches.

Never has a villainess been so amoral, merciless, and profitable as Ilsa, the queen-B anti-heroine
of the sexual-mutilation-and-mayhem circuses titled *Ilsa, She Wolf of the S.S.* (1974), *Ilsa, Harem
Keeper of the Oil Sheiks* (1976), *Ilsa, the Tigress of Siberia* (1977), and *Ilsa, the Wicked Warden*
(1980). Breastacular blonde Dyanne Thorne's on-screen incarnation as the domineering female
prison warden motivated by a hyper-spiteful libido guaranteed that *Ilsa, She Wolf of the S.S.*
would be a breakout abomination of female duress so cravenly nasty (in the most vile sense of
the word) that three sequels would be demanded. The swastikas and Nazi drag were not carried
over beyond the sinister and sinful *She Wolf* original, but Thorne is every bit as capricious, cruel,
and curvaceous in the Ilsa follow-ups.

Top 501 DVDs: *Ilsa, Harem Keeper of the Oil Sheiks* (1976), *Ilsa, She Wolf of the S.S.* (1974), *Ilsa, the
Wicked Warden* (1980)

Ilsa, the Wicked Warden (1980)

Director: Jess Franco

Breasts: 33; **Butts**: 12; **Bushes**: 16

Nude Stars: **Tania Busselier** (Full Frontal, Butt); **Lina Romay** (Breasts); **Esther Studer** (Left Breast, Butt); **Dyanne Thorne** (Full Frontal, Butt)

Anonymous Nudes: 14

Fans of concentration-camp sex crimes who don't like Nazis will find the perfect compromise in *Ilsa, the Wicked Warden*. Dyanne Thorne ravishes in the role of an überbitch commander of a Latin American lockup for deranged women. The camera work is clear and adroitly focused, the inmates make up for their wackiness with good looks, and the conflicts are primal and often resolved in the nude—as if there's any other way.

TOP 5

Movies for Bush

5. *Fantasm Comes Again* (1977) – 19 bushes

4. *Bloodsucking Freaks* (1976) – 21 bushes

3. *Salon Kitty* (1976) – 28 bushes

2. *Immoral Tales* (1974) – 31 bushes

1. Caligula (1979) 46 Bushes!

Immoral Tales (1974)

Director: Walerian Borowczyk

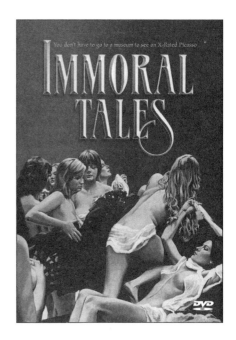

Breasts: 62; **Butts**: 31; **Bushes**: 31

Nude Stars: **Charlotte Alexandra** (Full Frontal, Butt);
Florence Bellamy (Full Frontal, Butt); **Pascale
Christophe** (Full Frontal, Butt); **Lise Danvers** (Breasts,
Butt, Bush); **Paloma Picasso** (Full Frontal, Butt)

Anonymous Nudes: 26

The arthouse sensation *Immoral Tales* presents four vignettes
by Polish auteur Walerian Borowczyk that illustrate sexual
misdeeds throughout history. The pope's daughter bears
his child. A depraved countess bathes in the blood of slain
damsels. Kissing cousins experiment with deep-throating.
A maiden and a cucumber reach orgasmic heights. The only
thing more impressive than the director's obsessive genius
is the vast pool of awe-inspiring skin here, including a
beautifully lit full-frontal display by Pascale Christophe
and Paloma Picasso.

The Initiation (1984)

Director: Larry Stewart

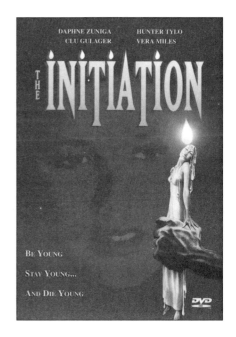

Breasts: 2; **Butts**: 2; **Bushes**: 1

Nude Stars: **Hunter Tylo** (Full Frontal); **Daphne
Zuniga** (Butt)

Anonymous Nudes: 1

A homicidal maniac provides sorority sisters with the
initiation of a lifetime. Trapped in a closed department store,
a group of perky pledges spends the night in the company of
a slain security guard, a half-dozen older girls, a few dudes,
and a leading lady about to confront childhood trauma. Plus,
one of the girls might be the psycho. The survivors will have
plenty to talk about at their ten-year reunion.

Innocent Blood (1992)

Director: John Landis

Breasts: 28; **Butts**: 1; **Bushes**: 1

Nude Stars: **Anne Parillaud** (Full Frontal, Butt);
 Teri Weigel (Breasts, Thong)

Anonymous Nudes: 12

Gangsters have long been viewed as drains on civil society, so it is only natural that director John Landis should combine the crime and vampire genres to create *Innocent Blood.* French fireball Anne Parillaud plays a succulent succubus who infects New York Mafiosi with the bloodsucking bug. With crag-faced costars on the order of Robert Loggia and Don Rickles, Anne is especially bewitching. She'll get your blood pumping.

In Praise of Older Women (1978)

Director: George Kaczender

Breasts: 15; **Butts**: 4; **Bushes**: 2

Nude Stars: **Karen Black** (Breasts); **Monique Lepage** (Breasts, Butt); **Marilyn Lightstone** (Right Breast); **Marianne McIsaac** (Breasts, Butt); **Helen Shaver** (Full Frontal, Butt); **Alexandra Stewart** (Breasts, Butt, Bush); **Susan Strasberg** (Breasts); **Alberta Watson** (Breasts)

Studly Tom Berenger plays an everyman in *In Praise of Older Women*—an everyman who beds down with every bangable woman he sees, which is the kind of everyman that every man dreams of being. Each of the lovelies shows skin. Rather than envy the man, thank him for bringing out the best in these experienced women for all to share.

In the Cut (2003)

Director: Jane Campion

Breasts: 11; **Butts**: 2; **Bushes**: 1

Nude Star: **Meg Ryan** (Full Frontal, Butt)

Anonymous Nudes: 5

Meg Ryan sheds her sunny image—and her clothes—for
In the Cut, playing a New York City teacher who indulges
in dangerous sex after a woman is murdered in her
neighborhood. She jills off, enjoys a grilling from homicide
detective Mark Ruffalo, and hangs out near a sex club.
Meg bares her pegs six different times, and you'll be
sleepless when Sally shows hairy.

Itty Bitty Titty Committee - *n.*

Unofficial support organization for bite-size-breasted
beauties worldwide who, ironically, don't need much
support up top.

"[It] turns me on because it's real."
— MADONNA

IN THE
REALM OF THE
SENSES
A FILM BY NAGISA OSHIMA

Subtitled
Version

"Spectacularly erotic"
— THE LOS ANGELES TIMES

FOX
LORBER
FILMS

WORLD CLASS CINEMA COLLECTION

NC-17   DVD

In the Realm of the Senses (1976)

Director: Nagisa Oshima

Breasts: 8; Butts: 2; Bushes: 3

Nude Star: **Eiko Matsuda** (Full Frontal, Butt)

Anonymous Nudes: 4

The Japanese arthouse classic *In the Realm of the Senses* spins a tale of sexual obsession that drives a man (Tatsuya Fuji) and his female servant (Eiko Matsuda) to the brink of oblivion. This film runs the gamut of kinky sex, ranging from strangulation to strange insertions, and there is very little that Eiko leaves to the imagination. It will leave your senses in the realm of pleasure.

Senses Overload

Throughout its history, *In the Realm of the Senses* has repeatedly fallen into the realm of the censors. Although it was filmed in Japan, *Senses* had to be shipped to France for lab work due to its native land's strict rules regarding nudity. Following the movie's premiere at the Berlin Film Festival, it was seized as pornography until a federal court allowed it to screen eighteen months later. Originally rated X in the United States, a subsequent rerelease earned an NC-17.

skinfo

Iris (2001)

Director: Richard Eyre

Breasts: 3; **Butts**: 1; **Bushes**: 1

Nude Stars: **Penelope Wilton** (Left Breast);
   Kate Winslet (Full Frontal, Butt)

In the biopic *Iris,* elderly Dame Judi Dench plays English novelist Iris Murdoch at the end of her life, as Alzheimer's disease claims the writer's mind. Sounds boring, huh? Well, fear not—things get lap-expandingly exciting during several flashbacks to Iris in her prime, where she's played by Kate Winslet. Throughout the movie, Kate-as-Iris claims to be devoted to her husband, but the curvaceous crumpet shares her bitable bits with any man she pleases. And that is one tasty English muffin.

Irréversible (2002)

Director: Gaspar Noé

Breasts: 2; **Butts**: 1; **Bushes**: 1

Nude Star: **Monica Bellucci** (Full Frontal, Butt)

Irréversible is told in reverse, starting with a murder and working backward to show the motivation. Vincent Cassel stars opposite Monica Bellucci, and the two have some great moments in the sack. During the film's notorious rape scene, you'll want to jump in and help Monica, but luckily, since the film is told backward, there are good times ahead of her. Or is it behind her?

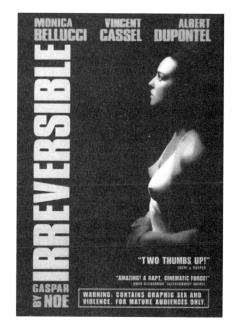

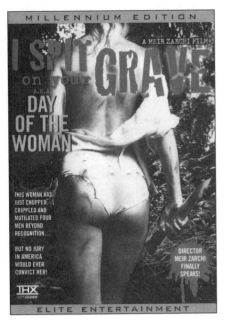

I Spit on Your Grave (1978)
Director: Meir Zarchi

Breasts: 2; **Butts**: 1; **Bushes**: 1

Nude Star: **Camille Keaton** (Full Frontal, Butt)

Camille Keaton is a big-city novelist in *I Spit on Your Grave* who's house-sitting and skinny-dipping in the country. Some rednecks rubberneck while Camille enjoys a full-frontal swing in her hammock and decide to show this urban cutie some backwoods brutality. That heinous act sets in motion the most skintense revenge movie ever made.

Rape and Revenge
What goes around, comes.

If a man, for whatever reason, desires to firmly entrench himself deep on a particular woman's bad side, there are few more effective means for doing so than forcing her to engage in sex. When a brute bullies a lass to bone, she doesn't simply pretend to be outraged. There is no afterglow following a nonconsensual encounter. She is murderously mad. Care to witness the wrath of a woman wronged without experiencing that feminine rage? Smarten up with a viewing of *House by the Lake* (1976), *I Spit on Your Grave* (1978), *Ms. 45* (1981), *Alley Cat* (1984), *Naked Vengeance* (1985), *Sudden Death* (1985), or *I Spit on Your Corpse, I Piss on Your Grave* (2001), and don't ever do what those dudes did.

Top 501 DVDs: *Alley Cat* (1984), *Body Shots* (1999), *I Spit on Your Grave* (1978), *Thriller: A Cruel Picture* (1974)

I Spit on Your Marriage Certificate

Camille Keaton is the grandniece of stone-faced silent-film legend Buster Keaton and was briefly wed to *I Spit on Your Grave* director Meir Zarchi after they collaborated on their mutual misanthropic masterwork. Imagine that honeymoon!

skinfo

Is There Sex After Death? (1971)

Directors: Alan Abel, Jeanne Abel

Breasts: 47; **Butts**: 11; **Bushes**: 16

Nude Stars: **Iris Brooks** (Breasts); **Helen Gross** (Full Frontal, Butt); **Mary Elaine Monti** (Breasts, Butt); **Stephanie Skura** (Right Breast, Butt); **Jennifer Welles** (Full Frontal, Butt)

Anonymous Nudes: 21

Director and star Alan Abel pursues the answer to the age-old question, *Is There Sex After Death?* In the course of this daffy documentary, he meets natural breast enlarger Buck Henry and a porno magician who pulls scarves from women's private parts. On the more skinful side are Iris Brooks as the breast development student and future porn star Jennifer Welles as the magician's (and masturbator's) assistant.

STALLONE

Italian Stallion (1970)
Director: Morton Lewis

Breasts: 12; **Butts**: 5; **Bushes**: 5

Nude Stars: **Janet Banzet** (Full Frontal);
   Henrietta Holm (Full Frontal, Butt)

Anonymous Nudes: 4

Long before Sylvester Stallone was Rocky, the young thespian came off cocky, as proved by the future superstar's performance in *Italian Stallion*. Stallone's *Stallion* character is known simply as Stud, derived from the movie's original title, *Party at Kitty and Stud's*. The plot complexities are easily summed up: Stud bangs his girlfriend, Kitty. Afterward, three more chicks show up, eager to party, and Stud goes a round with each. Ding! Ding!

Italian meatballs

Following its big mid-1980s release on VHS, *Italian Stallion* played trashpit porn theaters for years, including such New York City dens of disease as the Harem and the Venus. Whatever audiences hobbled into these video-projecting petri dishes were far more interested in conducting illegal and/or unsanitary transactions than in watching whatever might be on screen. Still, it's fun to imagine somebody looking up from God-knows-what and noticing, "Shee-yit! It's Rocky's ass!"

skinfo

J. D.'s Revenge (1976)

Director: Arthur Marks

Breasts: 14

Nude Stars: **Alice Jubert** (Breasts); **Joan Pringle**
(Breasts); **Barbara Tasker** (Breasts)

Anonymous Nudes: 4

J. D.'s Revenge attempts to expand the parameters of the
blaxploitation formula common to the typical Afrocentric
cinema offerings of the day, veering into horror-thriller
territory but never venturing far from a funky soundtrack.
Ironside star Joan Pringle shows up as the slapped and salami-
slammed girlfriend, and erotically multiracial multitasker
Barbara Tasker thrills while lying topless in bed and also
when she leaps out from beneath the sheet! Revenge is teat.

Jumbo Jackage - *n.*

Naturally super-sized bosoms; see also Breast Sizes:
JAMAMBO!

SKIN·finition

DAVID CARUSO
LINDA FIORENTINO
CHAZZ PALMINTERI

JADE

Jade (1995)

Director: William Friedkin

Breasts: 4; **Butts**: 2; **Bushes**: 2

Nude Stars: **Angie Everhart** (Full Frontal, Butt);
   Linda Fiorentino (Breasts, Butt, Bush, Thong)

Jade is a seedy, sexy thriller from the awesomely flesh-bent brain that brought us *Showgirls* (1995). It follows femme fatale Linda Fiorentino as a San Francisco woman who may be involved in a brutal murder. Chazz Palminteri and Richard Crenna provide the seedy, and Linda and red-maned Angie Everhart provide the sexy. David Caruso is the San Francisco district attorney who slowly realizes that Linda may be a killer. Just look at her—anybody that hot has to be guilty of *something!*

Jade-d

On the (high) heels of *Basic Instinct*, screenwriter Joe Eszterhas brokered record-shattering script deals for himself. The first result was *Showgirls* (1995), which was publicly bludgeoned on arrival before blossoming into a recognized masterpiece and enduring cult sensation. The second, based on a single-paragraph story description, was *Jade*, which is still just . . . *Jade.* Eszterhas elaborates on these and his other whacko movie-biz adventures in a highly entertaining pair of memoirs: *Hollywood Animal* and *The Devil's Guide to Hollywood: The Screenwriter as God!*

 skinfo

Jaded (1996)

Director: Caryn Krooth

Breasts: 6; **Butts**: 3; **Bushes**: 1

Nude Stars: **Carla Gugino** (Breasts, Butt); **Rya Kihlstedt** (Full Frontal, Butt); **Anna Levine** (Breasts, Butt)

Rarely, if ever, do musings on rape feature females as the perpetrators, but such is the premise of *Jaded*. A serious dramatization of the apathy endured by a woman who is sexually assaulted by two female acquaintances, *Jaded* raises unsettling questions of gender assumptions. Although softened with numerous nudes of the gorgeous Carla Gugino, even the most jaded filmgoer may find himself jolted.

The Janitor (2003)

Directors: T.J. Nordaker, Andy Signore

Breasts: 12

Nude Stars: **Rachael Ann Bennett** (Breasts); **Meghan Callihan** (Breasts); **Crystal LeBard** (Breasts); **Stephanie Christine Medina** (Breasts, Thong); **Tusdi Rodriguez** (Breasts)

Anonymous Nudes: 1

The mop-wielding hero of *The Janitor* is a sensitive soul, but when he snaps, he does much more than just trash talk. And this wouldn't be worthy of the description "B-movie gore" if there weren't copious amounts of T&A. Feast on the likes of Rachael Ann Bennett, Crystal LeBard, and Stephanie Christine Medina and get ready to do a little cleaning up of your own.

The Josephine Baker Story (1991)

Director: Brian Gibson

Breasts: 2; **Butts**: 1

Nude Star: **Lynn Whitfield** (Breasts, Butt)

The Josephine Baker Story packs more swivel in its sexy hips than a boatload of tropical fruit. Scandalously hot 1920s chanteuse Josephine Baker, who became known for her notorious "banana dance," is played by Lynn Whitfield. Seeing Lynn dance over and over again in nothing but a skirt made out of bananas will surely make your banana do a dance of its own.

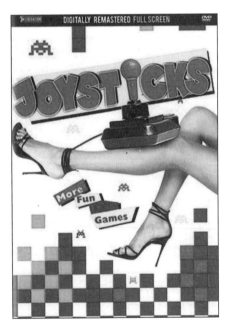

Joysticks (1983)

Director: Greydon Clark

Breasts: 15; **Butts**: 1; **Bushes**: 1

Nude Stars: **Erin Halligan** (Full Frontal, Butt);
   Kym Malin (Breasts); **Kim G. Michel** (Breasts)

Anonymous Nudes: 5

Before geek was chic there was *Joysticks,* where big-breasted bimbos terrorize a video-arcade worker by stealing his pants on his first day on the job. But his real problem is a group of sexy Pac Man–esque dolls sent by King Vidiot to take over the arcade. Boobs meet beeps, and everybody scores.

Just One of the Girls (1992)

Director: Michael Keusch

Breasts: 8; **Butts**: 3; **Bushes**: 4

Nude Stars: **Stacey Green** (Full Frontal, Thong);
  Lisha Snelgrove (Full Frontal, Butt)

Anonymous Nudes: 2

Warning: Do not catch yourself lusting over Corey Haim in drag! The cross-dressing comedy *Just One of the Girls* might mislead those who stumble across it on cable some night. Corey goes undercover in a high school as a girl. Fortunately, Nicole Eggert spices up the plot as Corey's new best friend. And in case of any gay feelings, break open the girls' locker room scene!

The Joy(sticks) of Sex

Ultracurvaceous Corinne Bohrer somehow turned up in two most totally awesome teen sex comedies of the 1980s–*Joysticks* and *Zapped!* (1982)–without exposing her udderly tremendous top. Then came the golf romance *Dead Solid Perfect* (1988), where Corrine finally delivered the goods with full-frontal nudity–while walking through a crowded hotel hallway!

skinfo

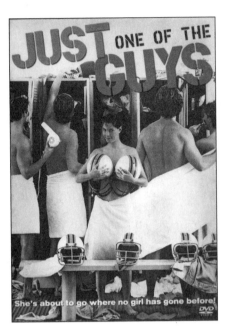

She's about to go where no girl has gone before!

Just One of the Guys (1985)

Director: Lisa Gottlieb

Breasts: 2

Nude Star: **Joyce Hyser** (Breasts)

Just One of the Guys casts Joyce Hyser as Terry, a female aspiring high-school journalist who goes undercover as a guy to prove a point about sexism . . . sexily. Trouble rears its twin torpedoes when she falls for Rick (Clayton Rohner). With the prom coming up, the pressure is on to come clean. When Terry finally opens her tuxedo to reveal her chest pieces, we witness the greatest case of accessorizing since the cummerbund.

Just *Two* of the Girl's

Just One of the Guys seems likely to hold some sort of record when it comes to repeated airings on a multitude of cable TV outlets throughout the decades since its release. It also contains the all-time favorite nude scene of MrSkin.com Editorial Director and handsome devil Mike McPadden.

skinfo

Kama Sutra: A Tale of Love (1996)

Director: Mira Nair

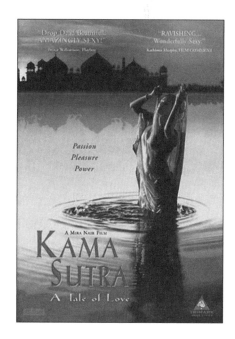

Breasts: 5; **Butts**: 1; **Bushes**: 2

Nude Stars: **Sarita Choudhury** (Full Frontal);
   Indira Varma (Full Frontal, Butt)

Anonymous Nudes: 1

She's supposed to be playing genuine royalty, but Sarita
Choudhury gets the royal shaft as Queen Tara. Her
Highness is basically locked up in a palace and forced to
serve as a sex toy for her husband. Her best friend and
servant, Indira Varma, is no prize, either, especially since
she's also slept with the king. Fortunately, the complex plot
of *Kama Sutra: A Tale of Love* includes a scene where the
queen and her former servant work out their differences
in lesbianic fashion.

Knobjob - *n.*
Oral sex, female gratifying male.

Ken Park (2002)

Directors: Larry Clark, Edward Lachman

Breasts: 4; **Butts**: 1; **Bushes**: 2

Nude Stars: **Tiffany Limos** (Full Frontal); **Maeve Quinlan** (Breasts, Butt, Bush)

Director Larry Clark's earlier forays into teenage excess, *Kids* (1995) and *Bully* (2001), exhibit a documentary feel. His exploration of southern California suburban screwups, *Ken Park,* does too. What distinguishes *Ken Park* is that the sex scenes are far and away the most erotic he has ever filmed, with Tiffany Limos flexing every fissure of her fine form while taking a pair of white punks on a tour of her tawny temptations. And that's saying a mouthful.

Larry Clark
Teen lust laid bare.

High-art photographer Larry Clark had long specialized in the hormonal antics of adolescent adventurers by the time he collaborated with screenwriter Harmony Korine on the 1995 arthouse outrage *Kids*. Clark has maintained his trademark passion for the rites of puberty in *Bully* (2001), *Teenage Caveman* (2001), *Ken Park* (2002), and the shockingly restrained *Wassup Rockers* (2005).

Top 501 DVDs: *Bully* (2001), *Ken Park* (2002), *Teenage Caveman* (2001)

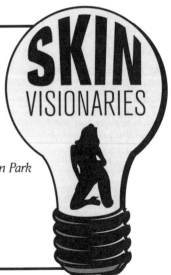

SKIN VISIONARIES

The Kentucky Fried Movie (1977)

Director: John Landis

Breasts: 12; **Butts**: 1

Nude Stars: **Uschi Digard** (Breasts); **Marilyn Joi** (Breasts); **Lenka Novak** (Breasts); **Tara Strohmeier** (Breasts)

Anonymous Nudes: 2

Before *Saturday Night Live,* hipster writers put together counterculture sketch comedy, and *The Kentucky Fried Movie* may be the best of the batch. Once you see the sex-flick send-up "Catholic High School Girls in Trouble," you'll agree—after you recover the power of speech. The other bits boast brazen beauties busting out of their bras, including Marilyn Joi, Lenka Novak, Tara Strohmeier, and Uschi Digard—who is the owner of the famously soaped-up supersoakers that bounce against the shower-stall door in *Kentucky's* "Catholic" high point(s).

This movie is *totally out of control!*

"Quite Hilarious...
Flawlessly Performed."
—*Kevin Thomas, L.A. Times*

My Old Kentucky Bone

The Kentucky Fried Movie launched the big-time career of director John Landis, who next helmed *Animal House* (1978), as well as the writing team Jerry Zucker, Jim Abrahams, and David Zucker. Their follow-up was *Airplane!* (1980), which features an unforgettable anonymous jug jostling by Francesca "Kitten" Natividad.

skinfo

Keys to Tulsa (1996)

Director: Leslie Greif

Breasts: 14; **Butts**: 3; **Bushes**: 2

Nude Stars: **Joanna Going** (Full Frontal, Butt, Thong);
   Dawn Warner Ramos (Breasts); **Deborah Kara
   Unger** (Bush)

Anonymous Nudes: 5

Keys to Tulsa is a tawdry tale of Tulsa society that stars Eric
Stoltz as a rich kid who gets caught up in the death of a
hooker. The film adeptly uses a mix of hipster dialogue and
loony star turns, but it's left to Deborah Kara Unger (who
offers a flash of muff) and Joanna Going to strip down in
search of the keys to revving up your crotch.

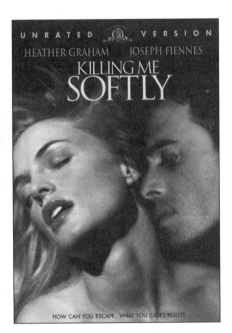

Killing Me Softly (2002)

Director: Kaige Chen

Breasts: 2; **Butts**: 1; **Bushes**: 1

Nude Star: **Heather Graham** (Full Frontal, Butt)

Heather Graham has moved to England and works as a web
designer in the erotic thriller *Killing Me Softly.* She throws
away job and boyfriend for the musty allure of a mysterious
stranger. She marries him only to discover he may have
murdered his last couple of girlfriends. Maybe they should
have dated longer. No, it makes for better skintertainment
that they get buck naked and go buck wild. Oh, those
golden Grahams!

Lady Chatterley's Lover (1981)

Director: Just Jaeckin

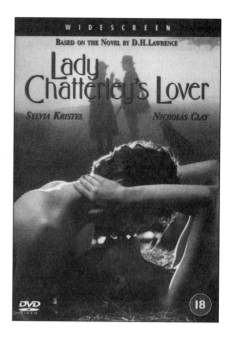

Breasts: 2; **Butts**: 1; **Bushes**: 1

Nude Star: **Sylvia Kristel** (Full Frontal, Butt)

Author D. H. Lawrence could not have imagined his masterpiece of a rich, neglected wife taking to the sheets with her groundskeeper being brought to visual life replete with the nips, buns, and pubic wisps of Sylvia Kristel. If Lawrence had foreseen the brazen nudity to come in *Lady Chatterley's Lover,* he might have been slightly less bold—so be grateful that the past's ignorance preserves the inspiration for today's bliss.

Lady Thrillers

As with *Emmanuelle* and *Fanny Hill*, the titular figure of *Lady Chatterley's Lover* has skinspired a bevy of movie adaptations, variations, and flat-out rip-offs. A French version hit the screen first in 1955. Harlee McBride (the real-life Mrs. Richard Belzer) became a softcore star in a pair of *Young Lady Chatterley* movies, while adult-video actress Chloe assumed the role for the softcore cable series *Lady Chatterley's Stories* in 2000. More fanciful takes on the erotic masterwork include *Fanny Hill Meets Lady Chatterley* (1967) and *Lady Chatterley in Tokyo* (1979).

skinfo

The Lady in Red (1979)

Director: Lewis Teague

Breasts: 33; **Bushes**: 3

Nude Stars: **Pamela Sue Martin** (Breasts);
   Francesca Natividad (Breasts)

Anonymous Nudes: 17

Pamela Sue Martin plays Polly, a 1930s girl who goes to Hollywood to find fame and fortune and winds up in dead-end Chicago instead in *The Lady in Red*. Polly can't catch a break—even ending up in prison and having to endure nude inspections—until she begins dating all-around great guy Robert Conrad. But as luck would have it, he's America's Most Wanted poster boy John Dillinger. Pamela, who played TV's Nancy Drew, will give you a hardy boy.

The Lair of the White Worm (1988)

Director: Ken Russell

Breasts: 4; **Butts**: 1; **Bushes**: 1

Nude Star: **Amanda Donohoe** (Full Frontal, Butt)

Anonymous Nudes: 1

Director Ken Russell goes all out in *The Lair of the White Worm,* a simple tale of legendary rustic Worm Gods that becomes a mad mix of rock and roll and sadomasochistic imagery. He chooses a properly shameless cast, too, with Sammi Davis and Catherine Oxenberg keeping their tongues firmly in cheek. Your hands, however, will be firmly in your pants once you check out Amanda Donohoe's kinky turn as the Priestess of the Worm.

Lake Consequence (1992)

Director: Rafael Eisenman

Breasts: 4; **Butts**: 1; **Bushes**: 2

Nude Stars: **May Karasun** (Full Frontal, Butt);
   Joan Severance (Full Frontal)

Lake Consequence chronicles Joan Severance as a repressed
housewife who runs off with gardener Billy Zane for a wild
weekend of sexual revelations. May Karasun plays Zane's
girlfriend, who doesn't mind at all when Joan shows up to
celebrate the Chinese New Year. It won't be just firecrackers
going off as Joan and May flash their full frontals in plenty
of nude scenes, ultimately leading to some hubba-hubba
hot-tub action!

Ken Russell
England's creaming.

Ken Russell established himself as the screaming-mad messiah of
British cinema with over-the-top exercises such as *The Devils* (1971),
Tommy (1975), *Lisztomania* (1976), and *Altered States* (1980). He also
specialized in literary adaptations and classical music biographies. The
one constant running through Russell's repertoire? Naked women. All hail
the insane genius!

Top 501 DVDs: *Lair of the White Worm* (1988)

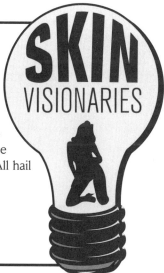

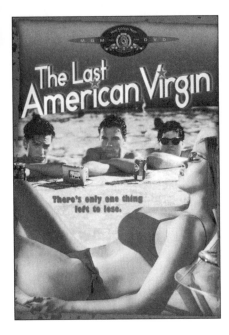

The Last American Virgin
(1982)
Director: Boaz Davidson

Breasts: 11; **Butts**: 3; **Bushes**: 2

Nude Stars: **Diane Franklin** (Full Frontal); **Gerri Idol** (Breasts); **Louisa Moritz** (Breasts, Butt, Bush); **Tessa Richarde** (Breasts)

Anonymous Nudes: 3

Mr. Skin's
TOP
69

38

The story line of *The Last American Virgin* involves a group of high-school pals vying for the attentions of lovely Diane Franklin. Don't be fooled by the classic setup, though, since *The Last American Virgin* is a truly innovative film. There are still plenty of old-fashioned sexcapades, as the horny teenagers get to ogle Tessa Richarde and stunning older woman Louisa Moritz (the poor boys don't get to see Diane's Franklin mints and short-and-curlies in the doctor's office, but we do!).

The Last House on the Left (1972)
Director: Wes Craven

Breasts: 5; **Butts**: 2; **Bushes**: 1

Nude Stars: **Sandra Cassel** (Right Breast, Butt, Bush); **Lucy Grantham** (Breasts, Butt); **Jeramie Rain** (Breasts)

Wes Craven's landmark shocker *The Last House on the Left* is a grueling tale of two teenagers who get kidnapped, humiliated, and murdered by psychos. The good news is that the creeps get punished. The bad news is that the revenge seems just as sleazy as the original crime. Just keep repeating, "It's only a movie, it's only a movie," so you'll feel okay about jerking off to it.

Teen Sex Comedies
Losing it in the locker room.

The nerds. The jocks. The pranks. The cheerleaders. The cheerleaders getting changed. The cheerleaders enjoying a group shower. The fascistic principal pooping the party . . . until he gets his! The Teen Sex Comedy is our collective adolescent id committed to celluloid. Birthed in the relatively squeaky-clean mid-'60s as beach-party movies, the Teen Sex Comedy erupted in all its naked glory throughout the pom-pom-girl-happy 1970s, smack up to changing the world via *Animal House* (1978). The form perfected itself in the early '80s, as crystallized in *Fast Times at Ridgemont High* (1982), *The Last American Virgin* (1982), *Porky's* (1982), *Risky Business* (1983), and *Revenge of the Nerds* (1984). So who ratted to the local authorities? A criminal filmmaker by the name of John Hughes, who castrated the Teen Sex Comedy, injected it with the sentimentality of prom-night poetry, and sanitized it for mass consumption. No wedgie on earth would be long, slow, or humiliating enough to properly punish Mr. Hughes for his unforgivable transgressions. Fortunately, *American Pie* (1999) and *Varsity Blues* (1999) broke The Curse of *The Breakfast Club* (1985) and reignited the horny high schooler as a cinematic icon.

Top 501 DVDs: *American Pie* (1999), *American Pie Presents Band Camp* (2005), *American Pie Presents The Naked Mile* (2006), *Animal House* (1978), *The Beach Girls* (1982), *Boarding School* (1978), *The Cheerleaders* (1973), *EuroTrip* (2004), *Fast Times at Ridgemont High* (1982), *Fraternity Vacation* (1985), *The Hollywood Knights* (1980), *Homework* (1982), *Hot Dog . . . The Movie* (1984), *Joysticks* (1983), *Just One of the Girls* (1992), *Just One of the Guys* (1995), *The Last American Virgin* (1982), *Loose Screws* (1985), *Malibu Beach* (1978), *The Pom Pom Girls* (1976), *Porky's* (1982), *Preppies* (1982), *Private School* (1983), *Revenge of the Cheerleaders* (1976), *Revenge of the Nerds* (1984), *Risky Business* (1983), *Road Trip* (2000), *School Spirit* (1985), *Screwballs* (1983), *The Swinging Cheerleaders* (1974), *Valley Girl* (1983), *Van Wilder* (2002), *Varsity Blues* (1999)

The Last Picture Show (1971)

Director: Peter Bogdanovich

Breasts: 10; **Butts**: 2; **Bushes**: 4

Nude Stars: **Kimberly Hyde** (Full Frontal, Butt); **Cybill Shepherd** (Breasts, Butt); **Sharon Ullrick** (Breasts)

Anonymous Nudes: 3

The Last Picture Show is the first word on Cybill Shepherd. The classic coming-of-age story takes place in a small Texas town. Cybill strips at a pool party in front of rich Wichita kids and makes movie history. Besides Cybill's cuties, Kimberly Hyde shows off her comely hide, and Sharon Ullrick lets Timothy Bottoms drive her in the backseat of his car.

Bernardo Bertolucci
Italian maestro with an eye for Alps.

Along with Fellini, Pasolini, and other icons of Italian film, Bernardo Bertolucci dazzled international audiences with his breakthrough hit *The Conformist* (1970). His 1972 collaboration with Marlon Brando, *Last Tango in Paris*, both scandalized the planet and broke new ground in fresh uses for dairy products. Since then, Bertolucci has regularly painted the screen with powerful nudity in titles such as *La Luna* (1979), *The Sheltering Sky* (1990), *Stealing Beauty* (1996), and his carnal comeback smash, *The Dreamers* (2003).

Top 501 DVDs: *The Dreamers* (2003), *Last Tango in Paris* (1972)

Last Tango in Paris (1972)

Director: Bernardo Bertolucci

Breasts: 2; **Butts**: 1; **Bushes**: 1

Nude Star: **Maria Schneider** (Full Frontal, Butt)

He's wacky, he's naked, and he's the greatest actor of his generation. Ladies and gentlemen, Marlon Brando! *Last Tango in Paris* isn't so much a story as it is a character study of grieving widower Brando as he hurls his beefy being into a desensitized physical relationship with brick-house-built submissive Maria Schneider. *Paris* is burning.

Tango and Gash

Last Tango in Paris was originally rated X and was ultimately released on video in both X and R versions. The scene that crosses the line is apparently one where Brando sneaks his Marlon up Maria's buttery back door. In the softer edit, the scene isn't cut, but a lamp is superimposed over the action. In 1997 *Last Tango* received an NC-17 rating.

skinfo

The Last Temptation of Christ (1988)

Director: Martin Scorsese

Breasts: 12; **Butts**: 1; **Bushes**: 4

Nude Star: **Barbara Hershey** (Breasts, Butt, Bush)

Anonymous Nudes: 5

In *The Last Temptation of Christ,* it seems that Jesus led a relatively productive life, with some unpleasantness at the end. *Last Temptation* dares to consider the Christian savior's life as an actual man, imbued with a common mortal's needs and desires, and on top of that possessed by the divine spirit. Playing a professional love object, darkly alluring damsel Barbara Hershey's slinky sales pitch includes teaser previews of pubes and pop-up breast tips. That's Barbara's cross to bare.

The Lickerish Quartet (1970)

Director: Radley Metzger

Breasts: 6; **Butts**: 3; **Bushes**: 3

Nude Stars: **Erika Remberg** (Full Frontal, Butt);
  Silvana Venturelli (Full Frontal, Butt)

Anonymous Nudes: 1

What goes down when a rich Italian family happens upon the lead actress from a smut film they've just viewed? If reality is dictated by director Radley Metzger, Mom, Dad, and son persuade the stacked blonde to accompany them back to their countryside villa for an orgy of surreal seduction. *The Lickerish Quartet* is deliberately mind-blowing and intends to penetrate the viewer's head as deeply as it does the seat of desire. Take a lick.

Lie with Me (2005)

Director: Clément Virgo

Breasts: 2; **Butts**: 2; **Bushes**: 1

Nude Stars: **Lauren Lee Smith** (Full Frontal, Butt)

Anonymous Nudes: 1

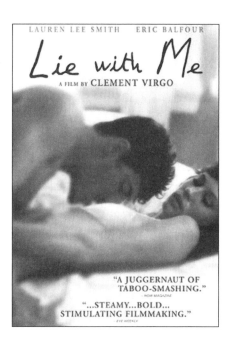

Lauren Lee Smith ignites the carnally charged indie romance *Lie with Me* with her naturally gorgeous looks and astonishing erotic screen presence. Lauren plays Leila, who beds a succession of partners and embarks on all manner of sexual escapades, including masturbating to porn and engaging in intercourse alongside another copulating couple. The nonstop onslaught of dirty doings gets complicated when Leila falls for one of her cocky conquests (Eric Balfour). But fear not, the graphically gratifying heat keeps coming— and Lauren's clothes keep coming off!

Radley Metzger
Euro-erotica at its most elegant.

Native New Yorker Radley Metzger first entered the skinema game by bringing the groundbreaking Swedish hit *I, a Woman* (1965) to the United States. Deigning to create his own movies, Metzger made *Carmen, Baby* (1967), *Therese and Isabelle* (1968), and *Camille 2000* (1969) in rapid succession, followed by his masterpiece *The Lickerish Quartet* (1970). Shot in Europe, Metzger's films are sumptuous visual and sensual accomplishments. With the rise of "porn chic," Metzger went hardcore under the name Henry Paris, directing what is hailed by many as the finest X-rated film of all time, *The Opening of Misty Beethoven* (1976).

Top 501 DVDs: *The Lickerish Quartet* (1970), *Therese and Isabelle* (1968)

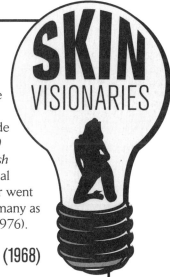

SKIN VISIONARIES

Lifeforce (1985)

Director: Tobe Hooper

Breasts: 2; **Butts**: 1; **Bushes**: 1

Nude Star: **Mathilda May** (Full Frontal, Butt)

How bad can an alien invasion be when the leader is megameloned Mathilda May? It's surprising that anybody even notices that London is overrun by shriveled zombies when Mathilda flaunts her three bangtabulous Bs walking nude throughout the sci-fi epic *Lifeforce*. American astronaut Steve Railsback still feels bad for bringing Mathilda to Earth, though, so he teams up with British military man Peter Firth to put an end to the shapely space vampire and her celestial body.

TOP 5

Vampire Movies

5. *The Forsaken* (2001)

4. *Innocent Blood* (1992)

3. *The Hunger* (1983)

2. *Lifeforce* (1985)

1. Embrace of the Vampire (1994)

Little Witches (1996)

Director: Jane Simpson

Breasts: 20; **Butts**: 5; **Bushes**: 2

Nude Stars: **Clea Duvall** (Breasts, Butt); **Lalaneya Hamilton** (Full Frontal, Butt); **Sheeri Rappaport** (Breasts, Butt); **Melissa Taub** (Full Frontal, Butt)

Anonymous Nudes: 6

The goth teens of *Little Witches* want to seduce the locals, so black magic is pursued and things get devilishly delicious. Clea Duvall does a dance and loses her underpants. Zoe Alexander gets topless but keeps her back to the camera. Melissa Taub's got a lot of what we like to call the moist. And although Lalaneya Hamilton's skin is steamy, it's Sheeri Rappaport who really puts a spell on spew. *Little Witches* will get you big in the britches.

Live Nude Girls (1995)

Director: Julianna Lavin

Breasts: 9; **Butts**: 2

Nude Stars: **Kim Cattrall** (Breasts, Thong); **Olivia d'Abo** (Breasts); **Dana Delany** (Butt); **Laila Robins** (Right Breast, Butt); **Cynthia Stevenson** (Breasts); **Lora Zane** (Breasts)

Kim Cattrall, Laila Robins, Dana Delany, Lora Zane, and Olivia d'Abo get together to raise a little hell in *Live Nude Girls*. Playing a B-movie actress (with A-plus B cups), Kim plans one last slumber party with her tarty playmates the night before she's set to be married. Soon penis-plumping pillow fights, cheap thrills, and frilly nightgowns abound from the giggly estrogen-induced group.

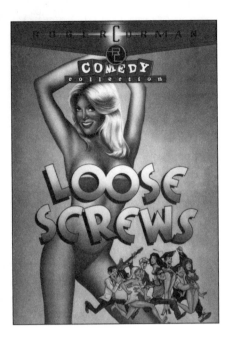

Loose Screws (1985)

Director: Rafal Zielinski

Breasts: 21; **Butts**: 6; **Bushes**: 1

Nude Stars: **Cynthia Belliveau** (Breasts, Butt); **C.J. Fidler** (Breasts, Butt, Bush); **Beth Gondek** (Breasts); **Susan Irvine** (Breasts, Butt); **Laura Potter** (Breasts); **Karen Wood** (Breasts)

Anonymous Nudes: 8

Stop us if you've heard this one before, but there's a fat guy, a nerdy guy, and a real Romeo who enjoy all kinds of merry misadventures while trying to get laid. Don't worry about the plot of *Loose Screws,* though. You'll be too busy screwing your zipper loose while enjoying a bounty of beauties like Cynthia Belliveau, C.J. Fidler, Susan Irvine, and more!

Lesbian - *n.*

For Mr. Skin's purposes, the term *lesbian* connotes any on-screen sensual contact—from kissing and canoodling to full-on cunnilingus—between two women. Or more. If we're lucky.

Lord of the G-Strings: The Femaleship of the String

(2002)

Director: Terry West

Breasts: 22; **Butts**: 8; **Bushes**: 9

Nude Stars: **Anoushka** (Full Frontal, Butt); **Darian Caine** (Full Frontal, Butt); **C.J. DiMarsico** (Full Frontal, Butt); **Chelsey Hampshire** (Full Frontal, Butt); **Barbara Joyce** (Breasts, Bush); **A.J. Khan** (Breasts, Bush); **Ruby Larocca** (Breasts, Butt); **Misty Mundae** (Full Frontal, Butt, Thong); **Allanah Rhodes** (Breasts, Butt, Bush); **Paige Richards** (Breasts); **Kelli Summers** (Breasts, Butt, Bush)

You'll pull your cord over Misty Mundae, Darian Caine, and A.J. Khan in *Lord of the G-Strings: The Femaleship of the String,* a sexy spoof on the *Lord of the Rings* trilogy. Misty's the Throbbit who gets stuck with the job of destroying the all-powerful G-string. Fortunately, this sacred mission involves hot lesbianic action from the likes of Anoushka, Barbara Joyce, and Ruby Larocca.

Lip-Slip - *n.*

An accidental, momentary revelation of an actress's crotch. Bijou Phillips provides a primo Lip-Slip twenty-three minutes into *Bully* (2001).

SKIN-finition

From the Director of LEAVING LAS VEGAS
the loss of sexual innocence

"One of the most daring and innovative films. It examines the way sex, guilt and knowledge interact." - Roger Ebert, CHICAGO SUN-TIMES

The Loss of Sexual Innocence (1999)

Director: Mike Figgis

Breasts: 4; Butts: 2; Bushes: 1

Nude Stars: **Saffron Burrows** (Left Breast, Butt); **Hanne Klintoe** (Full Frontal, Butt); **Johanna Torell** (Left Breast)

The Loss of Sexual Innocence finds director Mike Figgis following a long tradition of making an indulgent film that dwells on his own sexcapades. The really good news is that Mike seems to have dipped his fig into plenty of fine femmes. Even the silly segment about Adam and Eve offers alluring imagery of both nature and natural boobies. Besides, who needs dialogue when you've got nudity from the likes of Saffron Burrows, Hanne Klintoe, and Johanna Torell?

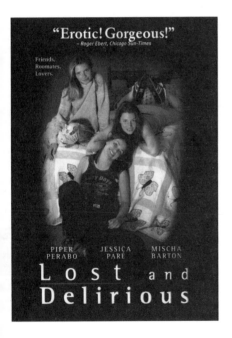

"Erotic! Gorgeous!"
– Roger Ebert, Chicago Sun-Times

Friends,
Roomates,
Lovers.

PIPER PERABO   JESSICA PARÉ   MISCHA BARTON

Lost and Delirious

Lost and Delirious (2001)

Director: Léa Pool

Breasts: 4

Nude Stars: **Jessica Paré** (Breasts); **Piper Perabo** (Breasts)

Mischa Barton's evil stepmother ships her off to boarding school in *Lost and Delirious*. We should all be so lucky, as Mischa finds herself boarding with lesbian lovers Piper Perabo and Jessica Paré. The lusty and delicious doings between Jessica and Piper will have you fingering your skin flute.

Lost Highway (1997)

Director: David Lynch

Breasts: 8; **Butts**: 1

Nude Stars: **Patricia Arquette** (Breasts, Butt); **Lisa Boyle** (Breasts); **Natasha Gregson Wagner** (Breasts)

Anonymous Nudes: 1

Director David Lynch weaves a weird world of misplaced identities in *Lost Highway*. It begins with jazzman Bill Pullman being sent a videotape of himself sleeping in his bed and gets even weirder when Balthazar Getty finds himself teleported into a prison cell. Mysterious Robert Blake doesn't do much of a job of explaining things, either. There's nothing mysterious, however, about the found curves of Patricia Arquette, Lisa Boyle, and Natasha Gregson Wagner.

Lust and *Delirious*

Piper Perabo ate up her role as a lesbian so convincingly in *Lost and Delirious* that she easily returned to playing Sapphic in the much less skintensive girl-girl love story *Imagine Me & You* (2005). Between sucking lady face on screen, Piper turns up in *Cheaper by the Dozen* movies.

skinfo

All the youthful beauties of Europe enslaved for the pleasure of the 3rd Reich

WE GUARANTEE YOU THAT YOU WILL NOT LIVE LONG ENOUGH TO FORGET THE THINGS YOU WILL WITNESS AND EXPERIENCE INSIDE...

LOVE CAMP 7

Maria Lease
Kathy Williams

color

Love Camp 7 (1969)
Director: Lee Frost

Breasts: 24; **Butts**: 12; **Bushes**: 9

Nude Stars: **Maria Lease** (Full Frontal, Butt);
   Kathy Williams (Full Frontal, Butt)

Anonymous Nudes: 10

An early high-water mark of the lower-than-lowbrow "Nazi-sploitation" genre, *Love Camp 7* concerns a pair of intrepid female agents for the Allies who slip undercover into the atrocity establishment of the title. Their aim is to witness and report back on the sexual grotesqueries of the Third Reich. And *Love Camp 7* provides them with plenty to write home about!

SKINEMA SENSATIONS!

Nazi-sploitation
Deutschland boober alles.

We all know that Hitler's sicko party was, ironically, no party. But being a part of the masturbation-race has been portrayed as a goose-stepping good time in a series of bad-taste sexploitation movies that still pack *das oomph* of a Gestapo heel to the gonads. It took a few decades after World War II until filmdom realized how sexy a thigh-high pair of leather boots looks on a half-naked hottie. Case in point, *The Night Porter* (1974), with Charlotte Rampling's petite pair making a blitzkrieg in your pants. Arthouses set the tone with *Salon Kitty* (1976), and, in *Ilsa, She Wolf of the S.S.* (1974), Dyanne Thorne created a character of such mamnificient proportions that she continues to make men quiver and quake. Lesser-known titles include *Fräuleins in Uniforms* (1973), *Gestapo's Last Orgy* (1977), *Nazi Love Camp 27* (1977), and *S.S. Girls* (1977).

Top 501 DVDs: *Ilsa, She Wolf of the S.S.* (1974), *Love Camp 7* (1969), *The Night Porter* (1974), *Salon Kitty* (1976)

Love Letters (1984)

Director: Amy Holden Jones

Breasts: 2; **Butts**: 1

Nude Star: **Jamie Lee Curtis** (Breasts, Butt)

What would someone do if they discovered a hidden stockpile of their mom's love letters? Well, if you're juggy Jamie Lee Curtis, first you'd read them, and then you'd find yourself a lover, quick. Turns out dear old Mom had a torrid affair that Jamie Lee knew nothing about until she found the purple prose. Jamie Lee decides adultery is all right and proceeds to take off her shirt a lot and let those flesh balloons fly.

Lovely & Amazing (2001)

Director: Nicole Holofcener

Breasts: 2; **Butts**: 1; **Bushes**: 1

Nude Star: **Emily Mortimer** (Full Frontal, Butt)

Lovely & Amazing brings us some mixed-up ladies. Brenda Blethyn goes under the knife to remove some unwanted fat and falls for the plastic surgeon. Catherine Keener strays from her dull husband. But breast of all is the insecure actress portrayed by Emily Mortimer, who, in the movie's moist infamous scene, gets dressed down by her lover while standing completely naked before him. Emily is lovely and amazing all over. And furry where it counts.

The Lover (1992)

Director: Jean-Jacques Annaud

Breasts: 3; **Butts**: 2; **Bushes**: 1

Nude Stars: **Lisa Faulkner** (Right Breast, Butt);
Jane March (Full Frontal, Butt)

The Lover takes place in French colonial Vietnam, and Jane March plays a teen who, on her way to boarding school, is waylaid (well, just plain laid) by an older Chinese businessman. Lisa Faulkner adds some more boob, including a DVD extra flash, but it's Jane who marches this flick into the hall of fame. You've got to love *The Lover*.

Love to *Lover*, Baby

The Lover is a semi-autobiographical account by French writer Marguerite Duras about how she lost her virginity. Thanks for sharing!

skinfo

Luscious (1997)

Director: Evan Georgiades

Breasts: 2; **Butts**: 1; **Bushes**: 1

Nude Star: **Kari Wuhrer** (Full Frontal, Butt)

Luscious is the greatest movie ever made about art. It stars Kari Wuhrer as a struggling fashion model. Her boyfriend is an artist plagued by self-doubt and impotence. In a rage, he tosses his paints on Kari's naked body. It arouses him so much that they start banging, and the resulting painting is a masturbation-piece! Kari is naked throughout the movie as they explore new sensual techniques. She even agrees to do anal for art's sake. What a master-*piece*.

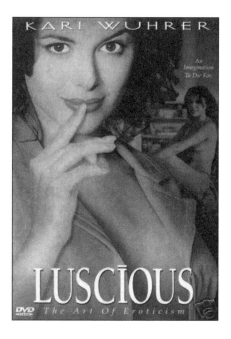

Luther the Geek (1990)

Director: Carlton J. Albright

Breasts: 2; **Butts**: 1

Nude Star: **Stacy Haiduk** (Breasts, Butt)

Luther the Geek warns of what can happen when a youngster witnesses a circus sideshow. That's what happened to Luther. Years later, grown-up Luther employs stainless-steel choppers to bite the necks of his victims. Stacy Haiduk is not about to become a finger-licking-good morsel, but it's understandable why he wants to cluck her, what with those large, juicy breasts. Step right up and get right off!

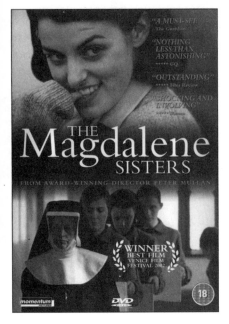

The Magdalene Sisters (2002)

Director: Peter Mullan

Breasts: 18; **Bushes**: 9

Nude Stars: **Anne-Marie Duff** (Full Frontal); **Dorothy Duffy** (Full Frontal); **Nora-Jane Noone** (Full Frontal); **Eileen Walsh** (Full Frontal)

Anonymous Nudes: 5

Based on true events, *The Magdalene Sisters* concerns itself with three bonny Irish lasses who are shuttled off to a brutal Catholic laundry to pay penance for having sex. Although the heroines are subjected to merciless abuse at the hands of the sadistic sisters, the audience gets a risqué respite when seven sets of bulging breasts and seven fluffy muffs line up and shiver in shame beneath the berating attention of an angry nun. Hail hairy!

Malibu Beach (1978)

Director: Robert J. Rosenthal

Breasts: 20; **Butts**: 2

Nude Stars: **Kim Lankford** (Breasts, Butt); **Susan Player** (Breasts, Butt); **Tara Strohmeier** (Breasts)

Anonymous Nudes: 7

Malibu Beach takes soap-opera drama, plays the arch villainy for laughs, pumps up the quotient of jiggling but firm breast flesh, and pops those quivering melons from the bikini tops. A tale of misplaced affections and well-meaning machinations, *Malibu Beach* is light, breezy, and glowing with orbicular delight from California-cool dirty blonde Kim Lankford, pert and perfectly blonde playmaker Susan Player, and outdoor-nookie-loving fun-time gal Tara Strohmeier.

Malibu Express (1985)

Director: Andy Sidaris

Breasts: 35; **Butts**: 2; **Bushes**: 1

Nude Stars: **Sybil Danning** (Breasts);
Barbara Edwards (Full Frontal, Butt);
Robyn Hilton (Right Breast); **Alex
Hinton** (Breasts); **Kimberly
McArthur** (Breasts); **Shanna McCullough** (Breasts);
Lorraine Michaels (Breasts); **Shelley Taylor Morgan**
(Breasts); **Suzanne M. Regard** (Breasts); **Lori Sutton**
(Breasts, Butt); **Lynda Wiesmeier** (Breasts)

Anonymous Nudes: 7

Down-and-out detective Darby Hinton is in desperate need of a moneymaking case in guns and gazongas auteur Andy Sidaris's *Malibu Express.* He hits the lusty mother lode when Sybil Danning hires him to investigate the murder of her husband. Stumbling upon international espionage and a barrage of half-naked centerfold foils, this private dick can hardly keep his eyes (and his fly) on the trail long enough to solve the mystery.

Mali-beauties

Although writer-director Andy Sidaris explored similar themes in his low-budget action hit *Seven* (1979), *Malibu Express* established his enduring movie formula of casting *Playboy* and *Penthouse* models as secret agents who career around exotic locales, igniting firestorms of bombs, bullets, blood, and boobs. *Especially* boobs.

skinfo

TOP 5

Andy Sidaris Movies

5. *Guns* (1990)

4. *Savage Beach* (1989)

3. *Picasso Trigger* (1988)

2. *Fit to Kill* (1993)

1. **Malibu Express (1985)**

Take A Ride On The

MANHATTAN *Gigolo*

GIANNI DEI • ANDREA THOMPSON

Manhattan Gigolo (1986)

Director: Amasi Damiani

Breasts: 7; **Butts**: 2; **Bushes**: 1

Nude Star: **Andrea Thompson** (Full Frontal, Butt)

Anonymous Nudes: 3

Lusty lass Leslie is in for the bopping of her life in the Big Apple when she stumbles upon two horny Italian stallions in *Manhattan Gigolo*. Former CNN front fox and *NYPD Blue* babe Andrea Thompson takes off the cuffs for some thoroughly skindecent sexposure as Leslie. Andrea breaks out her big guns and booming bush while she's sandwiched between two Italian meatballs. Who says New Yorkers aren't friendly?

Manhattan Eye-land

Manhattan Gigolo star Andrea Thompson later played a top-heavy flatfoot on *NYPD Blue* and then scored a news-reporter gig in 2001. When word (and internet clips) broke out about Andrea's full-frontal *Manhattan* antics, the network stood by its woman.
Did her bosses C her actual Ns?
Mr. Skin thinks so.

skinfo

Mantis in Lace (1968)

Director: William Rotsler

Breasts: 10; **Butts**: 1; **Bushes**: 1

Nude Stars: **Pat Barrington** (Breasts, Butt);
   Susan Stewart (Breasts)

Anonymous Nudes: 3

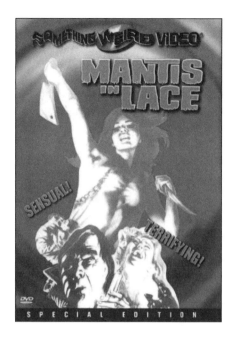

In *Mantis in Lace,* free-love stripper Pat Barrington uses her work environment as a dating pool. Her bag is to select a lucky stud from the crowd for after-hours depravity. One chosen swain unwisely slips the seductress a tab of LSD. She freaks out and stabs the generous fellow to death. What a trip!

The Man Who Fell to Earth (1976)

Director: Nicolas Roeg

Breasts: 10; **Butts**: 4; **Bushes**: 5

Nude Stars: **Candy Clark** (Full Frontal, Butt); **Hilary Holland** (Full Frontal, Butt); **Linda Hutton** (Breasts, Butt, Bush); **Claudia Jennings** (Full Frontal); **Adrienne Larussa** (Breasts, Butt, Bush)

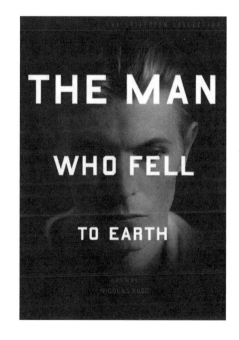

Being a freaky space alien who lands in the United States during the sexually active go-go 1970s is not without its privileges in *The Man Who Fell to Earth.* David Bowie plays the pale chap from another planet who comes across five human females who are willing to show indisputable physical proof of their gender, resulting in some of the most stimulating sex ever simulated—unless, as has been alleged, some of that copulation is without simulation.

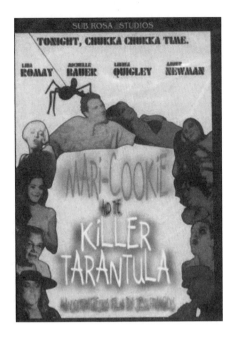

Mari-Cookie and the Killer Tarantula
(1998)

Director: Jesus Franco

Breasts: 14; **Butts**: 5; **Bushes**: 6

Nude Stars: **Michelle Bauer** (Breasts); **Analía Ivars** (Full Frontal, Butt); **Amber Newman** (Full Frontal, Butt, Thong); **Lina Romay** (Full Frontal, Butt)

Anonymous Nudes: 3

Mari-Cookie and the Killer Tarantula tells the sexorific tale of a human tarantula that's also a lesbian killer. Thrill to the spidery charms of Lina Romay as the lead—she spins her web at a strip bar, the better to meet naked chicks like B-movie queen Michelle Bauer, big-breasted Amber Newman, and spread-eagle Analía Ivars. In fact, all of these creepy crawlers spread their legs to enthrall and entrap you in their tangled bushes.

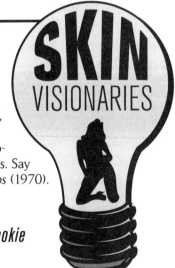

Jesus Franco
Spain's reigning baron of flesh and blood.

Jesus Franco is credited with directing more than 187 films (and counting) under more than 70 pseudonyms. Most are horror flicks, many are women-in-prison films, some are too bizarre to describe, and almost all are awash with nudity from the most gorgeous Euro-starlets of their day. As a youth, Franco studied under Orson Welles. Say what you will about *Citizen Kane* (1941), but it's no *Vampyros Lesbos* (1970).

Top 501 DVDs: *Eugenie… the Story of Her Journey into Perversion* (1970), *Ilsa, the Wicked Warden* (1980), *Mari-Cookie and the Killer Tarantula* (1998)

Marilyn Chambers' Bedtime Stories
(1993)
Director: Ernest G. Sauer

Breasts: 12; **Butts**: 3

Nude Stars: **Marilyn Chambers** (Breasts, Butt); **Camille Donatacci** (Breasts, Butt, Thong); **Isabelle Fortea** (Breasts, Butt, Thong); **Victoria Frost** (Breasts, Thong); **Theresa Lynn** (Breasts, Thong); **Donna Salvatore** (Breasts, Thong)

Marilyn Chambers' Bedtime Stories finds the former Ivory Snow girl getting her girlfriends together for a lingerie party. It's the best kind of lingerie party, one that involves very little lingerie. Of the big plastic boobies that join Marilyn for some naked fun, most familiar to a mainstream audience is Kelsey Grammer squeeze Camille Donatacci in her nude debut. She's something to *cheer* about!

Married People, Single Sex (1993)
Director: Mike Sedan

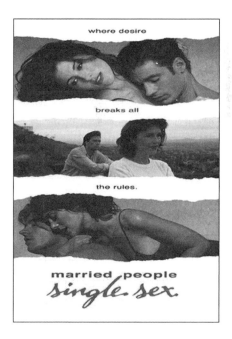

Breasts: 11; **Butts**: 4; **Bushes**: 3

Nude Stars: **Darla Haun** (Full Frontal, Butt); **Chase Masterson** (Breasts, Butt); **Shelley Michelle** (Breasts, Thong); **Teri Thompson** (Breasts, Butt); **Wendi Westbrook** (Breasts, Butt, Bush)

Anonymous Nudes: 1

Three married couples confess their marital sins in black and white only to illustrate them in glorious color in *Married People, Single Sex,* such as Wendi Westbrook's dalliances with dominant sexual fetishes. College coed Teri Thompson connects with a husband addicted to phone sex, Darla Haun flashes her hefty bags, and *Star Trek: Deep Space Nine* star Chase Masterson deep-sixes her top. Add video vixen Shelley Michelle to the mix, and you'll be mixing it up in your pants.

Massacre at Central High (1976)

Director: Rene Daalder

Breasts: 6; **Butts**: 2; **Bushes**: 2

Nude Stars: **Kimberly Beck** (Full Frontal, Butt);
  Lani O'Grady (Breasts); **Cheryl "Rainbeaux"
  Smith** (Breasts, Butt, Bush)

Being the new kid on campus is no picnic, but lucky for the hero in *Massacre at Central High,* the girls at his new school are rather indiscriminate in their affections. But tensions brew. A band of local bullies is firmly entrenched. Bad feelings lead to spilled blood. As the body count mounts, friends have a hard time distinguishing one another from foes. At least limber, blonde flesh icon Cheryl "Rainbeaux" Smith shows what legends are made of: beav, buns, and boobs all served alfresco.

Tits and *Massacre*

Massacre at Central High features nifty nudity from Lani O'Grady, who played sensible med-student daughter Mary on the ABC family hit *Eight Is Enough.* Her TV sister Joanie—a.k.a. Laurie Walters—bared all in *The Harrad Experiment* (1973), while their fictional sis-in-law Janet, portrayed by Joan Prather, went starkers in *Big Bad Mama* (1974), *Bloody Friday* (1974), and *Smile* (1975). Talk about pieces of *Eight*!

skinfo

Masseuse (1996)

Director: Fred Olen Ray

Breasts: 24; **Butts**: 2; **Bushes**: 1

Nude Stars: **Greta Carlson** (Breasts); **Griffin Drew** (Breasts, Butt); **Gail Harris** (Breasts, Butt); **J.J. Mantia** (Breasts); **Monique Parent** (Breasts, Bush); **Meaghan Prester** (Breasts, Thong); **Amy Rochelle** (Breasts, Butt); **Bianca Rocilili** (Breasts); **Brittany Rollins** (Breasts)

Anonymous Nudes: 3

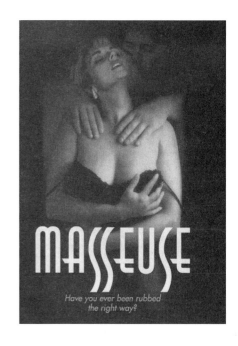

Have you ever been rubbed the right way?

Griffin Drew stars in *Masseuse* as the fiancée of a bum who makes off with her money. She seeks revenge by getting all the women who have ever slept with him to have an orgy. That's the kind of payback Mr. Skin can relate to! Among the many nudes who participate are Greta Carlson, J.J. Mantia, Amy Rochelle, Monique Parent, Bianca Roclili, and Gail Harris. *Masseuse* will rub you the right way.

Mata Hari (1985)

Director: Curtis Harrington

Breasts: 27; **Butts**: 2; **Bushes**: 6

Nude Star: **Sylvia Kristel** (Breasts, Butt)

Anonymous Nudes: 13

Sylvia Kristel

When she danced, their secrets flowed like wine.

The story of *Mata Hari* is so good, if it weren't true, somebody would have to make it up. Well, you get a little of both in this adaptation of the life of the World War I spy who ended up paying the ultimate price for her treason. But before lead Sylvia Kristel dies, she helps kill off millions of sperm cells in countless skin scenes, including some good old-fashioned lesbianism and a naked catfight.

Maze (2000)
Director: Rob Morrow

Breasts: 4; **Butts**: 2; **Bushes**: 2

Nude Stars: **Laura Linney** (Full Frontal, Butt);
  Sheila Zane (Full Frontal, Butt)

Rob Morrow directed, produced, and starred in *Maze* as an artist with Tourette's syndrome. But don't feel too bad for Rob, as he's got Laura Linney and Sheila Zane both eagerly posing in the buff for him. One-hundred-percent-natural-redhead Laura shows off her fair skin, buoyant bouncers, and luscious strawberry patch. It's a-maze-ing!

Moist, the - *n.*
Intangible sexual allure that elicits a fluid response in both a starlet and her stunned observer. Frequently invoked by MrSkin.com contributor Tyrone "Dollar" Green; for example, "She's got a lot of what I like to call the Moist."

SKIN·finition

Melvin and Howard (1980)

Director: Jonathan Demme

Breasts: 8; **Butts**: 1; **Bushes**: 1

Nude Star: **Mary Steenburgen** (Breasts, Butt, Bush)

Anonymous Nudes: 3

When eccentric millionaire Howard Hughes died, the reading of his will garnered some controversy, as he left much of his fortune to a loser who once gave him a ride when Hughes was stranded in the desert. That story is engagingly told in *Melvin and Howard*. Far more engaging, however, is Mary Steenburgen in her nude debut. She takes it all off in a crowded bar for a T&A-riffic look, a sight worth all of Hughes's riches.

Melvin and Hairless

Seek out a VHS copy of *Melvin and Howard* to see Mary Steenburgen's furry strip-club full frontal. The wide-screen DVD version trims the furburger, serving up only boobs and buns.

skinfo

Mercy (2000)

Director: Damian Harris

Breasts: 10; **Butts**: 2; **Bushes**: 4

Nude Stars: **Claire Burton** (Breasts, Butt); **Wendy Crewson** (Full Frontal); **Lara Daans** (Full Frontal); **Peta Wilson** (Full Frontal, Butt); **Karen Young** (Full Frontal)

Mercy revolves around a serial-killer plot populated by oft-nude lipstick lesbians—Mr. Skin's favorite kind! Ellen Barkin is the detective on the case of Peta Wilson, who tempts Ellen with the joys of girl-girl sex. Ellen never loses her trench coat, but Peta, as one of a troupe of tawdry lesbian call girls, is skinful enough for two. For those who have a fetish for females in chains and leather . . . have mercy.

Mischief (1985)

Director: Mel Damski

Breasts: 6; **Butts**: 4; **Bushes**: 1

Nude Star: **Kelly Preston** (Full Frontal, Butt)

Anonymous Nudes: 5

Mischief is a nostalgic comedy about a pair of adolescent males coming into a state of sexual hyperactivity along with the nation during the 1950s. Erotic mores were expanding. Social structures were straining. And Kelly Preston, as the good little rich girl fighting against her parents' control, frees her body and presents it to her rebel suitor. The future Mrs. John Travolta bares her flawless all, including her fuzzy Barbarino.

The Model Solution (2002)

Director: Edward Holzman

Breasts: 22; **Butts**: 10; **Bushes**: 11

Nude Stars: **Antoinette Abbott** (Full Frontal, Butt); **Kitana Baker** (Full Frontal, Butt); **Kimberly Fisher** (Full Frontal); **April Flowers** (Full Frontal, Butt); **Holly Hollywood** (Full Frontal, Butt); **Kim Laurel** (Full Frontal, Butt); **Katie Lohmann** (Full Frontal, Butt, Thong); **Kimber Lynn** (Full Frontal, Butt); **Sasha Peralto** (Full Frontal, Butt); **Regina Russell** (Full Frontal, Butt); **Candace Washington** (Full Frontal, Butt)

The Model Solution can be summed up simply as the story of two modeling agencies competing for a lucrative lingerie-catalog contract. By Mr. Skin's count, eleven actresses get naked, masturbate, shower, and make out with one another, but then it's hard to keep count with one hand. One of the sweetest buds belongs to April Flowers, who brings pants showers.

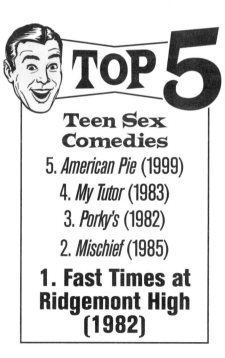

TOP **5**

Teen Sex Comedies

5. *American Pie* (1999)

4. *My Tutor* (1983)

3. *Porky's* (1982)

2. *Mischief* (1985)

1. Fast Times at Ridgemont High (1982)

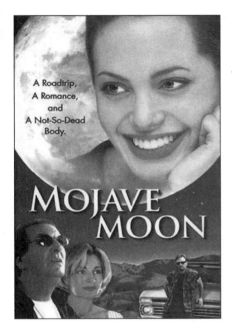

Mojave Moon (1996)

Director: Kevin Dowling

Breasts: 2

Nude Stars: **Angelina Jolie** (Breasts)

Angelina Jolie stars in *Mojave Moon* as an impossibly attractive young woman who is rather careless about where she strips down and is lax about shutting the bathroom door while taking her shower. A threadbare Danny Aiello is the failing used-car salesman being importuned upon by the young goddess. Aiello, naturally, conceives of himself as having a chance with the nymphet. He won't find true happiness until he settles for a shot at her mother.

Mondo Topless (1966)

Director: Russ Meyer

Breasts: 30; **Butts**: 1

Nude Stars: **Abundavita** (Breasts); **Babette Bardot** (Breasts, Thong); **Pat Barrington** (Breasts); **Donna X** (Breasts); **Denise Du Vall** (Breasts); **Veronique Gabriel** (Breasts); **Darlene Grey** (Breasts); **Gigi La Touche** (Breasts); **Yvette Le Grand** (Breasts); **Sin Lenee** (Breasts); **Lorna Maitland** (Breasts, Butt); **Darla Paris** (Breasts); **Heide Richter** (Breasts); **Greta Thorwald** (Breasts); **Diane Young** (Breasts)

Mondo Topless is the only documentary by the maven of all mammaries, Russ Meyer. It is, therefore, the greatest documentary ever made. *Mondo* assembles a skinternational array of strip-club peelers who, naturally, match the megaton top-heaviness of Meyer's most iconic bra busters.

The Monkey's Mask (2000)

Director: Samantha Lang

Breasts: 8; **Butts**: 2; **Bushes**: 1

Nude Stars: **Kelly McGillis** (Breasts, Butt);
   Susie Porter (Breasts, Butt, Bush)

Anonymous Nudes: 2

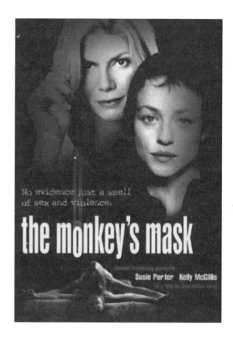

The Monkey's Mask stars Susie Porter as a lesbian private dick investigating the murder of a young girl. She ends up getting a little too close to Kelly McGillis, the victim's poetry teacher, and soon the two are writing love sonnets together between the sheets. The film contains a number of explicit sex scenes between Susie and Kelly, which a crew member claims "leave little to the imagination." What's behind the monkey's mask? One horny little beast!

Monster's Ball (2001)

Director: Marc Forster

Breasts: 4; **Butts**: 2; **Bushes**: 1

Nude Stars: **Halle Berry** (Breasts, Butt, Bush); **Amber Rules** (Breasts, Butt)

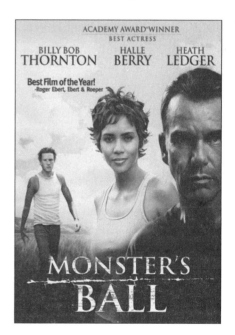

Academy Awards and slap-up sex scenes don't always go hand in hand, but the mammary glands of bravely stripped actress Halle Berry in *Monster's Ball* had Oscar voters rushing to stuff the ballot box. Berry and Billy Bob Thornton put the sparks into one of the most unlikely love connections in modern film history when they set to banging one another for what seems like an eternity. Have a ball!

Mood Swingers (2000)

Director: William Marsh

Breasts: 10; **Butts**: 1; **Bushes**: 1

Nude Stars: **Hayley Carr** (Full Frontal, Butt); **Alexandra Gilbreath** (Breasts); **Olivia Williams** (Breasts)

Anonymous Nudes: 2

Mood Swingers, based on the particularly unsexily monikered Martin Amis novel *Dead Babies,* squeezes kinetic life into the book's tale of privilege, perversion, and prigs gone wild. Alexandra Gilbreath, Olivia Williams, and Hayley Carr form a tool-tickling triumvirate of topless teatage when they relax outside before a runaway cow ruins their fun. And that's no bull!

Mountain of the Cannibal God (1978)

Director: Sergio Martino

Breasts: 8; **Butts**: 1; **Bushes**: 1

Nude Stars: **Ursula Andress** (Full Frontal, Butt); **Luigina Rocchi** (Breasts)

Anonymous Nudes: 2

It's a jungle out there in *Mountain of the Cannibal God.* Buxom Swiss miss Ursula Andress is a slave, and the cannibals are half-naked nubiles who live to strip our heroine and paint her orange. Ursula is searching the bush for her missing husband, but the natives are restless and more interested in her bush, displayed when she's bound and massaged by a pair of juggy jungle bunnies. The gods are happy, and you'll be slaphappy.

Ms. Don Juan (1973)

Director: Roger Vadim

Breasts: 11; **Butts**: 2; **Bushes**: 2

Nude Stars: **Brigitte Bardot** (Full Frontal, Butt);
    Jane Birkin (Full Frontal)

Anonymous Nudes: 4

Ms. Don Juan reunited director Roger Vadim with his
ex-wife and former muse, Brigitte Bardot, as the female
reincarnation of the libidinous Don Juan. In one of the great
Sapphic pairings of skinematic sirens, Brigitte and Jane Birkin
lie naked in bed together, a lit cigarette nested at Jane's
bush, like Brigitte's about to suck it with her sugar lips.
That must be the most coveted smoke in cinematic history.

BRIGITTE BARDOT
Don Juan
(or if Don Juan were a woman)
A FILM BY ROGER VADIM

We *Juan* More Brigitte!

Ms. Don Juan marks the final nude appearance of French
sex goddess Brigitte Bardot in a film to date.
Of course, it's *hard* to blame Brigitte for wanting to end
her legendary carnal career by bedding Jane Birkin.
Very hard. Indeed.

skinfo

Mudhoney (1965)
Director: Russ Meyer

Breasts: 8; **Butts**: 2

Nude Stars: **Lee Ballard** (Breasts); **Antoinette Christiani** (Breasts); **Rena Horten** (Breasts, Butt); **Lorna Maitland** (Breasts, Butt)

Ex-con John Furlong hires on as a farmhand in Missouri—and since *Mudhoney* is a Russ Meyer classic, there are plenty of udders to keep both hands busy. He's particularly fond of farmer's niece Antoinette Christiani. Antoinette's psycho husband has the decency to take us to the local whorehouse, where we can marvel at the mammaries of Lorna Maitland and her deaf sister, Rena Horten. Lee Ballard also makes her sole screen appearance as a gal who bares bosoms in the dirt. You catch more unzipped flies with *Mudhoney!*

Marty Feldman Boobs - *n.*
Breasts that have nipples pointing in opposite directions, much like the famously frazzled bug eyes of the late British funnyman from *Young Frankenstein.*

SKIN·finition

Mulholland Dr. (2001)
Director: David Lynch

Breasts: 4

Nude Stars: **Laura Harring** (Breasts);
Naomi Watts (Breasts)

The twisted David Lynch masterwork
Mulholland Dr. follows Naomi Watts as an aspiring actress
embroiled in numerous surreal escapades. Laura Harring
loses her memory after a car crash but remembers how to
kiss and fondle and suck and grind against Naomi when
their puzzling paths cross. Naomi loses her top and Laura
loses her mind (and eventually everything else) as they
Sapphically canoodle on a couch in one of Hollywood's
greatest girl-on-girl grapples.

Mulholland Tunnels
Writer-director David Lynch originally developed
Mulholland Dr. as a TV series pilot for ABC. Luckily
for graphic-Sapphic-sex fans, the network passed.
Also watch for blonde Rena Riffel as a streetwalker
in *Mulholland Dr.* Previously, Rena played (very
naked) strippers in the two premier peeler films of
all time, *Showgirls* (1995) and *Striptease* (1996).

skinfo

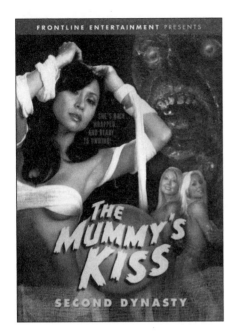

Mummy's Kiss: Second Dynasty (2006)

Director: Donald F. Glut

Breasts: 24; **Butts**: 6; **Bushes**: 4

Nude Stars: **Stacy Burke** (Full Frontal, Butt); **Belinda Gavin** (Breasts, Butt); **Lorielle New** (Breasts, Butt); **Christine Nguyen** (Full Frontal, Butt); **Sasha Peralto** (Breasts); **Crystal Potter** (Breasts); **Jocelyn Potter** (Breasts); **Cindy Pucci** (Full Frontal, Butt, Thong); **Andrea Smith** (Breasts); **Mia Zottoli** (Full Frontal, Butt)

Anonymous Nudes: 2

Mummy's Kiss (2002) was not enough. Fans are in luck if they were longing to see more (and see it *all!*) after the conclusion of the original ancient Egypt–flavored softcore skin epic. *Mummy's Kiss: Second Dynasty* picks up where the previous epic left off, prompting a whole new array of luscious beauties to unwrap their coverings and come clean. You'll see numerous lap pyramids and Tit-ankhamens along the Nile-wide pile of naked nubiles on display in the *Second Dynasty.* Oh, mummy!

Modern B - *n.*
Direct-to-video action/horror/thriller romps from the early 1990s to today.

Murder-Set-Pieces (2004)

Director: Nick Palumbo

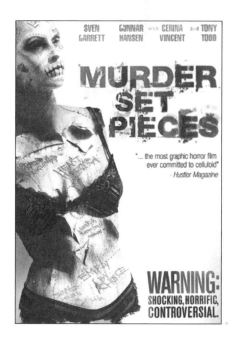

Breasts: 37; **Butts**: 9; **Bushes**: 10

Nude Stars: **Valerie Baber** (Breasts, Butt); **LeAnn Clinton** (Breasts); **Christina Holsinger** (Breasts, Thong); **Crissy Moran** (Breasts, Thong); **Lauren Palac** (Breasts, Butt); **Renee Sloan** (Breasts, Bush); **Jenna Velanni** (Breasts, Butt)

Anonymous Nudes: 22

Writer-director Nick Palumbo shocked even the most hard-core horror fans with his splatter-blasting, sexual-torturer, serial-killer freak-out *Murder-Set-Pieces*. Sven Garrett plays the Photographer, a Hitler-sympathizing German who shoots pictures of numerous Las Vegas sex workers before slicing, dicing, chopping, burning, brutalizing, and otherwise hideously disposing of these women. The good news is that we get to see each of them extremely naked first. *Murder-Set-Pieces* takes a convincing stab at the title of the ultimate exercise in flesh and blood.

My Breast (1994)

Director: Betty Thomas

Breasts: 1

Nude Star: **Meredith Baxter** (Left Breast)

Meredith Baxter plays a New York journalist who's jerked right out of the hustle-bustle of big-city newspaper life in the milestone NBC TV movie *My Breast*. After being informed of a malignancy growing in her breast, Meredith reevaluates her life while rewriting the history of network-television nudity. *My Breast* allows viewers a glimpse of mortality's unavoidable reality, along with a glorious gander at the tit-ular character, Meredith Baxter's mammoth left-side Alex P. Teat-on.

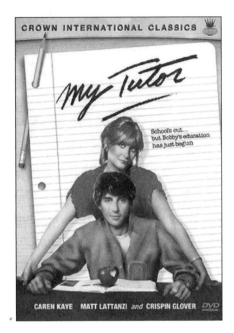

My Tutor (1983)

Director: George Bowers

Breasts: 9; **Butts**: 1

Nude Stars: **Caren Kaye** (Breasts,
    Butt); **Graem McGavin** (Breasts);
    Francesca Natividad (Breasts);
    Katt Shea (Breasts); **Jewel
    Shepard** (Left Breast)

When Matt Lattanzi fails French, he gets *My Tutor*, the luscious Caren Kaye. At first, she wants to help him conjugate his verbs, while he wants to learn how to French-kiss. But Caren is a serial skinny-dipper, so it's only a matter of time before he's sticking his baguette in her pastry. Legendary actress Francesca "Kitten" Natividad is a whore ready to relieve Matt of his virginity, but he passes out beneath the weight of her massive mams.

Hot for Teacher
Tits and class.

Many young scholars have one particular pedagogue to thank for instilling him with a thirst for knowledge. He remembers her, and he can pull up the details of her sheer-stockinged calves, of a sprig of her hair breaking loose from her tightly controlled bun, of her spry buns flexing beneath her fitted skirt, of the bra strap that slipped and showed every time she reached to the top of the chalkboard. Probably this particular teacher never paid enough attention to him while he was in her charge to be able to pick him out of a police lineup. In a better world, teacher-student relations would more often have been like *Summer School Teachers* (1975), *Private Lessons* (1981), and *My Tutor* (1983).

Top 501 DVDs: *Homework* (1982), *My Tutor* (1983), *Porky's* (1982), *Private Lessons* (1981), *They're Playing with Fire* (1984), *Varsity Blues* (1999)

Naked Souls (1995)

Director: Lyndon Chubbuck

Breasts: 12; **Butts**: 2; **Bushes**: 2

Nude Stars: **Pamela Anderson** (Breasts, Butt); **Chantel King** (Breasts); **Elizabeth Low** (Breasts); **Seana Ryan** (Full Frontal, Butt); **Justina Vail** (Full Frontal)

Anonymous Nudes: 1

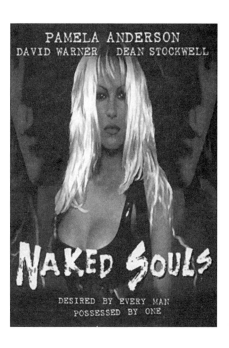

Pamela Anderson is an artist who makes impressions of busty beauties' bosoms in *Naked Souls*. Add that her boyfriend is a scientist experimenting with memory who stumbles onto the twisted brain waves of a serial killer, and you have a sci-fi thriller-diller. Pam's plump puppies, which she flashes during a torrid lovemaking scene, are the obvious draw, but even Pam has some stiff competition from Justina Vail, whose un-vail-ing is sure to make audiences stiff.

Night Call Nurses (1972)

Director: Jonathan Kaplan

Breasts: 16; **Butts**: 3

Nude Stars: **Patty Byrne** (Breasts); **Lynne Guthrie** (Breasts); **Barbara Keene** (Breasts, Butt); **Mittie Lawrence** (Breasts); **Dixie Peabody** (Breasts); **Alana Stewart** (Breasts, Butt)

Anonymous Nudes: 2

The drive-in classic *Night Call Nurses* mixes a classic thriller with touching social drama. Oh, and there are also a lot of titties being stalked as they escape from tight white uniforms. Your dick will require examination—*STAT!*—once you see a lucky guy getting his mitts on Mittie Lawrence's titties. And did we mention how the film boldly explores the effects of amphetamines on innocent truck drivers?

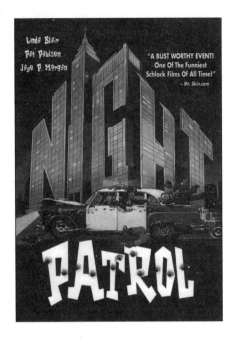

Night Patrol (1984)

Director: Jackie Kong

Breasts: 5

Nude Stars: **Linda Blair** (Left Breast); **Francesca Natividad** (Breasts); **Lori Sutton** (Breasts)

Former "Unknown Comic" Murray Langston stars in *Night Patrol* as a pathetic cop who moonlights as a stand-up comic with a bag over his head. Little person Billy Barty rants away as Murray's tyrannical superior, while Pat Paulsen deadpans as a cynical fellow officer. Your dick will be on constant patrol for the ladies, too. Jaye P. Morgan keeps her clothes on as Murray's horny agent, but Linda Blair, Lori Sutton, and Francesca "Kitten" Natividad make this a bust-worthy event.

Night Makes Right

The Anchor Bay DVD of *Night Patrol* was the very first title to ever include a quote of critical praise from Mr. Skin on its cover. The exact words: "A BUST WORTHY EVENT! One of the funniest schlock films of all time!"

skinfo

The Night Porter (1974)

Director: Liliana Cavani

Breasts: 12; **Butts**: 5; **Bushes**: 1

Nude Star: **Charlotte Rampling** (Breasts, Butt, Bush)

Anonymous Nudes: 8

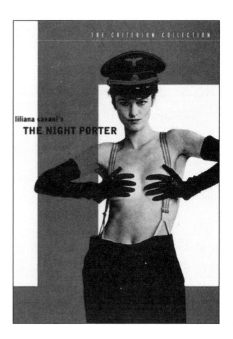

Dirk Bogarde stars in *The Night Porter* as a former Nazi officer who's now stuck carrying luggage in a Vienna hotel. In a just world, he'd spend eternity waiting on nagging customers with suitcases full of anvils. Instead, he gets lucky and runs into his former sex slave, Charlotte Rampling. Instead of turning him in, the former concentration-camp prisoner decides to revive their sexual relationship. It's daring stuff, and Charlotte elevates *Porter*'s hard kink to high art.

Night-see regime

Charlotte Rampling claims that the very first scene shot for *The Night Porter* was her bare-nippled song-and-dance number while she was (partially) clad in Nazi garb.

skinfo

Norma Jean and Marilyn (1996)
Director: Tim Fywell

Breasts: 5; **Butts**: 2; **Bushes**: 1

Nude Stars: **Ashley Judd** (Full Frontal, Butt); **Erika Nann** (Right Breast); **Mira Sorvino** (Breasts, Butt, Bush)

HBO's Marilyn Monroe biopic *Norma Jean and Marilyn* provides two nude beauties in one role. Ashley Judd portrays the starlet back when she was still known as Norma Jean Dougherty. Mira Sorvino then steps in to cover the legendary Hollywood years. Both beauties bare all, proving that dia-*mounds* are a guy's breast friend.

Hello, *Norma Jean*

Norma Jean and Marilyn represents a high-end, mainstream take on the tragic screen goddess. *Goodbye, Norma Jean* (1976) embodies another extreme: the wild-and-wooly 1970s exploitation version. Directed by schlockmeister Larry Buchanan (*Mars Needs Women*) and starring hay-stacked *Hee-Haw* honey Misty Rowe, *Goodbye, Norma Jean* played the drive-in circuit for more than a decade and contains one of the most memorable closing lines in all of skinema, spoken by Misty: "Well, that's the last cock I'll ever have to suck!"

skinfo

Normal Life (1996)

Director: John McNaughton

Breasts: 2

Nude Star: **Ashley Judd** (Breasts)

Hey, don't give fired cop Luke Perry a hard time for robbing banks in *Normal Life.* He's married to the incredibly hot Ashley Judd, a wild gal whose various addictions include a jones for Luke's johnson. She's also kind of a free spender. Besides, robbing banks is a fun activity for them to share as a couple. It's also a fun thing to share with skinema fans, especially when Ashley straps a bulletproof vest over her flawproof breasts . . . but not before blazing us with her milk bullets.

Nip-Slip - *n.*

An accidental, momentary revelation of the best part of the breast, typically from an open blouse or a deliciously deep-plunging neckline.

SKIN·finition

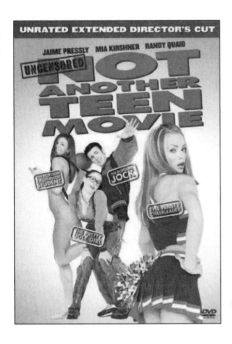

Not Another Teen Movie (2001)
Unrated Extended Director's Cut
Director: Joel Gallen

Breasts: 6; **Butts**: 3

Nude Stars: **Jesse Capelli** (Breasts); **Chyler Leigh**
   (Butt); **Cerina Vincent** (Breasts, Butt)

Anonymous Nudes: 1

Not Another Teen Movie is a parody of All Things Teen Sex
Comedy. You'll pop a woody watching wicked stereotypes
made sizzling flesh in the form of Jaime Pressly as the evil
cheerleader, Chyler Leigh as the shy girl with a bod of gold,
Mia Kirshner as an incest-mad rich bitch, and, in a skinstory-
making role, Cerina Vincent as foreign-exchange student
Areola, who is literally naked every moment she's on-screen.
You'll *nut* to this *Teen Movie*.

Nerps - *n. pl.*
Extra-long, mouthwateringly thick, and/or colorful
nipples.

Not of This Earth (1988)

Director: Jim Wynorski

Breasts: 12; **Butts**: 2

Nude Stars: **Ava Cadell** (Breasts); **Belinda Grant** (Breasts); **Roxanne Kernohan** (Breasts); **Becky LeBeau** (Breasts); **Traci Lords** (Breasts, Butt); **Taaffe O'Connell** (Breasts, Butt)

Scandalous underage porn star Traci Lords goes mainstream with *Not of This Earth*. Traci parades around as a private nurse to a bloodthirsty alien before mounting her man. Connoisseurs of red-blooded romance will be happy to note that the space freak feasts on a high-school hussy, three hookers, and a strip-o-gram gal, most of whom fish out the floppers prior to falling prey. As for Traci's T&A swan song— it's out of this world!

Jim Wynorski
Let the boob times roll!

Born in the wild suburbs of Glen Cove, New York, Jim Wynorski turned his passion for B-movies into a full-time job beginning with the affectionate sci-fi serial send-up *The Lost Empire* (1983) and culminating in more than 60 other romps to date.

Top 501 DVDs: *The Bare Wench Project* (1999), *Big Bad Mama II* (1987), *Not of This Earth* (1988), *Sorority House Massacre II* (1990)

The Notorious Bettie Page (2005)

Director: Mary Harron

Breasts: 6; **Butts**: 2; **Bushes**: 2

Nude Stars: **Gretchen Mol** (Full Frontal, Butt);
    Bettie Page (Breasts, Butt)

Anonymous Nudes: 1

The Notorious Bettie Page spans the entire life of the planet's most famous pageboy-haircut fetishist and pinup model and is filmed in black and white, with bursts of color for wild sex spreads. Audiences will burst, too, watching busty Gretchen Mol fill out Bettie's poses. Everything you love about Bettie is here—from her jungle-print nature shots to the more extreme S&M photos she did for Irving Klaw. You'll get more bangs for the buck (naked)!

Paging *Bettie*

In a battle of the biopics, *The Notorious Bettie Page* was beaten to the marketplace by the direct-to-DVD *Bettie Page: Dark Angel* (2004). In the video feature, the titular pinup is embodied by Paige Richards, who donned the trademark black coif but strained the flick's credibility by sporting breast implants.

skinfo

Irving Klaw
Brooklyn's pioneering firebrand of fetish.

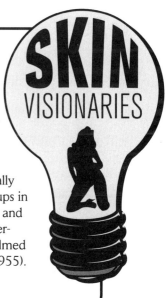

Irving Klaw was not only given a fitting name upon his 1910 birth in Brooklyn, New York; he also stood to inherit an outstanding family business—the still-thriving poster-and-photo outlet Movie Star News. As Irving grew up, he and his sister, Paula Klaw, noticed a demand for pictures of gorgeous girls creatively tied up. With Paula occasionally modeling, Irving became the world's foremost photographer of pin-ups in peril. Often his subjects were burlesque stars such as Tempest Storm and Lili St. Cyr. Still, the Klaws will forever be remembered as the brother-sister duo who initially brought the world Bettie Page. Irving later helmed burlesque feature films, including *Varietease* (1954) and *Teaserama* (1955). Klaw died in 1966.

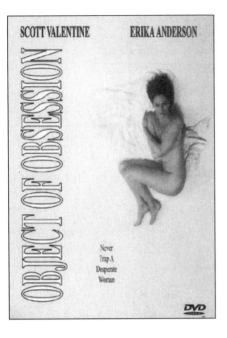

SCOTT VALENTINE   ERIKA ANDERSON

OBJECT OF OBSESSION

Never
Trap A
Desperate
Woman

DVD

Object of Obsession (1994)

Director: Gregory Dark

Breasts: 14; **Butts**: 2; **Bushes**: 4

Nude Stars: **Erika Anderson** (Breasts, Butt, Bush);
   Jennifer MacDonald (Full Frontal)

Anonymous Nudes: 5

The plot of *Object of Obsession* has something to do with
Erika Anderson hooking up with the wrong guy, in that
he imprisons her in a warehouse made especially for sex.
It doesn't sound that bad to Mr. Skin, and Erika makes
the breast of it in four skin scenes showing off her hidden
talents. Just for some variety, blonde Jennifer MacDonald
shows up in a videotape taking off her dress and revealing
her objects of obsession. Yummy.

Gregory Dark (Hippolyte)
From new-wave porn to late-night erotica to . . . Britney Spears?!

The X-rated *New Wave Hookers* (1985) ignited the career of its
director, Gregory Dark, as well as its underage lead starlet, Traci
Lords. In time, both Dark and Lords went from hardcore porn to
direct-to-video movies, but only one went on to work with A-list
talent. Bizarrely Greg Dark became one of the late-1990s most in-demand
MTV video directors. Among the acts Dark created clips for are Britney
Spears, Christina Aguilera, the Backstreet Boys, Sublime, and the Melvins.

Top 501 DVDs: *Animal Instincts* (1992), *Animal Instincts 2* (1994),
Animal Instincts III (1995), *Object of Obsession* (1994)

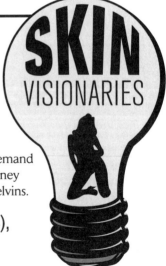

SKIN
VISIONARIES

Oh! Calcutta! (1972)

Director: Jacques Levy

Breasts: 10; **Butts**: 5; **Bushes**: 5

Nude Stars: **Raina Barrett** (Full Frontal, Butt); **Samantha Harper** (Full Frontal, Butt); **Patricia Hawkins** (Full Frontal, Butt); **Margo Sappington** (Full Frontal, Butt); **Nancy Tribush** (Full Frontal, Butt)

The two exclamation points are not a grammatical error in the title *Oh! Calcutta!* It is that good. This pay-per-view special is the only film documentation of the first nudie musical that put genitalia on Old Broadway. A musical comedy, *Oh! Calcutta!* features dance numbers that will make you feel groovy. It's one of the longest-running shows ever to hit the Great White Way, but this is the only way you'll get to see why. Do so, now. *Oh!*

Big *Oh!*

The theatrical production of *Oh! Calcutta!* proved to be a box-office sensation anyplace its cast dropped trou. Debuting in 1969, the show ran for more than 2,400 performances in London and more than 1,600 in New York. A 1976 Broadway revival packed houses at the Edison Theater for thirteen uninterrupted years, racking up 5,959 performances.

skinfo

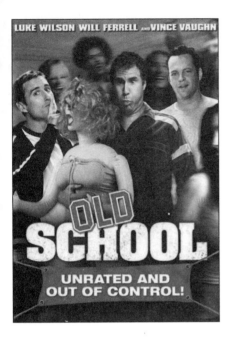

Old School (2003)

Director: Todd Phillips

Breasts: 6

Nude Stars: **Lisa Donatz** (Breasts); **Kristina Hughes** (Breasts); **Corinne Kingsbury** (Breasts)

Old School may not seem like much on paper (a trio of postcollegiate screwups sets up house next door to a college crawling with corruptible coeds), but hilarity does ensue. You'll be slapping your knee (along with parts farther north) when topless, auburn-haired Lisa Donatz prepares to wrestle shirt-free, flaxen-tressed Corinne Kingsbury in a vat of K-Y Jelly. K-Y don't you come up and see Mr. Skin sometime?

Bold *School*

Old School director Todd Phillips's debut was the shockumentary *Hated* (1994) about scum-rocker GG Allin, infamous for his nude, excrement-filled stage show. Phillips cleaned up his act with *Road Trip* (2000), starring Amy Smart's tasty torso tarts. In the meantime, GG died. Of unnatural causes.

skinfo

Original Sin (2001)

Director: Michael Cristofer

Breasts: 5; **Butts**: 1

Nude Stars: **Nitzi Arellano** (Right Breast);
Angelina Jolie (Breasts)

Anonymous Nudes: 1

In *Original Sin,* Angelina Jolie plays a mail-order bride who's delivered to the island of lonely Antonio Banderas. He was expecting somebody a lot less gorgeous, but Jolie explains that she sent an ugly picture so she wouldn't just be loved for her body. That's cool, since Antonio lied about being poor when he's really a millionaire. Good thing that the complicated plot also requires the unveiling of Angelina's assets and Nitzi Arellano's titzies.

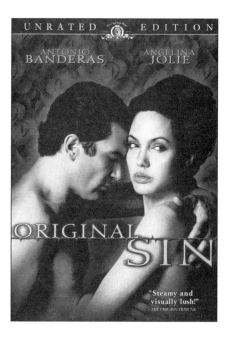

Orgy - *n.*
An on-screen sex act involving four or more participants. Hopefully more.

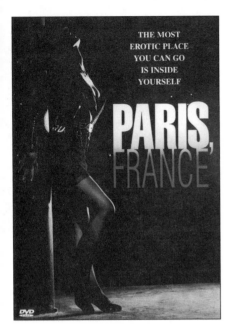

THE MOST
EROTIC PLACE
YOU CAN GO
IS INSIDE
YOURSELF

PARIS, FRANCE

DVD

Paris, France (1993)

Director: Jerry Ciccoritti

Breasts: 2; **Butts**: 1; **Bushes**: 1

Nude Star: **Leslie Hope** (Full Frontal, Butt)

Paris, France lights up early when Leslie Hope provides great glances at all three of her Bs while engaging in some heavy-duty humping with a dude. Leslie plays a saucy scribe who spends her fantasy time in an imaginary Paris as the real-life confidante of four male friends who indulge in progressive degrees of hetero-, bi-, and homodabbling. *France* looks best without pants.

Public Nudity - *n.*

Any exposure of the nipples, butt crack, pubic hair, or labia in an outdoor setting where passersby are likely to witness the revealed body parts.

SKIN·finition

Ss

The People vs. Larry Flynt (1996)

Director: Milos Forman

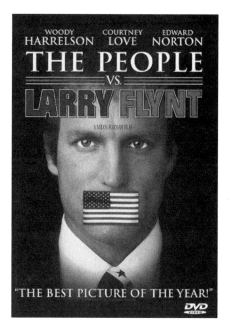

Breasts: 46; **Butts**: 17; **Bushes**: 5

Nude Star: **Courtney Love** (Full Frontal, Butt)

Anonymous Nudes: 43

National heroes don't come more unlikely than the publisher of *Hustler,* Larry Flynt. *The People vs. Larry Flynt* chronicles Flynt's defense of our right to see boobies (and more graphic things) and also displays the boobies (and more graphic things) of Flynt's stand-in wife, Courtney Love. You'll want to stand erect and salute the red-white-and-pink . . . with one hand over your hard, of course.

Not in Like *Flynt*

According to *The People vs. Larry Flynt* director Milos Forman, both Bill Murray and Tom Hanks were considered for the role of Flynt. Forman offered no word, however, on what repellant crack-harpies lost the female lead to Courtney Love.

skinfo

Picasso Trigger (1988)

Director: Andy Sidaris

Breasts: 12; **Butts**: 3

Nude Stars: **Cynthia Brimhall** (Breasts); **Hope Marie Carlton** (Breasts, Butt); **Patty Duffek** (Breasts, Butt); **Kym Malin** (Breasts); **Dona Speir** (Breasts, Butt); **Julie Strain** (Breasts)

Dona Speir and partner Hope Marie Carlton are two sexy secret agents sent to stop supervillain *Picasso Trigger*. But we know the real plot: babes running, skinny-dipping, and firing guns. You've got to love the fact that Dona can do her truly serious thinking only in the hot tub . . . and this gal's got a lot on her mind! Fellow bra busters Cynthia Brimhall and Julie Strain, among many others, are also on hand to pull your Picasso trigger!

Pick-up Summer (1980)

Director: George Mihalka

Breasts: 10

Nude Stars: **Joy Boushel** (Breasts); **Eve Robin** (Breasts); **Karen Stephen** (Breasts)

Anonymous Nudes: 3

Pick-up Summer is the Canadian version of a summer feel-good movie. Our heroes divide their time between a pinball arcade, chasing girls, and antagonizing a biker gang. Joy Boushel gives the comedy some much needed weight when her bikini top comes off and her beach balls bounce around to the joy of all. Eve Robin and Karen Stephen pop up—and out—for their only skin to date. They'll make your pinballs tilt!

The Pigkeeper's Daughter (1972)

Director: Bethel G. Buckalew

Breasts: 8; **Butts**: 4; **Bushes**: 4

Nude Stars: **Peggy Church** (Full Frontal, Butt);
Terry Gibson (Full Frontal, Butt); **Gina Paluzzi** (Full
Frontal, Butt)

Anonymous Nudes: 1

The plot of *The Pigkeeper's Daughter* is basically an illustration
of the old farmer's-daughter-and-traveling-salesman joke,
with the punch line packing more of a wallop to your boner
than your funny bone! For fans of B-movie siren Peggy
Church, this is her skinfining moment on-screen. The other
actresses involved—one-time skinster Terry Gibson and two-
timer Gina Paluzzi—do their best to make every sex scene
a booby-prize winner. Look closely, and you'll notice they
ain't acting!

Harry Novak
Cornpone soft-porn at its most rootin' two-tit.

Hicksploitation hit drive-in screens in the 1970s like a mouthful of
moonshine exploding in a hayseed's belly. Nobody better combined
Hee Haw hilarity with hot sex than exploitation vet Harry Novak.
Along with curiously monikered director Bethel G. Buckalew, Novak
produced numerous iconic titles on the order of *Country Cuzzins*
(1970), *Tobacco Roody* (1970), *Midnight Plowboy* (1971), *The Pigkeeper's
Daughter* (1972), and *Sassy Sue* (1972). Never one to exclusively work the
outhouse circuit, Novak also begat such softcore favorites as *Please Don't Eat
My Mother* (1972) and *Wham Bam Thank You Spaceman* (1975).

Top 501 DVDs: *Below the Belt* (1971), *The Pigkeeper's Daughter*
(1972), *Please Don't Eat My Mother* (1972), *Sassy Sue* (1972), *Tobacco
Roody* (1970), *Wham Bam Thank You Spaceman* (1975)

"One of the most vile, stupid and repulsive films ever made."

John Waters'
Pink Flamingos
25TH ANNIVERSARY EDITION
Starring DIVINE

DVD

Pink Flamingos (1972)

Director: John Waters

Breasts: 10; **Bushes**: 4

Nude Stars: **Elizabeth Coffey** (Right Breast, Bush);
Cookie Mueller (Full Frontal); **Mary Vivian Pearce**
(Breasts); **Mink Stole** (Full Frontal); **Susan Walsh**
(Right Breast)

Anonymous Nudes: 1

In what era other than the 1970s could obese transvestite
Divine become a star by eating dog shit on-screen? Such is
the genius of *Pink Flamingos,* cult director John Waters's
classic that offends and enthralls while following the exploits
of Baltimore's basest in a contest to determine the filthiest
people alive. Sweet Cookie Mueller shows all boning a
greaseball with a live chicken squawking between their
torsos, while skinny and shameless Mink Stole bares bush
and sucks toes. Now *that's* Divine!

TOP 5

Midnight Movies

5. *Café Flesh* (1982)

4. *Pink Flamingos* (1972)

3. *Forbidden Zone* (1980)

2. *Mulholland Dr.* (2001)

1. Showgirls (1995)

Playback (1996)

Director: Oley Sassone

Breasts: 14; **Butts**: 1

Nude Stars: **Tawny Kitaen** (Breasts, Thong);
   Shannon Whirry (Butt)

Anonymous Nudes: 6

Playback is part sexploitation, part thriller, and all hot! On
the thriller end, Tawny Kitaen and her hubby are suffering
from bedroom boo-boos thanks to the strain of his work.
They decide the cure is a bit of wife-swapping swinging. But
hubby's coworker, Shannon Whirry, blackmails the guy. On
the skin side, Tawny lets her big girls out for some sexual
healing, while Shannon gives a truly "cheeky" performance.
It's worth keeping at least one hand on the playback button.

The Players Club (1998)

Director: Ice Cube

Breasts: 16

Nude Stars: **LisaRaye** (Breasts, Thong);
   Monica Calhoun (Breasts); **Chrystale
   Wilson** (Breasts, Thong)

Anonymous Nudes: 6

LisaRaye is a college girl short on funds but long on looks
who strips for tuition in *The Players Club*. She finds sisters
like to do it with sisters, like the lesbian duo who run special
hotel parties and sell their hot plates to clients. Bernie Mac,
Jamie Foxx, and even 2 Live Crew make appearances, while
Monica Calhoun and Chrystale Wilson add to the playful
atmosphere with T&A. Girls just want to have fun—and guys
just want to watch!

Play-Mate of the Apes (2002)

Director: John Bacchus

Breasts: 10; **Butts**: 5; **Bushes**: 5

Nude Stars: **Anoushka** (Full Frontal, Butt); **Darian Caine** (Full Frontal, Butt, Thong); **Sharon Engert** (Full Frontal, Butt); **Misty Mundae** (Full Frontal, Butt); **Shelby Taylor** (Full Frontal, Butt)

Play-Mate of the Apes may be the pinnacle of the soft-porn parodies from Seduction Cinema. When a spaceship full of human women, including superstar Misty Mundae, lands on a planet where apes evolved into dominant creatures, our intrepid explorers do what any science-minded person would do: engage in nonstop lesbian sex. They even get human natives Darian Caine and Shelby Taylor into the act. *Apes* will have you spanking your monkey.

Seduction Cinema
New Jersey's softcore super-studio.

As the millennium drew to a close, a mighty nudie-movie powerbase arose from the Garden State, fueled by passionate filmmakers, an on-target sense of humor, and a bewitching B-movie superstarlet named Misty Mundae who lit up the screen like no one since the most dazzling drive-in divas of yore. Seduction Cinema is the company's name, and hot, funny, well-made soft-sex productions are their game. Along with trademark parodies such as *Kinky Kong* (2006), the studio's Retro Seduction Cinema wing reissues sexploitation classics, including those of pioneering eroticist Joseph W. Sarno.

Top 501 DVDs: *Lord of the G-Strings: The Femaleship of the String* (2002), *Play-Mate of the Apes* (2002), *The Seduction of Inga* (1969), *SpiderBabe* (2003)

Please Don't Eat My Mother (1972)

Director: Carl Monson

Breasts: 8; **Butts**: 3; **Bushes**: 4

Nude Stars: **Rene Bond** (Full Frontal, Butt);
   Alice Fredlund (Full Frontal)

Anonymous Nudes: 2

Please Don't Eat My Mother is a softcore take on *The Little Shop of Horrors* (1960), with a talking plant that demands to be fed people. Its owner lures hookers and swinging couples to his home and turns them into plant food, including carrot top (and bottom!) Alice Fredlund and hardcore hottie Rene Bond and her real-life husband, Ric Lutze. You'll have to keep one green thumb on the pause button . . . and the other in your pants!

Play-Mate of the Shipe's

At the offices of MrSkin.com, the spectral presence of beloved *Play-Mate of the Apes* star Misty Mundae seems to loom over everything we do. In fact, Associate Editor Keara Shipe even dreamed once that Misty was her best friend and that they liked to go shopping at thrift stores together. This is actually the kind of stuff we talk about here.

skinfo

Poison Ivy 2 (1996)

Director: Anne Goursaud

Breasts: 9; **Butts**: 1;

Nude Stars: **Tara Ellison** (Left Breast); **Victoria Haas** (Breasts); **Alyssa Milano** (Breasts, Butt); **Kate Rodger** (Breasts)

Anonymous Nudes: 1

For *Poison Ivy 2,* the titular trollop is Alyssa Milano, a nice girl who gets horny when she's shipped off to college. She lands at an artists' co-op and, after reading the diary of a previous coed who expanded her realm of experience in pursuit of harder education, seeks out her own sexual awakening via affairs with an older professor and the Big Sculptor on Campus.

Poison Ivy
Itchin' to get naked.

You can look but you better touch this Poison Ivy. This trilogy of titillation gets hotter with each new installment. *Poison Ivy* (1992) started with a simple premise: Introduce a young temptress into an unstable family and watch the sparks fly. Drew Barrymore was electric as the original lead. In *Poison Ivy 2* (1996), Alyssa Milano takes over the role of the young seductress . . . and takes it all off. But things really started to bloom with the third and final episode of erotic entertainment called *Poison Ivy 3: The New Seduction* (1997), in which Jaime Pressly gives one of filmdom's moist revealing performances. The plot is a return to the original, with Jaime destroying a family by sleeping with each one of them (what a way to go), but this time Jaime's naked abandon smokes her smoking predecessors.

Top 501 DVDs: *Poison Ivy 2* (1996), *Poison Ivy 3: The New Seduction* (1997)

Poison Ivy 3: The New Seduction (1997)

Director: Kurt Voss

Breasts: 4; **Butts**: 1

Nude Stars: **Athena Massey** (Breasts);
Jaime Pressly (Breasts, Butt, Thong)

Poison Ivy 3: The New Seduction? It's more like the nude seduction, as blonde, buxom, built-to-bang Jaime Pressly, as Violet, proves to be the most poisonous ivy yet. Jaime plays the sister of Drew Barrymore's character in the original *Poison Ivy* (1993). She's also a semipro dominatrix with a thirst for revenge. Her idea of revenge, naturally, involves end-to-end intercourse and tearing the family of Michael Des Barres asunder by sleeping with its multiple members one by one. When you come across this *Poison Ivy,* be sure to have lotion handy.

Pretty *Poison*

The first two entries in the fantastically trashy *Poison Ivy* film series cast bankable-name starlets in their lead strumpet roles–Drew Barrymore and Alyssa Milano, respectively. *The New Seduction* gambled on an unknown and won. Jaime Pressly became a skinstant star with the movie's debut, bolstered by repeated promos on HBO that featured the hard-bodied beauty ditching her robe for a skinny dip.

skinfo

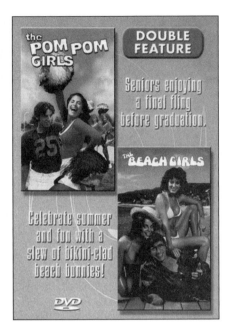

The Pom Pom Girls (1976)

Director: Joseph Ruben

Breasts: 10; Butts: 3

Nude Stars: **Jennifer Ashley** (Breasts, Butt); **Diane Lee Hart** (Breasts, Butt); **Susan Player** (Breasts, Butt); **Lisa Reeves** (Breasts); **Cheryl "Rainbeaux" Smith** (Breasts)

In a twisted story line that will appeal to athletes everywhere, the Pom Pom Girls plot to weaken their opposing team's players by luring the jocks into strength-sapping sexual situations. Any red-blooded baller would say nuts to the big game after seeing Jennifer Ashley, Lisa Reeves, Susan Player, Diane Lee Hart, and cheerleading specialist Cheryl "Rainbeaux" Smith in various stages of undress in the locker room. Being set up to be a loser never seemed like such a winning proposition.

Cheerleader Movies
Rah! Rah! Raw!

What's hotter than a young girl, wearing little more than a short pleated skirt, bouncing around with her pom poms out? The kickoff's in your pants when these sweater-betties get it on, whether it's Mena Suvari proving that every rose has a thorn in *American Beauty* (1999) or Bambi Woods giving audiences a woody in the X-rated *Debbie Does Dallas* (1978). Cheerleader flicks have been all over the stylistic map, from the good-natured teen comedy *Bring It On* (2000) and sexy spoof *Not Another Teen Movie* (2001), to the devilish *Satan's Cheerleaders* (1977) and ass-kicking *Cheerleader Ninjas* (1998). And if anyone has helped uplift the genre and put their pom poms beyond the call of booty, it has to be dearly departed damsel Cheryl "Rainbeaux" Smith. If there's a squad of hotties in heaven, she's at the top of that flesh pyramid.

Top 501 DVDs: *The Cheerleaders* (1973), *The Pom Pom Girls* (1976), *Revenge of the Cheerleaders* (1976), *The Swinging Cheerleaders* (1974)

Porky's (1982)

Director: Bob Clark

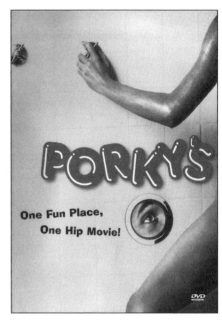

Breasts: 16; **Butts**: 9;
   Bushes: 6

Nude Stars: **Kim Cattrall** (Butt, Bush);
   Kaki Hunter (Breasts, Butt, Bush);
   Pat Lee (Breasts); **Allene Simmons**
   (Full Frontal)

Anonymous Nudes: 8

Porky's presents a nostalgia-based, nonstop barrage of lowbrow sight and sex gags that skewer adolescent male fixations that run the gamut from the girls' showers to the local whorehouse, Chez Porky. After the basketball team from Angel Beach High gets humiliated at the titular brothel, their raucous pranks escalate into epic revenge. Along the way there's Pee-Wee, the famous peepholes, Kim Cattrall as the howlingly hot (and hairy-lapped) Lassie, plus Bula Ballbricker attempting to tug a "tallywhacker" clear through the shower-room wall. *Porky's* is one of the true titans of the teen sex comedy.

TOP 5

Movies from 1982

5. *The Seduction*

4. *The Last American Virgin*

3. *Summer Lovers*

2. *Porky's*

1. Fast Times at Ridgemont High

Possessed by the Night (1994)

Director: Fred Olen Ray

Breasts: 8; **Butts**: 1

Nude Stars: **Sandahl Bergman** (Breasts, Butt); **Amy Rochelle** (Breasts); **Sandra Taylor** (Breasts, Thong); **Shannon Tweed** (Breasts, Thong)

The romantic author of *Possessed by the Night* can't get it up for another bodice ripper, so he ventures into Chinatown and purchases a one-eyed creature in a jar. Whether it helps unblock the flow of words is unclear. It does, however, undress everyone from the scribbler's wife (Sandahl Bergman) to his secretary, played by legendary skinstress Shannon Tweed. The monster turns Shannon into a sex-crazed psycho who bares her plastic-fantastic lovers and pleasures herself with a pistol. Talk about getting banged!

Preaching to the Perverted (1997)

Director: Stuart Urban

Breasts: 26; **Butts**: 6; **Bushes**: 2

Nude Stars: **Julie Graham** (Full Frontal, Butt, Thong); **Guinevere Turner** (Full Frontal, Butt)

Anonymous Nudes: 12

The irony of men of the cloth harassing persons who prefer to be unclothed is tackled in *Preaching to the Perverted*. Suffice it to say, you'll be destined for a conversion beyond your wickedest imagination after catching the sinful sight of bald-headed, fuzzy-mounded Julie Graham sauntering all curvy and pervy into full-frontal camera range.

Preppies (1982)

Director: Chuck Vincent

Breasts: 22; **Butts**: 1

Nude Stars: **Nitchie Barrett** (Breasts); **Cindy Manion** (Breasts); **Katt Shea** (Breasts, Butt); **Lynda Wiesmeier** (Breasts)

Anonymous Nudes: 9

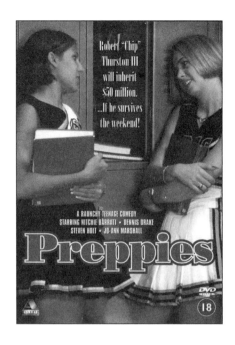

A pack of hotties attempts to distract a gaggle of unsuspecting Preppies so they fail their final exams. Nitchie Barrett dances topless, while Cindy Manion's bulbous breasts slip out of her racy lingerie. A topless Katt Shea puts her ass on glass. And Lynda Wiesmeier has an orgasm all by herself. Where do these preppies go, the School of Hard Knockers?

Pretty Baby (1978)

Director: Louis Malle

Breasts: 6; **Butts**: 2; **Bushes**: 1

Nude Stars: **Susan Sarandon** (Breasts); **Brooke Shields** (Breasts, Butt)

Anonymous Nudes: 1

The 1970s saw platform shoes for white guys, coke spoons dangling from the necks of insurance execs, and *Pretty Baby* playing in mainstream movie houses in all fifty of the United States. In Louisiana, 'round about a hundred years ago, a preadolescent girl of unparalleled charm (Brooke Shields) is being raised in the whorehouse where her mother—Susan Sarandon at her most superstacked magnificent—is a prostitute. Well, tit does run in the family.

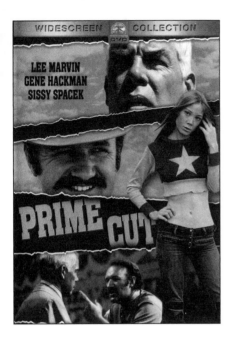

Prime Cut (1972)

Director: Michael Ritchie

Breasts: 14; **Butts**: 2; **Bushes**: 3

Nude Stars: **Janit Baldwin** (Full Frontal, Butt);
Sissy Spacek (Breasts, Butt, Bush);
Angel Tompkins (Breasts)

Anonymous Nudes: 6

The enduring image of gangster flick *Prime Cut* is of the pens that a cattle rancher stocks with nubile, naked females to be shopped as sex slaves to brothel keepers. This raunchy rancher also makes ends meet by grinding his business rivals into sausage filling. Life in these hard times was better lived as a man, especially when those men could catch a gander at brunette Janit Baldwin and rusty-top Sissy Spacek housed like triple-B-baring livestock in a straw-strewn pen, each in her prime.

Plumber's Crack - *n.*

Accidental exposure of the butt crack above the waistline of pants or a skirt, especially from bending over.

Private Lessons (1981)

Director: Alan Myerson

Breasts: 5; **Butts**: 1; **Bushes**: 1

Nude Stars: **Pamela Jean Bryant** (Right Breast);
   Sylvia Kristel (Breasts, Butt, Bush)

Anonymous Nudes: 1

Sylvia Kristel is the au pair with quite a pair in *Private Lessons*. Sylvia drives the young boy she's hired to care for wild. She quickly picks up on his carnal interest and figures to scam the kid out of his inheritance. Not only does Sylvia strip naked for the drooling pubescent, but she also spreads her legs and snatches his cherry. Then she pretends to die in the sack after coming so hard from his good loving. But the child has no point of reference—how could he know anything's up? Guess he'll need some more private lessons.

Private Parts

The most profitable independent-film release of 1981, *Private Lessons* was based on the novel *Philly* by Dan Greenburg. Interestingly, the book is a thriller with some pronounced horror overtones. The moviemakers wisely decided to wacky things up a bit for the big screen.

skinfo

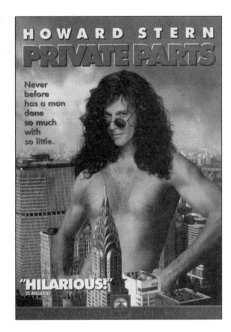

Private Parts (1997)

Director: Betty Thomas

Breasts: 18; **Butts**: 2;
   Bushes: 1

Nude Stars: **Carrie Flaska** (Breasts);
   Melanie Good (Breasts, Butt, Thong);
   Jenna Jameson (Full Frontal, Butt);
   Theresa Lynn (Breasts)

Anonymous Nudes: 7

Howard Stern lived up to his boast of being the King of All Media when he released *Private Parts,* his funny, frisky, and funbag-tastic biopic. The story follows his humble beginnings as a DJ; his fateful gathering of busty Robin Quivers, joke man Jackie Martling, and bizarro freak Fred Norris; and his rise to fame. Along the way, Howard fantasizes about lesbians, makes Theresa Lynn reach orgasm via stereo speaker, and gets porn star Jenna Jameson to bare all on the air.

TOP 5

Comedies

5. *Trading Places* (1983)

4. *Almost Pregnant* (1992)

3. *EuroTrip* (2004)

2. *Animal House* (1978)

1. Private Parts (1997)

Private School (1983)

Director: Noel Black

Breasts: 20; **Butts**: 11;
   Bushes: 8

Nude Stars: **Phoebe Cates** (Butt); **Kari
   Lizer** (Left Breast); **Julie Payne** (Left
   Breast); **Betsy Russell** (Full Frontal,
   Butt); **Brinke Stevens** (Breasts, Butt);
   Lynda Wiesmeier (Full Frontal, Butt)

Anonymous Nudes: 7

What they teach in *Private School* is how to ogle nude babes
and how to try anything to get laid. Roly-poly hero Bubba
Beauregard (Michael Zorek) and pals dress in drag to crash
the girls' dorm, and they hit it big. Among those cracking
open their school uniforms are Phoebe Cates and Betsy
Russell, who rides a horse topless. Brinke Stevens and Lynda
Wiesmeier shower, while Julie Payne and Kari Lizer pop
their cheerleader tops. *Private School* is the ultimate primer
in tits and class.

Puffy Nipples - *n. pl.*
Deliciously bulbous boob protrusions.

Promises! Promises! (1963)

Director: King Donovan

Breasts: 2; **Butts**: 1

Nude Star: **Jayne Mansfield** (Breasts, Butt)

Promises! Promises! is a groundbreaking landmark in bra-busting cinema featuring the legendary hills of blonde bombshell Jayne Mansfield. Juicy Jayne is itching to get pregnant and decides that a sea cruise is just the fluid but firm environment in which her ticket is likely to be punched in a manner that knocks her up. She lolls naked in her cabin, and the rise and swell of her breasts imprint an outline of eternal pleasure on the mass male consciousness. Bombshell Jayne will set you off. We promise! We promise!

Promises Keeper

The advent of the motion picture brought with it the promise of a medium unparalleled in excellence when it comes to delivering naked starlets to the masses. And several decades later, that promise was fulfilled, fittingly enough, by *Promises! Promises!* There were skincidents of on-camera nakedness prior to this Jayne Mansfield opus, but *Promises!* actually promoted itself as an opportunity to witness its buxom main attraction in the buff. And from there, an entire birthday-suit skindustry was born.

skinfo

Prozac Nation (2001)

Director: Erik Skjoldbjærg

Breasts: 2; **Bushes**: 1

Nude Star: **Christina Ricci** (Full Frontal)

What's a nut to do? If you're Christina Ricci as the messed-up heroine of *Prozac Nation,* it's pill-popping time. But if you're a viewer, then it's nut-draining time as Christina finally unloads her heavy sacks for the first time. She opens the picture with a bang, fully nude, with those honking hooters rising over her flat stomach like two dirigibles advertising something wild. Who could be depressed with pill-ows like those?

CHRISTINA RICCI · JASON BIGGS · ANNE HECHE · MICHELLE WILLIAMS AND JESSICA LANGE

PROZAC NATION

"Christina Ricci Gives A Standout Performance!"
– Roger Ebert

Based On *The New York Times* Best-Selling Book!

Prozac and Cons

Prozac Nation was adapted from a 1998 memoir by Elizabeth Wurtzel. The movie was made in 2000 for release a year later. Four years then passed until the film debuted on cable TV in 2005. Reasons for the delay have been credited to an unlikable central character and Wurtzel's own description of the movie as "horrible." Well, she might consider the source material.

skinfo

The Psycho Lover (1970)

Director: Robert Vincent O'Neill

Breasts: 13; **Butts**: 1; **Bushes**: 1

Nude Stars: **Diane Jones** (Left Breast); **Lynn Lyon** (Full Frontal, Butt); **Elizabeth Plumb** (Breasts)

Anonymous Nudes: 4

The Psycho Lover tells the story of a psychiatrist who doesn't have the guts to leave his abusive, drunken wife for his mistress. Then along comes a patient who just happens to be a psycho killer who preys only on females. The lightbulb goes on over the doctor's head, and the rest is a creepy and sexy thriller, thanks to toplessness from Diane Jones, Lynn Lyon, and Elizabeth Plumb. It'll drive you mad!

Punch (2002)

Director: Guy Bennett

Breasts: 10; **Butts**: 1; **Bushes**: 1

Nude Stars: **Sonja Bennett** (Breasts, Butt); **Kathryn Kirkpatrick** (Breasts); **Meredith McGeachie** (Breasts)

Anonymous Nudes: 2

In *Punch,* Sonja Bennett stars as a young gal who runs afoul of Meredith McGeachie as a topless boxer. We're not talking about foxy boxing, either—Meredith and her pals seriously slam each other while their titties go flying. Forget the creepy subplot about Sonja's relationship with her father, and marvel at a pleasing parade of punchy pretties. And fans of big girls should check out the big'uns of Kathryn Kirkpatrick, who's totally shameless in showing off her butch bod. *Punch* will provide you plenty to do with your fist.

Quest for Fire (1981)

Director: Jean-Jacques Annaud

Breasts: 20; **Butts**: 5; **Bushes**: 1

Nude Star: **Rae Dawn Chong** (Full Frontal, Butt)

Anonymous Nudes: 9

Rae Dawn Chong's performance in *Quest for Fire* is hotter than the subject of the title. The movie concerns a bunch of cavemen looking to relight their fire, which they do, metaphorically, when they meet Rae, who can not only light a fire but light their fire with her advanced missionary sex position. Since she's naked throughout most of the movie, orgasm for the audience is a given too. Prepare to beat your club.

Punch Munch

The power of *Punch* comes courtesy of Sonja Bennet as a scrappy teen who offers her nude body to her father. Sexy enough, you say? How about the fact that the movie was actually directed by Sonja's real-life father, Guy Bennet, who got to oversee a sumptuous scene of his darling offspring bottomlessly proving she's a natural blonde. Dad's our kind of Guy.

skinfo

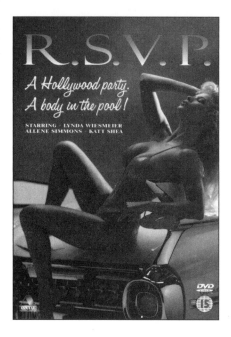

R.S.V.P. (1984)

Directors: John Amero, Lem Amero

Breasts: 18; **Butts**: 6; **Bushes**: 5

Nude Stars: **Tamara Landry** (Breasts); **Laurie
Senit** (Breasts); **Katt Shea** (Breasts, Butt);
Allene Simmons (Full Frontal, Butt); **Lynda
Wiesmeier** (Full Frontal, Butt)

Anonymous Nudes: 5

The premise of *R.S.V.P.* is that a best-selling author of a
roman à clef has gathered those wild people who inspired
the story, which is about to be made into a motion picture.
More like moanin' picture. Among those letting it all hang
out are video vixen Tamara Landry in her first on-screen
flash, Laurie Senit in her last, Katt Shea, and big-breasted
Lynda Wiesmeier. Mr. Skin is definitely RSVP-ing for this
party.

Ragtime (1981)

Director: Milos Forman

Breasts: 2; **Butts**: 1; **Bushes**: 1

Nude Star: **Elizabeth McGovern** (Full Frontal, Butt)

There's murder, racism, and a swan-song performance from
James Cagney, but the most resonating image from Milos
Forman's *Ragtime* is that of Elizabeth McGovern as Evelyn
Nesbit Thaw, a sixteen-year-old model whose sadistic
husband offs her sugar daddy. Liz treats us to one of
filmdom's most entrancing entrances when she streaks into
viewers' heart-ons, offering up every bit of her lucky charms.
At the time, she wasn't on the rag, but you'll definitely need
to wipe up after watching.

The Ranch (2004)

Director: Susan Seidelman

Breasts: 10

Nude Stars: **Jennifer Aspen** (Breasts); **Jessica Collins** (Breasts, Thong); **Samantha Ferris** (Breasts); **Nicki Micheaux** (Breasts, Thong); **Paige Moss** (Breasts)

The Showtime drama *The Ranch* revolves around the humpings and bumpings of pretty prostitutes at the fictional Diamond Ranch in Reno. With beautiful booby babes such as Jennifer Aspen, Jessica Collins, and Nicki Micheaux giving the good-time gals at the Bunny Ranch a skinematic run for their money, every cowboy worth his weight in pork butts will be pining for a poke or a stroke.

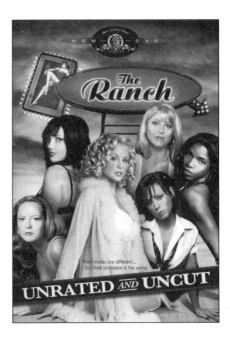

Rapa Nui (1994)

Director: Kevin Reynolds

Breasts: 97

Nude Star: **Sandrine Holt** (Breasts)

Anonymous Nudes: 50

If you ever wanted to know how those giant stone heads got erected on Easter Island, well, go to the library. But if you want to get erect from a movie based on the legend of that mysterious island, rent *Rapa Nui*. French-Chinese beauty Sandrine Holt stars as the love interest of one of the island's upper crusts. She spends much of the movie with her pagan idols showing, and viewers will want to worship them one-handedly.

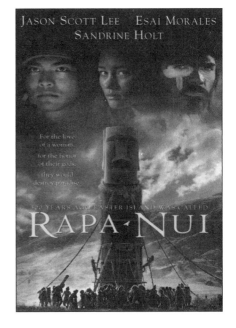

The Rapture (1991)

Director: Michael Tolkin

Breasts: 5; **Butts**: 1

Nude Stars: **Carole Davis** (Right Breast, Butt); **Stephanie Menuez** (Breasts); **Mimi Rogers** (Breasts)

Rapture (rap-chur): 1. ecstatic joy or delight; 2. a state of extreme sexual ecstasy; 3. the feeling of being transported to another sphere of existence; 4. the experience of being spirited away to heaven just before the Apocalypse; 5. seeing Mimi Rogers's boobies. In *The Rapture,* Michael Tolkin (writer of *The Player*) rides his flavor-of-the-year notoriety straight to an everlasting afterlife of bliss.

Rated X (2000)

Director: Emilio Estevez

Breasts: 32; **Butts**: 6; **Bushes**: 4

Nude Stars: **Joanne Boland** (Breasts); **Carolyn Goff** (Breasts); **Tracy Hutson** (Breasts); **Sadie Leblanc** (Breasts, Butt)

Anonymous Nudes: 13

Hollywood siblings Emilio Estevez and Charlie Sheen are a pair of bros whose combined labors yielded the Showtime movie *Rated X.* It's the story of blue-screen visionaries Jim and Artie Mitchell as they journey from film-school dropouts to '70s porn magnates. *Rated X,* as directed by Estevez and starring he and Sheen as the Mitchells, is a gritty, goofy, gut-grabbing, gazonga-baring depiction of a family bond that was fun before fraying into tragedy. Rate it seXy!

Raw Nerve (1999)

Director: Avi Nesher

Breasts: 4; **Butts**: 1

Nude Stars: **Nicollette Sheridan** (Breasts, Butt, Thong);
   Monica Trombetta (Breasts)

A cop under investigation for money laundering calls in a
favor from a scaredy-cat college teacher whose life the cop
had saved in the distant past. Add South American drug
lords with a penchant for throat-slitting vengeance, toss in
a few boob-baring broads (Nicollette Sheridan, anyone?)
susceptible to the charms of the rogue lawman, and garnish
with a side of inoperable cancer, and you have *Raw Nerve*,
a recipe for bang-up entertainment.

Racktastic - *adj.*

Breast-intensive. Actually, make that: breast-skintensive.

"An Exuberant Comedy!"
—Rolling Stone

A seductive and fashionable comedy!

ROBERT ALTMAN'S
READY TO WEAR

Ready to Wear (1994)

Director: Robert Altman

Breasts: 26; **Butts**: 14;
Bushes: 14

Nude Stars: **Rossy de Palma** (Bush); **Katarzyna Figura** (Butt); **Sally Kellerman** (Breasts); **Ute Lemper** (Butt, Bush); **Tara Leon** (Full Frontal, Butt); **Georgianna Robertson** (Full Frontal, Butt); **Ève Salvail** (Full Frontal, Butt)

Anonymous Nudes: 9

Director Robert Altman's *Ready to Wear* takes on the pretensions of the fashion industry, while providing actresses with ample opportunities to take off their fashions. The climactic scene of *Ready to Wear* features a gang of supermodels waltzing fully naked along the runway. The camera does not shy away from focusing on breasts, butts, and creases of crotch, and the viewer should not shy away either. Call it *Ready to Bare*.

Re-Masturbator

Don't miss the deleted scenes on the *Re-Animator* DVD. Somehow, they feature even more boobage from Barbara Crampton. We didn't think that was possible!

Ready to Bare

Two of the beautiful catwalkers on display at the climax of *Ready to Wear* are prominent real-life supermodels Georgianna Robertson and Ute Lemper. Ute is so pregnant that she looks like she might pop the kid out with the next pop of a flashbulb.

Robert Altman
Naked Hollywood maverick.

One of Tinseltown's true rebels, Robert Altman carved a unique niche in cinema via sprawling, multilevel films such as *M*A*S*H* (1970) and *Nashville* (1975), up to his death shortly after completing *A Prairie Home Companion* (2006). Along with overlapping dialogue and interwoven plots, Altman also reliably delivered piles of nude bodies with brazen gusto.

Top 501 DVDs: *Aria* (1987), *Dr. T and the Women* (2000), *Ready to Wear* (1994), *Short Cuts* (1993)

SKIN VISIONARIES

Re-Animator (1985)
Director: Stuart Gordon

Breasts: 6; **Butts**: 2; **Bushes**: 1
Nude Star: **Barbara Crampton** (Full Frontal, Butt)
Anonymous Nudes: 2

If scream queen Barbara Crampton never fails to raise the dead in your pants, then *Re-Animator* is the movie to release that pent-up appendage. She's never been more naked, and the flesh comes with enough gore and guffaws to keep everyone happy. *Re-Animator* is the first in a series of campy horror favorites about a mad scientist who develops a serum that, well, reanimates the dead. It does wonders for your dead wood, too!

MILLENNIUM EDITION
H.P. LOVECRAFT'S
Re-Animator
HERBERT WEST HAS A VERY GOOD HEAD ON HIS SHOULDERS...
AND ANOTHER ONE IN A DISH ON HIS DESK

THX
OPTIMIZER

ELITE ENTERTAINMENT

Reform School Girls (1986)

Director: Tom DeSimone

Breasts: 21; **Butts**: 12; **Bushes**: 5

Nude Stars: **Michelle Bauer** (Breasts); **Leslee Bremmer** (Full Frontal); **Linda Carol** (Full Frontal, Butt); **Andrea Darnell** (Full Frontal, Butt); **Darcy DeMoss** (Right Breast, Butt); **Sherri Stoner** (Breasts, Butt); **Wendy O. Williams** (Breasts, Butt, Bush, Thong)

Anonymous Nudes: 10

Some movies win your heart from the very title. With *Reform School Girls,* you just hit PLAY. Social contract dictates that such a film will feature nubile girls, several at a time, naked in showers, for a full ninety seconds. There will be clothing-optional catfights. And there will be a trail of dried drool when you wake up three hours later to the snowy buzz of the blank TV.

School Girls' Boy

Tom DeSimone, director of *Reform School Girls,* also helmed the talking-vagina masterpiece *Chatterbox* (1977), as well as the Linda Blair howler *Hell Night* (1981) and the babes-behind-bars hit *The Concrete Jungle* (1982). If it seems an amusing turn for a man whose career began with children's movies, consider that DeSimone was most prolific as "Lancer Brooks," one of the most esteemed gay-porn filmmakers of the 1970s.

 skinfo

Living Dead Girl

Mindy Clarke's voodoo-powered striptease/ mutation/body-modification in *Return of the Living Dead Part III* is skinema's single-greatest goth-girl-gone-wild moment to date. An even bigger shock came a decade later when Mindy expanded her name to Melinda and costarred on the Fox TV teen drama *The O.C.* as the MILF-eriffic mother of Mischa Barton's character.

 skinfo

Requiem for a Dream (2000)

Director: Darren Aronofsky

Breasts: 8; **Butts**: 1; **Bushes**: 2

Nude Stars: **Aliya Campbell** (Breasts, Bush); **Jennifer Connelly** (Butt, Bush)

Anonymous Nudes: 3

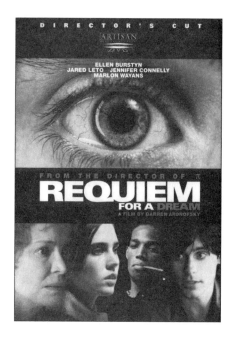

Requiem for a Dream, based on Hubert Selby Jr.'s novel, is a tough and unflinching depiction of drug addiction's downward spiral that will have viewers flinching and leave them feeling decidedly tender—tender in the trousers, that is. The view of miracle-bust brunette Jennifer Connelly's crotch fluff is the most potent drug of all.

Return of the Living Dead Part III (1993)

Director: Brian Yuzna

Breasts: 2

Nude Star: **Mindy Clarke** (Breasts)

Return of the Living Dead Part III chronicles the effects of corpse-reanimating gas on mesmerizing Mindy Clarke after she and her boyfriend stumble into a secret weapons test. When Mindy accidentally dies, her beau makes use of the opportunity to revive her. Although Mindy shows her supple sacks early on, her slinky, kinky reemergence as a self-mutilated, bare-mammaried ghoul is one of the most disturbingly erotic moments in the annals of horror movies.

Return to Savage Beach (1998)

Director: Andy Sidaris

Breasts: 8; **Butts**: 3; **Bushes**: 1

Nude Stars: **Shae Marks** (Full Frontal, Butt); **Julie K. Smith** (Breasts); **Julie Strain** (Breasts, Butt); **Carrie Westcott** (Breasts, Butt, Thong)

Return to Savage Beach reunites the double-D agents, this time working to foil a terrorist after some hidden World War II treasure. Julie Strain is back as the villain, but how bad can she be when she looks this good? The agents aren't outgunned by juggy Julie, not with Shae Marks on their side, who's been getting high marks from fans since her stint as a *Playboy* Playmate. Life is a beach with these savage beauties.

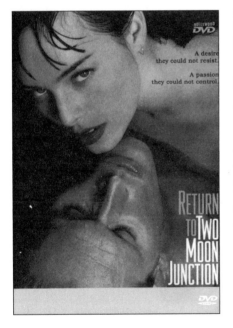

Return to Two Moon Junction (1994)

Director: Farhad Mann

Breasts: 2; **Butts**: 1

Nude Star: **Mindy Clarke** (Breasts, Butt)

A sequel to the original erotica, *Return to Two Moon Junction* tells the story of the sister of Sherilyn Fenn, the first movie's lead, played by Mindy Clarke. She takes up right where her sibling left off, which is naked and in bed. Mindy, now famous for her role on the hit series *The O.C.* and last skinfully seen in *Return of the Living Dead Part III* (1993), is a sight for sore eyes . . . and sorer crotches!

Revenge of the Cheerleaders (1976)

Director: Richard Lerner

Breasts: 8; **Butts**: 3; **Bushes**: 4

Nude Stars: **Susie Elene** (Full Frontal); **Helen Lang** (Full Frontal, Butt); **Patrice Rohmer** (Full Frontal, Butt); **Cheryl "Rainbeaux" Smith** (Breasts, Butt, Bush)

Revenge of the Cheerleaders is sweet—these pom-pom girls show their megaphones before the opening credits are finished rolling! Rather than transfer to an inner-city school, the girls seek the revenge of the title by spiking the cafeteria with drugs, banging the football team in the showers, and flashing a pregnant Cheryl "Rainbeaux" Smith for the big-tummy perverts out there. The other naked rah-rah girls include Susie Elene, Helen Lang, and Patrice Rohmer. Now that's something to cheer about.

Cheerleaders Chump

Before David Hasselhoff was famous for talking to cars or as a son of the beach, he played Boner in *Revenge of the Cheerleaders*. And then he seemed to continue on in that role in real life. Forever.

skinfo

Revenge of the Nerds (1984)

Director: Jeff Kanew

Breasts: 4; **Bushes**: 1

Nude Stars: **Colleen Madden** (Breasts, Bush); **Julia Montgomery** (Breasts)

Becoming rich and retired by forty-five would seem to be payback enough, but no limits can be placed on the *Revenge of the Nerds*. This '80s classic tracks the trials and triumphs of the Tri-Lambda house, led by Robert Carradine and Anthony Edwards. After being victimized by campus jocks, the nerds rise above through a series of comic comeuppances, including high-tech peeping on sorority-house hotties. Despite scoring straight A's, every nerd among them makes it onto the dishonor role.

Risky Business (1983)

Director: Paul Brickman

Breasts: 4; **Butts**: 2; **Bushes**: 1

Nude Stars: **Rebecca De Mornay** (Full Frontal, Butt); **Francine Locke** (Breasts, Butt)

On a wild weekend home alone, Tom Cruise cruises for action and finds it in the form of top-dollar hooker Rebecca De Mornay. After a skinful night with raunchy Rebecca, Cruise finds himself in a pickle thanks to dipping his pickle in something he can't pay for. What follows is the cream of the teen sex comedies of the '80s, which ends with Cruise pimping Rebecca's stable to his horny schoolmates. The only risk in *Risky Business* is soiling your pants.

River's Edge (1986)

Director: Tim Hunter

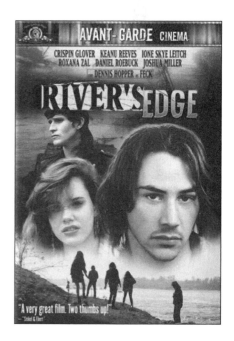

Breasts: 2; **Butts**: 1; **Bushes**: 1

Nude Star: **Danyi Deats** (Full Frontal, Butt)

At the *River's Edge* lies a dead and naked Danyi Deats. Her burnout high-school boyfriend killed her and is showing off her lifeless full-frontal shrubbery to his pals. Crispin Glover decides to cover up the crime, but Keanu Reeves rats. So good-bye gratuitous nudity from Danyi, and hello gratuitous kookiness from Dennis Hopper as a crippled ex-biker. He helps the kids, mostly by smoking pot with them, though he eventually wishes they didn't bogart Danyi.

Frisky *Business*

In 1983, 21-year-old Tom Cruise had four hit movies in circulation. The first was Curtis Hanson's Tijuana romp *Losin' It* (1983). Cruise followed that with Francis Ford Coppola's *The Outsiders* (1983). Then came *Risky Business* and *All The Right Moves* (1983), where he got to fondle the naked frames of Rebecca De Mornay and Lea Thompson, respectively. Praise Xenu!

skinfo

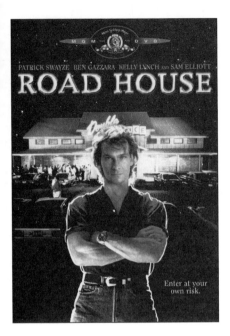

Road House (1989)

Director: Rowdy Herrington

Breasts: 6; **Butts**: 1

Nude Stars: **Laura Albert** (Breasts, Thong); **Kelly Lynch** (Breasts, Butt); **Julie Michaels** (Breasts)

Road House delivers an updated version of the classic western but with tits—*a lot* of tits. Patrick Swayze is a philosophy-spouting, martial-arts-expert bouncer who gets a job at the Double Deuce, which is a nice place to work if you like to fight or watch nearly naked ladies in the weekly G-string contests. But it's the gorgeous Kelly Lynch who's the biggest and barest winner of all!

Load *House*

Julie Michaels plays a topless dancer in *Road House.* She's also worked as a stunt double for such boobalicious talents as Pamela Anderson and Jaime Pressly, in *Barb Wire* (1995) and *Poor White Trash* (2000), respectively.

skinfo

The Road to Wellville (1994)

Director: Alan Parker

Breasts: 5; **Butts**: 2

Nude Stars: **Lara Flynn Boyle** (Breasts); **Bridget Fonda** (Breasts); **Traci Lind** (Left Breast, Butt); **Camryn Manheim** (Butt)

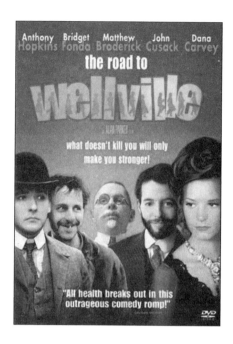

The Road to Wellville is paved with naked ladies. Bridget Fonda gets topless in a milk bath, which is sure to frost your flake. Matthew Broderick falls for his nurse, Traci Lind, when she gives him a moon and a glimpse of her left booby. Then there's Lara Flynn Boyle, who lets her jugs hang out in the room across the hall until Broderick doesn't know if he's coming or going. Even Camryn Manheim bares bombastic bumcakes. This road is a *hard* one.

Road Trip (2000)

Director: Todd Phillips

Breasts: 17; **Butts**: 3; **Bushes**: 2

Nude Stars: **Aliya Campbell** (Breasts); **Aerica D'Amaro** (Breasts); **Jaclyn DeSantis** (Breasts); **Amy Smart** (Breasts); **Bridgett Wise** (Breasts)

Anonymous Nudes: 4

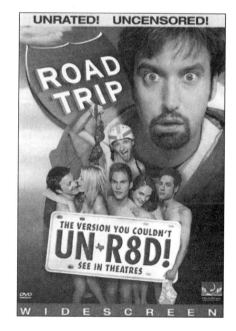

Road Trip tracks a college guy who's been dating his sweetheart since before he could get a hard-on. But when he finally strays, he records the tryst, and his roommate mistakenly sends the tape to his girlfriend. Tom Green relates the tale, which involves selling sperm for gas money and a lot of tits! Amy Smart is just one of the topless cuties who populate this zipper-popping comedy. See if you can stay on the road while watching.

Rod Steele 0014: You Only Live Until You Die (2002)

Director: Rolfe Kanefsky

Breasts: 24; **Butts**: 9; **Bushes**: 6

Nude Stars: **Tammi Fallon** (Full Frontal, Butt); **Gabriella Hall** (Breasts); **Holly Hollywood** (Full Frontal, Butt); **Jacqueline Lovell** (Breasts, Thong); **Delphine Pacific** (Breasts); **De'Ann Power** (Breasts, Butt); **Kira Reed** (Breasts, Butt); **Tracy Ryan** (Full Frontal, Butt); **Petra Sexton** (Full Frontal, Butt); **Sita Renne Thompson** (Full Frontal, Butt, Thong); **Sheila Vale** (Breasts, Butt)

Anonymous Nudes: 1

Rod Steele 0014: You Only Live Until You Die follows the intrepid spy as he tracks down a remote control that makes everyone horny little devils. He also battles an evil genius who wants to collect sperm from all the world's most powerful men. Meanwhile, all the world's sexiest women seem to have roles in the film, and some of them show off everything they've got!

Skingy - adj.

It rhymes with "stingy" and it means the same thing: an actress who is not generous when it comes to sharing her naked body with the camera.

SKIN·finition

S.O.B. (1981)

Director: Blake Edwards

The director who made the panther pink and taught you to count to 10 coins a new term for comedy.

Breasts: 6

Nude Stars: **Julie Andrews** (Breasts); **Rosanna Arquette** (Breasts); **Marisa Berenson** (Breasts)

S.O.B. is another Hollywood satire, but with one difference—actually two—Julie Andrews's naked boobies! This story of a director who decides to make a blockbuster by taking his G-rated, wholesome comedy script and star and converting it all to an arty musical sex film is funny and sexy. Besides Mary Poppins popping out, a young Rosanna Arquette flashes her heavy rack, and Marisa Berenson also shares her chesticles. Thanks to Julie's jugs, *S.O.B.* must stand for sexy old babe!

S.O.B.-cups

While the most common understanding of the term S.O.B. is as an acronym for "son of a bitch," in the movie the letters stand for "Standard Operational Bullshit." The most memorable dialogue, however, goes to Ms. Andrews herself. Upon entering the set where her hills will come alive, Julie announces: "I am going to show my boobies! Are you here to see my boobies?" Come on. We wouldn't be anywhere else.

skinfo

Salon Kitty (1976)

Director: Tinto Brass

Breasts: 60; **Butts**: 28;
   Bushes: 28

Nude Stars: **Tina Aumont** (Breasts);
   Rosemarie Lindt (Full Frontal, Butt);
   Teresa Ann Savoy (Full Frontal, Butt);
   Paola Senatore (Full Frontal, Butt);
   Ingrid Thulin (Breasts, Butt)

Anonymous Nudes: 25

Set in Nazi Germany, *Salon Kitty* exposes the Brown Shirts without their shirts in a brothel exclusively for top brass and war heroes. At this boot camp for booty, Teresa Ann Savoy, spicy Rosemarie Lindt, and many naked others are trained in all manner of illicit activity. No holes are barred, so grease your high boots and grab onto your Iron Cross, because the Third Reich is going to rise again . . . in your pants!

TOP 5

Movies from 1976

5. *Up!*

4. *The First Nudie Musical*

3. *Emanuelle in America*

2. *Fantasm*

1. Salon Kitty

Sassy Sue (1972)

Director: Bethel G. Buckalew

Breasts: 8; **Butts**: 2; **Bushes**: 4

Nude Stars: **Sandy Carey** (Breasts); **Tallie Cochrane**
(Full Frontal, Butt); **Karen Cooknell** (Full Frontal);
Sharon Kelly (Full Frontal)

Anonymous Nudes: 1

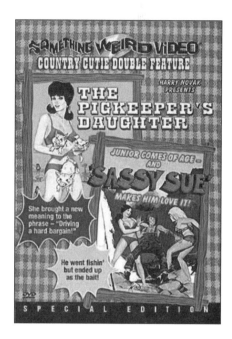

Sassy Sue will make you want to live down on a farm. This
ranch is raunchy, with the farmer selling moonshine, and
of course he's got to sample the goods—or is that goodies?
Sandy Carey and Tallie Cochrane expose everything from
their haylofts to their corn holes. Breast of all is Sharon
Kelly dangling her udders in some lucky guy's face while
Tallie rubs her hairy bits over his stiffy in the barn.
Cock-a-doodle-DO!

Savage Beach (1989)

Director: Andy Sidaris

Breasts: 12; **Butts**: 1; **Bushes**: 3

Nude Stars: **Hope Marie Carlton** (Full Frontal); **Patty
Duffek** (Breasts); **Lisa London** (Breasts); **Dona
Speir** (Full Frontal, Butt); **Maxine Wasa** (Breasts);
Teri Weigel (Breasts, Bush)

Director Andy Sidaris delivers the goods in *Savage Beach*,
those goods being the goodies of Hope Marie Carlton and
Dona Speir as federal drug agents. They work with Patty
Duffek and Lisa London, and more than her bridge is falling
down. The girls' boss also has a topless beauty by his side—
the top-heavenly Maxine Wasa. Even the bad guys are
naked and played by such sweet honeys as Teri Weigel!

Savage Streets (1984)

Director: Danny Steinmann

Breasts: 25; Butts: 6; Bushes: 8

Nude Stars: **Linda Blair** (Breasts); **Rebecca Perle** (Breasts); **Linnea Quigley** (Full Frontal); **Suzee Slater** (Breasts)

Anonymous Nudes: 15

Linda Blair fulfills everyone's breast wishes as she dons a skintight leather pantsuit in *Savage Streets*. A gang of local punks make the mistake of messing with Blair's sister, Linnea Quigley, so Blair breaks out a crossbow and starts handing out some street justice. First, though, she hands out a fine view of her Blair tits in the tub. Suzee Slater flashes her high beams, and of course garment-hating Quigley also shows up sans shirt. *Streets'* teats can't be beat!

Savage Meats

Savage Streets provides a rare opportunity to ogle future scream queen Linnea Quigley's delectably petite love pillows before she pumped them up with breast implants.

skinfo

Scandal (1989)

Director: Michael Caton-Jones

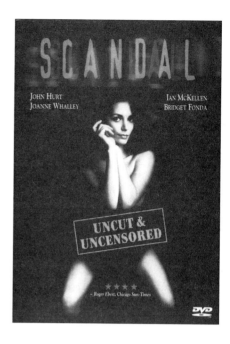

Breasts: 25; **Butts**: 6; **Bushes**: 4

Nude Stars: **Britt Ekland** (Breasts); **Bridget Fonda** (Breasts, Butt); **Tracy Kneale** (Breasts); **Susie Ann Watkins** (Breasts); **Joanne Whalley** (Full Frontal, Butt)

Anonymous Nudes: 12

In 1963, Britain's minister of war, John Profumo, was caught dipping his wick into sixteen-year-old prostitute Christine Keeler—which was made only more sensational by Christine's liaisons with various criminals and a Russian spy. The resulting sex scandal is recounted in the acclaimed film *Scandal*, with Ian McKellan as Profumo and Joanne Whalley making her first big splash (but using a body double for all nudity, alas) as Keeler. Drool, Britannia!

Scandalous Behavior (1998)

Director: James Hong

Breasts: 16; **Butts**: 3; **Bushes**: 3

Nude Stars: **Tiffany Bolton** (Breasts); **Lisa Comshaw** (Full Frontal, Butt, Thong); **Rena Riffel** (Breasts, Bush); **Shannon Tweed** (Full Frontal, Butt)

Anonymous Nudes: 4

An escape caper, crooks and crooked-cops drama, jewelry-heist saga, and softcore sexathon all wrapped into one brightly lit, crisply focused package, *Scandalous Behavior* is jam-packed with B-movie goodness. Director James Hong has invested the film with a richness of plot twists, shifting loyalties, and role reversals. And with a quartet of eagerly naked beauties jostling one another for skin-out screen time, it's all a director can do to cram them all in.

Scarlet Diva (2000)
Director: Asia Argento

Breasts: 6; **Butts**: 2; **Bushes**: 1

Nude Stars: **Asia Argento** (Full Frontal, Butt);
Vera Gemma (Breasts, Butt); **Selen** (Breasts)

In *Scarlet Diva,* writer, director, and star Asia Argento exposes herself to the world in her role as Anna Battista, a young star who's trying to become an artist by making a semiautobiographical film titled *Scarlet Diva.* Got it? She travels to Paris and experiences a depressing string of adventures, but your penis will perk up to sexy scenes by Asia, Vera Gemma, and Selen. Vera even claims in the DVD commentary that her sex scene consists of actual intercourse. That's *red* hot!

Daddy's (Not So) Little *Diva*

Scarlet Diva creator and star Asia Argento is the daughter of Italian horror maestro Dario Argento. Not only has Asia appeared in her father's films, but she also stripped nude for Dad's cam when she was seventeen in *Trauma* (1993), and again in *Phantom of the Opera* (1998).

skinfo

School Spirit (1985)

Director: Alan Holleb

Breasts: 23; **Butts**: 1

Nude Stars: **Leslee Bremmer** (Breasts); **Marlene
    Janssen** (Breasts, Thong); **Becky LeBeau** (Breasts);
    Pam Ward (Breasts, Butt)

Anonymous Nudes: 8

The premise of *School Spirit* is that a college dude has finally
persuaded the coed of his dreams to join him for bed-top
conjugation, but with one caveat—he must first obtain a
condom, and the rubber seeker dies in a car crash. But wait,
this is a comedy! If you were freshly dead and suddenly able
to venture unseen into any private place in the material
world, would your first stop be the girls' shower room?
That's the spirit.

Score (1972)
Unrated Edition
Director: Radley Metzger

Breasts: 4; **Butts**: 2; **Bushes**: 2

Nude Stars: **Lynn Lowry** (Full Frontal, Butt);
    Claire Wilbur (Full Frontal, Butt)

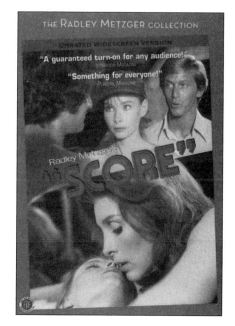

Radley Metzger's *Score* tracks a sophisticated couple who
preys on the insecurities and taboo desires of a naive and
troubled pair of young lovers. Stifling inhibitions and
outmoded gender roles have been overcome. The life-
affirming sexual energy has been unleashed. Homophobes
be alert! Avert your gazes, or else pretend that one of the
two dudes playing couch ball is actually a chick, which is
exactly what one of those dudes does.

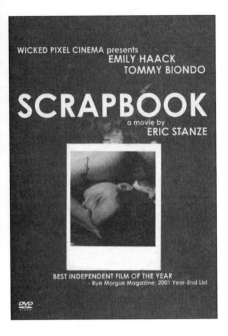

WICKED PIXEL CINEMA presents
EMILY HAACK
TOMMY BIONDO

SCRAPBOOK
a movie by
ERIC STANZE

BEST INDEPENDENT FILM OF THE YEAR
- Rue Morgue Magazine, 2001 Year-End List

DVD

Scrapbook (2000)

Director: Eric Stanze

Breasts: 4; **Butts**: 1; **Bushes**: 1

Nude Star: **Emily Haack** (Full Frontal, Butt)

Anonymous Nudes: 1

The powerful, inventive, micro-budget production *Scrapbook* isn't chintzy about disturbing imagery. Emily Haack puts herself through plenty of horrible scenes as a young woman captured by serial killer Tommy Biondo. The film follows a naked Emily throughout her miserable captivity, where she's forced to keep a diary of her degradation in Tommy's personal scrapbook. The good news is that Emily's fearless, indelible performance is frighteningly sexy.

SKINEMA SENSATIONS!

Skingoria
Flesh and blood.

Some men like women in bikinis, some in lingerie, and some in less than that. But there's a special brand of pervert who likes his women splattered in their own guts—and it's called Skingoria. Better this grindhouse ghoul crack his nuts on-screen than release such fantasies in the real world. That's why there are horror movies, and if a gal is going to take off her clothes in a scary movie, chances are she's going to end up covered in the sticky stuff—blood, that is. Cerina Vincent upholds the torrid tradition in *Cabin Fever* (2002), when she takes a bath and rubs soap not only over her hooters but also over the decomposing skin that drips off her sexy frame like the spunk it elicits from those watching. Talk about gross anatomy!

Top 501 DVDs: *Caligula* (1979), *Carrie* (1976), *The Devil's Advocate* (1997), *Frankenhooker* (1990), *Hollywood Chainsaw Hookers* (1988), *Humanoids from the Deep* (1980), *Immoral Tales* (1974), *Re-Animator* (1985), *Return of the Living Dead Part III* (1993), *Scrapbook* (2000)

Scream Queen Hot Tub Party (1991)

Directors: Fred Olen Ray, Jim Wynorski

Breasts: 22; **Butts**: 7; **Bushes**: 2

Nude Stars: **Michelle Bauer** (Full Frontal, Butt); **Bridget Carney** (Breasts, Butt); **Deborah Dutch** (Breasts); **Monique Gabrielle** (Breasts, Butt); **Roxanne Kernohan** (Breasts); **Kelli Maroney** (Breasts, Butt); **Michelle Michaels** (Breasts, Butt); **Melissa Anne Moore** (Breasts); **Linnea Quigley** (Breasts); **Brinke Stevens** (Full Frontal, Butt); **Stacia Zhivago** (Breasts, Butt)

How many scream queens can you fit into a hot tub? In the comedy *Scream Queen Hot Tub Party* there are eleven. Now how did they all get together in that hot tub? Count Byron Orlock invites the scream queens to his mansion, but the girls have no idea why. So they get out the Ouija board, put on the lingerie, and think. Thinking is hard work, so naturally they need to get into the hot tub and relax.

Tub Thumping

The *Scream Queen Hot Tub Party* DVD comes with a commentary by codirectors Fred Olen Ray and Jim Wynorski, who have great stories to tell about schlock cinema and the girls who make it click. There's also a featurette titled *One Million Heels B.C.*, which is a must-see for Michelle Bauer fans. Like you.

Second Time Lucky (1984)

Director: Michael Anderson

Breasts: 16; **Butts**: 2; **Bushes**: 1

Nude Star: **Diane Franklin** (Full Frontal, Butt)

Anonymous Nudes: 9

Second Time Lucky uses the familiar notion of one couple being reincarnated throughout time—in this case, as an experiment by a curious God. And you'll be thanking God once you see Diane Franklin as Eve in the Garden of Eden. Plenty of guys fell in love with Diane as the French babe in *Better Off Dead* (1985), but we're better off with her here, as she shows off her own hole-y trinity with perpetual boyfriend Roger Wilson.

Secretary (2002)

Director: Steven Shainberg

Breasts: 2; **Butts**: 1; **Bushes**: 1

Nude Star: **Maggie Gyllenhaal** (Full Frontal, Butt)

Maggie Gyllenhaal, fresh from a mental hospital and looking to be part of society, finds a job as a secretary at the firm of neurotic lawyer James Spader, who punishes his employee for typos. Maggie really responds to his stern ways, and it isn't long before things get downright sexretarial. There are plenty of hot scenes in *Secretary*, including a bath-bound flash of Maggie's monumentally massive triangle tangle that will get male viewers indulging in their own favorite kind of self-abuse.

The Seduction (1982)

Director: David Schmoeller

Breasts: 6; **Butts**: 2

Nude Star: **Morgan Fairchild** (Full Frontal, Butt)

Anonymous Nudes: 3

Morgan Fairchild stars in *The Seduction* as a gorgeous
television anchor whose orbit suddenly picks up a sad-sack
and threatening satellite in the form of a fan who can't take
"Go away" for a hint. You don't need a horoscope to know
that when planets collide, some would-be lover will be
in a spinning world of hurt, but not before he peeps her
heavenly hoots in the bath. Morgan will seduce your organ.

The Seduction of Inga (1969)

Director: Joseph W. Sarno

Breasts: 10; **Butts**: 4; **Bushes**: 2

Nude Stars: **Marie Liljedahl** (Full Frontal, Butt); **Inger
    Sundh** (Breasts, Butt, Bush)

Anonymous Nudes: 4

Marie Liljedahl returns as the titular triple-timing nympho
in *The Seduction of Inga*. She's already tearing off her clothes
while being torn between two male lovers—a young pop star
and an older writer—when Inger Sundh swings into town.
Inger's been enjoying the older writer, too, but the topless
twosome sorts things out after their slugfest turns Sapphic.
Will the poor, young Inga ever find true love? We'll let you
know after we're finished finding our zippers!

The Seniors (1978)

Director: Rodney Amateau

Breasts: 10; **Butts**: 1

Nude Stars: **Priscilla Barnes** (Breasts); **Ashley Cox** (Breasts); **Chantal Westerman** (Breasts)

Anonymous Nudes: 3

Using Priscilla Barnes as bait, a group of students loath to leave the cushy college life behind gets a grant to study the sex life of liberated college women. Viewers can watch in awe as the four seniors bang comely coeds such as Ashley Cox and Chantal Westerman. Cathryn Hartt shows up in a transparent bra, which in any other film would be the main course, but here is merely an appetizer. *The Seniors* earns a T&A-plus!

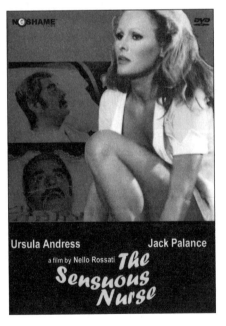

The Sensuous Nurse (1975)

Director: Nello Rossati

Breasts: 8; **Butts**: 3; **Bushes**: 3

Nude Stars: **Ursula Andress** (Full Frontal, Butt); **Luciana Paluzzi** (Breasts); **Carla Romanelli** (Full Frontal, Butt)

Anonymous Nudes: 1

What motivation would a hospital patient have to get well if he had sexy RN Ursula Andress bending over his bedside to take away his bedpan? *The Sensuous Nurse* is a frolicsome farce that begs just that question. The skinternational smash was lensed in Italy and embodies the pick of that country's sweet, ripe, orbicular femininity presented with a typical Continental eye for prurient detail.

Sex and Lucía (2001)

Director: Julio Medem

Breasts: 6; **Butts**: 3; **Bushes**: 3

Nude Stars: **Elena Anaya** (Full Frontal, Butt);
   Diana Suárez (Breasts, Butt, Bush);
   Paz Vega (Full Frontal, Butt)

Take one look at sweet-breasted, sugar-butt brunette Paz Vega in *Sex and Lucía*. How can her divinely balanced breasts and buns, not to mention the thick-spun wool of her crotch covering, be glimpsed without giving rise to considerations of fornication? Director Julio Medem's exercise in mistaken identity works on many counts, not least because he is every bit as fascinated with the heavenly Paz as is the eager audience.

a film by julio medem

sex and lucía

"ONE OF THE MOST EROTIC MOVIES EVER MADE"
MR. SKIN, CBS RADIO NETWORK

Softcore - *n.*

The sexy, fleshy naughty flicks from the late 1980s to today that keep late-night-cable-TV and home-video viewers up . . . way up.

Ss

SKIN·finition

The hunt for pleasure is the most basic instinct of all.

Sexual Predator (2001)

Directors: Robert Angelo, Rob Spera

Breasts: 18; **Butts**: 3; **Bushes**: 3

Nude Stars: **Angie Everhart** (Breasts, Butt); **McKayla** (Full Frontal, Butt); **Ray Valenti** (Full Frontal, Butt, Thong)

Anonymous Nudes: 6

A hedonistic photographer hooks up with a hot-crotch beauty who orders him to squeeze her neck at the moment of climax. Something goes amiss, and the adventurous miss goes limp. Furthermore, a Sexual Predator is on the loose, slaying babes in the same manner as the strangling administered by the photog. The probation officer is ready to round up a lynch mob, and our hero's only hope is to seduce her before she frames him. All this involves Angie Everhart, so prepare to be Ever-hard.

Sexual Red-Hair Protector

Fifty-four minutes into *Sexual Predator,* Angie Everhart jumps Richard Grieco while she's wearing only a crotch patch. Fire anyone who would dare obscure the view of a natural fire bush!

skinfo

Sheena (1984)

Director: John Guillermin

Breasts: 12; **Butts**: 2;
   Bushes: 1

Nude Stars: **Tanya Roberts** (Full
   Frontal, Butt); **France Zobda** (Left
   Breast, Butt)

Anonymous Nudes: 5

Who's the queen of the jungle? *Sheena,* that's who. The reigning female monarch of the African plain is a blonde white woman who cavorts, like the animals, wearing nothing beyond her bared fangs and fur. Succulent straw-top Tanya Roberts is perfectly natural sashaying au naturel into a Kenyan lake. Dusky delicacy France Zobda plays the luxuriating Countess Zanda, whose butt-naked pampering is the antithesis of earthy blonde Sheena's naturally nude philosophy.

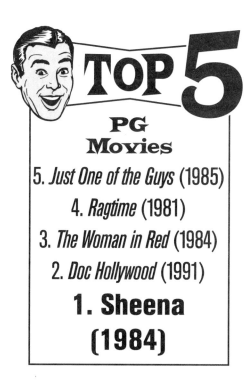

TOP 5
PG Movies

5. *Just One of the Guys* (1985)

4. *Ragtime* (1981)

3. *The Woman in Red* (1984)

2. *Doc Hollywood* (1991)

1. Sheena (1984)

Sherrybaby (2005)
Director: Laurie Collyer

Breasts: 2
Nude Star: **Maggie Gyllenhaal** (Breasts)

What was independent skinema before Maggie Gyllenhaal came along? Ever since her kinktastic bare debut in *Secretary*, she's been an absolute standout in numerous original roles. Best of all, many of them have prompted Maggie to peel down, including *Sherrybaby*. Here, Maggie plays a rough-edged New Jersey woman who gets out of prison and attempts to reestablish a connection with her young daughter. Her attempts to connect with other adults, however, frequently involve illicit sex and Maggie's mouthwateringly naked funbaggies.

Skinterracial - *adj.*
Naked on-camera sexual contact between members of different races.

SKIN·finition

Shortbus (2006)
Unrated & Uncut
Director: John Cameron Mitchell

Breasts: 24; **Butts**: 7;
   Bushes: 7

Nude Stars: **Lindsay Beamish** (Right
   Breast); **Shanti Carson** (Breasts);
   Sook-Yin Lee (Full Frontal, Butt, Thong)

Anonymous Nudes: 12

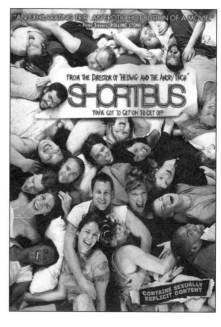

Shortbus chronicles the underground New York City club
of the title, where clothes come off and bodies get close—
regardless of size, shape, gender, or any other restrictions.
Sook-Yin Lee plays a couples therapist who has never
experienced an orgasm. Dealing with her patients ignites
a quest to achieve her own climax, inevitably leading her
to the omnisexual happenings at Shortbus. What Sook-Yin
finds there will prompt viewers to their own happy endings
as well.

The Long and Shortbus

Shortbus came by its cast the hard way. Each
potential performer was required to create a
ten-minute video in which he or she recalls an
important personal sexual experience. The number
of submissions totaled approximately
five hundred.

skinfo

Short Cuts (1993)

Director: Robert Altman

Breasts: 6; **Butts**: 3; **Bushes**: 4

Nude Stars: **Anne Archer** (Butt); **Frances McDormand** (Left Breast, Bush); **Julianne Moore** (Butt, Bush); **Lori Singer** (Full Frontal, Butt); **Madeleine Stowe** (Left Breast)

Anonymous Nudes: 1

Short Cuts strings together a series of interlocking vignettes that explore the quieter agonies of day-to-day existence. One sign of Robert Altman's deft and masterly touch with sensitive material is that a slew of A-list celebrity actresses show off everything from a humble nip slip from Madeleine Stowe to the blazing-red triangle of foliage flaunted by copper top Julianne Moore as she argues with her hubby. Makes you wonder why the movie's called *Short Cuts*.

Show, Girls

The most high-profile NC-17 release to date, *Showgirls* was initially lambasted by mainstream critics and mocked by a public that didn't bother to see it. However, *Showgirls* also developed an immediate cult following, and less than a year later Paramount reissued it as a midnight movie. The studio stocked theaters with drag queens and handed out sheets with lines for audiences to shout at the screen. It even altered the title in advertisements to read *sHOwgirls*. Director Paul Verhoeven, upon learning of his project's comeback, announced: "After the crucifixion, it's nice to have a resurrection."

skinfo

Showgirls (1995)

Director: Paul Verhoeven

Breasts: 48; **Butts**: 5;
Bushes: 4

Nude Stars: **Elizabeth Berkley** (Full
Frontal, Butt, Thong); **Ungela
Brockman** (Breasts, Thong);
Bethany Chesser (Breasts); **María Díaz** (Breasts);
Gina Gershon (Breasts, Thong); **Caroline Key
Johnson** (Breasts); **Mason Marconi** (Breasts, Butt);
Danté McCarthy (Breasts, Thong); **Bobbie
Phillips** (Breasts, Thong); **Gina Ravera** (Butt);
Rena Riffel (Breasts, Butt, Bush); **Melinda
Songer** (Breasts, Thong); **Lin Tucci** (Breasts);
Melissa Williams (Breasts, Thong)

Anonymous Nudes: 12

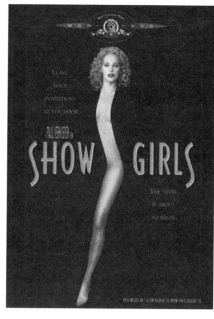

It is the best of films, it is the *breast* of films. Forget
everything you have ever heard about *Showgirls*—good,
bad, or indifferent. It is simply the greatest motion
picture experience ever rendered unto us mere
mortals. Screenwriter Joe Eszterhas and director Paul
Verhoeven have wrought nothing less than the alpha
and the omega of celebrity skin gone Hollywood (via
Vegas, of course), as well as a volcanic meditation on
girls gone way beyond wild and what it means to have
gonads and a dream in this lifetime. There is nothing
like *Showgirls*—not in this universe, anyway.

TOP 5

Paul Verhoeven Movies

5. *Starship Troopers* (1997)

4. *Turkish Delight* (1973)

3. *Flesh + Blood* (1985)

2. *Basic Instinct* (1992)

1. Showgirls (1995)

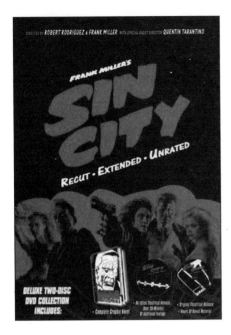

Sin City (2005)
Recut, Extended, and Unrated
Directors: Frank Miller, Robert Rodriguez

Breasts: 4; **Butts**: 1

Nude Stars: **Carla Gugino** (Breasts, Butt, Thong); **Jaime King** (Breasts)

Sin City is based on graphic novels by Frank Miller. Four intertwining stories of street fighters, street hookers, street cops, and street justice take place at the crossroads of sin and redemption in a steel-tinged world of dread. Jaime King gets porked by Mickey Rourke, showing a bevy of frighteningly flawless funbaggage when they go at it on a heart-shaped bed. Later, Carla Gugino glows while baring her gazongas and glutes to Mickey in her bathroom. Such sin is salvation.

Sin Titties

The *Recut, Extended, and Unrated* DVD of *Sin City* includes a bonus item that features full-color footage of the movie's black-and-white "green screen" shots. This enables viewers to get an eyeful of Carla Gugino's gorgeous gazongas in their natural flesh tones. Over and over. And over. Again.

skinfo

Single White Female (1992)

Director: Barbet Schroeder

Breasts: 4; **Butts**: 1; **Bushes**: 1

Nude Stars: **Bridget Fonda** (Breasts, Butt);
Jennifer Jason Leigh (Full Frontal)

Bridget Fonda has a sprawling Manhattan apartment in
Single White Female and after breaking up with her boyfriend
decides she needs to spice things up with a female roommate. She gets that and then some in Jennifer Jason Leigh,
who becomes fond of Fonda and proceeds to steal her
roomie's clothing, copy her haircut, and even sleep with
her boyfriend. The sexual tension is so thick you can cut it
with a knife . . . and Jennifer does.

Skingoria - *n.*

Nudity and blood/gore in the same scene. Where flesh
meats blood!

Sirens (1994)

Director: John Duigan

Breasts: 10; **Butts**: 3; **Bushes**: 5

Nude Stars: **Portia de Rossi** (Full Frontal, Butt); **Kate Fischer** (Full Frontal, Butt); **Tara Fitzgerald** (Full Frontal); **Elle MacPherson** (Full Frontal, Butt); **Pamela Rabe** (Full Frontal)

Sam Neill plays real-life artist Norman Lindsay in *Sirens*. He's working on a portrait of the Sirens, mythical hotties who lured sailors to a watery grave with their alluring song, played by Portia de Rossi, Pamela Rabe, Elle MacPherson, and Kate Fischer in all their full-frontal glory. On the male side, Mark Gerber is seen completely naked, including all his meat and potatoes as he poses. But Mr. Skin recommends viewing this movie à la Gerber in the scene in which he masturbates as Tara Fitzgerald watches. That way everybody has a good time.

TOP 5

Chick Flicks

5. *If These Walls Could Talk 2* (2000)

4. *Lovely & Amazing* (2001)

3. *Love Letters* (1984)

2. *Kama Sutra: A Tale of Love* (1996)

1. Sirens (1994)

Sizzle Beach, U.S.A. (1986)

Director: Richard Brander

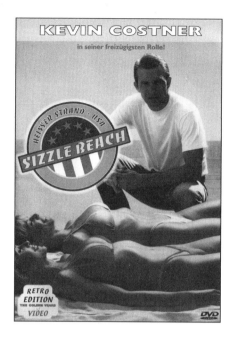

Breasts: 11; **Butts**: 4; **Bushes**: 4

Nude Stars: **Leslie Brander** (Right Breast); **Terry Congie** (Full Frontal); **Roselyn Royce** (Breasts, Butt); **Jennifer Stewart** (Full Frontal, Butt); **Victoria Taft** (Full Frontal, Butt); **Sylvia Wright** (Full Frontal, Butt)

Sizzle Beach, U.S.A. was filmed in 1974, but it wasn't released until 1986. It was worth the wait. A basically plotless tale of some hot tail trying to make it in Tinseltown, the movie captures the allure of La-La Land in all its naked glory. Leslie Brander, Terry Congie, Roselyn Royce, Jennifer Stewart, Victoria Taft, and Sylvia Wright will do anything to make it to the top, which usually means being topless, bottomless, and everything in between. Hooray for Hollywood!

Skyscraper (1997)

Director: Raymond Martino

Breasts: 2; **Butts**: 1

Nude Star: **Anna Nicole Smith** (Breasts, Butt)

Watching Anna Nicole Smith in *Skyscraper* take on foreign baddies is like seeing whole new episodes of *Twin Peaks* (get it?). Certainly, the two sex scenes, one shower scene, and even the rape scene are sure to erect something massive in your pants. Americans swell with patriotic pride as Anna kicks ass and shows much ass, too. Oh, Anna—how we miss you and those skyscrapers you could barely contain inside any bra.

Slackers (2002)

Director: Dewey Nicks

Breasts: 4

Nude Star: **Mamie Van Doren** (Breasts)

Anonymous Nudes: 1

Slackers is noteworthy for the appearance of *That '70s Show*'s redheaded siren, Laura Prepon. But it's nudeworthy for two of the oldest and boldest boobs ever exposed on a main-stream screen. There's a lengthy topless scene from a then seventy-one-year-old Mamie Van Doren, a veteran of forty-four films since her debut in 1951. There's also a comic romantic plot, but Laura and sexy Jamie King are criminally covered up throughout. Those slackers need to learn from the old-school bombshell what it takes to have a long and leeringly lustful movie career.

Slam Dance (1987)

Director: Wayne Wang

Breasts: 4; **Butts**: 1; **Bushes**: 1

Nude Stars: **Virginia Madsen** (Breasts);
    Lisa Niemi (Full Frontal, Butt)

It's a shame when a movie casts boobalicious Virginia Madsen only to kill her off in the beginning. But *Slam Dance* has some surprises to keep things interesting. Tom Hulce is suspected of murdering Virginia, and even his ex-wife, Mary Elizabeth Mastrantonio, doesn't trust him. But the flick gets freaky with the appearance of Lisa Niemi, who struts her stuff naked in a scene that's sure to make it hard for viewers to stand up. *Slam Dance* is a slam dunk.

Slap Shot (1977)

Director: George Roy Hill

Breasts: 2

Nude Star: **Melinda Dillon** (Breasts)

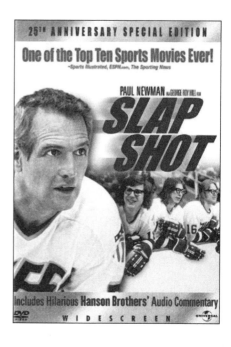

Slap Shot is not only one of the best sports films ever made but one of the funniest, too. Paul Newman is the manager of a third-tier hockey team that wins back fans through ultraviolence. After recruiting three greasy-haired, four-eyed, marginally intelligent bruisers, the blood flows as fast as the seats fill. The humor's raunchy, and Melinda Dillon exposes her MILFy mams for her first and only on-screen skin. That's enough to land your puck in the penalty box.

Slap Slot

Slap Shot was written by Nancy Dowd. That's right: a woman.

skinfo

TOP 5

Sports Movies

5. *Beer League* (2006)
4. *All the Right Moves* (1983)
3. *Youngblood* (1986)
2. *Varsity Blues* (1999)
1. **Slap Shot (1977)**

Slaughter (1972)

Director: Jack Starrett

Breasts: 3; **Butts**: 2

Nude Stars: **Marlene Clark** (Right Breast, Butt);
Stella Stevens (Breasts, Butt)

Jim Brown is *Slaughter,* a former Green Beret whose brother is killed by the Mob. Brown seeks revenge, but all beat-down and no play makes Jim a dull boy. That's where the ladies come in. On the dark side is Marlene Clark, who serves up a hefty side of breast with buns. For white-meat lovers, there's the blonde goodness of Stella Stevens, on the menu in two sex scenes and one shower scene. Gentlemen, prepare to slaughter your seed.

Slaves to the Underground (1997)

Director: Kristine Peterson

Breasts: 4; **Butts**: 2; **Bushes**: 1

Nude Stars: **Molly Gross** (Breasts, Butt, Bush);
Marisa Ryan (Breasts, Butt)

Slaves to the Underground exposes what really goes on within the ranks of a hard-rocking girl band—that is, hard-boffing, girl-girl action! Molly Gross and Marisa Ryan love each other's instruments, and eventually the two are tuning each other up in the nude. Each shows off her little cupfuls and meaty rump when they make beautiful music together. *Slaves to the Underground* doesn't hit a wrong note, and you'll be pulling your chord along with the ladies.

Snapdragon (1993)

Director: Worth Keeter

Breasts: 2; **Butts**: 1

Nude Star: **Pamela Anderson** (Breasts, Butt, Thong)

Pamela Anderson may have been at her hot peak in the thriller *Snapdragon*. Here she's involved in a murder mystery where men are being killed while banging hookers (well, if you have to go . . .). Pam plays an amnesia patient with nightmares in which she kills her lovers. It would seem to be an open-and-shut case, but when Pam opens her legs for several striking sex scenes, there's always more to investigate.

SNAPDRAGON

STEVEN BAUER

CHELSEA FIELD

PAMELA ANDERSON

A Psycho-Sexual Thriller

Underground Mound

As a girl, *Slaves to the Underground* star Marisa Ryan played one of the daughters on the CBS sitcom *Major Dad.* She's since grown up to be a major piece of ass—with a huge bum for such a tiny thing. In 2000 Marisa played Rhoda's daughter Mary in *Mary and Rhoda,* the *Mary Tyler Moore Show* reunion movie. She can turn the world on with her (vertical) smile.

skinfo

Something About Sex (1998)

Director: Adam Rifkin

Breasts: 18; **Butts**: 6

Nude Stars: **Shawnee Free Jones** (Breasts, Butt); **Leah Lail** (Breasts); **Chasey Lain** (Breasts); **Hudson Leick** (Breasts); **Janine Lindemulder** (Breasts)

Anonymous Nudes: 6

Dinner parties can be perilous undertakings. The überblowhard invited to supper in *Something About Sex* is an ego-driven writer who holds forth upon the impossibility of monogamy. Initially, the guests dismiss his theorizing as pompous rhetoric, but after the final course is served, zippers come down, breasts pop out, and sheets are rumpled. Be a lucky man and glom the bouncing mams of Hudson Leick.

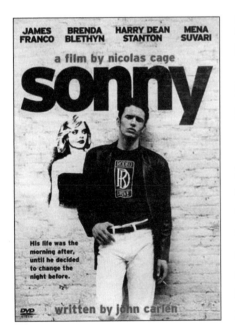

Sonny (2002)

Director: Nicolas Cage

Breasts: 6; **Butts**: 1; **Bushes**: 1

Nude Stars: **Josie Davis** (Breasts, Butt, Bush); **Janet Shea** (Breasts); **Brenda Vaccaro** (Breasts)

Nicolas Cage's directorial debut, *Sonny*, details the life of a lucky guy who happens to have been raised in a New Orleans bordello that his mother owns. And still the guy wants to break away from a life of promiscuous sex and easy money. *Charles in Charge* knockout Josie Davis bares it all, and for any lowborn brutes who long to see a rich bitch given the S&M bondage grinding she deserves, gird yourselves for Janet Shea getting her comeuppance.

Sorority Babes in the Slimeball Bowl-O-Rama (1988)

Director: David DeCoteau

Breasts: 4; **Butts**: 2; **Bushes**: 2

Nude Stars: **Michelle Bauer** (Full Frontal, Butt);
Brinke Stevens (Full Frontal, Butt)

Sorority Babes in the Slimeball Bowl-O-Rama opens with a pair of heterocurious fellas sneaking into the hot-chick sorority house and successfully spying naked, nubile nymphs. Upon being caught in their transgression, the dorky duo is subjected to a hazing form of campus justice before a jive-talking genie is released from a busted bowling trophy and murderous mayhem mixes with the mammaries and the muff mounds. Slime yourself.

Sorority House Massacre II (1990)

Director: Jim Wynorski

Breasts: 14; **Butts**: 3; **Bushes**: 1

Nude Stars: **Dana Bentley** (Breasts, Thong); **Bridget Carney** (Breasts, Thong); **Gail Harris** (Breasts); **Melissa Anne Moore** (Breasts, Butt); **Savannah** (Breasts, Thong); **Michelle Verran** (Breasts, Butt, Thong); **Stacia Zhivago** (Full Frontal, Butt)

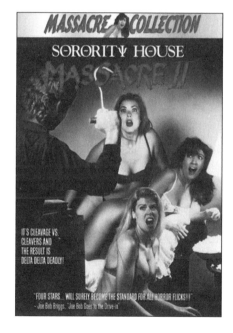

Sorority House Massacre II is worth the sacrifice of a half-dozen scantily clad sorority sisters at the hands of a homicidal maniac, because at least those coeds go down in a blaze of nakedness. Rather than give away the plot, let's just say that any film blessed with career-high performances from platinum-tressed stack of boobs Savannah, dirty-blonde bombshell Gail Harris, and curvilinear engineering triumph Stacia Zhivago has more well-rounded acting than any one film has a right to.

Species (1995)

Director: Roger Donaldson

Breasts: 5; **Butts**: 1; **Bushes**: 1

Nude Stars: **Marg Helgenberger** (Right Breast); **Natasha Henstridge** (Breasts, Bush)

Anonymous Nudes: 1

The animal kingdom is full of females who give their male mates a tough time. Be thankful you're not a penis-wielding preying mantis, a black widow dude, or one of the hapless guys of *Species*. Who could resist sultry, sexy blonde Natasha Henstridge as a space alien on a mission? Well, we're all space-man bait when Natasha transforms into a spike-spined alien and sucks our brains out. What a way to go . . . and come.

SpiderBabe (2003)
Unrated Edition

Director: Johnny Crash

Breasts: 20; **Butts**: 7; **Bushes**: 6

Nude Stars: **Darian Caine** (Full Frontal, Butt); **C.J. DiMarsico** (Breasts); **Chelsey Hampshire** (Breasts, Butt); **Ruby Larocca** (Breasts, Butt); **Bethany Lott** (Full Frontal); **Misty Mundae** (Full Frontal, Butt); **Tiffany Sinclair** (Breasts); **Kelli Summers** (Full Frontal, Butt, Thong); **Shelby Taylor** (Breasts, Butt, Bush); **Julian Wells** (Breasts, Butt, Bush)

Hot babes get caught in the sexy web of *SpiderBabe,* another welcome spoof from Seduction Cinema. Misty Mundae plays the hung-up hero who gets bitten by a radioactive spider and finds herself with her spidey senses on horny and the ability to shoot web from her muff. Misty eventually uses her powers to stop sex crimes but is nearly foiled by her archenemy, Julian Wells. *SpiderBabe* will have you slinging more than web fluid.

Spun (2002)

Director: Jonas Åkerlund

Breasts: 6; **Butts**: 1; **Bushes**: 1

Nude Star: **Chloe Hunter** (Full Frontal, Butt, Thong)

Anonymous Nudes: 2

In *Spun,* meth dabbler Jason Schwartzman falls under the speedy appeal of Brittany Murphy. He becomes so enraptured that he forgets about his girlfriend, Chloe Hunter (coincidentally, *Spun* costar Mena Suvari's body double for the *American Beauty* poster), who's tied to the bed at home. Things may start to rapidly unravel for poor Schwartzman, but they just get better and better for the viewer as we're treated to a thrill ride through the hills and valleys of Hunter's poster-girl bod.

Spider bite

In his Fifth Annual Anatomy Awards, Mr. Skin happily awarded Seduction Cinema's *SpiderBabe* the trophy of Best B-Movie. That same year, *SpiderBabe* herself—the incomparable Misty Mundae—served as the first ever Skinterview subject at MrSkin.com. Rightly celebrated as an extraordinary genre actress of larger-than-life grace, beauty, and luminous screen presence, Ms. Mundae has subsequently changed her professional name to Erin Brown, and she has appeared in more high-profile projects. We want only mega-success and world conquest for her. Still, when Misty turned down a follow-up Skinterview pitch from MrSkin.com's Mike McPadden, the Editorial Director could not help but whimper, "Misty Mundae hurt my feelings. In my heart. As a person."

skinfo

Star 80 (1983)

Director: Bob Fosse

Breasts: 4; **Butts**: 1

Nude Star: **Mariel Hemingway** (Breasts)

Anonymous Nudes: 1

Beauty is an element of all the most wrenching tragedies, and no tragic tale of doomed beauty is more wrenching than *Star 80*. Mariel Hemingway plays doomed real-life centerfold Dorothy Stratten, who was a *Playboy* model, plaything to the rich and powerful, and eventual victim of a murder-suicide perpetrated by her erotically entrepreneurial boyfriend (Eric Roberts). Moody, macabre, and emotionally draining, *Star 80* takes the audience on a disturbing descent.

Star Lady

In the 1982 lesbo classic *Personal Best*, Mariel Hemingway describes her naked body as "a carpenter's dream—flat as a board and easy to screw." To play voluptuous Playmate Dorothy Stratten in *Star 80*, Mariel very publicly underwent breast-augmentation surgery. She showed off her fresh silicone installations not only in the movie but also in a *Playboy* spread of her own.

skinfo

Starship Troopers (1997)

Director: Paul Verhoeven

Breasts: 7; **Butts**: 3

Nude Stars: **Tami-Adrian George** (Left Breast);
Blake Lindsley (Left Breast); **Dina Meyer** (Breasts);
Brooke Morales (Breasts, Butt)

Anonymous Nudes: 2

Starship Troopers transcends parody simply because it goes
beyond the kitschy space-invader genre to which it pays
homage. The excitement of battle rarely wanes, and when
there is a lapse in the spectacular special effects, the pause
serves only to increase the impact of the next grand-mal
attack. *Starship Troopers* is a seizure ready to strike, and strike
it does with a classic multigirl shower scene featuring Tami-
Adrian George, Blake Lindsley, Dina Meyer, and Brooke
Morales. That's a lot of *Starship* boobers.

Steambath (1972)

Director: Burt Brinckerhoff

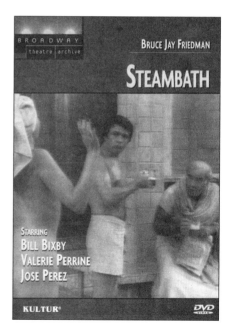

Breasts: 1; **Butts**: 1

Nude Star: **Valerie Perrine** (Right Breast, Butt)

Bill Bixby and some strangers unexpectedly wake up in a
steambath. They don't know how they got there or when
they got there; all they know is that it's gettin' hot in here!
They try to find a way out, but there isn't one. Our sweaty
stars begin telling each other their stories, and we slowly
realize—along with them—that they might be in the afterlife.
This is one of those great stories that could only be made
in the wacky, wonderful '70s!

Still Smokin' (1983)

Director: Tommy Chong

Breasts: 22; **Butts**: 3; **Bushes**: 1

Nude Star: **Linnea Quigley** (Breasts, Butt)

Anonymous Nudes: 10

Sex and dope are a combination that's always good for a few hearty laughs, especially when exploited by the smoked-out comedic vision of Cheech Marin and Tommy Chong in their midcareer highlight *Still Smokin'*. The overbaked duo star as themselves on a trip to that capital of legal prostitution and lawful marijuana capitalism, Amsterdam. Awash in a cluster of nameless health-club nudes, Linnea Quigley's chest bongs will get you high where it counts. She's smokin' hot.

Scream Queen - *n.*

A term popularized for Jamie Lee Curtis after her roles in *Halloween, The Fog,* and *Prom Night,* which was then seized in the '80s by topless gals in direct-to-video shriek fests. The Unholy Scream Queen triumvirate remains Michelle Bauer, Linnea Quigley, and Brinke Stevens.

SKIN·finition

The Story of O (1975)
Director: Just Jaeckin

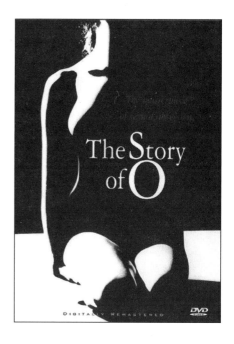

Breasts: 27; **Butts**: 4; **Bushes**: 6

Nude Stars: **Jehanne Blaise** (Full Frontal); **Ewa Carson** (Left Breast); **Corinne Clery** (Full Frontal, Butt); **Christiane Minazzoli** (Breasts, Butt); **Albane Navizet** (Breasts); **Sylvie Olivier** (Breasts, Bush); **Nadine Perles** (Full Frontal); **Li Sellgren** (Breasts)

Anonymous Nudes: 6

Corinne Clery, as the title character in *The Story of O*, joins boyfriend Udo Kier at a retreat in Spain, where she's taught the ropes, so to speak, of bondage and slavery. This comes in handy for Udo, who's in debt to his stepbrother. All is forgiven once he hands O over as property. And you'll also want to go "Ooh" over Jehanne Blaise, Ewa Carson, Christiane Minazzoli, Albane Navizet, Sylvie Olivier, Nadine Perles, and Li Sellgren. *O*, what a feeling!

Just Jaeckin
Eyeful tower.

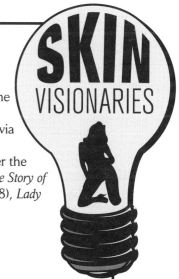

"I saw Sylvia with short hair, and she wasn't what I expected for the role. I don't know why I said, 'That's the girl.' It was an instinctual choice." So explains director Just Jaeckin of his decision to cast Sylvia Kristel in the lead of his world-changing erotic opus *Emmanuelle* (1974). The French filmmaker used his natural flair for arousal over the next decade to build an indelible body of sexy work, including *The Story of O* (1975), *The French Woman* (1977), *The Last Romantic Lover* (1978), *Lady Chatterley's Lover* (1981), and *Gwendoline* (1984).

Top 501 DVDs: *Emmanuelle* (1974), *Gwendoline* (1984), *Lady Chatterley's Lover* (1981), *The Story of O* (1975)

Storytelling (2001)

Director: Todd Solondz

Breasts: 4; Butts: 2; Bushes: 1

Nude Stars: **Selma Blair** (Breasts, Butt);
Aleksa Palladino (Full Frontal, Butt)

Director Todd Solondz spins a pair of potent yarns in *Storytelling,* the first of which features diminutive dreamboat Selma Blair as a gullible college student who ends up having some very non-PC sex with her college instructor. If you've ever wondered about the origin of Howard Stern's audio clip of a chick yelling a variation of the phrase "F me N word!" wonder no more.

Story Yelling

Storytelling's theatrical audiences didn't get the whole story. Pressured to make cuts to secure an R rating, director Todd Solondz opted to flip off the censors by covering Selma Blair and Robert Wisdom with a computer-generated big orange block during their skinfamously loud sex scene. The *Storytelling* DVD includes the option of viewing those altered scenes. Either way, nothing's there to impede one's enjoyment of Selma shouting, "Fuck me, [N word]!"

skinfo

Straw Dogs (1971)

Director: Sam Peckinpah

Breasts: 2

Nude Star: **Susan George** (Breasts)

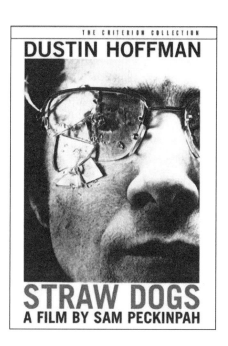

Straw Dogs casts Dustin Hoffman as a mathematician who moves back to his wife Susan George's hometown in Scotland so he can have some solitude and get some work done. The natives have some other plans, though . . . the most important of which involves getting their filthy mitts on Susan. Director Sam Peckinpah does an outstanding job blurring the lines of all the conflicts, except the revenge aspect, which exonerates Hoffman in the end—*after* Susan gets naked.

Dogs' Life

Straw Dogs was twice banned by the British Board of Film Classification in 1999 when the producers refused to cut the "rape scene" and any signs that George was "enjoying" the proceedings. The BBFC eventually caved, and by 2002, the uncut version was released on DVD and VHS.

skinfo

Stripped to Kill (1987)

Director: Katt Shea

Breasts: 16

Nude Stars: **Carlye Byron** (Breasts, Thong);
Tracey Crowder (Breasts, Thong); **Michelle
Foreman** (Breasts, Thong); **Pia Kamahaki** (Breasts);
Debra Lamb (Breasts, Thong); **Kay Lenz** (Breasts,
Thong); **Lucia Lexington** (Breasts, Thong); **Debbie
Nassar** (Breasts, Thong)

The innovative detective thriller *Stripped to Kill* places its
hard-nosed heroine cop (Kay Lenz) on a nightclub stage
and trains a spotlight on her as she peels off her tawdry
costume and reveals her concealed wonders. A sexually
frustrated homicidal freak has been knocking off exotic
dancers, and Kay's tender bits are dangled as murderer bait.
The mammary lures are bound to bring off any innocent
males who happen to gaze upon them as well.

Stripped to Thrill

Stripped to Kill director Katt Shea knows a thing or
(more specifically) two about peeling down on
camera. Katt is a former B-movie actress who
bared flesh in *My Tutor* (1983) and *Barbarian Queen*
(1985) among other grindhouse faves.

skinfo

Striptease (1996)

Director: Andrew Bergman

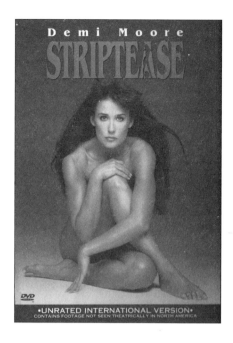

Breasts: 14; **Butts**: 1

Nude Stars: **Daphne Duplaix** (Breasts); **Demi Moore** (Breasts, Thong); **Pandora Peaks** (Breasts); **Rena Riffel** (Breasts, Thong); **Dina Spybey** (Breasts, Thong); **Barbara Alyn Woods** (Breasts, Thong)

Anonymous Nudes: 2

In *Striptease,* Demi Moore is a single mom who strips to pay the bills. She's trying to get back custody of her daughter and gets the chance to make a powerful friend once cuckoo congressman Burt Reynolds develops an understandable fixation on her. Demi and her peak-condition peaks give a fine perv-formance, but her rock-solid bod gets some stiff competition courtesy of top-heavy and shirt-free costars Daphne Duplaix, Pandora Peaks, Dina Spybey, and Barbara Alyn Woods.

The Stud (1978)

Director: Quentin Masters

Breasts: 16; **Butts**: 3; **Bushes**: 2

Nude Stars: **Minah Bird** (Breasts); **Felicity Buirski** (Breasts); **Joan Collins** (Breasts, Butt); **Emma Jacobs** (Breasts); **Sue Lloyd** (Breasts)

Anonymous Nudes: 3

Made at the tail end of the golden age of drive-in depravity, *The Stud* tells the tale of a hung, handsome, and hungry waiter who seeks to better his station by slipping double portions of dong to the boss's wife (Joan Collins). Of course, she, being a woman, can't keep the sexing a secret from her friends, and soon a whole pack of rich, love-addicted women are lined up hoping to give the waiter's career a hand.

Sugar Cookies (1973)

Director: Theodore Gershuny

Breasts: 8; **Butts**: 3; **Bushes**: 3

Nude Stars: **Maureen Byrnes** (Breasts, Butt); **Lynn Lowry** (Full Frontal, Butt); **Jennifer Welles** (Full Frontal); **Mary Woronov** (Full Frontal, Butt)

Sugar Cookies shows how an adult film could accommodate both hot sex and a compelling story line. Mary Woronov stars as a lesbian out for revenge on the porn director who caused her lover's death. Her plot involves seducing Lynn Lowry, who takes on a double role as both Woronov's former lover and her new replacement. There's plenty to make you toss off in *Cookies*.

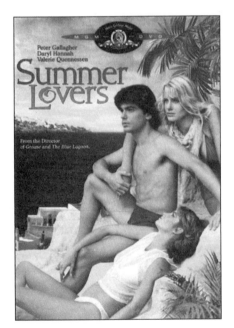

Summer Lovers (1982)

Director: Randal Kleiser

Breasts: 93; **Butts**: 17; **Bushes**: 10

Nude Stars: **Daryl Hannah** (Breasts, Butt); **Valérie Quennessen** (Full Frontal, Butt)

Anonymous Nudes: 65

Daryl Hannah and Peter Gallagher are young, beautiful, and on vacation in Greece in *Summer Lovers*. Their happiness hits a hitch, though, after Daryl learns that Peter's peter has had its way with local gal Valérie Quennessen. Maybe she's intoxicated by that Greek island air, but Daryl surprises everyone by deciding that Peter can certainly be shared by both of them. The ménage stays strictly heterosexual, but Daryl and Valérie sure seem to enjoy being around each other's nakedness.

Sunset Grill (1993)

Director: Kevin Connor

Breasts: 6; **Butts**: 3; **Bushes**: 2

Nude Stars: **Alexandra Paul** (Breasts, Butt);
Lori Singer (Breasts, Butt, Bush, Thong); **Sandra Wild** (Full Frontal, Butt)

In *Sunset Grill,* Peter Weller is a miserable ex-cop working as a private dick, and he's even more miserable when he has to team up with the lover of his ex-wife, Alexandra Paul. She's been murdered—which is a real crime against nature— and the trail leads to rich nutcases using illegal immigrants as organ banks. Meanwhile, you'll bank your organ at an angle once you see the sunny bods of Alexandra, Lori Singer, and Sandra Wild.

Sunset Strip (1992)

Director: Paul G. Volk

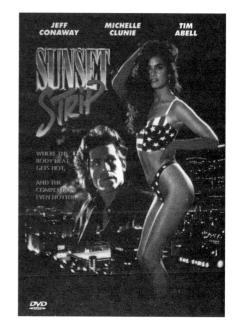

Breasts: 22

Nude Stars: **Cameron** (Breasts, Thong); **Michelle Clunie** (Breasts, Thong); **Michelle Foreman** (Breasts, Thong); **Lori Jo Hendrix** (Breasts, Thong); **Tanya Moon** (Breasts)

Anonymous Nudes: 6

Exotic dancer wannabe Heather (Michelle Foreman) is drawn to dropping her drawers at the sultriest nudie club in town in *Sunset Strip.* Heather becomes a pro at the pole, grooving and glistening among the groans of sex-happy, satisfied men. When Heather starts dancing in the pants of a conniving customer (Jeff Conaway) offstage, she starts to question her lusty lifestyle and wonders if she should change her skinful ways.

Superchick (1973)

Director: Ed Forsyth

Breasts: 9; **Butts**: 3; **Bushes**: 2

Nude Stars: **Uschi Digard** (Breasts, Butt, Bush); **Flo Gerrish** (Left Breast); **Joyce Jillson** (Breasts, Butt); **Candy Samples** (Breasts)

Anonymous Nudes: 1

Mousy stewardess Joyce Jillson leads a secret life as a golden-maned, karate-kicking nympho in *Superchick*. While her vagina encounters a bevy of men, Joyce encounters a supercast of kinky characters. Uschi Digard is a lesbian porn star showing off her amazing bod, Flo Gerrish livens up a party with her superbreasts, and Candy Samples goes naughty and nautical. But even though Jillson shows off plenty of her jujubes, you can still occasionally catch a not-so-superchick filling in as her body double.

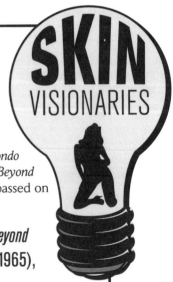

SKIN VISIONARIES

Russ Meyer
The Bosom King.

The Maven of All Things Mammary, war vet Russ Meyer trained his peacetime camera on explosive bombshells of another kind: Amazonian superwomen with impossibly expansive upper anatomies. Meyer's drive-in epics are two-of-a-kind cult classics: *Mondo Topless* (1966), *Vixen!* (1968), *Cherry, Harry & Raquel!* (1969), and *Beyond the Valley of the Dolls* (1970). In 2004 the Archduke of Amplitude passed on to the Maidenform Factory in the Sky.

Top 501 DVDs: *Beneath the Valley of the Ultra-Vixens* (1979), *Beyond the Valley of the Dolls* (1970), *Mondo Topless* (1966), *Mudhoney* (1965), *Supervixens* (1975), *Up!* (1976), *Vixen!* (1968)

Supervixens (1975)

Director: Russ Meyer

Breasts: 9; **Butts**: 3; **Bushes**: 3

Nude Stars: **Ann Marie** (Breasts);
Uschi Digard (Full Frontal, Butt);
Shari Eubank (Full Frontal, Butt);
Sharon Kelly (Left Breast); **Deborah McGuire** (Full Frontal, Butt)

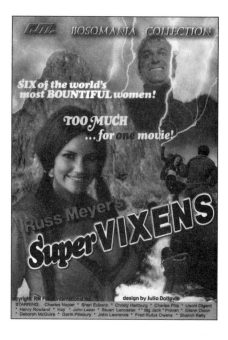

In Russ Meyer's comeback caper *Supervixens*, Charles Pitts is a gas jockey who has to take off after cop Charles Napier frames him for the murder of his wife. He soon discovers that America is full of crazy, huge-breasted nymphomaniacs who want to come to his assistance. The legendary Haji keeps her tight clothes on, but there's supernudity from the likes of Uschi Digard, Shari Eubank, Deborah McGuire, and more!

Superb *Vixens*

Supervixens, the first film written by mammary maestro Russ Meyer himself, is one of the great indie success stories of '70s cinema. It was shot for under $100,000 and went on to make $4 million during its initial release in North America alone. That buys a lot of F-cup bras!

skinfo

SCIENCE MADE HIM A MONSTER!

Swamp Thing (1982)

Director: Wes Craven

Breasts: 2

Nude Star: **Adrienne Barbeau** (Breasts)

Ray Wise has an accident in his swamp lab and ends up as
. . . well, a swamp thing. Louis Jourdan is the evil Arcane,
who's also anxious to become a marshy monster, while
Adrienne Barbeau plays a government agent who dips
skinny in a swamp. Adrienne's things will turn you swampy.

.

Swamp Things

The PG-rated *Swamp Thing* caused a ruckus when it
arrived on DVD. A Dallas woman rented it for her
kids and went into a tizzy upon seeing Adrienne
Barbeau's bombers. The irate lady actually got
MGM to recall the DVD. Thanks a lot, Mom.

skinfo

Sweet Justice (1992)

Director: Allen Plone

Breasts: 11; **Butts**: 3

Nude Stars: **Finn Carter** (Breasts); **Catherine Hickland** (Breasts, Butt); **Marjean Holden** (Breasts, Butt); **Kathleen Kinmont** (Breasts); **Michelle McCormick** (Left Breast, Butt); **Cheryl Paris** (Breasts)

Sweet Justice is kind of an environmental action movie about bad guys who dump toxic waste and threaten a town's drinking water. When Cheryl Paris, as the city councilor who tries to stop them, is murdered (thankfully, not before exposing her breasts), her sister forms an all-female martial-arts revenge squad. Before they fight, however, they need to get clean, and Catherine Hickland, Kathleen Kinmont, and Finn Carter show their floaters in a hot tub. Sweet!

Swimming Pool (2003)

Director: François Ozon

Breasts: 4; **Butts**: 1; **Bushes**: 2

Nude Stars: **Charlotte Rampling** (Full Frontal); **Ludivine Sagnier** (Full Frontal, Butt)

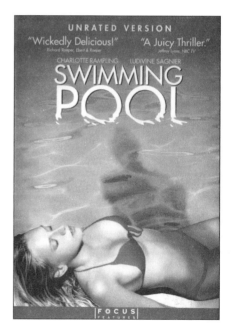

Mystery author Charlotte Rampling goes to France to stay at her publisher's summer digs and fight her writer's block. The old typewriter is humming along when Ludivine Sagnier unexpectedly shows up to administer hummers among the lucky villagers. She's the publisher's randy daughter and likes to use the swimming pool topless and ride the town's boys completely naked. Charlotte finds the sexually adventure-some girl an inspiration, and the pages keep coming, as does the audience.

The Swinging Cheerleaders (1974)

Director: Jack Hill

Breasts: 6; **Butts**: 1

Nude Stars: **Jo Johnston** (Breasts, Butt); **Rosanne Katon** (Breasts); **Cheryl "Rainbeaux" Smith** (Breasts)

The Swinging Cheerleaders is the Watergate of wank films. Aspiring muckraker Jo Johnston plays a radical college reporter intent on taking down the antifeminist cheerleading squad by infiltrating its ranks. But how can she resist the top-heavy charms of future *Playboy* Playmate Rosanne Katon and the studly quarterback? The addled hippies are vanquished, and Jo is saved from a life of dirty hair and love beads. Swing is in the air!

Jack Hill
Jack's Hills.

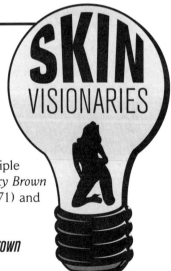

Described by Quentin Tarantino as "the Howard Hawks of exploitation," Jack Hill excelled in every B-movie genre he ever touched, from the whacked-out horror of *Spider Baby* (1968) to the pom-pom power of *The Swinging Cheerleaders* (1974) to the girl gangs of *Switchblade Sisters* (1975). Hill also helmed multiple masterworks in the fields of blaxploitation—*Coffy* (1973) and *Foxy Brown* (1974)—as well as women in prison, with *The Big Doll House* (1971) and *The Big Bird Cage* (1972).

Top 501 DVDs: *The Big Bird Cage* (1972), *Coffy* (1973), *Foxy Brown* (1974), *The Swinging Cheerleaders* (1974)

Swordfish (2001)

Director: Dominic Sena

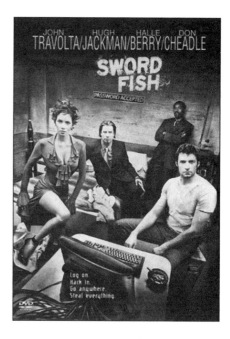

Breasts: 2

Nude Star: **Halle Berry** (Breasts)

Swordfish sees Hugh Jackman and Halle Berry joining forces with G-man John Travolta to form the covert counterterrorist unit Black Cell. They plan to gain access to powerful secrets and mountains of money with hopes of harpooning rebel sharks plaguing the city. Things go along swimmingly as soon as Halle storms them all with her form by dropping her top for some fun in the sun, giving her cocoa cans a sextraspecial splash of tan.

Swinging *Cheerleader*

Swinging Cheerleaders star Cheryl "Rainbeaux" Smith kept a big secret from the film's producers. Her eye-popping topless scene thirteen minutes in shocked Rainbeaux boosters, as the formerly demure-bosomed blonde babe had sprouted mightily buoyant milk balloons. The reason? She was three months pregnant. In *Revenge of the Cheerleaders* (1976), Rainbeaux bares her no-longer-secret nine-months-pregnant(!) body and appears with her real-life baby Justin after the movie's end credits.

skinfo

Sword Cash

Gossip tabloids reported that Halle Berry earned $500,000 for her topless moment in *Swordfish*. That's a cool quarter-mil for each hot Berry!

skinfo

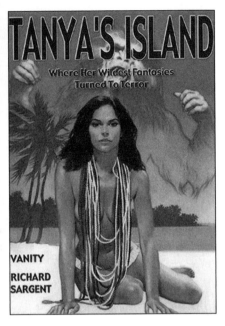

VANITY
RICHARD
SARGENT

Tanya's Island (1980)

Director: Alfred Sole

Breasts: 2; **Butts**: 1; **Bushes**: 1

Nude Stars: **Vanity** (Full Frontal, Butt)

In *Tanya's Island,* Vanity tries to escape an abusive boyfriend by delving into a fantasy that finds her on a deserted island . . . well, not so deserted. Her boyfriend is there, as is an antagonistic ape. Vanity then proceeds to get naked and bang her beau while the gorilla gets jealous. Can you blame him? No man is an island, true; but if Vanity is stranded there, no man wants to get off . . . that's because she's already gotten him off.

Tarzan, the Ape Man (1981)

Director: John Derek

Breasts: 37; **Butts**: 1; **Bushes**: 1

Nude Star: **Bo Derek** (Full Frontal, Butt)

Anonymous Nudes: 18

You meet the most interesting people when you venture into the African jungle, particularly if you happen to be a stunning blonde of the ilk so magnificently embodied by Bo Derek in *Tarzan, the Ape Man.* No trip to the Dark Continent is complete without being kidnapped by natives, menaced by fierce beasts, and creeped out by reptiles, of both the scaly and the human varieties. What is a defenseless girl to do? Purse her lips, drop her clothing, and wait for Tarzan to swing in for the rescue.

Teenage Caveman (2001)

Director: Larry Clark

Breasts: 8; **Butts**: 1

Nude Stars: **Crystal Celeste Grant** (Breasts);
   Hayley Keenan (Breasts); **Tiffany Limos** (Breasts,
   Butt); **Tara Subkoff** (Breasts)

Teenage Caveman takes place in an apocalyptic future, where
mankind has returned to cave dwelling. One band of rebels
ventures out, learns to read by picking up discarded porn
mags, and hooks up with a hedonistic couple. They turn the
primitives on to alcohol, drugs, and sex, which have been
outlawed back in the caves. Trouble is, once the ladies take
the cavemen's clubs between their legs, they explode!
You'll know the feeling.

Threesome - *n.*

The French call it ménage à trois, and everybody else just
refers to it as fantasy made flesh . . . times three! One
is never enough, and two is too much! There's nothing
better than three for the price of come!

Therese and Isabelle (1968)

Director: Radley Metzger

Breasts: 5; **Butts**: 5

Nude Stars: **Anna Gaël** (Breasts, Butt);
    Essy Persson (Breasts, Butt)

Anonymous Nudes: 3

All grown-up (and out) former prep-school student Therese (Essy Persson) returns to her old boarding school after a twenty-year absence in *Therese and Isabelle*. While tripping down mammary lane, the former coed delights in past intense skinstruction with her breast buddy, Isabelle (Anna Gaël). For the fine flashings of young gal Gaël mashing mounds with her mate, Mr. Skin gives both girls an A- (and T-) plus for high marks in Sapphic sex education.

They're Playing with Fire (1984)

Director: Howard Avedis

Breasts: 2; **Butts**: 1

Nude Star: **Sybil Danning** (Breasts, Butt)

Sybil Danning goes against type and plays a college professor in *They're Playing with Fire*. But don't fret; she's still scorching hot, especially when stripping for one of her pupils. But this is no mere sexploitation romp. There's also a thriller edge, with a scheme to embezzle a million-dollar inheritance. And a masked murderer is prowling the campus. You get gore, T&A, and the always alluring Sybil naked, which makes this a win-win-whack-off scenario.

Thief of Hearts (1984)

Director: Douglas Day Stewart

Breasts: 4; **Bushes**: 2

Nude Stars: **Barbara Williams** (Breasts, Bush);
Romy Windsor (Full Frontal)

Barbara Williams plays a bored, rich housewife in *Thief of Hearts* whose overworked hubby neglects what she needs most (hint: it's in his trousers). Enter Steven Bauer as a brooding cat burglar who slips inside Barbara's mansion and, after cleaning the joint out, notices a journal of the lonely lady's deepest thoughts and desires. Oh, does this put the horny housebreaker into a position of power, and, wow, does he use it!

This Girl's Life (2003)

Director: Ash

Breasts: 7; **Butts**: 1; **Bushes**: 2

Nude Stars: **Sung Hi Lee** (Left Breast); **Juliette Marquis** (Full Frontal, Butt, Thong); **Cheyenne Silver** (Breasts)

Anonymous Nudes: 1

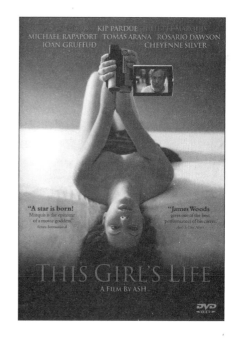

Juliette Marquis debuts as a porn star trying to make room in her life for ailing parent James Woods in *This Girl's Life*. That's not easy when your house is set up to accommodate the paying voyeurs on your website. Her gal pals Rosario Dawson and Kam Heskin are there for moral support, but Juliette provides all the support for that girder in your pants.

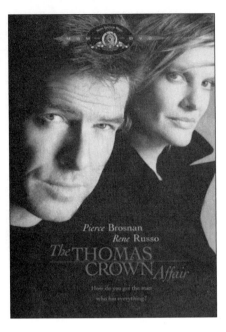

The Thomas Crown Affair (1999)

Director: John McTiernan

Breasts: 2

Nude Star: **Rene Russo** (Breasts)

A remake of the stylish '60s caper flick with Steve
McQueen and Faye Dunaway, *The Thomas Crown Affair*
does that classic one better by revealing the classic beauty of
star Rene Russo. Rene didn't let her advancing age stop her
from showing off her skintacular T&A for the only time on-
screen. Seeing her boobs is enough to start an affair
between your hand and your penis.

Thriller: A Cruel Picture (1974)

Director: Bo Arne Vibenius

Breasts: 4; **Butts**: 1; **Bushes**: 2

Nude Stars: **Christina Lindberg** (Full Frontal, Butt);
    Despina Tomazani (Full Frontal)

Thriller: A Cruel Picture features Christina Lindberg as Frigga,
a mute girl forced into a life of prostitution and drugs who
finally turns on her pimp and captors in an explosive orgy of
violent revenge. You'll be grabbing your one-eyed monster
when you see Christina surrender her body to kinky lesbian
trick Despina Tomazani in a fully nude and mind-bendingly
violent sex scene.

Thursday (1998)

Director: Skip Woods

Breasts: 2; **Butts**: 1

Nude Star: **Paulina Porizkova** (Breasts, Butt)

Thursday is the new hump day, thanks to Paulina Porizkova. The former model and current wife of Ric Ocasek of the Cars exposes her genetic perfection in this meaty nudie, sandwiched between her two other skin shows, *Her Alibi* (1989) and *Knots* (2004). It's a bit of a good-news-bad-news situation, though, as it's her best exposure on-screen to date, but she's getting raped and murdered in this ultraviolent drama. You've got to take it where you can.

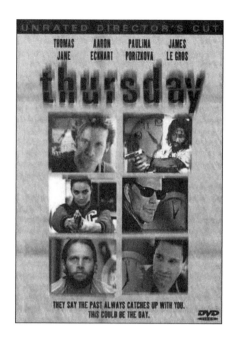

Thriller: A Cool Picture

Quentin Tarantino openly cites *Thriller* as an inspiration for his *Kill Bill* movies and especially for Daryl Hannah's one-eyed character. A long-standing rumor surrounding *Thriller* was that a real corpse was employed for an eye-removal scene. In a March 2006 interview, Christina Lindberg confirmed this. The body was of a young girl who had committed suicide. Makeup was added to the eye, and the shot was filmed in the hospital that had received the body.

skinfo

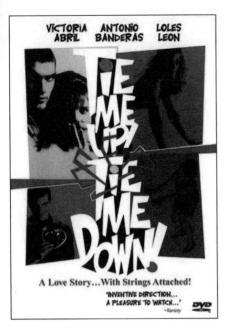

Tie Me Up! Tie Me Down! (1990)

Director: Pedro Almodóvar

Breasts: 2; **Butts**: 1; **Bushes**: 1

Nude Star: **Victoria Abril** (Full Frontal, Butt)

In *Tie Me Up! Tie Me Down!* Antonio Banderas plays a released mental patient who proceeds to track down drug-addicted porno star Victoria Abril, whom he ties up, as the title implies. When Banderas returns all beaten up after trying to score for her, she gives him a pity fuck. After that, he doesn't need rope to keep this sexy thing at his side. Bondage makes the heart grow fonder.

High *Tie*

Upon its debut, *Tie Me Up! Tie Me Down!* got tied down with an NC-17 rating. But director Pedro Almodóvar refused to make any cuts. He wasn't bound by the conventional tastes of the MPAA.

skinfo

Tightrope (1984)

Director: Richard Tuggle

Breasts: 8; **Butts**: 2; **Bushes**: 1

Nude Stars: **Randi Brooks** (Breasts, Butt);
Jamie Rose (Butt)

Anonymous Nudes: 4

Clint Eastwood pursues a serial killer in *Tightrope,* and the murderer has a penchant for raping and murdering pretty women, such as stereotypical blonde ditz Randi Brooks, who gets naked and dips into her hot tub before being killed. Jamie Rose flashes a big ass as a corpse belly-down on the bed. But the real victim here is your sperm. The loss is in the millions.

Tobacco Roody (1970)

Director: Bethel G. Buckalew

Breasts: 10; **Butts**: 4; **Bushes**: 5

Nude Stars: **Dixie Donovan** (Full Frontal, Butt); **Maxine DeVille France** (Full Frontal); **Debbie Osborne** (Full Frontal, Butt); **Gigi Perez** (Full Frontal, Butt); **Wendy Winders** (Full Frontal, Butt)

In Harry Novak's explicit hillbilly exploitation masturbation-piece *Tobacco Roody,* incest is best. A farmer plows niece Dixie Donovan, while wife Debbie Osborne is in the kitchen cooking something up with the sheriff. Daughters Wendy Winders and Gigi Perez cavort nude and fantasize about making it with men. And there's even a French-speaking motorist (Maxine DeVille France) who cruises the farmer for a 'ho-down. No surprise this turned out to be one of Novak's most financially successful corn-porn productions.

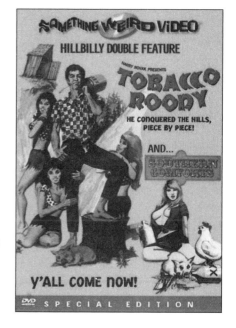

Tomboy (1985)

Director: Herb Freed

Breasts: 22; **Butts**: 2

Nude Stars: **Michelle Bauer** (Breasts); **Betsy Russell** (Breasts, Butt); **Kristi Somers** (Breasts); **Cynthia Thompson** (Breasts)

Anonymous Nudes: 9

One of the best sex comedies of the 1980s, *Tomboy* tells the story of a girl named Tommy who hates men until she meets a dreamy race-car driver. Betsy Russell plays the lead, and she pops her hood to show her beau her perky pistons.

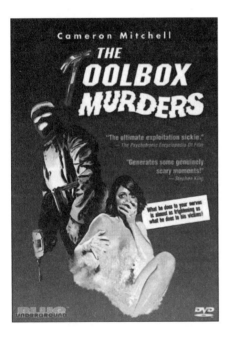

The Toolbox Murders (1978)

Director: Dennis Donnelly

Breasts: 4; **Butts**: 1; **Bushes**: 1

Nude Stars: **Marciee Drake** (Breasts); **Kelly Nichols** (Full Frontal, Butt)

The Toolbox Murders stars Cameron Mitchell as a distraught dad avenging his daughter's death at the hands of a drunk driver by . . . well, killing gorgeous gals with assorted power tools. There's gotta be some logic in there somewhere. You'll be hauling out your hammer while Marciee Drake gets out of a wet T-shirt and Kelly Nichols dips into her own toolbox in the bathtub. Marciee and Kelly will file a screwdriver in your tool drawers!

To the Limit (1995)

Director: Raymond Martino

Breasts: 12; **Bushes**: 1

Nude Stars: **Coralisa Gines** (Breasts, Thong); **Kathy Shower** (Breasts); **Anna Nicole Smith** (Full Frontal, Thong); **Catherine Weber** (Breasts)

Anonymous Nudes: 2

Secret agent Anna Nicole Smith is fighting software pirates in the swashbuckler *To the Limit,* where she not only gets her man but also shows off her mams! And she's not alone. Kathy Shower and Catherine Weber take the skin to the limit. Then there's Coralisa Gines, who is topless oiling down some poor schmuck with gasoline. Then she lights him aflame. If you've got to go . . .

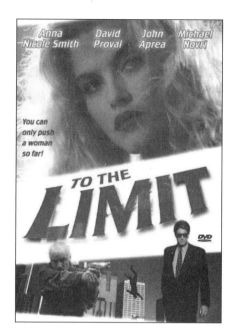

Trading Places (1983)

Director: John Landis

Breasts: 8

Nude Star: **Jamie Lee Curtis** (Breasts)

Anonymous Nudes: 3

Dan Aykroyd and Eddie Murphy star in *Trading Places,* a classic comedy about a Harvard-educated stockbroker and a streetwise con artist who get caught up in a bet by evil millionaires. The real stars, though, are Jamie Lee Curtis's breasts. She steals the film as a hooker who takes in the newly destitute Aykroyd. The unveiling of her vampish va-vooms wouldn't be equaled until the hype for Halle Berry in *Swordfish* (2001).

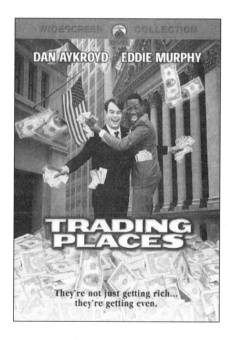

2 DVD COLLECTOR'S SET
"EXHILERATING... HAS POETRY TO MATCH ITS SEX AND GORE!" —*NY Times*
"SHAKESPEARE IS TRANSFORMED INTO A NO-HOLDS BARD!" —*Variety*

A LLOYD KAUFMAN / MICHAEL HERZ PRODUCTION

TROMEO & JULIET

10TH ANNIVERSARY EDITION
DIRECTED BY LLOYD KAUFMAN

BODY PIERCING. KINKY SEX. DISMEMBERMENT.
THE THINGS THAT MADE SHAKESPEARE GREAT!

Tromeo and Juliet (1996)

Director: Lloyd Kaufman

Breasts: 16

Nude Stars: **Jane Jensen** (Breasts); **Debbie Rochon** (Right Breast); **Jacqueline Tavarez** (Breasts)

Anonymous Nudes: 6

Troma Studios' *Tromeo and Juliet* is fairly loyal to the original, once you get past this new version's kinky sex, lesbian couplings, and mad mutant monsters. Debbie Rochon and Jacqueline Tavarez contribute some amazing sex scenes that would make the Bard hard, and Jane Jensen may not be the truest Juliet to ever grace the silver screen, but she certainly out-hussies Olivia Hussey and puts Claire Danes to shame.

Where for art thou, *Tromeo*

Tromeo and Juliet screenwriter James Gunn later penned the script for two *Scooby-Doo* movies and *Dawn of the Dead* (2004). Don't buy Troma's claim that the script is in iambic pentameter, though. Gunn gave that a shot but found out it was just easier to lie about it to Troma's Lloyd Kaufman. Nobody ever knew otherwise.

Turkish Delight (1973)

Director: Paul Verhoeven

Breasts: 19; **Butts**: 3; **Bushes**: 4

Nude Star: **Monique van de Ven** (Full Frontal, Butt)

Anonymous Nudes: 9

Turkish Delight is a delight for the eyes . . . and the hands.
Rutger Hauer plays a passionate artist, and Monique van
de Ven is his equally passionate model. She shows off her
entire canvas, from the hairy bristles to the soft, curvy frame.
Hauer goes wild, sticking a flower in her ass before spanking
that Teutonic tush. These dirty Euro hippies emphasize the
dirty, as in a kinky good time.

Twentynine Palms (2003)

Director: Bruno Dumont

Breasts: 2; **Butts**: 1; **Bushes**: 1

Nude Star: **Yekaterina Golubeva** (Full Frontal, Butt)

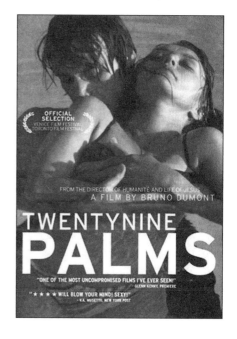

American photographer David (David Wissak) and his
Russian girlfriend, Katia (Yekaterina Golubeva), scout
locations in the desert town of *Twentynine Palms*. David
doesn't understand Russian. Katia doesn't speak English.
They communicate b(r)e(a)st in the language of love. The
carnal-crazy couple's days sizzle with sweat, until the night
when cactus baddies strip Katia and make her watch as
they ram David's own rear end. Bummer.

Twilight (1998)

Director: Robert Benton

Breasts: 3; **Butts**: 1

Nude Stars: **Susan Sarandon** (Right Breast, Butt); **Reese Witherspoon** (Breasts)

Twilight is a tribute to senior citizens, as retired cop Paul Newman serves as a live-in private investigator for dying movie star Gene Hackman and his actress wife, Susan Sarandon. Normally nude-friendly Susan uses a body double for her naked bits. Fortunately, the film also salutes the perky young talents of Reese Witherspoon, who starts the movie with a topless turn as Sarandon's runaway daughter. Your dick will be out of your pants by sundown once you ogle Reese's pieces in her bedroom.

David Lynch

Mam-happy midnight-movie madman.

One of the most admired and debated figures in all of cinema, there is one aspect of David Lynch's films on which everyone can agree: He sure gets hot chicks to take their clothes off and do wild stuff. Isabella Rossellini's rape and nude suburban stroll in *Blue Velvet* (1986) set a standard that Lynch has since exceeded with kinky doings in *Wild at Heart* (1990), *Twin Peaks: Fire Walk with Me* (1992), and *Lost Highway* (1997), culminating with his lesbian masterpiece *Mulholland Dr.* (2001).

Top 501 DVDs: *Blue Velvet* (1986), *Lost Highway* (1997), *Mulholland Dr.* (2001), *Twin Peaks: Fire Walk with Me* (1992), *Wild at Heart* (1990)

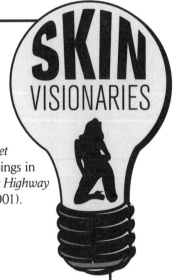

Twin Peaks: Fire Walk with Me (1992)

Director: David Lynch

Breasts: 6

Nude Stars: **Anne Gaybis** (Breasts); **Moira Kelly**
   (Breasts); **Sheryl Lee** (Breasts)

Twin Peaks: Fire Walk with Me is the prequel to David Lynch's
mysterious television series. Instead of "Who killed Laura
Palmer?" as the main impetus of the plot, here it's "When is
Laura getting naked?" Answer: a lot. Laura, played by Sheryl
Lee, shows off her boobs in a half-dozen scenes. In addition,
Moira Kelly flashes her divine pair, and MILFy Anne Gaybis
proves you're never too old to go-go dance topless. That's a
lot of *Peaks* peeks.

Twin Peeks

After being cast in *Twin Peaks: Fire Walk with Me*,
real-life Catholic girl Moira Kelly claims that she
got permission from a priest to do her first
sexual scene.

skinfo

From the Producer of "Nine 1/2 Weeks"

TWO MOON JUNCTION

Uncontrollable Passion. Undeniable Heat.

DVD

Two Moon Junction (1988)
Director: Zalman King

Breasts: 4; **Butts**: 1; **Bushes**: 1
Nude Stars: **Sherilyn Fenn** (Full Frontal, Butt); **Kristy McNichol** (Breasts)

Two Moon Junction casts Sherilyn Fenn as a senator's daughter who takes up with sexy roustabout Richard Tyson. Sheriff Burl Ives is brought in to break up the lovefest, but he can't stop some sizzling nude scenes from Fenn, as well as a fantastic turn from Kristy McNichol as a topless trucker! Beyond McNichol's McSilver Dollars, we also get to see Sherilyn Fenn's back door open so wide at *Two Moon*'s climax that it may constitute the greatest celebrity anus slip in skinema history.

Mr. Skin's TOP 69
3

Zalman King
Wear your red shoes to Two Moon Junction.

With his wild mane of hair, intense eyes, and passion for boundary-pushing erotic filmmaking, Zalman King naturally exudes the air of a foreign talent. Amazingly he was born in New Jersey. King initially broke into show business as an actor in the cult films *Trip with the Teacher* (1975) and *Blue Sunshine* (1976). He has subsequently become a brand name for highly polished sexual entertainment, beginning when he produced *9½ Weeks* (1986) and *Siesta* (1987) and directed *Two Moon Junction* (1988) and *Wild Orchid* (1990). King's late-night Showtime series *Red Shoe Diaries* is an archetype of 1990s softcore that was revived with a 2006 edition.

Top 501 DVDs: *9½ Weeks* (1986), *Delta of Venus* (1995), *Female Perversions* (1997), *Lake Consequence* (1992), *Two Moon Junction* (1988), *Wild Orchid* (1990), *Wild Orchid 2: Blue Movie Blue* (1992)

SKIN VISIONARIES

The Unbearable Lightness of Being
(1988)
Director: Philip Kaufman

Breasts: 41; **Butts**: 5; **Bushes**: 17

Nude Stars: **Juliette Binoche** (Breasts, Butt, Bush);
Consuelo De Haviland (Right Breast, Butt, Bush);
Pascale Kalensky (Breasts); **Lena Olin** (Full
Frontal, Butt)

Anonymous Nudes: 20

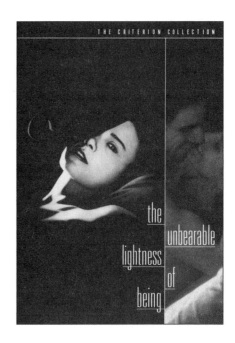

The Unbearable Lightness of Being is a Czech love story set
against the Soviet invasion of 1968. Tanks roll onto the
streets to crush the rebellion, but the big guns are fired by
naked Juliette Binoche and Lena Olin.

Under Lock and Key (1995)
Director: Henri Charr

Breasts: 22; **Butts**: 4; **Bushes**: 5

Nude Stars: **Trisha Berdot** (Full Frontal, Butt); **Stephanie
Ann Smith** (Full Frontal, Butt); **Sai Tyler** (Breasts);
Wendi Westbrook (Full Frontal, Butt)

Anonymous Nudes: 8

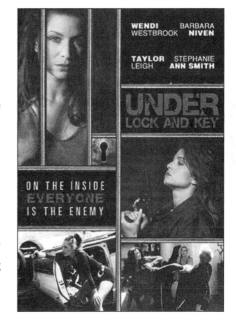

Under Lock and Key boasts busted beauties who will unlock
the bottled-up passion in your lusty loins. FBI eyeful
Danielle Peters (Wendi Westbrook) enters maximum-security
skincarceration to build a case against a drug lord. Befriending
the dealer's ex (Stephanie Ann Smith), she goes under the
covers with her new gal pal. When the druggie thug kidnaps
Danielle's young daughter, the fed enlists the help of her
skinmates to bust out and stop the sucker in his tracks.

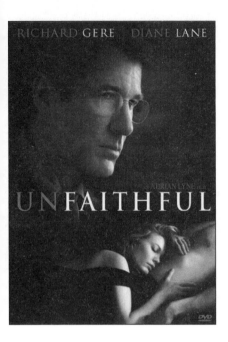

Unfaithful (2002)

Director: Adrian Lyne

Breasts: 2; **Butts**: 1

Nude Star: **Diane Lane** (Breasts, Butt)

Love and sex make the world go 'round, but as seen in *Unfaithful,* the forces of profound physical affection can also make worlds fall apart. Case in point: large-breasted, luscious Diane Lane soaks in a steamy tub and pulls her buzzer as a precursor to cheating on her husband (Richard Gere) and endlessly come-plicating their once-happy union.

Up-Skirt - *n.*

An unexpected peek between the thighs of a dress-clad starlet. Sometimes, but not as often as we'd like, resulting in a Lip-Slip.

SKIN·finition

Up! (1976)

Director: Russ Meyer

Breasts: 18; **Butts**: 8; **Bushes**: 6

Nude Stars: **Elaine Collins** (Breasts, Butt); **Raven De La Croix** (Full Frontal, Butt); **Foxy Lae** (Full Frontal, Butt); **Su Ling** (Full Frontal, Butt); **Marianne Marks** (Breasts); **Francesca Natividad** (Full Frontal, Butt); **Linda Sue Ragsdale** (Breasts, Butt); **Candy Samples** (Full Frontal, Butt); **Janet Wood** (Full Frontal, Butt)

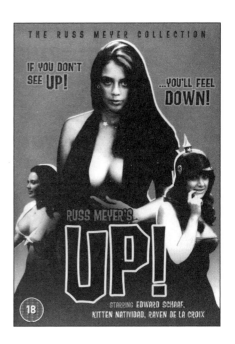

Hefty-hootered supervixens get down and dirty in boob-meister Russ Meyer's *Up!* As this fleshfest begins, a man dressed as Hitler gets his *heil* on licking the sweetbread of Candy Samples, Elaine Collins, and Su Ling. The rest is a whore-iffic whodunit with tyrannical-topped foxes Francesca "Kitten" Natividad, Raven De La Croix, and Janet Wood jumping in to lengthen timbers on- and offscreen.

TOP 5

Russ Meyer Movies

5. *Beneath the Valley of the Ultra-Vixens* (1979)

4. *Supervixens* (1975)

3. *Mondo Topless* (1966)

2. *Beyond the Valley of the Dolls* (1970)

1. Up! (1976)

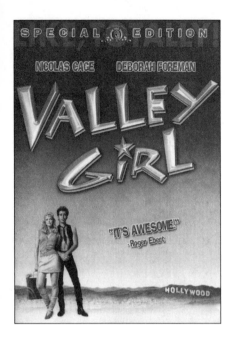

Valley Girl (1983)

Director: Martha Coolidge

Breasts: 5

Nude Stars: **Elizabeth Daily** (Breasts); **Michelle Meyrink** (Left Breast); **Tina Theberge** (Breasts)

Valley Girl is a quintessential 1980s teen sex comedy that captures status-conscious, consumer-driven, intellectually fallow, and sex-obsessed San Fernandans cruising their natural habitat in all their bra-popping, bikini-stuffing, shower-taking glory. And, fer shur, frosted blonde Elizabeth Daily takes male breath away with an on-her-back view of rack in the raw.

Hills and *Valley*

The new-wave *Valley Girl* soundtrack launched the inescapable smash hits "I Melt with You" by Modern English and "A Million Miles Away" by The Plimsouls. It has proven so enduring that Rhino Records issued a second volume more than ten years after the movie's release.

skinfo

Van Wilder (2002)

Director: Walt Becker

Breasts: 4

Nude Stars: **Ivana Bozilovic** (Breasts);
Jesse Capelli (Breasts, Thong)

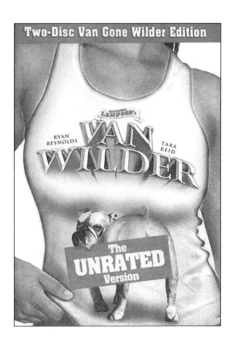

Van Wilder is a sort of revisitation of *Animal House* (1978),
with Tara Reid as the dream girl. The *Wilder* of the title is
provided by topless oil-massage recipient Ivana Bozilovic,
who sets a fire in her man's pants before he accidentally sets
fire to himself, and Jesse Capelli, who finds the secret to
studying is writing math problems on her cones. That sure
would have helped Mr. Skin learn the Pythagorean theorem.

Varsity Blues (1999)

Director: Brian Robbins

Breasts: 9

Nude Stars: **Bristi Havins** (Left Breast);
Tonie Perensky (Breasts, Thong)

Anonymous Nudes: 3

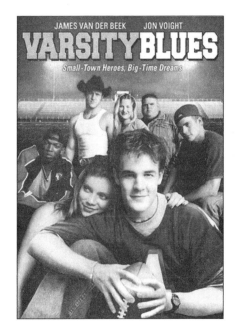

Varsity Blues is a high-school sports film that hits all the
required notes: The setting is small-town Texas. The coach
is a raging megalomaniac. The backup quarterback is thrust
into the starting role. The chicks are hot and willing to take
off their shirts. Teacher Tonie Perensky reveals her after-
hours gig at a strip club. Even a nonnude scene scores a
technical touchdown: Ali Larter's whipped-cream bikini
kicked off a confectionery trend as sweet as the most naked
of teats.

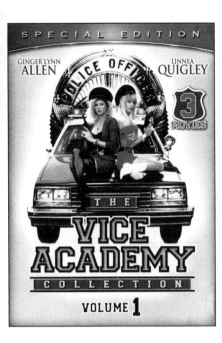

Vice Academy (1988)

Director: Rick Sloane

Breasts: 4

Nude Stars: **Linnea Quigley** (Breasts);
    Karen Russell (Breasts)

Vice Academy tells the story of a bunch of female cadets training to join the Hollywood vice squad whose first assignment is to infiltrate the seedy side of Tinseltown, which includes working as prostitutes. Some of those cadets know a thing or two about vice, such as porn star Ginger Lynn Allen in her first mainstream skin flick, scream queen Linnea Quigley, and first-timer Karen Russell. They make it a Vice Rack-ademy.

Vice Academy
Nice Academy.

This series made for two long-running franchises with "Academy" in the title—with the *Vice Academy* cast beating out Guttenberg with plenty of juttin' bergs. Linnea Quigley stars in the 1988 original as a cadet up against spoiled police chief's daughter Ginger Lynn Allen. The pair's pairs return for *Vice Academy 2* (1990) and *Vice Academy 3* (1991), before regular Veronica Carothers maintained the franchise in *Vice Academy 4* (1994). Recurring themes are sexy *Batman*-style villains, comic kicks to the crotch, plenty of disrobing in the name of the law, and Jay Richardson as the commissioner in every entry, right up to *Vice Academy 6* (1998). *Mortuary Academy* (1988) and *Ninja Academy* (1991) didn't fare as well.

Top 501 DVDs: *Vice Academy (1988)*

Video Vixens (1975)

Director: Henri Pachard

Breasts: 26; **Butts**: 5; **Bushes**: 8

Nude Stars: **Maria Aronoff** (Full Frontal); **Angela Carnon** (Full Frontal, Butt); **Sandy Dempsey** (Full Frontal); **Gil** (Breasts); **Robyn Hilton** (Breasts); **Terri Johnson** (Full Frontal, Butt); **Starlyn Simone** (Full Frontal, Butt); **Cheryl "Rainbeaux" Smith** (Full Frontal); **Robyn Whitting** (Full Frontal, Butt); **Linda York** (Breasts, Butt, Bush)

Anonymous Nudes: 5

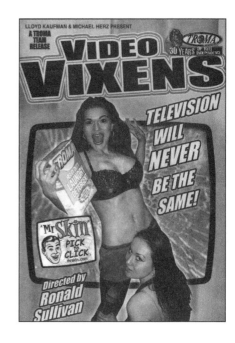

In the visionary world of softcore sexploitation cinema, corporate conglomeration of the mass media was once a major concern. The hero of *Video Vixens* exults in the revolutionary act of liberating a broadcast outlet from the stifling commercial interests controlling it and televises a bastardized awards show dedicated to glorifying stag films. Do we need to point out that this paean to all things erotic is in effect a loosely connected sketch-comedy vehicle that is every bit as puerile as it is prurient?

Video Fixin's

Fans of *Video Vixens'* "Twinkle Twat Girl"–played by eternal drive-in goddess Cheryl "Rainbeaux" Smith–should note that this is the very best place to see our beloved pom-pom icon prove her natural blondeness . . . by the *bushel.*

skinfo

Virtual Encounters (1996)

Director: Cybil Richards

Breasts: 20; **Butts**: 8; **Bushes**: 9

Nude Stars: **Michelle Barry** (Full Frontal, Butt); **Roxanne Blaze** (Full Frontal, Butt); **Sindee Coxx** (Full Frontal, Butt); **Elizabeth Kaitan** (Breasts, Butt, Bush); **Jill Kelly** (Breasts, Butt, Bush); **Jacqueline Lovell** (Full Frontal); **Lori Morrissey** (Breasts, Butt, Bush); **Cathleen Raymond** (Full Frontal, Butt); **Taylor St. Clair** (Breasts, Butt, Bush); **Tricia Yen** (Breasts)

When uptight glamour puss Elizabeth Kaitan refuses to give it up for her beau, he gives her the virtual sex game *Virtual Encounters* for her birthday. Wired up to a sexcellent virtual-reality machine in an abandoned warehouse, clad only in curve-clutching spandex, Elizabeth's soon flashing her birthday suit for everyone and thoroughly skinjoying the packages of lusty lasses Lori Morrissey, Tricia Yen, Jacqueline Lovell, and Taylor St. Clair.

Vixen! (1968)

Director: Russ Meyer

Breasts: 4; **Butts**: 2

Nude Stars: **Erica Gavin** (Breasts, Butt); **Vincene Wallace** (Breasts, Butt)

There is nothing Russ Meyer likes more than a bountiful pair of boobies—except maybe a good belly laugh. Both are plentiful in *Vixen!* with Erica Gavin filling the titular role. The chest cannons and the giggles you expect from Meyer, but what you might not expect is a critique of the Vietnam War. *Vixen!* proves that social commentary is best served with an extra helping of disrobed double Ds.

TOP 5

Russ Meyer Mamazons

5. Raven De La Croix - *Up!* (1976)

4. Lorna Maitland - *Mudhoney* (1965),
Mondo Topless (1966)

3. Francesca "Kitten" Natividad - *Up!* (1976)

2. Uschi Digard - *Supervixens* (2003), *Up!* (1976)

1. Erica Gavin
Vixen! (1968), *Beyond the Valley of the Dolls* (1970)

Video Vixen - *n.*

A B-movie starlet of the post-VCR era who peels down and packs sex into low-budget, direct-to-video, and late-night-cable-TV movies.

SKIN·finition

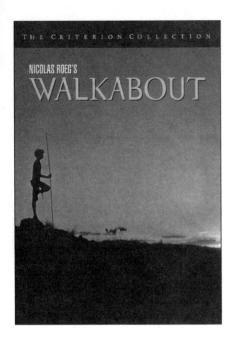

Walkabout (1971)

Director: Nicolas Roeg

Breasts: 18; **Butts**: 1; **Bushes**: 1

Nude Star: **Jenny Agutter** (Full Frontal, Butt)

Anonymous Nudes: 8

Director Nicolas Roeg's *Walkabout* tracks two white city kids, a brother and sister, lost and on their own in the remote Australian outback. An aboriginal boy appears to guide them homeward. The cinematography captures the natural wonders of the raw terrain with such grandeur that the awestruck viewer may need a few moments to realize that formative fox Jenny Agutter is going native in her embrace of nudity as a natural clothing option.

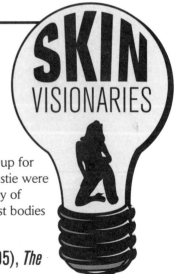

Nicolas Roeg
Roeg's gallery.

Nicolas Roeg first cut his professional teeth as a cinematographer, working with greats such as François Truffaut, Roger Corman, and David Lean. Once he was allowed to point the camera wherever he wanted, Roeg immediately focused on naked female flesh. The psychotically kinky *Performance* (1970) proved to be a mere warm-up for *Don't Look Now* (1973), in which Donald Sutherland and Julie Christie were rumored to have actually copulated for Roeg's camera. Roeg's body of work since then has been admirably populated by many of the best bodies ever filmed in the buff.

Top 501 DVDs: *Don't Look Now* (1973), *Full Body Massage* (1995), *The Man Who Fell to Earth* (1976), *Walkabout* (1971)

SKIN VISIONARIES

Warm Summer Rain (1989)

Director: Joe Gayton

Breasts: 2; **Butts**: 1; **Bushes**: 1

Nude Star: **Kelly Lynch** (Full Frontal, Butt)

Kelly Lynch kicks off *Warm Summer Rain* right—buck naked!—after attempting suicide in a mental hospital. Afterward, she escapes and wanders the desert. The next day, she wakes up in bed with a mysterious stranger and discovers they are married. What's a girl to do? Apparently, strip down to some dark bush and bang the guy in one of filmdom's most kinetic wango-tangos!

Warm Texas Rain (1998)

Director: Daniel Rogosin

Breasts: 10; **Butts**: 1; **Bushes**: 1

Nude Stars: **Annette Chavez** (Breasts);
    Frankie Thorn (Full Frontal, Butt)

Anonymous Nudes: 3

Warm Texas Rain chronicles the life of a career soldier who kills a man after the punk tries to rape sexy redhead Frankie Thorn. The movie opens in a strip bar with Annette Chavez in a silver bikini bottom and nothing else. That's a good start. It gets even better when flaming carrot-top Frankie exposes her scarlet roots. The warm rain in Texas won't be the only thing wet when watching this flick.

The Warrior and the Sorceress (1984)

Director: John Broderick

Breasts: 11; **Butts**: 2; **Bushes**: 1

Nude Stars: **Lillian Cameron** (Full Frontal, Butt); **Cecilia North** (Breasts, Thong); **Maria Socas** (Breasts)

Anonymous Nudes: 3

The Warrior and the Sorceress stars David Carradine as the former and Maria Socas as the latter. Carradine rides into a town where two rival gangs are fighting for control. They're probably fighting over the naked slave girls or four-boobed Cecilia North (she has pretty convincing fakes, too). Lillian Cameron also shows up for full-frontal exposure while being drowned in a tank full of water. Watch that bush float!

Sword & Sorcery Sirens
Dungeons and milk wagons.

Despite the overwhelming Sapphic slant of *Xena: Warrior Princess*, a cinema aesthete need not be a muff-munching lesbian in order to reap tingling erotic benefits from the Sword & Sorcery genre of live-action entertainment. No one figured out how to fully capitalize on all the potential for warrior-woman allure until the 1980s, when *Barbarian Queen* (1985) and *Barbarian Queen II: The Empress Strikes Back* (1989) made a cult sensation of battling bosom-barer Lana Clarkson. Now the formula is so well established that it reigns on screens big and small. High points include Sandahl Bergman in *Conan the Barbarian* (1982), Barbi Benton in *Deathstalker* (1984), and Misty Mundae in *Gladiator Eroticus* (2001).

Top 501 DVDs: *Barbarian Queen* (1985), *Deathstalker* (1984), *Flesh + Blood* (1985), *The Warrior and the Sorceress* (1984)

The Waterdance (1992)

Director: Neal Jimenez, Michael Steinberg

Breasts: 6; **Butts**: 2

Nude Stars: **Adriana Barbor** (Breasts, Butt); **Helen Hunt** (Breasts, Butt); **Jennifer Ryan** (Breasts, Thong)

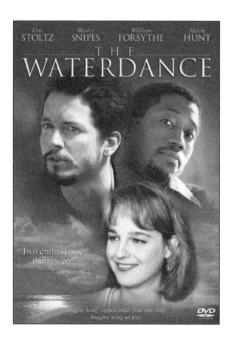

The Waterdance proves that just because a guy can't walk doesn't mean his third leg can't kick. Dead-legged Eric Stoltz rolls into a topless bar where Jennifer Ryan and Adriana Barbor are jiggling their tits and asses onstage. Stoltz is well on his way to recovery thanks to some girl-on-top sex from Helen Hunt, whose breasts and buns make a fine meal. It's sure to set your water dancing. *Mad About You*'s Helen will give you a Reiser.

Wham Bam Thank You Spaceman (1975)

Director: William A. Levey

Breasts: 22; **Butts**: 7; **Bushes**: 8

Nude Stars: **Maria Aronoff** (Full Frontal, Butt); **Sandy Carey** (Full Frontal, Butt); **Anne Gaybis** (Full Frontal, Butt); **April Grant** (Full Frontal); **Valda Hansen** (Breasts, Butt, Bush); **Joyce Mandel** (Left Breast); **Valerie Nicorre** (Full Frontal, Butt); **Gayna Shireen** (Full Frontal); **Dyanne Thorne** (Breasts); **Talle Wright** (Full Frontal, Butt)

Anonymous Nudes: 4

Wham Bam Thank You Spaceman is pure sci-fi, as a dying planet's only hope for salvation is to breed with earthlings, which is also a great conceit for a movie ripe with lesbianism, masturbation, rape, and other more vanilla flavors of sex. To get a feel for the movie, check out the character names of Dyanne Thorne (Hooker), Valerie Nicorre (Sheik's Slave), and Gayna Shireen (Rape Victim). Now get a feel of yourself.

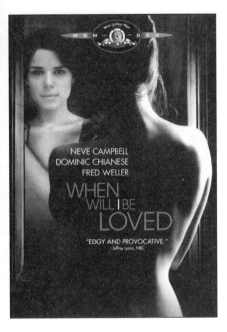

When Will I Be Loved (2004)

Director: James Toback

Breasts: 3; **Butts**: 2; **Bushes**: 1

Nude Star: **Neve Campbell** (Breasts, Butt)

Anonymous Nudes: 2

When Will I Be Loved begins with Neve Campbell's party of two and sitter appearing while wandering après shower, and it just gets better as she dives into casual sex, erotic manipulation, and videotaping her bicurious impulses. When a fast-talking boyfriend and an Italian count attempt to exploit our heroine, the tables turn, and the men are forced to admit just how little they understood of the bright girl after all.

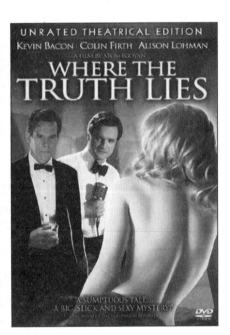

Where the Truth Lies (2005)
Unrated Edition

Director: Atom Egoyan

Breasts: 8; **Butts**: 5; **Bushes**: 2

Nude Stars: **Kristin Adams** (Breasts); **Rachel Blanchard** (Full Frontal, Butt); **Rebecca Davis** (Full Frontal, Butt); **Alison Lohman** (Breasts, Butt)

Anonymous Nudes: 2

The mysterious death of a young woman breaks up popular comedy team Kevin Bacon and Colin Firth in *Where the Truth Lies*. They share not only their box-office success but girls as well, as Rachel Blanchard gets topless in a threesome with the two showbiz players. Alison Lohman, Kristin Adams, and Rebecca Davis also contribute to the film's NC-17 rating. The truth lies where there's skin.

The Whole Nine Yards (2000)

Director: Jonathan Lynn

Breasts: 2

Nude Star: **Amanda Peet** (Breasts)

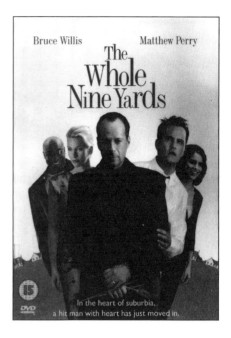

The Whole Nine Yards is a complex farce. It stars Bruce Willis as a mobster in witness protection, Matthew Perry as a dentist in a loveless marriage to French Canadian bitch Rosanna Arquette, and hit woman in training Amanda Peet as Perry's assistant. Natasha Henstridge is the femme fatale, and bodies do drop in this black comedy. But so do clothes, specifically the amazing Amanda's. Viewers will grow nine inches after catching her carnal performance, even if we don't see Amanda's Peet moss.

The Wicker Man (1973)

Director: Robin Hardy

Breasts: 31; **Butts**: 13

Nude Stars: **Britt Ekland** (Breasts, Butt); **Lorraine Peters** (Right Breast); **Ingrid Pitt** (Breasts)

Anonymous Nudes: 14

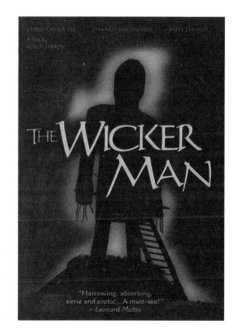

Edward Woodward stars as a devout Christian policeman summoned to a Scottish island to investigate a young girl's disappearance in *The Wicker Man*. He's soon disturbed to find that the pagan ladies of the place are quick to doff their clothes—and the heavenly lineup of heathens includes Ingrid Pitt and Lorraine Peters. This amazing thriller may lead to a shocking climax, but the femme cast does its best to prompt many more pleasant ones.

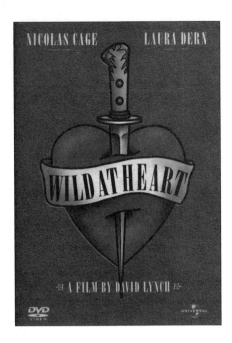

Wild at Heart (1990)

Director: David Lynch

Breasts: 20

Nude Stars: **Lisa Ann Cabasa** (Breasts); **Laura Dern** (Breasts); **Valli Leigh** (Breasts); **Mia M. Ruiz** (Breasts); **Charlie Spradling** (Breasts)

Anonymous Nudes: 5

David Lynch's *Wild at Heart* chronicles rock-and-roll lovers Laura Dern and Nicolas Cage. Laura's loony mom (Diane Ladd) deals with her own hots for Cage by trying to have him killed, so Cage takes Dern on a good old-fashioned road trip to try to outrun the hit man. Lynch assembles his usual stellar collection of bizarre villains and friendly weirdos, augmented by plenty of decadent disrobing by the likes of Lisa Ann Cabasa, Mia M. Ruiz, and Charlie Spradling.

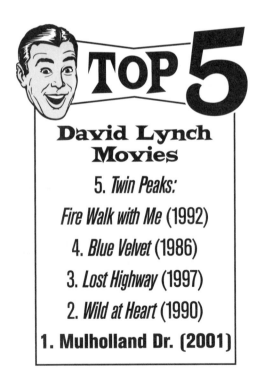

TOP 5

David Lynch Movies

5. *Twin Peaks: Fire Walk with Me* (1992)

4. *Blue Velvet* (1986)

3. *Lost Highway* (1997)

2. *Wild at Heart* (1990)

1. **Mulholland Dr. (2001)**

Wild Orchid (1990)

Director: Zalman King

Breasts: 20; **Butts**: 4;
Bushes: 2

Nude Stars: **Carré Otis** (Full Frontal);
Anya Sartor (Full Frontal);
Assumpta Serna (Breasts)

Anonymous Nudes: 9

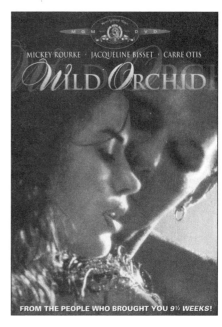

Carré Otis is a sexy young lawyer sent to Brazil with sexy old lawyer Jacqueline Bisset in *Wild Orchid*. That tropical weather has quite an effect on the amorous attorney, and millionaire Mickey Rourke inducts her into a new world of decadent dicking. Director Zalman King packs this steamy drama with too many nude bodies to count and credit. Offscreen lovers Carré Otis and Mickey Rourke are rumored to have been doing it for real in the notorious sex scene, but we're still not quite sure. Guess we'll have to watch one more time!

Wild Orchid 2: Blue Movie Blue (1992)

Director: Zalman King

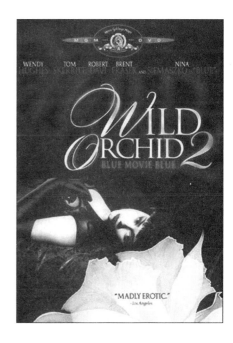

Breasts: 20; **Butts**: 3; **Bushes**: 5

Nude Stars: **Lydie Denier** (Breasts); **Gloria Reuben** (Breasts); **Nina Siemaszko** (Full Frontal, Butt)

Anonymous Nudes: 7

When a bebopping daddy sickens and dies in *Wild Orchid 2: Blue Movie Blue,* he leaves behind no life insurance or IRA, and his baby, Blue (Nina Siemaszko), is left to rely on the guidance of the questionable characters from Daddy's low-life milieu. Taken under the wing of a bordello madam, Blue resolves to fly that carnal coop, and that's when her perverting protectress reveals her true talons.

Wild Side (1995)

Director: Donald Cammell

Breasts: 6; **Butts**: 2

Nude Stars: **Joan Chen** (Breasts);
   Anne Heche (Breasts, Butt)

Anonymous Nudes: 1

Anne Heche is a corporate banker cum call girl who hooks up with seedy bad guy Christopher Walken in *Wild Side*, but Anne proves to be more interested in his wife, Joan Chen. The two hot ladies decide to send Daddy up the river so they'll have more time to play. But can they pull it off? Who cares, as long as they pull their tops off!

TOP 5

Lesbian Movies

5. *Bound* (1996)

4. *The Monkey's Mask* (2000)

3. *Desert Hearts* (1985)

2. *Mercy* (2000)

1. Wild Side (1995)

Wild Things (1998)

Director: John McNaughton

Breasts: 4; **Butts**: 1

Nude Stars: **Denise Richards** (Breasts);
  Theresa Russell (Breasts, Butt)

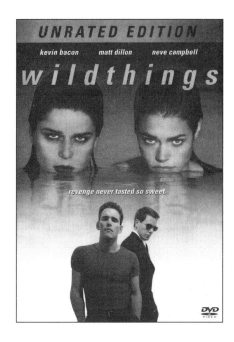

The plot is complicated, but the pleasures are simple in *Wild Things*. Never mind if teacher Matt Dillon assaulted sexy schoolgirls Denise Richards and Neve Campbell. Instead, just catalog the unforgettable moments. There's Theresa Russell baring her breasts as Denise's delicious MILF; the ménage between Matt, a topless Denise, and Neve; and, of course, Denise and Neve's poolside catfight that leads to Sapphic submission. Kevin Bacon even gets skinspired and shows off his pork roll—but we don't really need to see that.

The Woman in Red (1984)

Director: Gene Wilder

Breasts: 2; **Butts**: 1; **Bushes**: 1

Nude Star: **Kelly LeBrock** (Breasts, Butt, Bush)

Director Gene Wilder—who narrates *The Woman in Red* while standing on a ledge—also stars as a normal guy whose life goes to hell after he spies Kelly LeBrock in a red silk dress. Complications include secretary Gilda-Radner's mistaken conviction that Wilder's madly in lust with her, and there's also the large matter of LeBrock's husband. This was the film debut for LeBrock, and the former Pantene spokesmodel shows plenty of skinsational qualifications for being a dream girl.

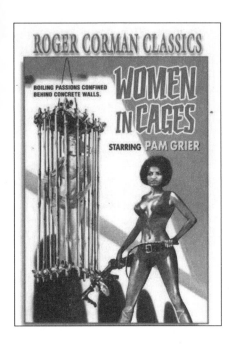

Women in Cages (1971)

Director: Gerardo de Leon

Breasts: 30; **Butts**: 11

Nude Stars: **Judith M. Brown** (Breasts); **Roberta Collins** (Breasts); **Pam Grier** (Breasts); **Sofia Moran** (Breasts, Butt)

Anonymous Nudes: 11

Jennifer Gan must be the innocent gal sent to the savage women's prison in *Women in Cages,* as she's the only one who doesn't get naked. Roberta Collins and Sofia Moran make for intimate inmates, though, as does Judith M. Brown as a junkie who's always fixin' to doff her top. Pam Grier rules as the sadistic lesbian warden.

W.I.P. - *n.*

A Women-in-Prison film.

SKIN·finition

Women in Film (2001)

Director: Bruce Wagner

Breasts: 4; **Butts**: 1; **Bushes**: 1

Nude Stars: **Beverly D'Angelo** (Breasts);
   Portia de Rossi (Full Frontal, Butt)

The bizarre feature *Women in Film* is a sexy experiment, with Beverly D'Angelo, Portia de Rossi, and Marianne Jean-Baptiste all speaking directly to the camera during some very private moments. There's an intersecting story that comes together with the three vignettes, but it's hard to pay attention to the plot when Portia and Beverly keep dropping their duds.

The woman who loves *Women*

The same year that *Women in Film* was released, co-star Portia de Rossi was photographed in intimate embrace with gorgeous singer Francesca Gregorini, the stepdaughter of Beatle Ringo Starr. In 2005 Portia revealed to gay magazine *The Advocate* that she and Francesca had been a lesbian couple for four years. Shortly thereafter Portia found love anew with America's favorite Sapphist, Ellen DeGeneres.

skinfo

Youngblood (1986)

Director: Peter Markle

Breasts: 2; **Butts**: 1
Nude Star: **Cynthia Gibb** (Breasts, Butt)

It's mullet madness as hockey players Rob Lowe and Patrick Swayze try to score their way out of the Canadian minor leagues in *Youngblood*. Lowe also has to beat a bad reputation as a wimp, thanks to his ability to dart around brawls. Good thing Cynthia Gibb can swear that Lowe's able to drive it through the 3-hole any way he wants. Fionnula Flanagan also heats up the rink as a MILF who'll have you slapping your shot.

Young, Too - *adj.*
The reason that this book only points out Susan Sarandon's nudity in *Pretty Baby* (1978).

SKIN·finition

Young Lady Chatterley (1977)

Director: Alan Roberts

Breasts: 8; **Butts**: 4; **Bushes**: 2

Nude Stars: **Mary Forbes** (Full Frontal, Butt); **Lindsay Freeman** (Left Breast); **Harlee McBride** (Full Frontal, Butt); **Kelly Ann Page** (Breasts, Butt)

Anonymous Nudes: 1

Scientists claim time is a continuum. Skinthusiasts know time flies when you're having funbags. *Young Lady Chatterley* plays with the audience's sense of time when Mary Forbes inherits her aunt's estate, finds her diary, and starts fantasizing about the explicit tales therein. Suddenly, the deceased aunt (Harlee McBride) becomes a real-life Mrs. Skin and illustrates the words of her journal in all their softcore glory! Soon Mary is getting laid in present day, inspired by her relation from the past.

Lay, *Lady,* Lay

For decades, radio maven Howard Stern has taunted regular guest Richard Belzer about the stand-up funnyman and *Law & Order: SVU* actor being married to "a porn star." Howard cites the *Young Lady Chatterley* movies, which showcase Mrs. Belzer–a.k.a. Harlee McBride–at her bare, although not quite pornographic, best.

skinfo

The Young Nurses (1973)

Director: Clint Kimbrough

Breasts: 16; **Butts**: 4; **Bushes**: 5

Nude Stars: **Angela Gibbs** (Breasts, Butt); **Kimberly Hyde** (Breasts); **Terrill Maguire** (Butt); **Jeane Manson** (Full Frontal, Butt); **Ashley Porter** (Breasts, Butt, Bush)

Anonymous Nudes: 4

The Young Nurses has everything a body needs for its sexual good health: Jeane Manson and Ashley Porter reveal their untrimmed '70s bushes, and Kimberly Hyde and Terrill Maguire round out the T&A. Even Sally Kirkland gets into the mix in a transparent bra. These young nurses go head-to-head with big issues of the day like abortion, but the film really sizzles when they're just giving head.

Up-and-Comers
"Young" "Student" "Nurse" "Teachers" at your beck and call!

The Young Nurses (1973) is a typical entry in a cycle from Roger Corman's New World studio. This particular spate of drive-in flicks focused on a group of often racially mixed but always uniformly gorgeous and new-to-the-business female professionals. Related titles include: *Night Call Nurses* (1972), *The Student Teachers* (1973), *Candy Stripe Nurses* (1974), and *Summer School Teachers* (1975). This trend was echoed later when the focus shifted to those being served in teen sex comedies such as *My Tutor* (1983) and *My Chauffeur* (1986).

Top 501 DVDs: *Candy Stripe Nurses* (1974), *My Tutor* (1983), *Night Call Nurses* (1972), *The Young Nurses* (1973)

Y tu mamá también (2001)

Director: Alfonso Cuarón

Breasts: 4; **Butts**: 1; **Bushes**: 2

Nude Stars: **María Aura** (Bush); **Ana López Mercado**
(Full Frontal); **Maribel Verdú** (Breasts, Butt, Thong)

Two teens in Mexico get their summer—and *Y tu mamá
también*—off to a good start by boffing their girlfriends. The
ladies are heading off to vacation, but don't worry about our
young heroes. They soon discover attractive older woman
Maribel Verdú, who's pissed off about her cheating husband.
The threesome takes off on a road trip, and Maribel teaches
the young men all about sharing. Specifically, she means
sharing her incredibly hot bod.

Hoochie *Mamá*

The unrated DVD of *Y tu mamá también* contains five
more minutes than the R-rated U.S. cut. Oddly, the
Region Four DVD includes a special PG version.

skinfo

Zandalee (1991)
Director: Sam Pillsbury

Breasts: 12; **Butts**: 3; **Bushes**: 3

Nude Star: **Erika Anderson** (Full
Frontal, Butt)

Anonymous Nudes: 5

Erika Anderson is very believable as a wild New Orleans gal
bored by her poet-turned-yuppie husband, Judge Reinhold,
in *Zandalee*. When his wild artist pal Nicolas Cage comes to
town, Erika's quick to indulge in some adulterous antics.
Nic and Erika delight in some serious banging—including
Erika giving boobs 'n' beav while Nic gives her a massage
with hot oils and cocaine. *Zandalee* is a toot!

NC-Zandalee

Zandalee was initially rated NC-17, then edited down
for an R rating. The original version has
never been released.

skinfo

Zipper - *n.*

What you should examine after watching any of the
DVDs reviewed in this book.

"My All-time Favorite Movies for Sex and Nudity on DVD!"

1. Showgirls (1995)
2. Fast Times at Ridgemont High (1982)
3. Two Moon Junction (1988)
4. Full Body Massage (1995)
5. Basic Instinct (1992)
6. Mischief (1985)
7. The Dreamers (2003)
8. Sirens (1994)
9. Porky's (1982)
10. The Hot Spot (1990)
11. 9½ Weeks (1986)
12. Blame It on Rio (1984)
13. H.O.T.S. (1979)
14. Big Bad Mama (1974)
15. 10 (1979)
16. American Pie Presents: The Naked Mile (2006)
17. Caligula (1979)
18. Dancing at the Blue Iguana (2000)
19. Last Tango in Paris (1972)
20. Secretary (2002)
21. Gia (1998)
22. Monster's Ball (2001)
23. My Tutor (1983)
24. The Devil's Advocate (1997)
25. Boogie Nights (1997)
26. Wild Orchid (1990)
27. Sensuous Nurse (1975)
28. Blown Away (1992)
29. Gwendoline (1984)
30. Exit to Eden (1994)
31. Havoc (2005)
32. Poison Ivy 3 (1997)
33. Summer Lovers (1982)
34. Wild Side (1995)
35. Salon Kitty (1976)
36. Private School (1983)
37. Eyes Wide Shut (1999)
38. Last American Virgin (1982)
39. Coffy (1973)
40. Embrace of the Vampire (1994)
41. Supervixens (1975)
42. Mulholland Dr. (2001)
43. Malibu Express (1985)
44. Hostel (2005)
45. Private Parts (1997)
46. Animal House (1978)
47. Sheena (1984)
48. Bully (2001)
49. The Cheerleaders (1973)
50. Ready to Wear (1994)
51. Don't Look Now (1973)
52. Breast Men (1997)
53. Carnal Knowledge (1971)
54. Zandalee (1991)
55. Body Double (1984)
56. Lord of the G-Strings: The Femaleship of the String (2002)
57. Barbarian Queen (1985)
58. Ginger (1971)
59. Henry & June (1990)
60. Bloodsucking Freaks (1976)
61. Lifeforce (1985)
62. Female Perversions (1997)
63. Caged Heat (1974)
64. Mercy (2000)
65. Species (1995)
66. Emmanuelle (1974)
67. Shortbus (2006)
68. My Breast (1994)
69. Ilsa, She Wolf of the S.S. (1974)

JACK NICHOLSON

ARTHUR GARFUNKEL
CANDICE BERGEN

ANN-MARGRET
RITA MORENO

DER OBSZÖNE
VOGEL DER LUST

«CARNAL KNOWLEDGE»

ASCOT

ASCOT

Mr. Skin's Top 69 Movies NOT on DVD (Yet)

Titles listed in alphabetical order.

...All the Marbles (1981)
Nudes: Angela Aames, Vicki Frederick
The Skinny: Gorgeous ladies of wrestling gone wild, and with Peter Falk, too!

American Nightmare (1983)
Nudes: Alexandra Paul, Lora Staley, Claudia Udy, Lenore Zann
The Skinny: Gore-gore girls galore in a smashing slasher flick, noteworthy for Joy herself, as well as the bitsy-bosomed *Baywatch* babe.

Around the World with Fanny Hill (1974)
Nudes: Shirley Corrigan, Marie Ekorre, Gaby Fuchs, Christina Lindberg
The Skinny: The stalwart sex tale gets a skinternational jet-set makeover—and strip-down.

Auditions (1978)
Nudes: Linnea Quigley, Idy Tripoldi
The Skinny: This skinnovative feature is a mock-documentary on the process of trying out for a big-screen smut production.

The Best of Sex and Violence (1981)
Nudes: Elvira, Vanity, Angela Aames, Phyllis Davis, Uschi Digard, Laura Gemser, Claudia Jennings, Joan Prather, Cheryl "Rainbeaux" Smith
The Skinny: Killer compilation of vintage grindhouse trailers hosted by John Carradine (with a cameo by sons David and Keith). This actually played in theaters!

Bonnie's Kids (1973)
Nudes: Tiffany Bolling, Robin Mattson
The Skinny: Drive-in divas Tiffany and Robin rebel first against their horny stepfather, then against Society itself as they morph into shotgun-blasting bandits.

Castaway (1987)
Nudes: Amanda Donohoe
The Skinny: Amanda and Oliver Reed crash on a tropical island. She gets, and stays, naked.

Chained Heat (1983)
Nudes: Linda Blair, Sybil Danning, Monique Gabrielle, Sharon Hughes, Marcia Karr, Edy Williams
The Skinny: The Wicked Warden of all Women-in-Prison films.

Cherry Hill High (1977)
Nudes: Rebecca Brooke, Nina Carson, Lynn Hastings, Stephanie Lawlor, Linda McInerney, Carrie Olson, Gloria Upson
The Skinny: Tawdry teens and their liberated teacher embark on a bicycle journey that becomes a contest to see which girl can most creatively pop free of her virginity.

Chatterbox (1977)
Nudes: Candice Rialson
The Skinny: The greatest talking-vagina film of all-time. Period.

Cheerleaders' Wild Weekend (1979)
Nudes: Elizabeth Halsey, Marilyn Joi, Lenka Novak, Janie Squire, Wally Ann Wharton
The Skinny: Mix part Patty Hearst with pom-pom hijinks. Shake well and serve giddy.

Cinderella (1977)
Nudes: Marilyn Corwin, Linda Gildersleeve, Elizabeth Halsey, Yana Nirvana, Cheryl "Rainbeaux" Smith
The Skinny: The very best dirty-fairy-tale movie of the 1970s is also our very favorite showcase for our very dearly and severely beloved Rainbeaux Smith.

The Concrete Jungle (1982)
Nudes: Camille Keaton, anonymous nudes
The Skinny: Harsh babes-behind-bars doings, including the final (to date) screen skin from *I Spit on Your Grave*'s enduring icon.

The Devils (1971)
Nudes: Georgina Hale, Carolyn Jones, Gemma Jones, anonymous nudes
The Skinny: Graphic Sapphic nunsploitation gets possessed by delirious high art in Ken Russell's bewitching brew based on true 17th-century religious outrages.

Dr. Minx (1975)
Nudes: Edy Williams
The Skinny: The last, best superstar showcase for Russ Meyer's racktastic Edy as a movie's central figure. And what a figure!

Dragonard (1987)
Nudes: Annabel Schofield, Claudia Udy
The Skinny: *Mandingo*-mania reignites a decade or so later in a sweaty saga of slave rebellion, where the best hills that get stormed are the meaty tips of Claudia's tits.

The Executioner's Song (1982)
Nude: Rosanna Arquette
The Skinny: The made-for-TV adaptation of Norman Mailer's true-crime book played uncut in European theaters, starring young Rosanna Arquette's rack and rump.

Fast Walking (1981)
Nude: Kay Lenz
The Skinny: An early James Woods vehicle that provides a picturesque display of Kay Lenz's lacto-launchers.

The Fifth Floor (1978)
Nudes: Dianne Hull
The Skinny: Insane-asylum eyefuls get bare and go bonkers. Whackers will dig these crackers.

Games Girls Play (1974)
Nudes: Jane Anthony, Jill Damas, Erin Geraghty, Christina Hart, Drina Pavlovic
The Skinny: It's hopscotch, hula-hoop, and hide-the-baloney in this very '70s, very endearing British bedroom farce.

Gemini Affair (1975)
Nudes: Kathy Kersh, Marta Kristen
The Skinny: *Lost in Space*'s Judy Robinson gets lost atop the face of co-starlet Kathy Kersh in a rocket-launching lesbian treasure.

The Happy Hooker Goes to Washington (1977)
Nudes: Dana Baker, Cisse Cameron, Dawn Clark, Raven De La Croix, Linda Gildersleeve, Marilyn Joi, Bonnie Large, Louisa Moritz, Pamela Zinszer
The Skinny: What happens when her professional T&A meats the boobs in D.C.

A Hard Gay's Night (2007)
Nudes: Oosha Boom, Julie Fabulous, Kate Fallon, Alix Lakehurst, Kim Martin, Lil Princess, anonymous nudes
The Skinny: The great psychedelic opus of Chicago noise-rock mavens Gays in the Military. Will Lil Princess make it to the Gays concert at the Bijou porn theater? Hundreds of nude weirdos turn up (and on) to help.

Hardbodies (1984)
Nudes: Julie Always, Leslee Bremme, Darcy DeMoss, Teal Roberts, Kristi Somers
The Skinny: A trio of (hilarious) middle-aged goofs hit the beach in pursuit of the bikini-adorned (and unadorned) physiques of the title.

The Harrad Summer (1974)
Nudes: Victoria Thompson, Laurie Walters
The Skinny: The see-quel to *The Harrad Experiment* (1973).

Hellhole (1985)
Nudes: Lamya Derval, Edy Williams
The Skinny: Bad things go down among loony lovelies in a brazen booby-hatch blowout.

Hit Man (1972)
Nude: Pam Grier
The Skinny: British gangster basher *Get Carter* (1971) gets a blaxploitation makeover, including the installation of Pam Grier in the nudity department.

The Hot Box (1972)
Nudes: Jennifer Brooks, Andrea Cagan, Margaret Markov, Rickey Richardson
The Skinny: Yet another Philippines-shot Women-in-Prison adventure, yet another must-see, only-in-the-'70s wonder.

Hot Splash (1987)

Nude: Andrea Thompson
The Skinny: Knuckleheaded sex farce features all-points nudity from *NYPD Blue*'s Andrea.

Human Experiments (1980)

Nudes: Gayle Ganne, Linda Haynes
The Skinny: Brainwashing gets added to the W.I.P. mix here, but fret not—there's still plenty of body washing, too.

I, the Jury (1982)

Nudes: Bobbi Burns, Barbara Carrera, Leigh Harris, Lynette Harris
The Skinny: Armand Assante plays tough dick Mike Hammer in an ultra-hardboiled whodunit with as many babes as bullets. Among them: naked twins Leigh and Lynette Harris.

Inner Sanctum (1991)

Nudes: Michelle Bauer, Tanya Roberts, Valerie Wildman
The Skinny: Tawdry marital mayhem drives Margaux Hemingway to attempt suicide in the movie and for her Body Double to take her clothes off. Miss Roberts, on the other gland, is the real deal.

Lunch Wagon (1980)

Nudes: Pamela Jean Bryant, Rosanne Katon, Candy Moore, Louisa Moritz
The Skinny: Mid-day snacking gets more mouth-watering than ever as a gaggle of glamazons takes over a catering truck.

Mandingo (1975)

Nudes: Susan George, Debbi Morgan, Laura Misch Owens, Brenda Sykes, Reda Wyatt
The Skinny: The ultimate big-budget exploitation potboiler set in the Old South during the dirty days of sex between master and slave, as interpreted by ham actors and B-movie babes.

Mama's Dirty Girls (1974)

Nudes: Candice Rialson
The Skinny: Sexbomb siblings find, fleece, and fry lonely men, as trained in the art of seduction-and-slaughter by their darling mother.

Mean Dog Blues (1978)

Nudes: Christina Hart, Kay Lenz, Tina Louise
The Skinny: Here's where to see Ginger from *Gilligan's Island* get naked, Little Buddy.

The Naked Cage (1986)

Nudes: Lisa London, Valerie McIntosh, Shari Shattuck, Angel Tompkins
The Skinny: Late-era entry in the vintage Women-in-Prison cycle delivers the badass goods like the best of them.

Naked Obsession (1990)

Nudes: Michelle Bauer, Ria Coyne, Maria Ford, Wendy MacDonald, Elena Sahagun
The Skinny: William Katt plays a mugged city councilman who may or may not be saved by Jesus Himself. Either way, it happens outside a strip club and a hallucinatory spelunk into professional sex ensues.

Night Games (1980)

Nudes: Joanna Cassidy, Cindy Pickett
The Skinny: "After Bardot, Deneuve, Fonda, Roger Vadim unveils a new kind of woman . . . Cindy Pickett in . . . *Night Games*." So went the movie's tagline, if not Pickett's stardom. See where the pub(l)ic failed her.

Nightmare in Badham County (1976)

Nudes: Denise Dillaway, Lynne Moody, Tonea Stewart
The Skinny: Sexy African-American coed Lynne Moody tastes the ugly side of Southern justice when she's tossed in the clink. Fortunately we then see the pretty sides (and fronts) of girls in jail.

Object of Desire (1989)

Nudes: Tara Buckman
The Skinny: Political skullduggery injected into tits-and-assery.

Opposing Force (1986)

Nude: Lisa Eichhorn
The Skinny: Crack commando Lisa Eichhorn is held in a POW camp and put through hell, which just happens to be a heavenly forced-to-strip scene of the 1980s.

Out of Control (1984)
Nudes: Cindi Dietrich, Betsy Russell, Claudia Udy
The Skinny: A prom party crashes on a tropical island and celebrates by tearing off their tuxes and gowns. Then pirates crash the bash.

Paradise (1982)
Nudes: Phoebe Cates
The Skinny: Believe it or not, the all-time greatest movie in which to see Phoebe Cates naked is not *Fast Times at Ridgemont High*. It is *Paradise*, an Israeli-made *Blue Lagoon* rip-off that features Phoebe repeatedly in the raw, along with some pre-*Bible Man* Willie Aames.

Perfect Timing (1986)
Nudes: Nancy Cser, Papusha Demitro, Alexandra Innes, Beth Rubens, Michele Scarabelli
The Skinny: Bozo brothers devise a scheme that has them posing as nude photographers. Lucky for viewers, it works.

Pets (1974)
Nudes: Candice Rialson
The Skinny: A kinky curiosity that showcases grindhouse goddess Candice Rialson as lethally sexy prey for various male and female predators.

Pretty Maids All in a Row (1971)
Nudes: Joy Bang, Gretchen Burrell, Angie Dickinson, Aimée Eccles, June Fairchild
The Skinny: Black comedy starring Rock Hudson as a ladies' man guidance counselor at a school where the most statuesque female students are getting bumped off. Hmm, Rock . . . got any issues? Theme song by the Osmonds.

Prison Girls (1972)
Nudes: Uschi Digard, Candy Samples, Donna Sutter
The Skinny: Uschi Digard in 3-D! Uschi Digard in 3-D! Uschi Digard in 3-D!

Rape Squad (1974)
Nudes: Anneka Di Lorenzo, Jo Ann Harris, Connie Strickland
The Skinny: The naked fury—and just plain nakedness—of *I Spit on Your Grave* multiplied many times.

Roller Blade (1985)
Nudes: Michelle Bauer, Crystal Breeze, Barbara Peckinpaugh
The Skinny: Post-nuke nuns of the future roller skate, fight fascists, and indulge in long, crowded group hot-tub sessions.

Rolling Thunder (1977)
Nudes: Cassie Yates
The Skinny: William Devane and Tommy Lee Jones team up as wronged Vietnam vets out to even a vicious score. Cassie Yates brings her bazookas to the showdown.

Savage Messiah (1972)
Nudes: Maggy Maxwell, Helen Mirren
The Skinny: Sculptor Henri Gaudier-Brzeska gets the Ken Russell biopic treatment. Maggy and Helen get undressed.

Separate Vacations (1986)
Nudes: Susan Almgren, Jennifer Dale, Blanca Guerra
The Skinny: A troubled wife and hubby split up during their time away from work, prompting various ladies to split from their clothing.

The Sex Symbol (1974)
Nudes: Connie Stevens
The Skinny: Connie Stevens embodies a thinly veiled Marilyn Monroe figure and unveils her own figure in the process.

Screwballs (1983)
Nudes: Astrid Brandt, Raven De La Croix, Terrea Foster, Jennifer Inch, Linda Shayne, Linda Speciale
The Skinny: Arguably the most insane '80s teen comedy and arguably the funniest as well. In a plot lifted by *The Usual Suspects*, five high-school archetypes meet in detention and plot to expose the bare parts of local prude Purity Busch.

Slumber Party '57 (1977)
Nudes: Mary Ann Appleseth, Janice Karman, Noelle North, Cheryl "Rainbeaux" Smith, Debra Winger, Janet Wood
The Skinny: The titular get-together occurs at the home of the teenage character portrayed by Debra Winger. We learn that chicks took their pajamas off even way back when.

The Stewardesses (1969)
Nudes: Monica Gayle, Christina Hart
The Skinny: A perennial high-flying midnight-movie favorite. In 3-D even!

Streetwalkin' (1985)
Nudes: Samantha Fox, Melissa Leo
The Skinny: Taut redhead Melissa Leo plies her bodily trade along Manhattan's underappreciated mid-'80s sleaze hub of 14th Street and 3rd Avenue. Julie Newmar and vintage porn queen Samantha Fox are selling too.

Strip Search (2004)
Nudes: Maggie Gyllenhaal
The Skinny: As a political prisoner made to peel down and then prodded all over, Maggie Gyllenhaal exposes her very being way beyond even her soul-baring *Secretary* role. And she shows her pubes, too.

Subliminal Seduction (1996)
Nudes: Griffin Drew, Rainer Grant, Katherine Kelly Lang
The Skinny: A mad scientist plots to subdue the earth via subtle suggestions, but there's nothing subtle about the naked knockouts he encounters along the way.

Summer School Teachers (1975)
Nudes: Pat Anderson, Candice Rialson
The Skinny: These educators put some real lead in your pencil.

Surf II (1984)
Nudes: Britt Helfer, Joy Michael
The Skinny: Über-nerd Eddie Deezen attempts world conquest with mind-controlling soda pop while an army of bikini chicks obeys his every bidding.

Takin' It All Off (1987)
Nudes: Candie Evans, Lauri Gilbert, Gail Harris, Becky LeBeau, Francesca "Kitten" Natividad, Diane Pedersen
The Skinny: The follow-up to *Takin' It Off* goes its predecessor two better: It's bolder and more bust-baring throughout.

Teachers (1984)
Nudes: Julia Jennings, JoBeth Williams
The Skinny: Social commentary sold as a tits-and-zits farce, climaxes with the mom from *Poltergeist* running naked down a crowded high-school hallway. Welcome to the honor roll, JoBeth.

Unholy Rollers (1972)
Nudes: Claudia Jennings, Candice Roman
The Skinny: Free-wheeling roller-derby ravishers—raw, raunchy, and roughin' it up.

Up the Creek (1984)
Nudes: Lori Sutton, Peggy Trentini
The Skinny: Otter and Flounder from *Animal House* team with Pee-Wee from *Porky's* to take the title in a collegiate white-water-rafting race. Those wanting to see naked coeds are the victors.

Vampire Strangler (1999)
Nudes: Misty Mundae
The Skinny: Misty Mundae sucks in this movie—literally. Here lies the skinfamous hardcore oral enchantment scene between Misty and the boner of her then-boyfriend, William Hellfire.

What Do You Say to a Naked Lady? (1970)
Nudes: Joie Addison, Joan Bell, anonymous nudes
The Skinny: Allen Funt indulges the carnal possibilities of his *Candid Camera* franchise with a formerly-X-rated romp that reigned for years as the highest-grossing documentary of all time.

Zapped! (1982)
Nudes: Jewel Shepard, Heather Thomas's Body Double
The Skinny: The incandescent '80s duo Scott Baio and Willie Aames was born with this telekinesis comedy in which the former Chachi can pop girls' tops open with his mind.

FIDAEXPORT presents

LAURA GEMSER

(Black Emanuelle)

in the NEW
and
continuing
adventures
of

EMANUELLE
in AMERICA

No one is ever the same after...

Emanuelle

A new experience
in sensuality

starring **GABRIELE TINTI · ROGER BROWNE · RICCARDO SALVINO**
MARIA PIERA REGOLI · MATILDE DELL'AGLIO · STEFANIA NOCILLI
special guest star **PAOLA SENATORE**
music by NICO FIDENCO · directed by JOE D'AMATO · a production NEW FILM PRODUCTION - Rome

Video Resources

The following top-tier video companies have proven to be indispensable in the world of MrSkin.com, as well as in the creation of this book. We thank them, and we hope you will support them. Truly, these are the best of the best.

Anchor Bay Entertainment
AnchorBayEntertainment.com

Blue Underground
Blue-Underground.com

Brain Damage Films
BrainDamageFilms.com

Camp Motion Pictures
CampMotionPictures.com

Central Park Media
CentralParkMedia.com

Code Red DVD
CodeRedDVD.com

Cult Epics
CultEpics.com

Dark Sky Films
DarkSkyFilms.com

Dreamworks
Dreamworks.com

Echo Bridge
EchoBridgeHE.com

Facets Multimedia
Facets.org

Fantoma
Fantoma.com

First Look Media
FirstLookMedia.com

First Run Features
FirstRunFeatures.com

Fox Home Entertainment
FoxHome.com

Genius Products
GeniusProducts.com

Hart Sharp Video
HartSharpVideo.com

Hen's Tooth Video
HensToothVideo.com

Indican Pictures
IndicanPictures.com

Koch Entertainment
KochEnt.com

Laguna Productions
LagunaProductions.com

Life Size Entertainment
LifeSizeEntertainment.com

Lions Gate Home Video
LionsGate.com

Magnolia Pictures
MagPictures.com

MGM Home Video
MGM.com

MPI Home Video
MPIHomeVideo.com

MTI
MTIvideo.com

Music Video Distributors
MVDb2b.com

New Line
NewLine.com

New Yorker Films
NewYorkerFilms.com

Paramount
Paramount.com

Pathfinder Pictures
PathfinderPictures.com

Private Screening Collection
PrivateScreeningCollection.com

Peach DVD
PeachDVD.com

Seduction Cinema
SeductionCinema.com

Severin Films
Severin-Films.com

Shock-O-Rama
Shock-O-Rama.com

Something Weird Video
SomethingWeird.com

Sony Pictures
SonyPictures.com

Subversive Cinema
SubversiveCinema.com

Synapse Films
Synapse-Films.com

THINKFilm
ThinkFilmCompany.com

TLA Releasing
TLAvideo.com

Troma Entertainment
Troma.com

Universal
UniversalStudios.com

Vanguard
VanguardCinema.com

Wicked Pixel
WickedPixel.com

Xenon Pictures
XenonPictures.com

At Porky's a kid can get anything he wants.
And a couple of things no one wants.

GET IT AT *Porky's*

PORKY'S

MELVIN SIMON PRODUCTIONS/ASTRAL BELLEVUE PATHE INC. Presents "PORKY'S" KIM CATTRALL
SCOTT COLOMBY · KAKI HUNTER · NANCY PARSONS · ALEX KARRAS as the Sheriff · SUSAN CLARK as Cherry Forever
Executive Producers HAROLD GREENBERG and MELVIN SIMON Produced by BOB CLARK and DON CARMODY
Written and Directed by BOB CLARK

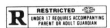

R RESTRICTED
UNDER 17 REQUIRES ACCOMPANYING
PARENT OR ADULT GUARDIAN

1981 TWENTIETH CENTURY-FOX

Actress Skindex

Bella Donna, 19
Bellamy, Florence, 175
Beller, Kathleen, 44
Belli, Agostina, 62
Belliveau, Cynthia, 204
Bello, Maria, 28, 94
Bellucci, Monica, 179
Bening, Annette, 154
Bennett, Rachael Ann, 185
Bennett, Sonja, 266
Bentley, Dana, 33, 311
Benton, Barbi, 104, 356
Berdot, Trisha, 345
Berenson, Marisa, 17, 283
Bergen, Candice, 82
Bergman, Jaime, 101
Bergman, Sandahl, 258, 356
Berkley, Elizabeth, 301
Berry, Halle, 225, 329, 339
Bingham, Traci, 31, 105
Binoche, Juliette, 345
Bird, Minah, 321
Birkin, Jane, 227
Bisset, Jacqueline, 361
Bissett, Josie, 163
Biton, Charlene, 41
Bittner, Carrie, 52
Black, Karen, 176
Blair, Linda, 234, 274, 286,
    375
Blair, Selma, 318
Blaise, Jehanne, 317
Blanchard, Rachel, 358
Blanchett, Cate, 149
Blaze, Roxanne, 52, 352
Blee, Debra, 40
Blethyn, Brenda, 209
Bloom, Lindsay, 157
Blue, Skye, 68
Bodnar, Jenna, 86
Boehrs, Jessica, 125
Bogart, Andrea, 101
Bohrer, Corinne, 187
Boisson, Christine, 122
Boland, Joanne, 270
Bolling, Tiffany, 79, 376
Bolton, Tiffany, 287
Bond, Rene, 42, 129, 130, 153,
    253
Bonet, Lisa, 21
Bonet, Nai, 128
Bontempi, Loredana, 84

Boom, Oosha, 376
Bottrell, Laura, 2
Boushel, Joy, 248
Boyd, Tanya, 56, 172
Boyle, Lara Flynn, 281
Boyle, Lisa, 207
Bozilovic, Ivana, 349
Bracci, Teda, 49
Bragg, Sherry, 128
Brander, Leslie, 305
Brando, Rikki, 51
Brandt, Astrid, 378
Bravo, Lucia, 145
Breeze, Crystal, 378
Bremme, Leslee, 376
Bremmer, Leslee, 274, 289
Brentano, Amy, 71
Brettschweiderova, Tereza, 125
Brewer, Roxanne, 129
Brimhall, Cynthia, 111, 137, 155,
    159, 160, 248
Brisebois, Danielle, 48
Brockman, Ungela, 301
Bronson, Gerie, 7
Brooke, Rebecca, 375
Brooks, Deanna, 64
Brooks, Iris, 181
Brooks, Jennifer, 7, 376
Brooks, Randi, 337
Brown, Erin (Misty Mundae),
    35, 152, 170, 205, 252, 253,
    312, 313, 356
Brown, Juanita, 77
Brown, Judith M., 364
Brown, Sara Suzanne, 51
Brown, Stacy Lynn, 123
Bryant, Pamela Jean, 157, 261,
    377
Buckman, Tara, 377
Buick, Denise, 20
Buirski, Felicity, 321
Burch, Tracey, 99
Burke, Stacy, 230
Burns, Bobbi, 377
Burns, Tricia, 164
Burrell, Gretchen, 378
Burress, Hedy, 142
Burrows, Saffron, 206
Burton, Claire, 222
Bush, Jovita, 87
Busselier, Tania, 174
Byrne, Patty, 233

Byrnes, Maureen, 98, 322
Byron, Carlye, 320

Cabasa, Lisa Ann, 360
Cadell, Ava, 111, 137, 159, 239
Caffaro, Cheri, 7, 150, 151
Caggan, Andrea, 376
Caine, Darian, 152, 205, 252,
    312
Calhoun, Monica, 251
Callihan, Meghan, 185
Cameron, 323
Cameron, Cisse, 376
Cameron, Lillian, 356
Camp, Colleen, 103
Campbell, Aliya, 275, 281
Campbell, Neve, 358, 363
Capelli, Jesse, 238, 349
Carey, Sandy, 285, 357
Carlson, Greta, 33, 219
Carlton, Hope Marie, 160, 248,
    285
Carney, Bridget, 291, 311
Carnon, Angela, 351
Carol, Linda, 274
Caron, Leslie, 96
Carothers, Veronica, 350
Carr, Hayley, 226
Carrera, Barbara, 377
Carson, Ewa, 317
Carson, Nina, 375
Carson, Kimberly, 157
Carson, Shanti, 299
Carter, Finn, 327
Cartwright, Nancy, 138
Casey, Elana, 80
Cassel, Sandra, 196
Cassidy, Joanna, 377
Cates, Phoebe, 26, 131, 263,
    378
Cattrall, Kim, 203, 257
Cavanaugh, Wendy, 129
Célarié, Clémentine, 45
Chambers, Marilyn, 22, 51, 217
Charbonneau, Patricia, 106
Chavez, Annette, 355
Cheek, Jeanie, 101
Chen, Joan, 362
Chesser, Bethany, 301
Chloe, 193
Chong, Rae Dawn, 132, 267
Choudhury, Sarita, 189

Christiani, Antoinette, 228
Christie, Julie, 110, 354
Christie, Shannon, 47
Christine, Heidi, 152
Christophe, Pascale, 175
Church, Peggy, 249
Churchill, Marguerite, 170
Ciardi, Francesca, 81
Clark, Candy, 215
Clark, Dawn, 165, 376
Clark, Marlene, 308
Clarke, Mindy/Melinda, 274, 275, 276
Clarkson, Lana, 36, 59, 104, 356
Clery, Corinne, 317
Clinton, LeAnn, 231
Clunie, Michelle, 123, 323
Cobbs, Renata, 32
Cochrane, Tallie, 285
Coeur, Joëlle, 29
Coffey, Elizabeth, 250
Cole, Debra, 169
Cole, Petina, 3
Colletin, Jeanne, 122
Collette, Toni, 1
Collins, Elaine, 130, 347
Collins, Jessica, 269
Collins, Joan, 55, 166, 321
Collins, Roberta, 77, 103, 364
Collins, Tai, 123
Comshaw, Lisa, 13, 287
Congie, Terry, 305
Connelly, Jennifer, 35, 169, 275
Conroy, Frances, 72
Cooknell, Karen, 285
Coolidge, Jennifer, 14
Copeland, Terri, 76
Cormier, Michelle, 16
Corri, Adrienne, 89
Corrigan, Shirley, 375
Corwin, Marilyn, 375
Coyne, Ria, 377
Cox, Amiee, 101
Cox, Ashley, 294
Coxx, Sindee, 352
Crampton, Barbara, 65, 145, 272, 273
Crewson, Wendy, 222
Crosby, Cathy Lee, 91
Cross, Becki, 22
Cross, Marcia, 133

Crow, Emilia, 132
Crowder, Tracey, 320
Cruz, Cintia, 3
Cser, Nancy, 378
Cummings, Summer, 68
Curtis, Jamie Lee, 158, 209, 316, 339

Daans, Lara, 222
d'Abo, Olivia, 67, 203
Daily, Elizabeth, 348
Dale, Jennifer, 378
Dali, Tracy, 52
Dalle, Béatrice, 45
D'Amaro, Aerica, 281
Damas, Jill, 376
Danes, Claire, 340
D'Angelo, Beverly, 365
D'Angelo, Mirella, 78
Daniel, Brittany, 90
Daniels, Stormy, 2
Danner, Joyce, 41
Danning, Sybil, 62, 213, 332, 375
Danvers, Lise, 175
D'Arbanville, Patti, 53
Dare, Barbara, 125
Darnell, Andrea, 274
Darnell, Vicki, 144
Davila, Azalea, 133
Davis, Carole, 270
Davis, Ilah, 158
Davis, Josie, 310
Davis, Julienne, 127
Davis, Neriah, 51
Davis, Neva, 22
Davis, Phyllis, 375
Davis, Rebecca, 358
Davis, Sammi, 194
Dawson, Rosario, 333
Deats, Danyi, 279
DeBell, Kristine, 10
De Borghese, Brigitte, 29
De Chadwick, Orita, 152
DeGeneres, Ellen, 171, 365
De Haviland, Consuelo, 345
De La Croix, Raven, 347, 376, 378
de La Fontaine, Agathe, 26
Delany, Dana, 126, 203
Delbourg, Véronique, 63
Delon, Nathalie, 62

Delora, Jennifer, 32, 144
Delpy, Julie, 72
Del Rio, Vanessa, 61
de Medeiros, Maria, 162
Demitro, Papusha, 378
De Mornay, Rebecca, 278, 279
Demos, Athena, 29
DeMoss, Darcy, 274, 376
Dempsey, Sandy, 351
Dench, Judi, 179
Deneuve, Catherine, 170
Denier, Lydie, 361
Deno, Mary, 70
de Palma, Rossy, 272
Derek, Bo, 4, 67, 330
Dern, Laura, 360
de Rossi, Portia, 304, 365
Derval, Lamya, 376
DeSantis, Jaclyn, 281
De Selle, Lorraine, 120
De Shaffer, Christine, 130
DeVasquez, Devin, 74, 155
Deveroux, Edita, 125
Dewar, Bettie, 29
Díaz, María, 301
Dickens, Kim, 163
Dickinson, Angie, 47, 48, 116, 378
Dietrich, Cindi, 378
Digard, Uschi, 35, 42, 43, 129, 130, 152, 172, 173, 191, 324, 325, 375, 378
Di Lazzaro, Dalila, 138
Dillaway, Denise, 87, 377
Dillon, Melinda, 307
Di Lorenzo, Anneka, 78, 378
DiMarsico, C.J., 205, 312
Ditmar, Marita, 128
Divine, Maya, 50
Dockery, Erika, 40
Donadio, Jane, 32
Donatacci, Camille, 217
Donatz, Lisa, 244
Donna X, 224
Donohoe, Amanda, 194, 375
Donovan, Dixie, 337
Dorian, Antonia, 37
Dougherty, Norma Jean (Marilyn Monroe), 236
Down, Lesley-Anne, 44
Drake, Maricee, 338
Drake, Michele, 165

Drew, Griffin, 74, 140, 219, 379
Drew, Linzi, 27
Drinkwater, Carol, 89
Duboir, Jade, 152
Ducati, Kristi, 51
Duchkova, Eva, 104
Duff, Anne-Marie, 212
Duffek, Patty, 160, 248, 285
Duffy, Dorothy, 212
Dunaway, Faye, 334
Dunlap, Dawn, 36
Dunphy, Jessica, 101
Duplaix, Daphne, 321
Dusenberry, Ann, 40
Dutch, Deborah, 29, 52, 291
Duvall, Clea, 203
Du Vall, Denise, 224
Dziena, Alexis, 72

Éccles, Aimee, 378
Eckert, Charmagne, 32
Edwards, Barbara, 213
Eggers, Kira, 31
Eggert, Nicole, 61, 187
Eichhorn, Lisa, 377
Ekland, Britt, 17, 287, 359
Ekore, Marie, 375
Elene, Susie, 277
Elfman, Marie-Pascale, 140, 141
Elise, Esther, 164
Elizabeth, Shannon, 14, 15
Ellison, Tara, 254
Elvira, 375
Engert, Sharon, 252
England, Audie, 104
Eskra, Donna, 32
Eubank, Shari, 325
Evans, Candie, 379
Evans, Sandy, 87
Everhart, Angie, 26, 38, 184, 296

Fabia, Rizza, 49
Fabian, Ava, 74
Fabulous, Julie, 376
Fairchild, June, 378
Fairchild, Morgan, 293
Falcone, Lisa, 70
Fallon, Kate, 376
Fallon, Tammi, 282
Farley, Teresa, 71
Farringer, Lisa, 92

Faulkner, Lisa, 210
Fawcett, Farrah, 115
Faye, Denise, 15
Fenn, Sherilyn, 276, 344
Ferrell, Jami, 64
Ferris, Samantha, 269
Ferroll, Liz, 98
Fidler, C.J., 204
Figura, Katarzyna, 272
Fiorentino, Linda, 184
Fischer, Kate, 304
Fisher, Frances, 133
Fisher, Kimberly, 223
Fitzgerald, Tara, 304
Flaherty, Maureen, 52
Flanagan, Fionnula, 366
Flaska, Carrie, 262
Flowers, April, 223
Flynn, Joni, 132
Fogarty, Brenda, 128, 130
Fonda, Bridget, 27, 281, 287, 303
Fonda, Jane, 35
Fondue, Stephanie, 87
Forbes, Mary, 367
Ford, Anitra, 49, 153
Ford, Maria, 377
Foreman, Amanda, 70
Foreman, Michelle, 320, 323
Fortea, Isabelle, 51, 217
Foster, Lisa, 129
Foster, Terrea, 378
Fox, Samantha, 379
France, Maxine DeVille, 337
Franklin, Diane, 196, 292
Frederick, Vicki, 375
Fredlund, Alice, 253
Freeman, Lindsay, 128, 367
Fritz, Nikki, 37, 52
Frost, Sadie, 139
Frost, Victoria, 217
Fuchs, Gaby, 375
Fulton, Kristina, 112

Gabriel, Veronique, 224
Gabrielle, Monique, 13, 30, 56, 125, 291, 375
Gaël, Anna, 332
Gan, Jennifer, 364
Ganne, Gayle, 377
Garner, Kelli, 73
Gavin, Belinda, 31, 50, 230

Gavin, Erica, 46, 77, 352
Gaybis, Anne, 128, 343, 357
Gayle, Gretchen, 129
Gayle, Monica, 379
Geary, Teri, 28
Gemma, Vera, 288
Gemser, Laura, 120, 122, 375
George, Rita, 164
George, Susan, 319, 377
George, Tami-Adrian, 315
Geraghty, Erin, 376
Geraghty, Finola, 30
Gerardi, Joan, 51
Gerrish, Flo, 324
Gershon, Gina, 35, 68, 301
Gibb, Cynthia, 366
Gibbs, Angela, 368
Gibson, Terry, 249
Gil, 351
Gilbert, June, 5
Gilbert, Lauri, 379
Gilbreath, Alexandra, 226
Gildersleeve, Linda, 375
Gines, Coralisa, 339
Giroux, Jackie, 173
Glaser, Lisa, 169
Goding, Gittan, 144
Goff, Carolyn, 270
Gogovacinschi, Silvia, 84
Going, Joanna, 192
Gold, Glori, 121
Gold, Lynda, 77
Golubeva, Yekaterina, 341
Gondek, Beth, 204
Good, Abigail, 127
Good, Melanie, 262
Graham, Heather, 68, 192
Graham, Julie, 258
Graham, Juliet, 10
Granath, Tiffany, 70
Grant, April, 357
Grant, Belinda, 239
Grant, Crystal Celeste, 331
Grant, Rainier, 379
Grantham, Lucy, 196
Gray, Julie, 114
Greco, Kristine, 91
Green, Eva, 115
Green, Marika, 122
Green, Stacey, 187
Green, Wendy, 49, 55
Greer, Ingrid, 65

Grey, Darlene, 224
Griebel, Amber, 28
Grier, Pam, 49, 55, 92, 117,
   143, 364, 376
Griffeth, Simone, 103
Griffin, Nikki, 118
Griffith, Melanie, 64, 65, 132
Gross, Helen, 181
Gross, Molly, 308
Gruen, Pamela, 98
Grunwald, Cheryl, 89
Guérin, Florence, 56
Guerra, Blanca, 378
Guerrero, Evelyn, 128
Gugino, Carla, 185, 302
Guthrie, Lynne, 233
Gyllenhaal, Maggie, 35, 292,
   298, 379

Haack, Emily, 290
Haas, Victoria, 254
Hahn, Jessica, 52
Haiduk, Stacy, 211
Haji, 172, 325
Hale, Georgina, 376
Hall, Gabriella, 109, 146, 282
Hall, Landon, 109
Halligan, Erin, 186
Halsey, Elizabeth, 375
Hamilton, Lelaneya, 203
Hamilton, Suzanna, 4
Hamilton, Wendy, 99
Hammon, Jennifer, 12
Hammond, Barbara, 19
Hampshire, Chelsey, 205, 312
Hannah, Daryl, 100, 322, 335
Hansen, Valda, 357
Hanson, Jody, 132
Harper, Maria, 129
Harper, Samantha, 243
Harring, Laura, 229
Harris, Gail, 86, 140, 219, 311,
   379
Harris, Jo Ann, 378
Harris, Leigh, 377
Harris, Lynette, 377
Hart, Christina, 376, 377, 379
Hart, Diane Lee, 256
Hartley, Nina, 68
Hartt, Cathryn, 294
Hastings, Lynn, 375
Hatcher, Teri, 6, 95

Hathaway, Anne, 161
Haun, Darla, 217
Haven, Annette, 4, 5, 64
Havins, Bristi, 349
Hawkins, Patricia, 243
Hayek, Salma, 27, 145
Hayes, Taylor, 25
Haynes, Linda, 376
Heart, Ashley, 152
Heatherton, Joey, 62
Heche, Anne, 151, 362
Hecht, Jessica, 18
Helfer, Britt, 11, 379
Helgenberger, Marg, 312
Helmer, Jessica, 108
Helmkamp, Charlotte J., 144
Hemingway, Mariel, 314
Hendrix, Lori Jo, 323
Henstridge, Natasha, 312, 359
Hernandez, Roxanna, 19
Hershey, Barbara, 200
Heskin, Kam, 333
Heyman, Elizabeth, 72
Hickland, Catherine, 327
Hill, Kathy, 59
Hill, Sharon, 43
Hills, Gillian, 89
Hilton, Robyn, 213, 351
Hinton, Alex, 213
Holcomb, Sarah, 23, 75
Holden, Gloria, 170
Holden, Marjean, 327
Holland, Hilary, 215
Hollimon, Tina, 105
Hollywood, Holly, 223, 282
Holm, Henrietta, 182
Holmes, Katie, 149
Holsinger, Christina, 231
Holt, Sandrine, 269
Hope, Leslie, 246
Hopkins, Kim, 165
Horten, Rena, 228
House, Joey, 108
Hrubesová, Markéta, 104
Hubley, Season, 158, 159
Hudson, Kate, 115
Hughes, Julie, 126
Hughes, Kristina, 244
Hughes, Sharon, 375
Hull, Dianne, 376
Hunt, Helen, 115, 357
Hunter, Chloe, 313

Hunter, Heather, 144
Hunter, Holly, 95
Hunter, Kaki, 257
Hurley, Elizabeth, 27
Hussey, Olivia, 340
Huston, Anjelica, 154
Hutchinson, Tracy, 13
Hutson, Tracy, 270
Hutton, Linda, 215
Hyde, Kimberly, 80, 87, 198,
   368
Hyser, Joyce, 188

Idol, Gerri, 196
Inch, Jennifer, 378
Innes, Alexandra, 378
Inoh, Annie Shizuka, 1
Irvine, Susan, 204
Irving, Amy, 83
Ivars, Analía, 216

Jacobs, Emma, 321
Jaffe, Shirley, 89
Jameson, Jenna, 262
Janssen, Marlene, 289
Jasae, 33
Jean-Baptiste, Marianne, 365
Jeníčková, Eva, 108
Jennings, Claudia, 215, 375,
   379
Jennings, Julia, 379
Jensen, Jane, 340
Jenteal, 25
Jillson, Joyce, 324
Johari, Azizi, 65
Johnson, Caroline Key, 301
Johnson, Michelle, 57
Johnson, Sandy, 157, 158
Johnson, Terri, 42, 351
Johnson, Victoria Lynn, 116
Johnston, Jo, 328
Joi, Marilyn, 92, 172, 191, 375,
   376
Jolie, Angelina, 142, 149, 224,
   245
Jones, Carolyn, 376
Jones, Diane, 266
Jones, Gemma, 376
Jones, Josephine Jacqueline, 56
Jones, Shawnee Free, 310
Jordan, Katie, 125, 152
Joyce, Barbara, 205

Jubert, Alice, 183
Judd, Ashley, 145, 236, 237
Julian, Yolande, 95

Kachtikova, Lucie, 125
Kaderabkova, Jana, 167
Kaitan, Elizabeth, 352
Kalensky, Pascale, 345
Kamahaki, Pia, 320
Kaniak, Aleksandra, 140
Kaprisky, Valérie, 71
Kapture, Mitzi, 19
Karasun, May, 195
Karman, Janice, 378
Karney, Amber, 84
Karr, Marcia, 375
Katon, Rosanne, 65, 91, 328, 377
Kaye, Caren, 232
Keaton, Camille, 180, 181, 375
Keenan, Hayley, 331
Keene, Barbara, 233
Keener, Catherine, 2, 209
Keisha, 41
Kellerman, Sally, 272
Kelley, Sheila, 100
Kelly, Jill, 352
Kelly, Moira, 343
Kelly, Sharon, 143, 153, 172, 173, 285, 325
Kennedy, Jayne, 65
Kernohan, Roxanne, 239, 291
Kersh, Kathy, 376
Khan, A.J., 152, 205
Kidman, Nicole, 54, 127
Kiger, Susan Lynn, 157
Kihlstedt, Rya, 185
Killian, Tara, 15
King, Chantel, 233
King, Jaime, 302
King, Jamie, 306
Kingsbury, Corinne, 244
Kinmont, Kathleen, 145, 327
Kinski, Nastassja, 63, 85, 108
Kirkland, Sally, 47, 368
Kirkpatrick, Kathryn, 266
Kirshner, Mia, 238
Kitaen, Tawny, 30, 156, 251
Klass, Alisha, 86
Kline, Val, 40
Klintoe, Hanne, 206
Kneale, Tracy, 287

Koscina, Sylva, 17
Kracht, Marion, 63
Krakowski, Jane, 9
Krem, Viju, 60
Kristel, Sylvia, 21, 120, 122, 193, 219, 261, 317
Kristen, Marta, 376
Kristensen, Mona, 53
Kroslak, Candace, 16

Ladd, Diane, 360
Ladd, Jordan, 90
Lae, Foxy, 347
La Fontaine, Agathe de, 26
Lahaie, Brigitte, 162
Lail, Leah, 310
Lain, Chasey, 105, 310
Lakehurst, Alix, 376
Lamb, Debra, 320
Landers, Audrey, 114
Landers, Judy, 114
Landry, Tamara, 268
Lane, Diane, 346
Lang, Helen, 277
Lange, Jessica, 72
Lang, Katherine Kelly, 379
Lankford, Kim, 212
Large, Bonnie, 376
Larocca, Ruby, 152, 205, 312
Larranaga, Catalina, 38, 84
Larter, Ali, 349
Larussa, Adrienne, 215
La Touche, Gigi, 224
Laurel, Kim, 223
Lawlor, Stephanie, 375
Lawrence, Mittie, 233
Leachman, Cloris, 47
Lease, Maria, 208
LeBard, Crystal, 185
LeBeau, Becky, 52, 239, 289, 379
Leblanc, Sadie, 270
LeBrock, Kelly, 363
Lee, Adriane, 71
Lee, Pat, 257
Lee, Robbie, 47
Lee, Sarah, 132
Lee, Sheryl, 30, 60, 343
Lee, Sook-Yin, 299
Lee, Sung Hi, 333
Le Grand, Yvette, 224
Leick, Hudson, 310

Leigh, Chyler, 238
Leigh, Jennifer Jason, 26, 131, 138, 303
Leigh, Shannan, 108
Leigh, Valli, 360
Le May, Dorothy, 4, 5
Lemper, Ute, 272
Lenee, Sin, 224
Lenz, Kay, 320, 376, 377
Leo, Melissa, 379
Leon, Tara, 272
Lepage, Monique, 176
Leprince, Catherine, 53
Le Roux, Madeleine, 41, 98
Levine, Anna, 135, 185
Levitt, Dee Dee, 129, 130
Lewis, Angel, 16
Lewis, Charlotte, 121, 170
Lewis, Fiona, 117
Lexington, Lucia, 320
Lightstone, Marilyn, 176
Liljedahl, Marie, 124, 293
Limos, Tiffany, 190, 331
Lind, Traci, 281
Lindberg, Christina, 334, 335, 375
Lindemulder, Janine, 310
Lindley, Gisele, 140, 141
Lindsay, Amy, 50
Lindsley, Blake, 315
Lindt, Rosemarie, 284
Ling, Su, 172, 347
Linne, Jeanette, 40
Linney, Laura, 220
LisaRaye, 251
Little, Angela, 15
Liu, Carolyn, 111, 137, 159
Liu, Lucy, 88, 139
Lizer, Kari, 263
Lloyd, Sue, 55, 321
Locane, Amy, 83
Locke, Francine, 278
Locke, Sondra, 103
Lohman, Alison, 358
Lohmann, Katie, 28, 101, 223
London, Lisa, 157, 285, 377
Long, Nia, 9
Lopez, Aida, 60
Lopez-Dawson, Kamala, 123
Lords, Traci, 239, 242
Lorén, Alicia, 97
Lott, Bethany, 312

Louise, Tina, 377
Love, Courtney, 247
Lovell, Jacqueline, 25, 133, 282, 352
Low, Elizabeth, 233
Lowe, Crystal, 134
Lowry, Lynn, 85, 289, 322
Lutra, Maria, 129
Lynch, Kelly, 280, 355
Lynn, Kimber, 50, 223
Lynn, Theresa, 217, 262
Lynn, Toni, 52
Lyon, Lynn, 266
Lyons, Elena, 90

MacDonald, Jennifer, 242
MacDonald, Wendy, 391
Mack, June, 43
MacPherson, Elle, 304
Madden, Colleen, 278
Maddox, Kim, 31
Madigan, Amy, 133
Madnadraszky, Mirka, 42
Madonna, 66
Madsen, Virginia, 169, 306
Maestro, Mia, 145
Magnuson, Ann, 170
Maguire, Terrill, 368
Mahoney, Sean'a, 99
Maillé, Maïté, 162
Maitland, Lorna, 224, 228
Malin, Kym, 155, 186, 248
Malove, Minia, 29
Man, Hayley, 123
Mandel, Joyce, 357
Mani, Karin, 11
Manion, Cindy, 259
Mann, Jamie Elle, 2
Mann, Nancy, 130
Mannheim, Camryn, 281
Mano, Kirina, 1
Mansfield, Jayne, 264
Manson, Jeane, 5, 368
Mantia, J.J., 219
Marani, Imelde, 138
Marcel, Tammy, 52
March, Jane, 93, 210
Marconi, Mason, 301
Markov, Margaret, 55, 376
Marks, Marianne, 347
Marks, Shae, 276
Maroney, Kelli, 291

Marquis, Juliette, 333
Marsillach, Blanca, 138
Martin, Kim, 376
Martin, Pamela Sue, 194
Marx, Maria, 173
Masselli, Fiorella, 138
Massey, Athena, 255
Masterson, Chase, 217
Mastrantonio, Mary Elizabeth, 306
Mathews, Phillipa, 26
Mathis, Samantha, 17
Matsuda, Eiko, 178
Mattson, Robin, 80, 375
Maxwell, Jacqui, 118
Maxwell, Maggy, 378
May, Mathilda, 202
McArthur, Kimberly, 213
McBride, Harlee, 193, 367
McBroom, Marcia, 46
McCarthy, Danté, 301
McClure, Tane, 52
McComas, Lorissa, 37
McCormick, Michelle, 327
McCullough, Julie, 48
McCullough, Shanna, 213
McDaniel, Donna, 18
McDormand, Frances, 300
McGavin, Graem, 18, 232
McGeachie, Meredith, 266
McGillis, Kelly, 84, 85, 225
McGovern, Elizabeth, 268
McGuire, Deborah, 152, 325
McInerney, Linda, 375
McIntosh,Valerie, 377
McIsaac, Marianne, 176
McKayla, 296
McKevic, Karen, 49
McLeod, Shannon, 24
McNichol, Kristy, 344
Medina, Stephanie Christine, 185
Mell, Marisa, 17
Meneses, Alex, 28
Menuez, Stephanie, 270
Menzel, Idina, 27
Menzies-Wills, Angela, 130, 132
Mercado, Ana López, 369
Meyer, Dina, 315
Meyrink, Michelle, 348
Michael, Joy, 166, 379

Michaels, Julie, 280
Michaels, Lorraine, 213
Michaels, Michelle, 291
Micheaux, Nicki, 269
Michel, Kim G., 186
Michelle, Shelley, 217
Miko, Izabella, 141
Milano, Alyssa, 121, 170, 254, 255
Miller, Mindi, 65
Miller, Mirta, 67
Miller, Penelope Ann, 82
Miller, Sienna, 9
Minazzoli, Christiane, 317
Miner, Rachel, 73
Miranda, Soledad, 170
Mirren, Helen, 78, 378
Mitchell, Elizabeth, 149
Mitchell, Lois, 152
Moir, Alison, 126
Mol, Gretchen, 240
Molnar, Linda, 38
Money, Constance, 4, 5
Monroe, Marilyn (Norma Jean Dougherty), 236
Montgomery, Julia, 278
Monti, Mary Elaine, 181
Moody, Lynn, 377
Moon, Sheri, 108
Moon, Tanya, 323
Moore, Candy, 377
Moore, Demi, 8, 57, 321
Moore, Julianne, 66, 68, 300
Moore, Melissa Anne, 20, 52, 291, 311
Morales, Brooke, 315
Moran, Crissy, 231
Moran, Sofia, 364
Morel, Marie-France, 29
Morell, Linda, 158
Moreno, Rita, 82
Morgan, Alexandra, 136
Morgan, Chesty (Liliana Wilczkowska), 102, 113
Morgan, Cindy, 75
Morgan, Debbi, 98, 377
Morgan, Jaye P., 234
Morgan, Mariana, 74
Morgan, Shelley Taylor, 213
Moritz, Louisa, 103, 196, 376, 377
Morrissey, Lori, 352

Mortimer, Emily, 209
Moss, Paige, 269
Mueller, Cookie, 250
Mulhern, Alyssa, 135
Mullen, Becky, 140, 159
Mullen, Patty, 144
Müller, Lillian, 17
Mundae, Misty (Erin Brown),
    35, 152, 170, 205, 252, 253,
    312, 313, 356, 379
Murphy, Brittany, 313
Myers, Cynthia, 46
Myers, T.J., 99

Nann, Erika, 236
Napoli, Susan, 144
Nassar, Debbie, 320
Natividad, Francesca "Kitten,"
    43, 191, 194, 232, 234, 347,
    379
Navizet, Albane, 317
Navratilova, Barbora, 125
Nedeljakova, Barbara, 167
New, Lorielle, 230
Newman, Amber, 216
Nguyen, Christine, 230
Nichols, Kelly, 338
Nicorre, Valerie, 357
Nielsen, Connie, 107
Niemi, Lisa, 306
Nirvana, Yana, 375
Niznik, Stephanie, 126
Noone, Nora-Jane, 212
Norby, Kate, 108
Norris, Michele, 150
North, Cecilia, 356
North, Noelle, 378
Novak, Lenka, 91, 191, 375
Nygren, Mia, 122

Obregón, Ana, 67
O'Brien, Shauna, 29
O'Connell, Helen, 129, 130
O'Connell, Lynette, 24
O'Connell, Natalie, 32, 71
O'Connell, Taaffe, 239
O'Donnell, Rosie, 126
O'Grady, Joanie (Laurie
    Walters), 218
O'Grady, Lani, 218
Oh, Sandra, 100
Ohana, Cláudia, 123

Ohrner, Carolin, 63
Olin, Lena, 345
Olivier, Sylvie, 317
Olsen, Carrie, 375
O'Neill, Remy, 22
Ormond, Julia, 1
Oruche, Phina, 141
Osborne, Debbie, 337
Otis, Carré, 361
O'Toole, Annette, 85
Otsuki, Tamayo, 18
Owens, Laura Misch, 377
Owens, Lois, 130
Oxenberg, Catherine, 194

Pacific, Delphine, 282
Page, Bettie, 240
Page, Brook Lynn, 51
Page, Kelly Ann, 367
Page, Kimberly, 2
Palac, Lauren, 231
Palladino, Aleksa, 318
Pallett, Alyssa Nicole, 16
Paltrow, Gwyneth, 26
Paluzzi, Gina, 249
Paluzzi, Luciana, 294
Paré, Jessica, 206
Parent, Monique, 74, 219
Parillaud, Anne, 176
Paris, Cheryl, 327
Paris, Darla, 224
Parker, Molly, 86
Parker, Nicole Ari, 68
Pascal, Olivia, 17
Pascual, Evita, 84
Paul, Alexandra, 323, 375
Pavlovic, Drina, 376
Payne, Julie, 263
Peabody, Dixie, 233
Peaks, Pandora, 111, 321
Pearce, Mary Vivian, 250
Peckinpaugh, Barbara, 40, 65,
    166, 378
Pederson, Diane, 379
Pederson, Kathleen, 20
Peet, Amanda, 67, 359
Pelham, Holly, 115
Perabo, Piper, 206, 207
Peralto, Sasha, 29, 223, 230
Perensky, Tonie, 349
Perez, Gigi, 337
Perle, Rebecca, 286

Perles, Nadine, 317
Perrine, Valerie, 315
Persson, Essy, 332
Peters, Jocelyne, 151
Peters, Lorraine, 359
Peterson, Marion, 27
Peterson, Martha, 135
Pettyjohn, Angelique, 148
Phillips, Bijou, 73, 161, 205
Phillips, Bobbie, 301
Phillips, Samantha, 99
Picasso, Paloma, 175
Pickett, Cindy, 377
Pierce, Jill, 99
Pitt, Ingrid, 170, 359
Plantadit-Bageot, Karine, 145
Plato, Dana, 109
Player, Susan, 153, 212, 256
Plumb, Elizabeth, 266
Plummer, Amanda, 1, 106
Pohle, Robyn, 91
Ponczkowski, Sue, 135
Poon, Alice, 95
Porizkova, Paulina, 335
Porter, Ashley, 368
Porter, Susie, 225
Posey, Parker, 26, 35
Potter, Crystal, 230
Potter, Jocelyn, 230
Potter, Laura, 204
Power, De'Ann, 282
Powers, Beverly, 153
Prather, Joan, 47, 218, 375
Pratt, Keri Lynn, 97
Prepon, Laura, 306
Pressly, Jaime, 238, 254, 255,
    280
Prester, Meaghan, 219
Preston, Kelly, 222
Princess, Lil, 376
Pringle, Joan, 183
Procter, Emily, 67, 70
Pucci, Cindy, 230

Quennessen, Valérie, 322
Quigley, Linnea, 114, 128, 164,
    286, 291, 316, 350, 375
Quinlan, Kathleen, 112
Quinlan, Maeve, 190
Quinones, Jackie, 160
Quintard, Mika, 159
Quivers, Robin, 262

Simmons, Chelan, 134
Simone, Starlyn, 351
Simova, Kristyna, 125
Simpson, Jessica, 118
Simpson, Suzi, 123
Sinclair, Tiffany, 312
Singer, Lori, 300, 323
Sirtis, Marina, 59
Skura, Stephanie, 181
Skye, Ione, 151
Slater, Suzee, 286
Sloan, Renee, 231
Smart, Amy, 244, 281
Smith, Andrea, 230
Smith, Anna Nicole, 305, 339
Smith, Cheryl "Rainbeaux," 77,
    117, 130, 218, 256, 277, 328,
    329, 351, 375, 378
Smith, Crystal, 168
Smith, Jaclyn A., 16
Smith, Julie K., 19, 29, 31, 37,
    99, 276
Smith, Lauren Lee, 201
Smith, Stephanie Ann, 345
Smith, Tracy, 168
Snelgrove, Lisha, 187
Socas, Maria, 356
Søeberg, Camilla, 123
Sokolova, Natalia, 64
Soles, P.J., 158
Som, Ined, 7
Somers, Kristi, 338, 377
Songer, Melinda, 301
Sorell, Annie, 97
Sorvino, Mira, 236
Soto, Talisa, 139
Spacek, Sissy, 83, 260
Spangler, Donna, 155
Spears, Britney, 242
Speciale, Linda, 378
Speed, Carol, 49
Speir, Dona, 111, 137, 155, 159,
    160, 248, 285
Spradling, Charlie, 360
Spybey, Dina, 321
Squire, Janie, 375
Stahl, Jennifer, 135
Staley, Lora, 375
Starr, Blaze, 58
St. Clair, Diana, 56
St. Clair, Taylor, 133, 352
Steele, Jennifer, 153

Steenburgen, Mary, 221
Stelfox, Shirley, 4
Stephen, Karen, 248
Stevens, Brinke, 33, 65, 263,
    291, 311, 316
Stevens, Connie, 378
Stevens, Stella, 308
Stevenson, Cynthia, 203
Stewart, Alana, 233
Stewart, Alexandra, 176
Stewart, Jennifer, 305
Stewart, Susan, 136, 215
Stewart,Tonea, 377
Stole, Mink, 250
Stone, Madison, 125
Stone, Sharon, 8, 39, 72, 171
Stoner, Sherri, 274
Storm, Tempest, 113
Stowe, Madeleine, 300
Strain, Julie, 29, 37, 74, 99, 123,
    137, 160, 248, 276
Strasberg, Susan, 176
Strickland, Connie, 378
Strohmeier, Tara, 164, 191, 212
Strömberg, Ewa, 170
Stroud, Sally Ann, 143
Studer, Esther, 174
Style, Sandy, 167
Styne, Beth Ann, 141
Suárez, Diana, 295
Subkoff, Tara, 331
Summers, Kelli, 205, 312
Sundh, Inger, 293
Susoeff, Linda, 150
Sutter, Donna, 378
Sutton, Krista, 17
Sutton, Lori, 213, 234, 379
Suvari, Mena, 256, 313
Swank, Hilary, 69, 106
Swinton, Tilda, 72, 133
Swisten, Amanda, 15
Sykes, Brenda, 117, 377

Taft, Victoria, 305
Talor, Venesa, 133
Tasker, Barbara, 183
Taub, Melissa, 203
Tavarez, Jacqueline, 340
Taylor, Delores, 54
Taylor, Kimberly, 144
Taylor, Sandra, 126, 258
Taylor, Shelby, 252, 312

Teague, Terri, 87
Texter, Gilda, 22
Theberge, Tina, 348
Theel, Lynn, 169
Theron, Charlize, 6, 106, 107
Thomas, Heather, 379
Thompson, Andrea, 154, 214,
    377
Thompson, Cynthia, 338
Thompson, Lea, 11, 279
Thompson, Sita Renne, 282
Thompson, Teri, 217
Thompson, Victoria, 376
Thorn, Frankie, 34, 355
Thorne, Dyanne, 172, 173, 174,
    208, 357
Thorwald, Greta, 224
Thulin, Ingrid, 284
Thurman, Uma, 162
Tiger, Lilly, 152
Tilly, Jennifer, 68, 100, 148
Tippo, Patti, 5
Tolo, Marilù, 62
Tomankova, Petra, 125
Tomasina, Jeana, 40
Tomazani, Despina, 334
Tompkins, Angel, 260, 377
Torell, Johanna, 206
Torosh, Rosita, 138
Tothova, Natali, 167
Traverso, Susana, 36
Trentini, Peggy, 105, 379
Tribush, Nancy, 243
Tripoldi, Idy, 128, 375
Tripplehorn, Jeanne, 39
Trochu, Jenny, 29
Trombetta, Monica, 271
Trongone, Michelle, 109
Tsengoles, Sue, 10
Tsentas, Jane, 42
Tucci, Lin, 301
Tunie, Tamara, 107
Turner, Guinevere, 17, 258
Turner, Janine, 115
Turner, Kathleen, 66
Turpin, Bahni, 151
Tweed, Shannon, 38, 168, 258,
    287
Tyler, Liv, 115
Tyler, Sai, 345
Tylo, Hunter, 175
Tyrrell, Susan, 138, 140, 141

Udy, Claudia, 375, 376, 378
Ullrick, Sharon, 198
Unger, Deborah Kara, 95, 192
Upson, Gloria, 375
Utal, Melinda, 128

Vaccaro, Brenda, 310
Vail, Justina, 233
Vale, Sheila, 282
Valenti, Ray, 296
van de Ven, Monique, 341
van Vooren, Monique, 138
Van Doren, Mamie, 306
Vanity, 8, 330, 375
Varma, Indira, 189
Vasquez, Roberta, 111, 137, 155, 159
Vega, Isela, 117
Vega, Paz, 295
Vega, Victoria, 152
Velanni, Jenna, 231
Veltri, Rachel, 15
Ven, Monique van de, 341
Venturelli, Silvana, 200
Verdú, Maribel, 369
Verran, Michelle, 311
Vetri, Victoria, 153
Vincent, Cerina, 167, 238, 290
Vooren, Monique van, 138
Vorgan, Gigi, 158
Vox, Linda, 29

Wagner, Lori, 78
Wagner, Natasha Gregson, 207
Wahl, Corinne, 13
Walcott, Jennifer, 15
Walker, Polly, 1
Wallace, Vincene, 352
Wallace-Stone, Dee, 4
Walsh, Eileen, 212
Walsh, Susan, 250
Walters, Laurie (Joanie O'Grady), 218, 376
Ward, Pam, 289
Warner, Julie, 110
Warner, Missy, 51
Wasa, Maxine, 285
Washington, Candace, 223

Watkins, Susie Ann, 287
Watson, Alberta, 176
Watts, Naomi, 229
Weber, Amy, 140
Weber, Catherine, 339
Weigel, Teri, 176, 285
Weintraub, Cindy, 169
Welch, Racquel, 62
Well, Honey, 7
Weller, Mary Louise, 23
Welles, Jennifer, 181, 322
Wells, Julian, 312
Welton, Maria, 129
Westbrook, Wendi, 217, 345
Westcott, Carrie, 276
Westerman, Chantal, 294
Wetherell, Virginia, 89
Whalley, Joanne, 287
Wharton, Wally Ann, 375
Whirry, Shannon, 24, 38, 251
Whitcraft, Elizabeth, 21
Whitfield, Lynn, 186
Whitting, Robyn, 351
Wiesmeier, Lynda, 213, 259, 263, 268
Wilbur, Claire, 289
Wilczkowska, Liliana (Chesty Morgan), 102, 113
Wild, Paula, 167
Wild, Sandra, 137, 323
Wildman, Valerie, 377
Wilkes, Donna, 18
Williams, Barbara, 333
Williams, Carol Ann, 165
Williams, Edy, 33, 46, 114, 375, 376
Williams, JoBeth, 379
Williams, Kathy, 208
Williams, Melissa, 301
Williams, Michelle, 171
Williams, Olivia, 226
Williams, Sasha, 101
Williams, Wendy O., 274
Wilson, Chrystale, 251
Wilson, Peta, 222
Wilson, Sheree J., 145
Wilson, Susie, 164
Wilton, Penelope, 179

Winders, Wendy, 337
Windsor, Keri, 38
Windsor, Romy, 333
Winger, Debra, 378
Winkler, K.C., 157
Winslet, Kate, 165, 179
Winters, Shelley, 47, 129
Wise, Bridgett, 281
Witherspoon, Reese, 17, 342
Wolfe, Liz, 130
Wood, Annie, 86
Wood, Janet, 22, 148, 347, 378
Wood, Karen, 204
Wood, Lana, 105
Woods, Bambi, 256
Woods, Barbara Alyn, 99, 321
Woods, Brandy, 87
Woronov, Mary, 22, 103, 119, 164, 322
Wright, Angela, 123
Wright, Sylvia, 305
Wright, Talle, 357
Wuhrer, Kari, 211
Wyatt, Reda, 377
Wyeth, Katya, 89

Yates, Cassie, 378
Yen, Tricia, 352
York, Linda, 351
Young, Diane, 224
Young, Donna, 173
Young, Karen, 222

Zabou, 156
Zane, Lora, 203
Zane, Sheila, 220
Zann, Lenore, 375
Zen, 28, 29
Zero, 28, 29
Zhivago, Stacia, 291, 311
Ziering, Nikki Schieler, 15
Zimova, Tereza, 125
Zinszer, Pamela, 376
Zobda, France, 297
Zottoli, Mia, 31, 230
Zuniga, Daphne, 175
Zuris, Carey, 32

Director Skindex

Abel, Alan, 181
Abel, Jeanne, 181
Adler, Gilbert, 105
Åkerlund, Jonas, 313
Albright, Carlton J., 211
Almodóvar, Pedro, 336
Altman, Robert, 27, 115, 272, 273, 300
Amateau, Rodney, 294
Amero, John, 268
Amero, Lem, 268
Ames, Stefani, 154
Anderson, Jane, 171
Anderson, Michael, 292
Anderson, Paul Thomas, 68
Angelo, Robert, 296
Anjou, Erik, 95
Annaud, Jean-Jacques, 210, 267
Antel, Franz, 17
Apatow, Judd, 2
Argento, Asia, 288
Argento, Dario, 288
Arkush, Allan, 164
Aronofsky, Darren, 275
Ash, 333
Avedis, Howard, 332
Avildsen, John G., 98

Bacchus, John, 152, 252
Barreto, Bruno, 83
Bartel, Paul, 103, 119
Baxley, Craig R., 8
Becker, Walt, 349
Beineix, Jean-Jacques, 45
Bennett, Guy, 266
Benton, Robert, 54, 342
Beresford, Bruce, 27
Bergman, Andrew, 321

Bertolucci, Bernardo, 115, 198, 199
Beshears, James, 166
Black, Noel, 263
Blank, Jonathan, 18
Bogdanovich, Peter, 198
Borden, Lizzie, 123
Borowczyk, Walerian, 175
Bowers, George, 65, 232
Brander, Richard, 305
Brass, Tinto, 78, 79, 284
Brickman, Paul, 278
Brinckerhoff, Burt, 315
Broderick, John, 356
Brutsman, Joseph, 108
Bryden, Bill, 27
Buchanan, Larry, 236
Buckalew, Bethel G., 42, 249, 285, 337

Cage, Nicolas, 310
Cammell, Donald, 362
Campion, Jane, 165, 177
Cardone, J.S., 141
Carpenter, John, 158
Carver, Steve, 47, 117
Caton-Jones, Michael, 110, 287
Cauthen, Kelley, 38
Cavani, Liliana, 235
Chandrasekhar, Jay, 90, 118
Chapman, Michael, 11
Charr, Henri, 86, 345
Chen, Kaige, 192
Chong, Tommy, 316
Chubbuck, Lyndon, 233
Ciccoritti, Jerry, 246
Cirino, Chuck, 29
Clark, Bob, 257

Clark, Greydon, 56, 186
Clark, Larry, 73, 190, 331
Collyer, Laurie, 298
Conaway, Jeff, 52
Connor, Kevin, 323
Coolidge, Martha, 171, 348
Coppola, Francis Ford, 279
Corman, Roger, 119, 354, 368
Crash, Johnny, 312
Craven, Wes, 196, 326
Cristofer, Michael, 67, 149, 245
Cronenberg, David, 95, 120
Cuarón, Alfonso, 369
Cumming, Alan, 26

Daalder, Rene, 218
D'Amato, Joe, 120
Damiani, Amasi, 214
Damski, Mel, 222
Dante, Joe, 13, 164
Dark, Gregory (Gregory Hippolyte), 24, 25, 38, 242
Davidson, Boaz, 196
DeCoteau, David, 114, 311
Deitch, Donna, 106
de Leon, Gerardo, 364
DeLuise, Michael, 13
Demme, Jonathan, 77, 119, 221
Deodato, Ruggero, 81
De Palma, Brian, 64, 65, 82, 83, 116, 117
Derek, John, 67, 330
DeSimone, Tom, 19, 274
Dickerson, Ernest R., 105
Dmytryk, Edward, 62
Donaldson, Roger, 148, 312
Donen, Stanley, 57
Donnelly, Dennis, 338

Masters, Quentin, 321
Mastorakis, Nico, 59
McBride, Jim, 71
McNaughton, John, 151, 237, 363
McTiernan, John, 334
Medem, Julio, 295
Metzger, Radley (Henry Paris), 200, 201, 289, 332
Meyer, Russ, 43, 46, 224, 228, 324, 325, 347, 352, 353
Mihalka, George, 248
Miller, Frank, 302
Mitchell, John Cameron, 299
Monroe, Madison, 84
Monson, Carl, 253
Moore, Charles Philip, 99
Moore, Paul, 101
Morrissey, Paul, 138
Morrow, Rob, 220
Mullan, Peter, 212
Mulot, Claude, 56
Mutrux, Floyd, 165
Myerson, Alan, 261

Nair, Mira, 189
Nathan, Mort, 64
Nesher, Avi, 271
Nichols, Mike, 82
Nicks, Dewey, 306
Noé, Gaspar, 179
Nordaker, T.J., 185
Novak, Harry, 249
Nussbaum, Joe, 16

O'Hara, Gerry, 55, 129
Olivera Héctor, 36
O'Neil, Lawrence, 70
O'Neill, Robert Vincent, 18, 266
Oshima, Nagisa, 178
Ozon, François, 327

Pachard, Henri, 351
Palumbo, Nick, 231
Paris, Henry (Radley Metzger), 200, 201, 289, 332
Parker, Alan, 21, 281
Peckinpah, Sam, 319
Peirce, Kimberly, 69
Peters, Barbara, 169
Peterson, Kristine, 308
Petrie, Daniel, 44

Phillips, Todd, 244, 281
Pillsbury, Sam, 370
Plone, Allen, 327
Polakof, James, 105
Pool, Léa, 206
Procko, Steve, 153

Radford, Michael, 4, 100
Raimi, Sam, 149
Ramis, Harold, 75
Rash, Steve, 15
Ray, Fred Olen, 33, 50, 52, 125, 164, 219, 258, 291
Reed, Joel M., 60, 148
Reynolds, Kevin, 269
Richards, Cybil, 133, 352
Rifkin, Adam, 310
Ritchie, Michael, 260
Rivette, Jacques, 42
Robbins, Brian, 349
Roberts, Alan, 367
Roddam, Franc, 27
Rodriguez, Robert, 302
Roeg, Nicolas, 27, 110, 146, 215, 354
Rogosin, Daniel, 355
Rollin, Jean, 29
Romero, Eddie, 55
Romine, Charles, 41
Rosenthal, Robert J., 212
Rossati, Nello, 294
Roth, Eli, 167
Rotsler, William, 152, 215
Ruben, Joseph, 256
Rush, Richard, 93
Russell, Ken, 27, 194, 195

Sacripanti, Luciano, 62
Sanders, Denis, 153
Santiago, Cirio H., 20
Sarno, Joseph W., 252, 293
Sassone, Oley, 251
Sauer, Ernest G., 51, 72, 217
Sayadian, Stephen, 76
Schaffer, Jeff, 125
Schain, Don, 7, 150, 151
Schmoeller, David, 293
Schrader, Paul, 28, 85, 158
Schreibman, Myrl A., 22
Schroeder, Barbet, 303
Scorsese, Martin, 119, 200
Scott, Tony, 170

Sedan, Mike, 217
Seidelman, Susan, 269
Sena, Dominic, 329
Shainberg, Steven, 292
Shea, Katt, 320
Shyer, Charles, 9
Sidaris, Andy, 111, 137, 155, 160, 213, 248, 276, 285
Sidaris, Christian Drew, 99, 123, 159
Signore, Andy, 185
Simpson, Jane, 203
Sindell, Gerald Seth, 157
Skjoldbjaerg, Erik, 265
Sloane, Rick, 350
Softley, Iain, 30
Sole, Alfred, 330
Solondz, Todd, 318
Spencer, Brenton, 61
Spera, Rob, 296
Stanze, Eric, 290
Starrett, Jack, 308
Steinberg, Michael, 357
Steinmann, Danny, 286
Stewart, Douglas Day, 333
Stewart, Larry, 175
Stone, Oliver, 112
Streitfeld, Susan, 133
Sturridge, Charles, 27
Sugerman, Andrew, 40

Tarantino, Quentin, 328, 335
Taymor, Julie, 145
Teague, Lewis, 194
Temple, Julien, 27
Thomas, Betty, 231, 262
Thompson, J. Lee, 5
Toback, James, 358
Tolkin, Michael, 270
Towne, Robert, 27
Townsend, Bud, 10, 40, 41, 91
Traynor, Peter S., 103
Treut, Monika, 123
Trueblood, Guerdon, 79
Truffaut, François, 354
Tuggle, Richard, 337

Urban, Stuart, 258

Vadim, Roger, 35, 227
Van Peebles, Mario, 160
Ventilla, István, 96